Wildlife Dies Without Making a Sound: Vol. II

Terry Grosz

Wildlife Dies Without Making a Sound:

The Adventures of a State Wildlife Officer in
the Wildlife Wars
Volume 2

by

Terry L. Grosz

WOLFPACK
PUBLISHING
—— EST 2013 ——

Print Edition

© Copyright 2015 Terry Grosz (as revised)

Wolfpack Publishing
48 Rock Creek Road
Clinton, Montana 59825

IBSN: 978-1-64119-056-5

Dedication

This book is dedicated to Amanda Grosz, Katelyn Grosz, Bria Jackson, Bryce Jackson, Bryant Jackson, Laurel Grosz, Gabriel Grosz, Nobuchika Takamiya, Kanako Takamiya, and Sawa Takamiya, grand kids and grandkids, one and all.

This book is dedicated to you, my dear grandchildren, that, through these real-life experiences I have had as a fish and game warden, you will see what natural treasures people used to be able to experience in the wonderful world of wildlife in the United States of America. However, you may never experience many of these natural resources firsthand because of man's inhumanity to man through the greedy exploitation of those natural resources by many of those humans "walking on the dark side" of the state and federal wildlife conservation laws.

Through these adventure stories I hope you will come to appreciate the many lonely hours Grandpa spent attempting to control those "walking on the dark side" in the world of wildlife. In these adventures I tried controlling those poachers who illegally destroyed your shares of the wildlife resources from Mother Nature's Treasure House. I also hope you will come to appreciate the many lonely hours your grandmother and parents (including Yumiko) spent when Grandpa was absent from their lives while hot on the trail of those "walking on the dark side" in the world of wildlife.

Through these stories you will also come to understand and appreciate that your grandfather had two great loves in his life.

First, your grandmother (or Oba-chan), who still is and always will be the first love of his life and his best friend. Your grandmother is a blessing and will continue to be for your grandfather until the day he dies. Your grandfather will always love your grandmother, forever and a day...

The second great love in your grandfather's life was his intense love for those critters in the world of wildlife who had little or no voice. Those wildlife critters had no voice and died without making a sound other than that of your grandfather's many times lone law-enforcement voice in the wilderness. But clearly understand, Grandpa was always out there squallin' like a smashed cat when it came to giving a voice to Mother Nature's voiceless ones. In his squallin,' he had the "teeth" and authority to make those pay who violated the laws of man and Mother Nature...

Suffice to say, many of those walking and killing on the dark side of Mother Nature came to know me "up close and personally" by my first name. Unfortunately my efforts on your and many others' behalf were not enough. Today, this great country of ours has suffered many losses in the world of wildlife. Many critters have now slipped into the dusty pages of natural history, because of those destroying forces of man in the world of wildlife who came before you and cared little for those yet to come.

I did the best I could, kids, to stop the outright slaughter of God's creatures. However, I am sorry to say, in many instances, my efforts were not enough...

I love all of you!

Grandpa, A.K.A.* Big Paw, A.K.A.* Grandpaw, A.K.A. Oji-chan

*A.K.A.-Also Known As (That is police talk...)

Table of Contents

Wildlife Dies Without Making a Sound, Volume II

Chapter One: The Colusa District: Part II

My Colusa County game warden law enforcement district laid smack dab in the historic Northern Sacramento Valley of California. A unique landed area that is rich in the aspects of its natural history, its earliest settlers namely the Ancient Ones, and the historical growth and settlement of the California portion of the Great American West in the years that followed. Two of those aspects of Americana, one involving the natural resource world and the other of the humanity that migrated into that area and evolved, were initially to be historically intertwined as much as brother and sister. Yet both aspects ultimately became wildly divergent when it came to growth, opportunity, outcome, and, their current day histories—divergent in that in one aspect, specifically involving the impact of humankind, would ultimately lead to a clash between all things natural and that dynamic stain called humanity. One force was movable and the other, as history would ultimately relate, was immovable, as is the great and majestic Sierra Nevada Mountain range forming the eastern backbone of the historic Sacramento Valley region of Northern California.

The natural history of the area fed and clothed its archeological and then its later day historically primitive peoples for many thousands of years. That world of wildlife fed and clothed them in the forms of meat, fur, feathers, leather, as well as other wildlife parts and products that multiplied the primitives' numbers and in part, helped in defining their individual cultures. As a result, that ruggedly beautiful aspect of ancient and later historic life flourished in its simplest of forms, culturally dignifying them for many years. Then came the quiet pastoral days of Old Mexico, followed by the invading and conquering Spanish, establishment of the Russian sea otter hunters along the northern Pacific seaboard, the invasion of the rough and tumble Mountain Men fur trappers, and finally the explosive California Gold Rush, all of which eventually led to the massive settlement by modern-day man throughout the land.

Those combinations of human events quickly led into present times, ultimately changing the environment, its peoples, and rich history forever because of the inevitable conflicts between man and all things natural. With that evolution and the advent of historic to modern-day history of humankind, California's civilization expanded explosively, tumultuously and many times without regard for the consequences. Technological advances, exploitation of new markets, along with man's exploratory and settlement presence blossomed into every corner of California. In particular, settlement into the resource rich and extremely fertile breadbasket that came to be known as the Sacramento Valley. With that early-day population expansion came new and expanded agricultural land use practices, and initially, all things natural and native to the area flourished together as one. Then with the increasing white Europeans explosive population growth pressures, natural history's flame in that shared environment and relationship began to flicker and then rapidly dwindled. Dwindled especially under such destructive forces as disease among the Ancients, loss of wildlife resources because of commercial market hunting, over fishing of pelagic and freshwater fisheries, destruction of large predators, which upset the natural balance of all things wild, and major environmental land use changes made through the initiation of many new and intensive agricultural practices. All of which ultimately resulted in the near total displacement of the original land dwelling ancient peoples, often times violently, at the hands of the lands newest inhabitants. In later years as well, that was followed ultimately with the near outright expulsion or physical destruction of many things wild and naturally occurring—destruction through the mass killings and sale by the unrelenting new and increasing vast swarms of land hungry, protein-starved immigrants streaming into California, the new fabled golden land of plenty.

My presence entered this swirling mass of Nature's and civilization's natural shifting balance of forces in 1967 as a local State of California fish and game warden. From my first day in that new environment, I was swept into this rapidly changing dynamic swirl of humanity and all things natural and never once looked back. Never looked back because I didn't want to see what destructive forces of inevitability were fast approaching my miserable carcass from behind as well... However, into that swirl I found myself rapidly drawn by resource and law enforcement adventure after adventure, until I also began aging through my existence the same as those members from "The Thin Green Line" who had come before me; came before me and had now long ago since aged out of existence as of recent memory and had turned to dust as we all must do. However, as the valley's newest wildlife officer, I was soon experiencing the whispers in the wind and the echoes of the living dust from the lands rising up around me, spurring me to carry on in their historic law enforcement traditions. A feeling I had not experienced at my previous North Coast duty station but there in the Sacramento Valley, that presence was almost physical in nature and constantly beckoning...and to that siren song, I soon fell.

"I NEED SOME HELP!"

The annual summer striped bass, sturgeon and king salmon runs were now migrating by the many hundreds of thousands throughout the historic Sacramento River. With the occurrence of such events, the river and its collateral fisheries migrations were to be a large part of my law enforcement home as the Colusa game warden for the next several weeks. Home because of the thousands of fishermen those runs attracted from far and wide, with all their warts, in an attempt to utilize those valuable fisheries resources. In short, I had a thirteen-mile stretch of the mighty Sacramento River running through the eastern portion of my assigned six-hundred-square- mile patrol district. My, how I grinned when I reread those lines just written. When I retired years later as the U.S. Fish and Wildlife Service's Special Agent in Charge of Region 6 in Denver, Colorado in 1998, my assigned law enforcement district of responsibility encompassed eight states, and three quarters of a million square miles; all in all, an area larger than the entire State of Alaska! How times and the man with his wildlife law enforcement responsibilities had changed since those halcyon days in California as a state fish and game warden...

Having spent the morning down river patrolling and checking numerous fishermen, I headed back once again to the Colusa Marina where I normally berthed the state's patrol boat. Taking care of a call of nature while there and grabbing a candy bar, I began servicing my eighteen-foot patrol boat for a subsequent afternoon patrol. After pouring in a quart of oil—my engine was a two-cycle inboard-outboard—I filled the gas tank and pumped the bilges. Taking a cold drink of tea from my ever-present stainless steel Stanley Thermos, I was just in the process of leaving the boat dock when a shout brought me up short. Looking up at the marina office, I saw Don, the owner, trotting down the ramp toward the boat dock where I sat in my patrol boat.

"Terry, hold up. I need some help!" Don yelled as he trotted toward my boat slip.

"What can I do you in for, Don?" I asked as he approached.

Arriving at my slip, Don grabbed the side of my boat and took a moment to gather his breath. "Terry, I need some help. I rented one of my boats and motor to a couple of fishermen from Marysville earlier this morning and they went upstream to fish for stripers. I don't know exactly what happened but when they were trying to land a really large striper, they got overly excited, and in that excitement trying to land such a monster, swamped and sank my boat in the river! Another nearby fisherman saw the accident and rescued the two men. But my boat is now sitting on the bottom of the Sacramento River in six feet of water. From what I gathered from the badly shaken men, I think they both leaned over the same side of the boat to land that big striper. When they did, their combined weight rolled the boat, dumping them and all their fishing gear into the river. Right now, I am extremely busy with striper and salmon fishermen needing everything under the sun from bait to boat rentals. There is no way I can leave the marina right now to try and recover my boat if that is even possible. Is there any way you can help me?"

"Sure, Don, I can try. Where did your lads sink her?" I asked.

"Being new to that part of the river, they don't have any idea. However, the fisherman who rescued and brought them back to the marina said it was about two miles upstream on the west side of the river. Fortunately they had the anchor out, and that is keeping the boat from moving downstream into deeper water and eventually being smashed into a million pieces on the nearest set of riffles according to their rescuer."

"I think I can handle that, Don. Let me head upstream and see if I can find the boat. If I do and can retrieve it, I will," I said.

"Damn, man. If you could find it, that would be one big help. I would hate to lose that boat from my fleet right now during the peak of the striper and salmon run. You know those dopes at the insurance company. It will take them a month to settle up with me over the loss. And then by the time I can finally replace that boat and motor, I have lost the money I could have earned this season on its rental," he said.

Don had been very helpful to me since I had arrived as the local Colusa game warden some months earlier.

And even if he hadn't been, I was still part of that small farming community, and I would just find the time to help him out and squeeze that in as part of my upstream patrol work. That's what a good neighbor would do, I thought.

Our discussion over, I moved out through the marina channel and out onto the fast flowing Sacramento River once again. Heading upstream, I kept a watch out on the fishermen I was passing making sure they were legally fishing as well as looking out for Don's sunken boat. Just about two miles upstream, I observed a sunken boat in the crystal clear waters near the west bank of the river. Since the river was low and clear as a bell, finding the sunken boat was a fairly easy matter. However, getting it off the bottom in six feet of water while fighting the collateral swift moving downstream currents would be a chore, I grimly thought as I slowly circled the sunken vessel with my patrol boat examining the situation at hand.

Slowing my patrol boat to a crawl as I moved against the current, I maneuvered up alongside the sunken boat. Looking down into the water's depths, I could see the chaps' fishing rods still lying in the bottom of the boat. However, everything else that could float, like tackle boxes, oars, and life preservers, had long since drifted off down the Sacramento River. Moving upstream above the sunken boat, I dropped my anchor. Slowly letting the anchor line through my fingers, I played it out until I was once again alongside the sunken boat. Fastening my anchor line so I wouldn't drift back any further, I grabbed my grappling hook. After trying a few times to hook the sunken boat with the grappling hook, I soon gave that up as a bad idea. There was nothing really substantial inside the sunken boat onto which I could grab and lift such a heavy weight. The seats were the only really secure anchor points, but my grappling hook kept slipping off every time I tried to lift the boat. Besides, whatever I grappled had to hold when I lifted the entire weight of the boat, water and all, against the swiftly moving river current. I also discovered, every time I tried lifting the boat by grappling the bench seats, its anchor ominously slipped a little bit, letting the sunken boat move even further dangerously downstream toward a massive set of boulder strewn riffles on the west side of the river.

That won't do, I thought after a couple of fruitless tries. Not one hundred yards below my position in the river was a long, deep, boulder-strewn set of riffles that was sure to smash the sunken boat to pieces if it drifted that far. Standing in my boat looking for the longest time down at the sunken boat, I kept coming back to the same damn conclusion and it was a wet and cold one...Stripping off my uniform shirt, gun belt, shoes, socks, leather belt holding up my pants and removing my wallet, into the cold, swiftly moving Sacramento River I went as I slipped over the side of my boat.

Now in those days, I was a rather stout fellow. Not the broken down and just waiting-to-die chap I am today, but a horse. I stood 6-foot 4-inches in my stocking feet and weighed in around 320 pretty solid pounds on a good day. That, plus I could dead lift over five hundred pounds in those days and had done so a fair number of times when called upon to do so. Maybe that is why I am so broken down in the lower back and barely able to wiggle today, eh? Ah, but those were the days when I was young at heart, many times foolish and of course, immortal...

The shock from the cold river took my breath away for a moment as it rose up to my neck, then moments later, I was at home with the elements. Hell, to be frank, the water temperature that day was a lot better than the 36-degree water I had been dumped into while working in

Alaska during my summer college days... Now, that little experience was a shock to the system! But that is a story for another time. If interested in my Alaskan adventures, one can find them in my book titled, Genesis of a Duck Cop, Chapter 12. It is well worth the read. Hanging onto the side of my boat for a few seconds, I gathered in several deep breaths and then dove down to the sunken boat below. While on the bottom, I drifted back toward the stern of the boat, moving hand over hand alongside the side rail with the current, until I arrived at the sunken boat's transom. There I loosened their outboard motor's fasts from the boat's transom. Returning to the surface alongside my boat, I grabbed hold of the side, took a couple more deep breaths and dove once again. When I surfaced that second time, I was carrying the boat's 25-horse outboard motor in my arms. Gathering up my breath and strength as I treaded water, I hefted the motor out of the river and let it tumble onto the floor in the bow of my boat. Then taking the gasoline hose that was still attached to the motor, I reeled in the nearby floating gas tank. That in turn was also loaded onto the floor of my boat. Next, I dove for the men's four valuable fishing rods snagged under the bench seats in the bottom of their boat. Surfacing moments later, I put three fishing rods into the open bow area of my boat. However, the fourth rod was wedged underneath one of the seats and damned if I could pull it out. Its terminal gear had hung up onto something pretty stout downstream and I couldn't dislodge it from under the seat while battling the river's strong current at the same time. That in mind, I left that fishing rod for later, because in its stuck position under the seat it wasn't going anywhere soon to my way of thinking. Gathering in my breath once again and now beginning to feel the adverse effects of the cold river waters on my miserable carcass, I dove again. On the river bottom that time, I grabbed one side of the sunken boat while standing in a crouching position and then stood up. In so doing, I was able to heft the boat upward to where one side was up and eventually partially out of the water. Bouncing the stern of the boat along the bottom, I moved it shoreward into about five feet of water, forcefully dragging the boat's anchor as I went. After catching my breath standing there in neck deep water, I horsed the boat up onto its side once again as far as I could lift it. Then I quickly let it settle back down on its keel. Doing that, I had emptied out about half the water from inside the boat. Now the boat's flotation took over and the vessel did not sink under the weight of the remaining inside water. Swimming back to and reaching into my boat, I grabbed a short piece of rope from the bow, swam back, then pulled and eventually tied the partially sunken boat alongside my patrol boat. After hanging onto the side of my boat for another long moment gathering in my breath, I hoisted myself back into my boat. Once out of the water and into the warmer summer air, I realized just how cold I was. Then I heard the oddest noise. Turning, I looked out into the center portion of the river. There sat three boats full of fishermen watching the crazy game warden swimming in the cold, swift-flowing Sacramento River. The strange noises I had heard were the fishermen clapping their approval over my successful boat retrieval. I think I would have preferred them lending a helping hand to my scraggly cold and sopping wet as a muskrat carcass instead...

Getting my wind and warmth back, I took a bucket from my boat and bailed out the one-time sunken boat until it floated as good as it was going to get. Reaching inside, I grabbed the stubborn fishing rod still wedged under the boat's seat so I could reel in its line and put that into my boat for safekeeping as well.

Jerking it out from under the seat in its stuck position with difficulty, I was surprised to find it still had a fish on its terminal gear! And what a fish it was! It took me about ten minutes to reel in all the line that huge fish had taken off the spool of the reel since the boat had been flipped onto its side and sunk. With that effort, I was finally able to get the big striper in sight. The fish was a giant striper who was pissed off to say the least, if his degree of pulling and tugging had anything to do with his ire! Finally getting the fish alongside the boat, you should have heard all the fishermen sitting in their boats in the middle of the river whooping and hollering in glee. As it turned out, the striper was about a fifty-pounder! Man, now my observing fishermen were really hollering and yelling encouragement. Then you should have heard them when I let the fish go after I had successfully removed the terminal gear from its mouth. For the longest moment, you could have heard a mouse pissin' on a ball of cotton in an Oklahoma Type-5 tornado over their surprise with my release of such a whopper. Then there was an obvious course of discouraging sounds sailing over the water over the fact I had released the fish instead of giving that monster striper to one of them. Now where was all that applause I had heard earlier when I had finally retrieved the sunken boat? I noticed that none of their stringers trailing their boats had any fish approaching the weight or size of the one I had just released. Maybe that is why they weren't saying much of anything encouraging or flattering to the wet as a muskrat game warden, eh?

Finished with the work at hand, I dragged in my previously sunken boat's anchor line and placed it and the anchor into the bottom of my boat after tying off part of its line to my vessel's stern. Reeling my patrol boat in on its anchor line, I finally lifted free. Drifting downstream, I slowly towed the boat back toward the marina. On the way back, I spotted a blue tackle box tangled up in the brush alongside the river on the west bank. Making a slow turn with my towed boat so I wouldn't sink it in the process, I retrieved the tackle box, which was still full of fishing gear. Figuring it had originally come from the fishermen's sunken boat, I placed it on board my boat with the rest of their fishing gear for safekeeping.

Well, I thought. I hadn't done too badly. I had managed to retrieve the boat, motor, and most of the fishermen's gear. Even caught a nice striper in the process, my very first ever of that species of fish landed and my first of the year.

TURNABOUT IS FAIR PLAY

Returning from the upstream portion of the Sacramento River at the end of my sunken boat retrieval mission, I turned into and idled down the narrow channel into the Colusa marina. Arriving at the marina proper with the retrieved boat in tow, I discovered Don, the marina owner, gassing up another fisherman's boat. Hearing the sounds of my approaching motor, he looked up and then jumped for joy on the boat dock like a mad man over what he was seeing. After I had pulled into a nearby empty boat slip, he ran over to me just a-whooping and a-hollering for joy at what he was gleefully witnessing.

"Damn, Terry. I thought you being able to retrieve my boat in that deep and cold damn river was a lost cause. The two fishermen who sunk the boat are upstairs in my office filling out an accident report with Deputy Sheriff

Del Garrison as we speak. I will help you get my boat into another slip and then go up and give those fishermen the good news," he happily chattered like a gray squirrel over another squirrel's newly discovered and unguarded cache of nuts in late summer under a chestnut tree.

With that, Don reached over and untied his boat from my patrol craft. Hauling it over to an empty slip, he knelt down and began tying it to a tie-down on the dock. As he did, I removed the sunken boat's motor and gas tank from my boat and placed them on the boat dock. I did so because if the motor had been running when it was immersed in the cold water, it would need some mechanical work before it could be used once again. Gathering up the rest of the recently retrieved loose gear from my boat, I ambled over to where Don was kneeling, with an armful of fishing rods, tackle box and reels to put back into his boat. As I approached, Don said loudly, "Terry, help me with this dang rope, will you?"

What the hell? I thought. Why does he need me to help him tie up a boat? He sure as hell doesn't need to ask for assistance in such a loud voice.

Walking over to Don, I laid down all the fishing gear, and then knelt down to give him a hand. As I did, he quietly said, "Terry, don't look around and make our conversation obvious! In trailer space No. 4 is a Fleetwood Trailer. Three men from Yuba City rented that space and they have been here for three days. Every day they go out fishing in the morning and evening. And every day, they have been bringing in double limits of stripers. When they came back this morning, they each had a limit of three fish apiece. They took those fish up to their trailer just like any other fisherman would. Somewhat later, two of the men returned to their boat and removed from it a heavy ice chest and took it up the walkway to their trailer.

Just before they got to their trailer, the handle on one end of the ice chest broke and spilled out its contents onto the ground. Terry, that ice chest was clear full of striped bass! There must have been at least another ten fish in that cooler. That was about an hour ago and they have been cleaning fish ever since. But they only take a limit to the fish cleaning station each time and only when no one else is there cleaning fish or looking on. Now here is the good thing. I was in the office looking out when the handle on their red ice chest broke. I saw all that, as did Deputy Del Garrison who was in the office at the same time taking statements from my two fellows who sank my boat! Del was going to hold the fellows with all those fish until you got back but now that won't be necessary. I will let him know you are here." Getting up from tying the boat, Don quietly said, "Terry, you didn't hear that from me. Because if word was ever to get out that I am helping the local game warden by ratting on my clients, well, it ain't good for business, if you get my drift."

With that, he trotted up the ramp to the office with the good news for his two fishermen on the recovery of the boat and their fishing gear. He wasn't gone two minutes when here came my dear friend, Deputy Sheriff Del Garrison. As an aside, my good friend Del died from the ravaging effects diabetes can have on a body some years later. Ironically as I was writing these words to this story in 2012, my wife was playing back some old recorded telephone messages from my children and their kids as they were growing up. It was then that I heard the unmistakable voice of my old friend on the recordings, his voice wracked with emotion, thanking my wife and me for the $250 we had sent him as a Christmas present. As it turned out, we had been the only ones to remember him on that Christmas day... Also, Del had been robbed of his

Social Security check just two days before! Until our Christmas money arrived, he had nothing in the way of money and had been eating one can of beans per day borrowed from a neighbor in order to have something to eat... It was hard for me to continue writing this story for the next few minutes after hearing his voice from the hereafter in the back of the beyond... May you rest in peace, my dear friend, one who was always there for me in my time of need when I was a fish and game warden needing a damn good backup and prisoner transport officer. Not to mention, just a damn good human being and dear friend.

"Hello, Hoss," he said, as his big hand engulfed mine. "Looks like you and I have some unfinished business to attend to. But I would first suggest that you get some clothes on that ugly carcass of yours that says who the hell you really are," as he laughed gently. It was then that I realized I was standing on the boat dock in my wet pants, t-shirt and bare feet. Five minutes later, the deputy and his still-wet-as-a-muskrat but now fully-dressed game warden friend ambled up to the suspect trailer like a couple of bears working the migrating salmon on a spawning stream in Alaska; Del was a larger man than I was.

Knocking on the door of the trailer, the two of us heard some shuffling noises inside like humans make when moving around. Then the door opened and that man, seeing the two of us grinning, monster-sized law dogs, just gasped in shock.

"Gentlemen," began Del. "At 11:51 this morning, I saw you and your partner there sitting at the table drop an ice chest in front of this here trailer. When it hit the ground, it spilled open. I saw at least ten striped bass fall from that cooler. Additionally, just before that time, I saw all three of you here in this trailer come in with nine striped bass on your fish stringers. I now have my little friend the local game warden with me and he would like to check all you fellows' fish." With that, Del turned saying, "It is all yours, Little Buddy."

Stepping around my bear-sized friend, I said, "Afternoon, Lads. My name is Terry Grosz and as you can see, I am a state fish and game warden. A wet one from a recent dip in the Sacramento River, but a warden just the same. Deputy Garrison here tells me you lads have a fish or two too many. Now before any of you embarrass yourselves with some denials, here is where we are as I see it. I didn't see any of these reported over limits of fish or you fellows fishing. Therefore, I have no legal right under the Fourth Amendment of the Constitution to search any of you personally or your trailer. That amendment guarantees one against an unreasonable search and seizure of their person, place or things. And since I did not see any of the alleged illegal activity, any subsequent search of your trailer on my part would be unreasonable under the law and illegal. However, the deputy here is not only a law enforcement officer of the state but an expert striped bass fisherman as well. And he knows the current fishing regulations like the back of his hand. He directly saw the three of you each bring a legal limit of stripers to your trailer earlier this morning. Then he saw two of you go back to your boat and bring up a heavy ice chest. Lastly, he saw a handle on that ice chest break, probably from carrying too much weight. When the ice chest hit the ground, he saw at least ten stripers fall out. With the nine fish the three of you brought up earlier and at least ten more in the ice chest, that puts you lads a tad over the limit." The limit was three striped bass per person per day and the possession limit was also limited to three. "Now we can do this one of two ways. The three of you can grant me full and complete inspection rights of the trailer and ice chests on a voluntary basis. Or, Deputy Garrison will stay right here and I will record his information on what he saw earlier. With that firsthand information, I will go to the county attorney here in Colusa, get a search warrant based on the deputy's firsthand information and return. With that search warrant, I will then conduct a full and lawful search of the trailer and your ice chests. The choice is yours, Gentlemen, but only with the full and complete understanding that any right of search you give me must be totally voluntary. And, realizing full well if I discover anything illegal during that search, those goods will be seized and the resultant case will be handled accordingly in a court of law at the Colusa Justice Court here in town."

With that I stood back and just looked at the lads. In fact, from where I stood in the open doorway of the trailer, I could see what looked like an over limit of undersize stripers lying every which way in their small kitchen sink! Now in those days, the legal size length for striped bass was a minimum of fifteen inches or the fish had to be returned unharmed back to the river. The reason for that length requirement, according to the fisheries biologists, was that striped bass didn't spawn unless they achieved at least that minimum length. Bottom line, to catch and destroy your fisheries resource before it had a chance to mature and spawn is a one-way ticket to biological ruination of a wild population. I don't think any of the bass in that sink waiting to be cleaned, from what I could see from where I stood, were over that minimum length! Just another foolish example of Man's greed destroying his resource before it could procreate. Hell, I never found striped bass such good eating that one had to take over limits or short fish anyway. Now take a mess of pink-meated pan-fried brook trout and you have some good eats.

The lad standing at the door turned and looked at his buddies. They, in turn, looked back at him like a couple of African meerkats who had just seen a bird of prey circling close-at-hand overhead. One that was to close for comfort and their burrow was no way close enough to guarantee a successful escape.

"Well, what do you guys want to do?" he asked his buddies with resignation in his voice.

"I don't think we have much choice," said the heavy set one. "Either way, he has us," the man continued glumly.

"I will tell you what. The deputy and I will wait outside. In the meantime, the three of you lads fetch out all the stripers you have caught since you rented this trailer space several days ago. Do that full well knowing that I am still going to search your trailer anyway when you are done, with your consent or with a warrant. And in the process, I don't want to hear any toilet flushing," I continued Flushing short striper filets down a toilet was a common practice when one was cornered in a house trailer or motor home during a fish and game inspection.

For the next five minutes, that trailer fairly rained stripers! Whole fish, gutted fish, frozen fish, and fish fillets fairly rained from within as Del and I stood there in disbelief. When the striper rain stopped, there were 59 striped bass or parts thereof laid out on the grass of their trailer space in front of God and everybody. And I do mean everybody. By now, Del and I had attracted quite a crowd of curious on-lookers. Other campers and fishermen staying in the trailer park at that marina had also gathered around looking on in disbelief at the rain of stripers. At first there was a lot of muttering, shaking of heads and clucking of tongues. That was soon followed by outright choruses of disgust for the fish hogs greed raining down around their heads from the curious crowd of onlookers. Finally, entering their trailer after the rain of stripers had subsided, I discovered a large plate full of freshly fried fillets hidden in the oven. Taking those out and counting two fillets to make a fish, I added another seven illegal fish to their over limits! That was, of course, after the lads admitted to the fact they were also some of the over limits of stripers they had caught days earlier and had forgotten to declare during their moment of shame.

Picture that scene from so long ago if you will. Two bear-like officers, one dripping wet but still beautiful of course, confronting three whipped illegal fishermen now looking like a mess of cornered African meerkats. A disgusted crowd grumbling at the fish hogs, in tones now clearly understood by all, that a necktie party was too good for my chaps with the gross over limits. And now, after adding the plate of fried filets, 66 unfortunate stripers representative of three men's greed, all laid out in front of God and everybody. A pretty picture it did not make unless you were a hunter of humans...

Asking for and receiving the lads' fishing and driver's licenses, I began the citation paperwork. A citation for each of my chaps for possession of gross over limits of striped bass and under-sized fish seemed to make the gathered crowd less grumpy. They went from restive to extremely happy when the three fishermen's fishing gear was also seized. When the paperwork was done, I got a not-too-unusual surprise from the crowd of legal fishermen. The "fair chase" fishermen standing around after I had taken pictures of the evidence ended up expertly cleaning all the fish! Previously, they had asked what was going to happen to all the seized fish. I explained that the county attorney always let me give them to those less fortunate souls who were considered needy. When they heard that, they asked permission and the fish were filleted out in fine style by a small group of "happy to be of service," good-natured fishermen.

Of note, one of that group of fish cleaners was a man and recent friend named George Elliott. He had told me earlier in our relationship when I had checked him river fishing one evening, that he was one of the Army chaps—the other was Joe McDonald—who many years earlier had spotted huge flights of aircraft approaching Hawaii on his new and still experimental radar set. You know, the ones approaching Pearl Harbor on December 7th, 1941... He radioed his superior with the news and was told to shut down his radar and go get some breakfast. His superior contended that the flights George was probably seeing were from an expected flight of B-17s coming in that morning from the mainland. The only thing was that the flight of aircraft George was seeing were coming from the opposite direction of the mainland... George pointed out that fact but was rebuffed once again by his officer of the day, told to shut down his radar set and go and get some breakfast. George never forgave himself after that for not being more forceful and getting the warnings out in time. He died a bitter man several years later, still blaming himself for all the deaths that followed after the Japanese had bombed our naval base at Pearl Harbor. It always amazed me over the years, just how many bits and pieces of American history I ran across while performing my duties as a state fish and game warden. Pieces of history that, for the most part along with their storytellers, are now lost to the ages...

Realizing I had citations to file in court and fish to distribute to disadvantaged families before they spoiled, I shut down the rest of my planned river patrols for the day. Walking back down toward the dock to retrieve my law enforcement equipment from the patrol boat, I began preparations in my mind for the next day's river patrols. In the process, I passed Don on the boat ramp leading up to the marina office.

As we passed and without any noticeable movement of recognition on his part, he quietly said, "Turnabout is fair play." With that, he proceeded on his way because to do any more in front of God and everybody openly visiting with the local game warden, might just be misconstrued by some on-lookers and bad for business... It was surprising to me the number of tips I got from Don after that. Particularly, those relating to over limits being landed and smuggled into the Colusa Marina. Especially after I had retrieved his sunken boat...

My three lads each later forfeited $500 bail for their over limit and short bass possessions. They also lost all their fishing gear to the State of California. The only good thing about the loss of so many fish, if there ever is any good that comes from such resource thievery, was that the fish appeared to be mostly all males instead of the more valuable egg-laying females.

THE FISH OF A LIFETIME

In addition to the striper and salmon runs in the Sacramento River, the white and green sturgeon were migrating in the river on their way to spawn as well. To my non-fishing readers, salmon are anadromous species of fish. That is, they migrate from saltwater into fresh water to spawn. Sturgeon, on the other hand, are catadromous. That means they migrate downstream from freshwater into a brackish marine environment in which to spawn. Many a hopeful fisherman staked out the sturgeons' historically known, deep resting pools in the river for an opportunity at catching these gentle, great eating, especially smoked, giants of the river. Once again to my non-fishing readers, white sturgeon can attain weights of over one thousand pounds and the green sturgeon, their smaller cousins, can weigh upwards of four hundred pounds. In fact, I can remember vividly many of my Sacramento River patrol experiences when it came to this noble and ancient fish. A creature that has remained basically unchanged for the last 65 million years! More than a dozen times on the river during my adventures as a game warden, I got the neatest of natural history surprises that one can ever hope to experience. All such happenings were garnered while on my Sacramento River patrols with "Mr. White Sturgeon." My fish and game patrol boat was eighteen feet in length and had an eight-foot beam. During those memorable times while flying upstream on step, I met Mr. White Sturgeon up close and personal-like in his own world of wildlife. Numerous times I had these great fish suddenly porpoise alongside my patrol boat as I zipped along at twenty miles per hour. And when that happened, they would porpoise right alongside my patrol boat no more than a few feet distant! Many of those that did were longer than my patrol boat, and I never saw their heads or tails! I also experienced the same thing when they crossed right, and I do mean right, in front of my speeding patrol boat. Many times they were so close that I would try quickly chopping the throttle for fear of collision and injuring the fish. It was during those times I never saw their heads or tails either, as they were longer than my boat was wide! It was easy to understand, when a wildlife officer experienced such occasions as described above, that working seven-day weeks and sixteen-hour days seemed so insignificant when it came to the officer's wellbeing when it came to protecting such noble and unique critters...

In those days, the State of California did not let anyone keep any sturgeon taken on a hook and line if it was shorter than four feet in total length. Any longer than that and one could keep them providing they were lawfully taken by the hook in the mouth method. And believe me, that great eating species had many a die-hard fisherman hot after such critters. It was during one of my many Sacramento River patrols that I ran across a special adventure and memory that is still vivid in my old carcass even to this day. And, that is some 45- plus years after the event!

One fine summer morning while zipping along up on step on the river to reduce my wake so I wouldn't disturb any nearby quietly anchored fishing boats, I passed a down river fisherman standing up in the front of his boat. His partner in the stern of the boat was keeping the boat slowly idling in gear and mid-river in position. The man in the bow appeared to be using a four-foot ocean rod and a Penn 9/0 reel holding at least eighty-pound test monofilament fishing line. It didn't take a genius to realize the man was a dyed- in-the-wool sturgeon fisherman and had one on the end of his line. And from all appearances, what a sturgeon he had hooked! The fish was so large, it was actually dragging the fishermen and their boat upstream against the current! Sensing an epic battle to the death, I slid my patrol boat onto the opposite shore and quietly parked it up on the edge of the bank and out of the way. There I quietly sat fascinated as I watched man battling nature's giant in its purest of forms. And what an epic battle it turned out to be!

The man running the boat would warn off any other passing boatmen with a wave of his arms in order not to have their boat's propellers inadvertently cut the hard working sturgeon fisherman's line. Soon there were about six or seven boats full of curious fishermen sitting in the river out of the way watching the man battle his still yet unseen river monster. This epic battle continued for over the next hour without anyone seeing neither hide nor hair, eh, scutes (bony external plates or highly modified scales) of the great fish!

In fact, the battle was so strenuous, the bowman would relinquish his fishing pole to the stern man who would take a turn at the monster. At the same time, the bowman would take his turn at running the motor in order to get some rest and his arm strength back. Then when he had recovered his arm and shoulder strength sufficiently, he would return to the epic battle trading positions with the man in the bow of the boat to take his place once again in battling the monster, here-to-fore unseen fish.

An hour and forty minutes into the battle, I could see the giant fish was beginning to tire. Sometimes his tail could be seen slapping the water's surface. And what a huge tail it was! But the river monster was not ready to yield up its life so easily and would once again sound for the protection the comforting depths of the river offered. Then the man with the rod and reel would start all over again struggling to reel in the giant fish. This seesaw battle went on for another fifteen minutes and finally I could see the fisherman was winning the battle with what had to be the biggest fish of his lifetime.

Slowly, ever so slowly, the river giant was succumbing to the greater force of man with a geared fishing reel. Then another fisherman moved his boat over to the boat fighting the sturgeon and transferred one of his passengers into that boat to assist. The new man assumed the operation of the motor. The original motor operator then walked forward in his boat and retrieved a giant gaff. In the meantime, the man fighting the fish, sensing his imminent victory, continued horsing the now tiring sturgeon up from the depths of the river and closer to his boat. Finally, all of us could see the great fish occasionally tiredly rolling on the surface. By now, a dozen boats had gathered to silently watch this epic, probably a once in a lifetime battle between man and his much-prized river monster.

However, lost in the crowd of gathered fishermen was one quiet tule-creeper of game warden flavor. He may have been lost in the crowd but he was watching the battle intently. For some reason, my guardian angels were raising hell with my inner being over what I had been witnessing for some time. Raising hell like something was wrong or out of place in this man versus sturgeon epic battle. Having been there before with my guardian angels and sensing they were signaling me to be alert, I paid heed...

Moments later the great fish finally gave up in exhaustion, rolled over onto its back and allowed itself to be slowly reeled into the range of the man standing in the boat with the deadly gaff. That was my cue. Starting up my patrol boat's engine, I slowly idled closer to the ending battle between man and the great fish. The fish was at least fifteen to sixteen feet in length and was a white sturgeon, the largest of the U.S. species. A white sturgeon weighing in at what had to be somewhere between seven hundred and a thousand pounds! Now really exhausted, the great fish allowed itself to be dragged even closer toward the boat and the man with his deadly gaff poised to soon end a magnificent life. A life of a great fish that to my way of thinking because of its huge size, had to be at least a hundred years old! Yes my readers, seventy- to one-hundred-year- old sturgeon were not that uncommon in California's major rivers in that day. However, in 2012, because of habitat loss, unfavorable water temperatures, pollution, legal over fishing and illegal fishing, the sturgeon populations in many of California's major rivers, especially the northern waterways, have been extirpated or are in jeopardy.

Then I noticed something! The fish had been foul-hooked because clearly stuck in its back, in front of its dorsal fin, was a large treble hook still holding some of its original bait! To be a lawful catch, the State of California required a fish to take the hook into its mouth. Hooked anywhere else was considered a foul hooked or snagged fish and was illegal to take and possess! It quickly became apparent that the location of that hook awkwardly placed far back near its dorsal fin and the huge size of the fish, had accounted for the long battle to drag it up from the bottom of the river!

With that discovery, I yelled for the man with the gaff to back off and not gaff the fish!

"What?" he said in utter disbelief as he looked over at a man whom he now realized was obviously a uniformed fish and game officer.

"That fish is foul-hooked and cannot lawfully be taken," I yelled back. "Do not gaff that fish! It cannot legally be taken or possessed."

By now all the boat traffic, silent up to that time, began to hoot and holler at me for not letting the man land and keep his fish of a lifetime. I just ignored those not in the know with their alligator mouths and hummingbird hind ends flapping in the breeze. Like an old-time game warden once told me, "Terry, if you do your job right, you will be called a son-of-a-bitch. And if you don't do your job right, you will be called a son-of-a-bitch. So, what kind of a son- of-a-bitch do you want to be?" Well, the adjacent river fishermen raising hell over my warning actions were about to discover what I already knew...

Idling my patrol boat over to the fishermen's boat with the snagged fish, I approached from the stern so as not to cut the fisherman's line with my propeller. Confirming that the fish was indeed foul-hooked, I pointed that out to the boat's occupants. Then I had the man running the motor slowly move their boat over to the west bank of the river where the water was shallower and less swift. Doing so, he dragged the exhausted monster sturgeon slowly along with him. Quickly stripping down to just my pants and t- shirt, I hastily anchored my boat and slipped overboard into the river. Standing in neck-deep water, I moved over and tried wrapping my arms around the girth of that exhausted giant fish so I could turn him belly-side down. There was no way that was going to happen! The fish was just too large for me to do that! And remember, I stood 6-foot 4-inches in height and had a set of arms, the length of which that would have made an orangutan proud. Grabbing the fish around its body as best as I could, I righted the river monster upright from its now exhausted belly-up position. That allowed the fish to breathe more normally and began reducing its shock and stress from the exhausting fight. Then I reached up and, with a requested fillet knife handed to me from a nearby boat crew, carefully removed the treble hook deeply snagged in one of the bony scutes in its back.

As expected, the fisherman catching the sturgeon was now not only exhausted from the long battle but almost physically sick over the prospect of losing his catch of a lifetime. He had just caught the largest fish of his life and had fought a hard battle for it in the process. Now the fish of a lifetime was being taken from him, due to no intentional fault of his own, and soon to be released if the man in green up to his neck in river waters, had his druthers. The fisherman was horribly disappointed as he resignedly looked at his monster fish of a lifetime lying close at hand in the water next to the side of his boat, soon to be released.

In the meantime, I was concerned as well. I was holding onto a fish of monstrous proportions with numerous wicked rows of scutes (heavy bony scales with hooks) running the full length of its body. If the fish suddenly decided to take off, it could tear my flesh with those barbed scutes like a warm knife going through a cube of butter! Then I had another major concern. The fish was so weakened from the hours-long battle, that it could not normally right itself. In short, it was near death from exhaustion, which was not uncommon in many large fish species after a long and exhausting fight due to the lactic acid buildup in its musculature! Moving forward on the fish in the neck-deep water, I looped my arms around its body in front of its pectoral fins as best as I could. However, I made sure my arms were not impeding the sturgeon's gill plates so it could continue breathing. Then I slowly began moving the fish back and forth in the water. By so doing, I was running extra-oxygenated water across its gill filaments hoping to revive the fish. For the longest time, the fish barely moved in my arms. And if I hadn't been moving the extra-oxygenated water across its gills, I doubt it would have had the strength to do so by itself. Then after about thirty minutes of moving it back and forth in the water, I could feel the fish slowly growing stronger in my arms. Now it could hold itself upright but it was still pretty weak. So, I continued my back-and-forth movement in the water, running extra-oxygenated water over its gills for about another twenty minutes. Soon the sturgeon was slowly moving its tail back and forth but was still too weak to right itself and swim off normally in the river's swift currents. Realizing there was no way I was going to release that magnificent fish in such a weakened condition, I hung on. After continuing my oxygenating treatment for another twenty minutes, I could now feel the sturgeon getting ever stronger in my arms. Then it began slowly moving its tail and other fins with purpose. Finally, I felt the great fish give a shudder to rid itself of me as it slowly swam out of my loosening grasp. Moments later the great fish swam away and disappeared into the Sacramento River's depths. That was the last I saw of my friend.

Turning and now starting to shake uncontrollably from the river water's cold, I attempted to hoist myself back into my nearby boat. It took two tries but soon I was back shivering like a dog crapping peach pits in my patrol boat. Then a cheer went up from the fishermen in the many boats now anchored nearby in the river watching the unfolding drama between man and an ancient fish of storied size. I even got a cheer from my fisherman who had caught the fish of a lifetime, only to watch it, because of unusual legal circumstances, slip away forever. In the rush of that moment, I discovered many fishermen had moved closer to the action and had taken numerous pictures of the great fish. Some even with their Polaroid cameras. My fisherman was only too happy to get those proffered forms of evidence documenting the biggest fish tale of his young life. It seemed once my gathered fishermen realized that the fish had been foul-hooked by mistake and had to be released under the law, they had warmed up to and finally applauded the catch-and-release efforts on my part.

Speaking of warming up, I was sure glad to get out of the cold river water, back into the boat and into the sun's warming rays. Sitting there half-dressed, I once again explained to my sturgeon fisherman why his fish was released and he concurred with my decision. My guess was the fish had made a huge lunge for his bait, misjudged the target of his intentions and had snagged itself on its back. However, that clumsy yet lucky maneuver saved its life. That and having the resident game warden close at hand to see what had unintentionally happened and ultimately looking out for the welfare of the ancient monster fish.

That incident occurred in 1968. Most of my dyed-in-the-wool sturgeon fishermen reading these lines also realize something else. That long-lived fish could still be alive today if it hasn't run afoul of an illegal net being run in the Sacramento River delta or from the hook of another fisherman.

Even today as I edit these words about my monster fish some 46 years later, I consider it some of my finest law enforcement work as a game warden. Being a game warden isn't always just about catching folks doing what they shouldn't be doing in the world of wildlife. It is about far more than that with conservation education of the masses being at the top of the list. But let me tell you, releasing a fish of such size and age is one great feeling that is not easily replicated during one's lifetime. And to those fishermen who were floating around near at hand that fine day watching on, I hope they learned a valuable lesson about caring for our nation's dwindling natural resources. I wonder if any of that monster fish's progeny are still alive today as a result of my lucky presence on the Sacramento River during that unique moment in time so long ago? If so, then living in this shell of a broken down and worn out old body today, as a result of my many hours of hard labor in and for the world of wildlife throughout the years, is certainly well worth it.

THE JUDGE TAKES A SWIM

Judge Weyand was my eastern district of Colusa County Justice Court Judge. He was an elderly, kind-hearted gentleman who many times caused me fits through some of his oddball judicial courtroom decisions. Since my arrival as one of the Colusa district's game wardens, I had managed to redo our county's antiquated fish and game bail schedule. One that I had inherited from my predecessor, Warden C. J. "Feather-Foot" Winn, upon my arrival as the new local Colusa game warden in 1967. In so doing, I began creating a new administrative system of minimum bail schedules that reflected an appropriate modern day, real-life penalty situation as it related to fish and wildlife violations. Heretofore, the fish and game bail schedule had been set so low that its deterrent value was basically non-existent. Twenty-five dollar fines for a large over limit of ducks or geese were just not cutting it when it came to taming my wildlife outlaw crowd! And in many other like cases involving really serious wildlife violations, the fines being levied by my judge weren't much better in the deterrent department either. So, off to the salt mines I went to change the antiquated bail schedule. That meant endless meetings with the county attorney and both Colusa County judges, trying to justify higher minimum bail figures that properly addressed modern day wildlife violations. Finally getting the bail schedule up into the realm of Twentieth Century reality and getting it signed off on by both my two judges, I was finally pleased with my efforts in addressing that issue. In short, the more serious the fish and game violation, the higher the bail and/or time incarcerated. Shortly thereafter, I ran afoul of what I came to call the "Judge Weyand Factor." Many times I would catch a chap with large over limits of wildlife, really serious late or early shooting violations—in excess of one hour—taking game during the closed season, spotlighting deer or the closed season taking of our rare in population numbers, resident California tule elk, the smallest sub-species of our three species of elk in north America; cases that I considered intentional and seriously destructive in nature. Then as I was soon to discover, once that chap stood before the mast in the Colusa Justice Court, the kindly old judge would reduce the fine, sometimes return the illegal game, or even let the outlaw go free altogether. Especially if the miscreant was a local and had a sob story! Soon the deterrent value of my newly increased bail schedule on the eastern side of my district, had been more or less reduced to zippo! Fortunately, I had a different justice court judge on the western side of my patrol district and he didn't need any help in fairly adjudicating the legal issues at hand if you get my drift... However, my enforcement related problems on the eastern side of my patrol district continued to mount and multiply. Especially when the really bad guys, many times my local dyed in the wool wildlife outlaws, realized all they had to do in front of the old judge, was to roll around on the courtroom floor, wail, cry crocodile tears, and say they would never do it again. And all too frequently if they did all that, they were more or less rewarded with severely reduced fines or being let completely off the hook and allowed to roam free in their killing sort of ways once again! As one can plainly see, not a really good recipe for holding the line against the march of fish and game violations or reining in the violating SOB's committing such crimes. Particularly since the natural resources of this great land of ours are limited in their scope and nature. And I just couldn't shoot my outlaws once apprehended in the field for the wildlife crimes they had committed because that type of reaction on the part of the law enforcement officer, had gone the way of the cowboy and hanging horse thieves... Damn, I was fit to be hog tied and fed to the valley's nearest yellow billed magpies over my judge's many times lenient courtroom decisions.

One day shaking my head over the latest serious wildlife case in which Judge Weyand had essentially pissed backwards, I got a goofy idea up my sleeve. Keep in mind my patient readers, sometimes wild-eyed desperation can lead one to take a bath in one's own endeavors if that chap is not careful... Maybe if I could get the old judge to go out with me on an actual patrol and see the scope and degree of the problems in the wildlife law enforcement arena that would help me be more effective. Particularly, those situations he was causing me fits over because of his low fines and other activist decisions. The more I thought that brilliant idea over, the more I liked it. Sharing my concerns and idea with Bonny Grussenmeyer, the Colusa Justice Court Clerk, I got her support and the green light to give my idea a try. Thereafter, every chance I got, I went to work on the old judge. And in so doing, quietly softening him up to the idea of a "ride-along-and-a-look-see-for himself" with the local game warden. It took several weeks of hard work but I finally succeeded in convincing the old judge of the value of the ride-along with the local game warden. Then "dag nab it," he would get a real taste of the wildlife law enforcement world and some of its problems. Especially some of the problems he created on what I considered serious wildlife crimes through his lowered damn penalties. But, I didn't mention that second part of the basis of my scheme to the judge for obvious reasons...

Next, I figured I had to pick the right kind of patrol for the ride-along or my idea would backfire. Backfire, because running around in the outback and outside the courtroom was not one of the judge's strong points. That deduction was based on the fact that he was pretty old and out of shape. So, I didn't figure into the equation having him running across the countryside chasing down a poacher. Somehow, I just didn't figure that was too judge-like and one in which he would consider a good learning experience... Plus, I figured I would only get one time in the barrel so, my field patrol lesson laid out before the old judge had to be a good teaching and learning moment.

Then to my way of thinking, the right occasion soon arose. It was a typical Sacramento Valley summer day, hot and humid. The stripers and sturgeon were in full run on the Sacramento River, as was the summer run of monster-sized king salmon. A river run in my patrol boat was always a great ride because of the cooling surrounding river waters and the heaps of fishing activity, both legal and illegal to keep ones interest up. Yep, I thought, that is what I am going to do. I will take the old judge out for a great river ride, show him lots of action, and buy him a cold beer at the distant down river Grimes Marina when all was said and done. Yes sir, that will give the old judge a real taste of the fish and game action, I happily concluded. Little did I realize, he was going to get more action on that kind of patrol then either of us ever realized or anticipated...!

Come the anointed day to take the old judge out for a ride on the river, I was ready. Hell, I was more than ready! The unmarked patrol boat, which looked like any other fishermen's craft, had been cleaned from stem to stern, was all gassed up, and ready to go. My patrol truck had been washed from stem to stern, the first time in a year, was for once spic and span and all gussied up. My uniform was in such great condition that I looked the part of a full-fledged Mexican general in the bright sunlight! Hell, I was beautiful... Yes, I was more than ready for my judge's soon to be joyous and enlightening ride-along. Now there you cautious readers go again. Just stop it! No, I didn't run over anyone or swamp the boat with the kindly old judge in it. I can't believe you non-trusting chaps reading these lines. The judge was taking a trip with the valley's Teutonic knight, also known as "The Great Grotz," not some damned knot head. You chaps reading these lines need to get with the program and have more confidence in your storyteller. Zuh!

Sliding by the judge's residence on a perfectly beautiful Saturday morning late, I gathered him up at the chosen hour and off we merrily went. Now for you unwashed, I had several methods of operation when working my assigned thirteen miles of Sacramento River fishermen. I could quietly anchor my patrol boat at the faraway head or tail end of a long line of fishermen as they fished from their boats. Sitting there anchored in an unmarked boat, I would quietly sit and watch my fishermen with my naked eyes or with the sly use and aid of a pair of binoculars. Upon spotting a violation, I would motor over to my miscreant and take care of business. Or, I could fly down the river with my patrol boat. Once up and on step, the boat would leave little or no wake to offend any close-at-hand fishermen anchored in their boats. As I roared by far off to one side of my unsuspecting fishermen and before anyone could clean up their illegal activity, like using extra fishing lines, I could look them over closely. If I saw a violation, I could snap my boat around on a dime, drop the throttle to avoid cavitation, and then slam the throttle forward once again. By operating in that cowboy manner, I would be on my violators almost every time before they could get rid of the suspected evidence of any wrongdoing. But if they did get rid of their wrongdoing, I would still have the observed evidence of illegality in my mind's eye and that was all I needed for a court of law. All methods worked very well and today just for the judge's enjoyment and learning experience, I chose the speeding-patrol- boat-routine. That way, he would get a nice ride, we could avoid the valley's heat with the cooling air flowing over the windshield once I was up on step and maybe even catch a chap or two screwing up in front of the judge in the process. Then the old judge could see the load of fishing traffic I had to deal with on a daily basis, maybe witness the numerous violations firsthand, and still have a nice morning ride out on the Sacramento River's cooling waters. With that, he could multiply those river situations with all the other wildlife related adventure problems I had in my patrol district and get a damn good idea of the workload I carried and the problems I faced. Yep, I had it all figured out down to a small bug's eyebrow. Except, I had forgotten that bugs didn't have eyebrows...!

Judge Weyand and I boarded my patrol boat at the Colusa Marina and, while preparing for our trip, I briefed the judge on my anticipated patrol procedures. He seemed pleased to be going for a pleasant boat ride and extremely happy with the thought of a cold beer at the end of the first leg of the trip. I figured with all that initial judicial feedback I was receiving, I was getting an A-plus so far...

Oh, one other thing before we hit the waterways. In California in those days, a freshwater inland fisherman could only use one line while fishing. A favorite ploy of my river fishermen, especially when the stripers were running hot and heavy, was to use two or more lines. Plain and simple, the more lines overboard meant better chances to catch more fish for the illegal fishermen. And man, I had a mess of illegal fishermen on the river in those days! Their favorite illegal fishing tactic was to anchor one decoy pole high in the air with a line over the side where it could readily be seen by any passing game warden. Then my chaps wanting to violate the law and increase their chances of catching more stripers would do the following. When they thought no one was watching their little sleight of hand, they would bait up another fishing rig and quietly, without any fanfare, let the terminal gear from that set-up slip the appropriate fishing distance behind them by letting the line run over the stern of their boat by hand. Then they would lay that fishing rod down flat in the bottom of their boat, so it would look like they were only fishing with one rod and line. If the badge carrier wasn't really on his toes, that ploy would work slicker than cow slobbers because one could easily overlook the extra fishing line lying just over the transom and almost out of sight trailing into the water behind the boat.

However, my illegal fishermen didn't realize they had a local game warden that had the eyes of an eagle—20/10 vision in those days—plus the apprehension and closing speed of a peregrine falcon in a dive on an unsuspecting rabbit. Well, maybe a rather large falcon ... but a highly beautiful one as all my readers have come to know. I had a trick I used that most fishermen didn't realize was smoother than a schoolmarm's thigh. I would zoom by in my patrol boat and, from a distance off to one side, quick-check my fishermen and their stringers of fish floating in the water behind their boats. As I steamed by, I would always look just behind the transoms of their boats. If they were running more than one fishing line, unbeknownst to my illegal fishermen, that extra monofilament line would be seen glistening in the sunlight as it laid over the stern. So it was an easy task on my sharp-eyed part to just count the glistening fishing lines as I roared by. And if I spotted more than one line per fisherman hanging over the stern leading from the end of a cleverly hidden fishing pole laying down in the bottom of the boat, I would snap my speeding boat around so fast that the illegal fisherman would hardly have any time to react. And when I did a quick turn around, I would always bark out, "State fish and game warden. Don't touch that extra line! I want to check it." If they did not comply and managed to cut the offending illegal line before I got alongside which was a common occurrence, I had another charge to lie on them beside the "fishing with two poles" violation. One called "Failure To Show" under section 2012 of the California Fish and Game Code. And that count was an additional fifty dollars per charge for failure to comply with the officer's order. That was if Judge Weyand subsequently didn't mess around with the citations in open court, believe the violator's sob story, and reduce their fine in the process... For my sharper thinking readers, you have to be asking yourselves why I didn't object in open court when such "cry me a river" situations occurred. Simple. A violator could appear in court at any time before his appearance date after the citation had been issued to settle the matter. And many times when that occurred, I would be out and about on a backcountry patrol and unavailable for said unplanned courtroom appearances or out of radio contact and couldn't be reached. And, when I didn't or couldn't show up for my violator's appearances, that is when the courtroom chicanery would take place. And it was only then after the miscreant's solo appearance, that I would discover the many times sad disposition of said case.

Moving out through the marina channel, we slowly entered the mighty Sacramento River. Checking to make sure no other boats were nearby to avoid a collision and finding the way clear, I fire- walled the throttle of my speedy, eighteen-foot inboard-outboard patrol boat. Within moments, we were up on step and fairly flying down the picturesque and historic river. I looked over at the old judge and he seemed to be having a grand time. Good, I thought. Maybe he will see how hard I work and let that be reflected in the future fines department when the bad guys are brought before his court for screwing with Mother Nature.

Down river we flew until I spotted a suspect stringer holding way too many stripers trailing from a boat holding three fishermen. The daily limit of stripers per fisherman in those days was three. The stringer on my suspect boat appeared to be holding way more fish than the nine they could collectively possess and my lads were still fishing! Snapping the boat around, I saw one of the fishermen near the stern, realizing that I might be a game warden by my radical boat actions, lunge for the stringer of striped bass trailing behind their boat in plain view. "Don't touch that stringer of fish!" I bellowed as my patrol boat snapped around. "State fish and game warden and I want to check that stringer of fish," I yelled. My efforts were to no avail as the man released the entire stringer of fish hanging from the side of his boat and it quickly sank out of sight into the Sacramento River. Gone and wasted forever were those poor live fish still hooked to the stringer and unable to escape! Fish that would hang there on that stringer until they slowly and cruelly starved to death at the bottom of the river or were eaten alive by the crawdads!

Pulling up alongside their boat, I said, "Didn't you hear me tell you not to touch that stringer of fish, that I wanted to check them?"

The man who had released the stringer of fish just shrugged his shoulders like "no big deal." Without showing my red over such a waste, not to mention the cruelty involved to the critters still fatally hooked to the stringer and now more than likely bouncing along on the bottom of the river heading downstream, I asked the men for their fishing licenses. They all checked out legal like on their fishing licenses. It was then that I asked my smart aleck who had illegally released the stringer of fish and had disobeyed my earlier order for him not to do so, for his driver's license.

"What for?" he mouthed off. "I ain't driving."

"I asked to check that stringer of fish because it appeared to me that there were a number of short bass on it and an over limit as well. However, you chose not to let me check the stringer, even though I gave you a verbal command not to release it. Now you will be receiving a citation for 'Failure To Show Upon Demand' for releasing that stringer after being told not to do so."

"You think so? Where is your evidence that we had any fish, you goofy hind end of a state parasite?" he retorted in a rather sour, having had too many beers manner. It always amazed me what a few beers could do to mess up one's common sense. And in so doing, always seemed to lead to one running his alligator mouth and overloading his hummingbird ass at the wrong time in the wrong place...

"That evidence is in my head. I saw the stringer of fish. And when I saw you move toward them, I shouted for you to leave that stringer alone because I wanted to check them. You disobeyed that verbal command and chose to do otherwise. That illegal action just guaranteed you a citation for 'Failure to Show Upon Demand' which will later be filed into the Colusa Justice Court."

"The hell you say," he said. "There are three witnesses in this boat who will testify there were no fish on any stringer. Me and my two buddies here. So, I will see your sorry ass in court," he growled. There went that "alligator mouth overloading one's hummingbird ass" thing once again, all fueled by a couple of beers too many.

I never said a thing in return and neither did my judge. I prayed with all my heart that my chap would later personally show up in court in front of the very judge who had seen his illegal fish dumping actions as well. Then let my outlaw try running a sob story by my judge. My chap was then issued a citation over his grumbling that he would see me in court ringing in my ears. With that work finished, we took off once again heading downstream. Man, was I ever glad the judge had just witnessed what some of my river problems were like, particularly when the stripers were running heavy. I could only pray that chap would personally show up in Judge Weyand's court with the same sour attitude just exhibited in front of God and everybody on the river.

Roaring downstream once again, I looked over at my judge out of the corner of my eyes to see if he had anything to say about what had just occurred. He was just looking downstream once again enjoying the brisk ride and the cooling wind over the windshield. Then he stood up in the boat and sat down on the top of the back of his seat. That way he could see more of what was going on around him and enjoy the cooling air flowing over the bow even more. Looking over at me with a big grin he said, "I am having a grand time." Then he said, "I can see better this way, plus the onrushing air is really cooling me off in this dang summer heat."

Now really pleased the judge was thoroughly getting into the patrol, I stepped up the speed. Zipping along about thirty miles per hour, about a mile further downstream we passed a boat with two fishermen. As I always did when we passed, I counted the lines glistening as they lay over the stern of their boat. There were four lines hanging over the transom of that boat! Two of those lines were legal since each fisherman could lawfully fish with one line and two were illegal. Without a moment's hesitation or second thought, I spun the wheel of my speeding patrol boat and snapped its direction hard-a-port—to the left, you landlubbers—toward my two illegal fishermen. "Don't touch those lines, I want to check them!" I yelled, as both of the men, now figuring out I might just be the law, leaned forward toward the offending extra lines with filet knives in hand to cut the evidence of their illegal actions. Within an instant, two of the lines had been cut and their terminal gear and my evidence drifted out of sight over the transom and into the river's depths. It was about then I heard a loud *ker-splash* as the patrol boat, reacting to my hard turn to port, leveled out in its abrupt turn!

Looking over at my judge's seat, I saw he was gone! Holy Buckets! I thought. When I made my high-speed, abrupt turn, I had launched my judge off the top of his seat and into the cold Sacramento River while traveling about thirty miles per hour! Looking downstream, I could see my judge's partially bald head floating in the frothy wake and waves with a panicked look on his surprised face! You think he had a surprised look on his face, you should have seen mine! Snapping my boat back around, I zipped over to my floating judge. Stopping alongside, I reached down and in the emotion of the moment, bodily lifted his portly frame into the boat. He was still choking for air but when I saw he was somewhat settled down, I said, "Damn, Judge, I am so sorry. I should have given you some warning I was coming around, but I just didn't think about it since I am so used to running this river patrol by myself." He just looked at me with a set of wild looking eyes that were still full of surprise and a touch of fright. Well, there goes my program to get the old judge on my side when it came to decent fish and game dispositions, I thought with a rapidly sinking heart. You readers remember what another writer said many years earlier about "the best laid plans of mice and men often go astray..."

Then I remembered my two anglers who had the four fishing lines earlier hanging over their boat's transom. Easing my boat back into gear, I motored back upstream and slid alongside my two line- cutting fishermen. They were still laughing loudly over my rider's rather swift dip into the river and his subsequent discomfort over now being as wet as a muskrat and shivering like a dog pooping peach pits. Then they more than quieted down when I asked to see their driver's licenses as well as their fishing licenses.

"Why do you need to see our driver's licenses?" the bearded one asked.

Not mincing any words because I was so pissed off at myself for dumping my judge into the swiftly flowing and cold Sacramento River at a high rate of speed, I said, "Because each of you were fishing with extra lines when I passed earlier."

Those words of accusation elicited a storm of denials. However, they saw I was pissed at something and they quickly complied with my request for their licenses. Then as I started issuing them citations for fishing with two extra poles and "Failure To Show Upon Demand," the denials once again flew like snowflakes in a November blizzard in the Sierra Nevada Mountains over the ill-fated Donner Party in the 1800s during supper time when those unfortunate souls were roasting something over their cooking fires other than a leg of lamb...

Ignoring their storms of protest, I continued writing out their fish and game citations. When finished I said, "Gentlemen, when I sped by, I saw four taut fishing lines hanging over the transom of your boat, two legal and two illegal. When I came about to check, both of you made furtive moves toward those lines and once cut [the two illegal lines], your terminal gear drifted over your transom and into the river. When I observed the two of you with knives in hand moving to cut your extra lines, I told you not to touch those lines. You both ignored my warnings and cut the extra lines anyway. So, both of you are receiving a citation for 'Failure To Show Upon Demand.' Additionally since both of you cut the extra lines, you will be getting tickets for fishing with extra lines as well. Are there any questions as to my reasoning?" I quietly and very professionally asked. But let me tell you readers out there, I was still very pissed over the event that had just occurred when I snapped my patrol boat around at a high rate of speed and had vaulted my judge up off his seat and into the river!

Terry Grosz

"We both will see your sorry ass in court because you don't have a scrap of evidence proving what you are saying," said the bearded one.

"That is fine with me," I said. "I get paid the same whether I am in court or out in the field," I snapped right back, still very much pissed over my neglect to warn the judge to hang on when I snapped the boat around upon observing a violation in progress.

In the meantime, my judge said nothing. He just sat there and shivered. To be frank, I think he was scared the confrontation would boil over into a full-scale fistfight right there on the river. With that, the judge and I motored off into the center of the river and out of earshot of my two just recently cited fishermen.

"Judge, I had better get you back to Colusa. There you can get into some dry clothing," I suggested. He never said a word, just nodded in the affirmative at my suggestion.

Back at the marina, I loaded him into my patrol truck and took him home. He exited the truck without saying a word and just gave me a wave of the hand over his shoulder as he headed for the front door of his residence. At least, it wasn't one with a one-fingered salute...

There goes my law enforcement program for the entire eastern side of the county, I sadly thought as I shifted my patrol truck into gear and returned to the river to finish my patrol. You readers can bet your bottom dollar there was no quarter given the rest of that day to any violators discovered on the river breaking the fish and game laws...

Two weeks later, Bonny, the Court Clerk, had the sheriff's office reach me in the field on my fish and game radio to let me know my two, two-extra-pole fishermen from the judge's recent ill-fated boating trip were in court wanting a court trial. To you unwashed, a court trial means in front of only a judge not a jury. Since for once I was close to home, I headed back for the Town of Colusa. Entering the court, I tried to read the Clerk of the Court's face. What I saw on her face said nothing of the judge's current temperament or state of mind relative to the case at hand... Man, I am a had dad! I quietly thought to myself, as I headed into the courtroom for a trial by the judge over the matter at hand. You know, the fishing matter that caused me to spin the judge off the back of his seat and into that damn cold river going about thirty miles per hour!

Quietly sitting in the courtroom with my duo of still-grumbling, illegal two-pole fishing knot heads, the judge finally streamed in from his chambers. Sitting at his desk, he quietly began reading the charges off my citation laid against my two fishermen. The same two fishermen fishing with the two lines the judge and I had spied well into our ill-fated boat patrol. The same two fishermen who had cut their lines as I spun the boat around to apprehend them. The same damn two fishermen who had caused me to dump my judge into the cold Sacramento River, who had hit the rock-hard water surface at thirty miles per hour! Yeah, suffice to say, I was still pissed off at myself over the incident!

When he quietly finished without any show of emotion reading the charges off my citations, the judge looked up and asked how the two men pled. They both pled not guilty and demanded a court trial. Then it dawned on me! Neither of the two men recognized the man they had laughed at upon getting dumped into the river. The very man who was none other than the judge sitting before them! Then contrary to court procedure, the judge allowed the two men to be sworn in and testify so they could give their side of the story. Usually, he called the charging officer first as legal procedure dictated and then the defendants for their side of the story. Not the other way around! What the hell is going on? Is this going to be another one of those situations in which the judge craps backwards and gives away the farm? I quietly asked myself nervously.

The judge professionally sat there quietly listening to the two men's story. Then as I prepared to get up and testify after the two had finished testifying and had sat back down, Judge Weyand waved me back into my seat. Oh boy, the judge is still so pissed at being dumped into the river that he isn't even going to let me testify! I now thought glumly as I quietly took my seat in the courtroom once again.

"Gentlemen," the judge began, "I find the two of you guilty on the charges. That will be $150 per offense (normally $50 per offense) or $300 each! Additionally, I am suspending your fishing licenses for 180 days!"

"But, Judge, that means we will miss the rest of the striper run," the bearded one blurted out in extreme surprise over the judgment rendered and the degree of penalties being laid on the two parties!

"You are right," said Judge Weyand thoughtfully. "I now change your 180-day suspension of all fishing rights to 360 days! That way, you will miss fishing for two striper seasons! Is there anything else you might want to say before this court today?"

Man, you could have heard a mouse passing gas in the next room it got so quiet over the judge's changed suspension order. Brother, you talk about shock! The two men couldn't believe the high cost of their fines or the length of their fishing suspensions, and neither could I!

Then the crap really hit the fan! "Judge, we both object. These fines are outrageous for the violations charged. Neither of us makes $300 a month at our jobs," complained the bearded one who had the big mouth while out on the river when I had initially confronted him over the violations.

"You can object all you want. The next time the two of you come into my courtroom and lie about what happened, and under oath at that, you can plan on spending some time in the Colusa County Jail," said Judge Weyand in stern-tones-like I had never ever heard him use in his courtroom! Both men were shocked at the sternness of his words and then the bearded one started once again to argue with the judge. That was when the judge beckoned Deputy Sheriff Ray Murillo, the Bailiff, over to the bench.

"Officer Murillo. I am about to reopen this hearing. If I do, it will also be for lying under oath as well. If that happens, I want you to go and get the Colusa County District Attorney and have him come over to this courtroom right away. I will need him for those new proceedings, which will start immediately if that is the choice of the defendants."

"Yes, sir," said the bailiff with a knowing grin. Ray Murillo was a good Christian man, a damn good deputy sheriff and dear friend. He was a big old dude and for the most part when among his peers, was as quiet as a snake sliding across a wet lawn. But like I said, he was a good man. May you rest in peace, my friend. Damn, this getting old is sure a privilege!

With that said, the judge just sternly looked at the two men saying, "Well, the ball is now in your court, Gentlemen. Open your mouth in this court one more time and you will be seeing the inside of the Colusa County Jail if I have my way!"

"Where do we pay?" said the bearded one's partner, now almost in a state of panic over the latest turn of events and the possibility of serving time for what he considered a lowly fishing violation and a subsequent courtroom appearance that had gone rather badly.

"Bailiff, will you kindly show these two gentlemen the way to the Clerk's Office so they can settle up with the court?" said Judge Weyand.

"Yes, sir," said the bailiff. "This way, Gentlemen," he said as he led the way to the Clerk's Office. I noticed as he led the men off to the clerk's office, that Ray had a grin on his ugly mug as wide as the Sacramento River is long.

Me, I just sat there with eyes the size of garbage-can lids and in shock over the high fines and the terms of the fishing license suspension! As the men left the courtroom to pay their fines, I got a second shock for the day. The Clerk of the Court entered and quietly advised the judge there were several more men who wanted to see him over fish and game citations they had recently received while fishing on the Sacramento River. With that, she handed him a citation that looked strangely like one of mine.

Then in walked my chap that had cut the stringer of fish loose before I could check the fish for short stripers or numbers of fish in possession on the day when I had the judge with me in the patrol boat! The one I had cited just glared at me like what one would do when looking at what horses leave in the street after a July 4th parade and he had just stepped in it with his expensive Sunday-go-to-meeting alligator leather shoes. His other two buddies did not look at me as they also passed by. A look that told me they were uncomfortable at being there that day, but just the same, took their seats in the courtroom like the whipped pups they appeared to be.

"Your Honor, I would like to plead my case before you if you have the time," said my ticketed chap before the judge had said anything.

The judge just sat back down and, with a wave of his hand to seat my chap who had cut the stringer of fish loose, quietly read the charges on my citation.

Then the judge did the same as before. He had my outlaw testify before he allowed me to testify. Once again, I was waved back to my seat when it came time for me to testify. Being the dense block of clay I was, I was once again chagrined over the judge's backwards courtroom legal procedure when it came to the order of those testifying before him.

Asking my chap to resume his seat after he had testified, the judge once again studied my citation for the longest time as if trying to figure out a way to reduce the charges against the man in light of the lack of physical evidence, particularly since the stringer of fish were now long gone and on the bottom of the Sacramento River probably now being worked over by a happy mess of striper-eating crawdads.

Then in a surprise move, my chap stood up and advised the judge that he had two witnesses that could testify as well on his behalf as to his innocence. The judge looked up from studying my citation saying, "That won't be necessary, Mr. Bell. I find you guilty for the offense of 'Failure To Show' and fine you $500! As for the two gentlemen you brought along, if they testify like I think they will, they will be going to jail for lying under oath. That is, going to jail for lying under oath if they decide to come forward and testify on your behalf and support your testimony presented here this morning as to the events that took place on the day this citation was issued."

Then Judge Weyand looked down at the two witnesses saying, "Do either of you want to testify on this man's behalf? Because if you do, I have no choice but to have you incarcerated for lying under oath. For you see, I am the man who was with Officer Grosz that day. And I saw everything that happened relative to the genesis of this citation."

There was nothing but stunned silence in the courtroom after those words and the revelation over what the judge had just said sank in. The man who had let the fish stringer go was still sitting there in shock at the high fine as if he couldn't believe what he was hearing. The other two members of his party just sat there not wanting to move for fear of going to jail if they even breathed too deeply. Suffice to say, there was another astonished chap in the courtroom that day as well...me! My bad guy left the courtroom without another word to go and pay his fine. His two whipped- pup witnesses, glad to be getting the hell out of the courtroom with their lives, trailed happily along behind the now guilty fish-string- dumper who was soon to be $500 poorer.

Then Judge Weyand left the bench and approached one overawed game warden that was still sitting down as he had been told to do earlier by his judge, one who was sitting there still in disbelief over what had just transpired in the normally lenient judge's courtroom.

"How was that, Terry? Any better in the fines department?" he asked with a sly smile crossing his face. "When are we going to take another boat ride? After all, you still owe me that cold beer at the Grimes Marina," he cackled. Then with a wink and a nod, he left the courtroom just as casually as a gunfighter of old who, after making one hell of a long-range pistol shot, slowly blew the smoke off the end of the gun barrel before placing his pistol back into the holster...

I never again had any problems with my Colusa Justice Court bail schedule and the judge. And yes, Judge Weyand did get another boat ride and his well-earned beer later in the week from a very thankful and overworked game warden. However, a free swim in the cold Sacramento River for the judge on that second trip was not in the offing...

SACRAMENTO RIVER BOUNTY

My second year working on the Sacramento River as the local Colusa County game warden during the annual sturgeon, striper, shad, and salmon runs went much more smoothly than did my first. I now had the hang of the river and knew all its dangerous riffles and potential trouble spots. By that time, I had also figured out my river-fishing clientele, especially those of my many river outlaws, their favorite haunts, and their crooked tricks of the trade when it came to stealing from Mother Nature's piscatorial storehouse. During that second year, I had one river patrol run that is still memorable in the annals of my mind because of its uniqueness and extensive series of illegal events that took place. But before you readers swing into this next series of adventures, you need to be reminded that my river patrols were just a small part of my law enforcement duties as a game warden. I still had the rest of the northern half of Colusa County, all six hundred square miles of it, and its related world of wildlife problems to try and keep a handle on. To all you mothers out there, remember the country and western song that advises, "Don't let your sons grow up to be cowboys." My advice to all you loving moms out there is to add "game wardens" to that sulfurous mix as well. That is because the work of a good wildlife officer is never done and if your son does not marry well, he will not be successful as a wildlife officer or as a family man. For without a great mate who always has his back, an officer of the law cannot run at the 110 percent level in his chosen field of law enforcement. And the graveyards are full of officers who were running at less than the 110 percent level... Then you have the issues of living through a collection of dangerous, life-threatening experiences, long days, many times no dependable backup, bad weather, crappy eating habits induced by the job's rigors, and mean-assed critters, all supported by questionable equipment provided to the wildlife officer by the lowest bidder. Think that over all you loving moms out there. However, if your son gets that faraway look at every sunrise and sunset, catches fish and then skillfully releases them back to the water, loves and lives for the hunt and is of great common sense, be prepared. You may have a wildlife officer in the making and he will need all the family support and encouragement he can gather unto his kilts...

Leaving the Colusa Marina early on an already hot summer morning, I headed upstream on the Sacramento River in my patrol boat. As I did, I kept passing empty Olympia beer cans floating by me in the river like ornaments flung around a liquid Christmas tree. California had a litter law in those days that prohibited tossing litter into the inland waterways or within one hundred feet of the high water mark of said waterways. Swinging by one floating beer can, I scooped it up with my dip net while on the fly. Smelling its pop-top opening,

I could still smell the yeasty odor of fresh beer. Turning the can over, I looked at the lot number stamped on its bottom in black ink as its beer-dregs foamed out the opening and onto the bottom of my boat. Those beer can lot numbers were something to keep in mind as an evidentiary lead if the thrower is ever captured, I thought, as I continued thundering upstream. Especially if I ran into my can thrower and the lot number on the bottom of my can matches any of the full cans remaining in my drinker's possession. Rounding a turn in the river a few miles later, I spotted a large pontoon houseboat some distance above me anchored out in the middle of the river. On it were a bunch of scantily clad young ladies moving around along with a number of men fishing for stripers off the stern and sides of the roomy vessel. Figuring that might be my beer can littering party, I slowed my boat and then stopped in a likely looking fishing spot shaded by trees growing along the river's edge. Throwing out my anchor, I drifted back to a stop that was a good one hundred yards below my suspect houseboat. Making sure at that distance I looked like any other fisherman, I raised up a fishing pole but only with a lead weight attached to the line so no one could me accuse me of fishing while on government time. With that, I cast my lead ruse out into the river. Realizing what might be coming next, I got out my notebook, pencil, and binoculars. Sitting there more or less semi-concealed in the tree shade of the riverbank like any other river fisherman, I slyly glassed my houseboat crew with my 7x50 binoculars. Sure as God makes salmon flies great for sure-fire rainbow trout bait, my houseboat folks were swilling down what appeared to be Olympia beer. In fact, dozens of cans of it! It seemed everyone on board had an open can of beer and were having one hell of a good time. And shortly thereafter, as

I had suspected would occur, I would see an empty beer can loft high into the air and sail overboard into the river from one of my folks on the houseboat. When that happened, I would identify the can flipper by dress or any other identifier and note the time. I had also brought along my Super 8mm movie camera with a telephoto lens and when it became obvious someone was swilling down the last drop based on the high tipping of the can to get at that last ounce of beer, I would start filming. Following that, out would go the empty can into the river, all duly caught on film I might add. And as a final act, I would then zoom in on my thrower's face with my telephoto lens for final identification in case this beer-can littering event ever went to trial in a court of law. I did so because the fine was one hundred dollars for littering, which was pretty big money in those days of the late 1960s. Gasoline was 34 cents per gallon, coffee was 5 cents per cup with unlimited refills, hamburgers were 25 cents, ice cream cones were 10 cents, T-bone steak at the butcher shop was 89 cents per pound...I think you readers get the picture and the meaning and value of a $100 dollar bill.

After sitting there for about an hour, I had all the evidence for littering I needed on each and every one of the thirteen people on board the houseboat! Getting ready to shake, rattle, and roll toward my houseboat and put an end to this littering foolishness, I was quickly brought up short with another potential moneymaking observation! One of the lads on the stern of the boat brought out an ice chest from the front of their vessel. Opening up the lid, he brought out what appeared to be a short striper or one that appeared to be less than fifteen inches in length. Within minutes, that fish had been filleted on a filet board, washed off in the river, sprayed with cooking oil from a can and laid on a hot barbecue grill located near the stern of the boat. This he did eight more times with what also appeared to be more short bass, or the best eating, if you like eating stripers that is. Finally, the ice chest holding the suspect illegal short fish was once again taken back to the frontal portion of the boat and covered up with a blanket to make it look like it was nothing but another seat. It was no wonder they had an ice chest possibly full of short stripers. From what I could tell, they had thirteen fishing lines over the stern and sides of the houseboat, and many of them were regularly catching stripers of all sizes!

Figuring I had seen enough, I retrieved my anchor, started up my boat and went to pay a visit to my thirteen happy partygoers. Moving slowly up to their pontoon houseboat in full uniform, I slid alongside and fastened my boat to the side of theirs on one of their tie-downs. As I did, an Olympia beer can sailed over the top of the houseboat from its far side. The drunken thrower, unaware of the game warden now alongside, pitched it perfectly into my boat! With that, the lads in the stern got everyone quickly under control before anything else embarrassing occurred. But by then, it was too late. You know what I say about moments of opportunity. Sometimes you eat the bear and sometimes the bear eats you...

Well, that was just the start of that frog-festival on the Sacramento River. Before it was all said and done, everyone on board had received a littering citation. That was made even more embarrassing, when I matched the Olympia can fetched from the river earlier to the lot numbers of full cans still on board. Then more surprises were in the offing. As it turned out, all six of the ladies on board were found to be fishing without licenses and were cited accordingly. Lastly, as the now burning smell of grilling short stripers filled the air, I climbed on board their vessel and retrieved the suspect ice chest out from under its covering in the front of the boat. In it was a short white sturgeon, one less than four feet in length as required by law. One which had been cut in half in order to fit into the ice chest and sixteen more short striped bass! It always amazed me on how whisper quiet it got when one carrying a badge reached into the very bowels of a nest of outlaws and fetched out the illegality in front of God and everybody. As a hunter of humans, I always appreciated those whisper quiet moments in time, especially when the long arm of the law was needed but not appreciated by those rank and file touched by such a representative of The Thin Green Line.

Shortly thereafter, I left the houseboat now holding a mess of somewhat scorched and subdued partygoers from the nearby Town of Marysville. That was after issuing twenty-three total citations, which tallied for littering ($1,300), possession of short stripers ($400), no fishing licenses in possession ($210), and possession of one short sturgeon ($150), for a total of $2,060! All of those cases were quietly and subsequently settled up with the Colusa Justice Court days later. Figuratively speaking, that one river stop alone paid for all the gas and oil the Williams game warden, the officer who patrolled the southern half of Colusa County, and I used on that shared patrol boat for the rest of the year. That was except when the Williams game warden and our illustrious squad's patrol captain, "Captain Lemon," weren't using the patrol boat as their own personal fishing vessel under the official covering guise of checking fishermen...

Moving further upstream, I passed another twenty fishing boats located along various likely fishing spots. None had that look or gave me a heads-up from my guardian angels as to existing violations, so, I passed on all of them. Rounding another turn in the river, I spotted three lads fishing on the bank of a sand dune. Knowing there was no access road to their little fishing spot, I decided to pay the lads an official visit. They wouldn't walk a long way through the vegetative jungle along the river to get to such a fishing spot unless they didn't want to be bothered for some reason. It was either one hell of a great fishing spot, or they had something to hide, I thought. That inner feeling of possible violations was validated when, as I approached, I spotted what appeared to be a short green sturgeon in the water tied to a fish stringer anchored on the bank. Nosing my patrol boat up onto the sand dune so that it wouldn't drift off, I cut the engine. Then I opened up my walk-through window, walked across the front deck, and tossed out my anchor onto the shore. Looking back over at my lads, there were now only two chaps left! What the hell? I thought as I raced up the sand dune only to spot one of my three fishermen hotfooting it across the sand dunes as he headed for the dense vegetative cover alongside the river and potential escape. Well, here was a race fit for a fat guy like me. I had size 14EEEE feet that made like snowshoes on a dromedary camel as I raced after my chap across the loose sand. My chap, on the other hand, had dinky feet— smaller than 14EEEE—and I soon ran him to ground. Well, not really running him to ground. Following my interception of his miserable sprinting carcass with a bellowed warning to stop, and when that was ignored, a rather rough around the edges horse- collar tackle soon followed!

Escorting my runner back to his buddies, I asked him why he ran. "I don't have a fishing license," he quietly admitted.

My remaining two fishermen checked out fine with their licenses. When I asked my chap without any fishing license to produce his driver's license so a citation could be issued, he said he had no identification on his person. I told the lad that without any form of good identification, I would have to place him under arrest and take him forthwith as was agency policy since he had violated the fish and game regulations. With those words, he just shrugged his shoulders like it was no big deal being incarcerated. With that very obvious bit of indifference, I went into high alert. His actions were reflective of the many hardened chaps with criminal records I had apprehended in the past for fish and game violations! Those folks had also shown indications of previous incarcerations through their behavioral actions same as my runner was now exhibiting. Turning him around before he tried to jack rabbit once again or tried something even more serious, I slipped the bracelets on his wrists. Then I let him know he was under arrest for fishing without a license. Once again, an indifferent shrug followed. Placing him in the passenger seat of my patrol boat after a thorough search of his person, I reached over and removed my ignition keys to preclude any subsequent escape actions on the part of my prisoner. Following that, I went back ashore to ascertain who had caught the short and illegal appearing sturgeon. One of the other chaps admitted to the error on the sturgeon claiming ignorance over the required minimum size limit. As he dug out his driver's license, I took a look at the live sturgeon on the end of the thin cotton rope fish stringer. It was on a fish stringer in the shallow water and, other than being captured, appeared to be none the worse for wear. Getting out my point-and-shoot camera, I took its picture tied to the fish stringer. Then I carefully measured it to ascertain if it was indeed less than four feet in total length, which it was. With that, I carefully removed the fish from the rope stringer, which had been run through the mouth and out the gill plate so as not to damage its gills, and gently released it. That was one happy fish as it swam off into the river from whence it came. To me, sturgeon were not only neat critters but needed all the protection they could gather around their scute-covered carcasses because of all the other humankind impacts being heaped on their population numbers. I just found it amazing to believe that they had remained basically unchanged for the last 65 million years! And if my hard-nosed protective efforts meant anything to the casual onlooker, the sturgeon species would remain on this planet in the lakes and river systems for another 65 million years! For you readers who are dyed in the wool sturgeon fishermen, read the story titled, "Ishi-Pishi Falls" in my National-Outdoor-Book-Award-winning book titled, *Wildlife Wars*. In that book, you will see to what lengths I went to protect both the white and green sturgeon in the rivers of Northern California as a rookie game warden. It is not often one lone officer can bring in eleven case hardened, sturgeon snagging wildlife outlaws with just one set of handcuffs. And did so with the nearest backup being sixty-seven miles away! The way I brought those chaps to justice was illegal in those days and is illegal in the field of law enforcement today. But I would be damned if I was going to let those hard cases go with just a citation and then have them disappear into the woodwork since all were temporary construction workers. So, the whole damn bunch went to the bucket courtesy the game warden. Of further note and possible interest, that adventure went into the two-hour movie made for Animal Planet, which was also titled *Wildlife Wars*. By the way, all those chaps were found guilty and ended up paying $500 each for snagging surgeon, $250 apiece for the use of illegal snagging terminal gear and another $250 for taking over limits. You might want to check that adventure out. But, back to the Sacramento River story at hand.

I was soon finished with writing up my short sturgeon-catching chap, boarded the boat, and then headed downstream with my prisoner who was now in a life jacket. But not before approaching my houseboat just in time to see one of my previously cited chaps, drunk as a British Lord, toss another empty Olympia beer can into the river. Receiving his second citation in the same day for littering, my chap was not pleased. Plus, it later cost him another $100 for being stupid and unlucky to the nth degree all at the same time.

Pulling into the marina, I walked my prisoner up to the office and called the Colusa County Sheriff's Office for a transport officer. They soon had a deputy on site that transported my prisoner to the local lockup. Following in my patrol truck, I finished booking my prisoner. When the dispatcher ran my prisoner for any previous records or priors on the Teletype, the machine remained silent for the longest time as I stood there patiently waiting for its response. Then the machine thump-thump-thumped as they were want to do in those days before computers, noisily grinding out the requested information on sheet paper. All of a sudden, it suddenly quit just as fast as it had started after the initial request for said information had been made.

Damn, I thought, this chap must not have a record as I had figured earlier on the river based on his cold-blooded behavioral reaction to being apprehended and then arrested.

Looking at the Teletype printout, it read, "Record too lengthy to send by Teletype, will mail!" It was following that revelation as I stood there in the cool quiet of the sheriff's office, that I once again realized why game wardens in the United States have a mortality rate far higher than any other type of law enforcement officer. Like I have written many times in my other books, "God loves little children, fools and game wardens..." I later discovered my chap had a violent rap sheet a mile long. In fact, he was soon returned to Sutter and then Sacramento Counties because of outstanding felony warrants. Just think, I had tangled with a violent wanted felon over not having his fishing license in possession. Thank goodness God watches over little children, fools, and game wardens, I once again quietly thought.

Returning to the marina after booking my prisoner, I headed back out onto the river and this time went downstream. Only that time instead of bothering anyone, I sped all the way south to the Grimes Marina, which was at the end of my river patrol district. In the process, I must have passed at least one hundred boats full of fishermen. Once at the Grimes Marina in the hot summer heat, I stopped and got myself a cold bottle of Coca-Cola. Then, since everyone had forgotten the game warden's boat speeding by almost an hour earlier, I began slowly working my way back upstream. Soon, I was in the process of checking numerous boats and their fishermen. As was usual, my fishermen were happy to see some kind of law on the river and were talkative, especially as to where the best fishing spots on the river were located and what fish were being caught. No citations surfaced for the longest time until I caught several chaps with over limits of stripers. That seemed to open up the can of worms— no pun intended—and I ended up catching more than two dozen additional chaps breaking the fish and game laws as I proceeded the rest of the way upstream. The citations were for using more than one line, over limits, short stripers, no fishing licenses, littering, another short sturgeon—I let that chap go because the fish was only half-an-inch too short, but the fish was returned back to the river to live another day—and on it went into the late afternoon. However, before that patrol stint on the river ended, I had written over $4,000 worth of citations during a ten-hour time period! Never again did I have such a day on the Sacramento River as I did that day. It just seemed like illegal bounty was at the height of its bloom and I was there gathering in the proverbial sheaves. And, my successes in catching folks doing what they shouldn't have been doing to Mother Nature in her world of wildlife, sadly, didn't end there.

Slowly motoring further upstream, I began seeing swirls of numerous stripers spawning on the top of the water as they are sometimes known to do. It was always such a pleasure and great delight for me seeing Mother Nature up close and personal-like. To me, it was always a reminder of the conservation work done by my badge carrying counterparts early on in the century. And as a result of their efforts and sacrifices, those of us modern day badge carriers got to still enjoy Mother Nature at her very best. Badge carrying counterparts of yesteryear, now long gone but not forgotten by the likes of appreciating chaps like me. Rounding another turn in the river, I spotted a good friend of mine from Colusa. He was slowly trolling upriver for stripers. But that wasn't what caught my eye. He was standing up in the stern of his boat with a huge, long handled dip net. Throwing up my binoculars to see what the heck he was doing, I got surprised! Stripers were spawning by the dozens in the wake created by his outboard motor's propeller! And Tom was dip netting the spawners out from the motor's disturbance and slipstream to his heart's content!

Dang it, Tom, that isn't legal! Stripers in the river must he taken only by hook and line, I thought. Laying down my binoculars, I sped up to my dip-netting friend before he got himself deeper into legal trouble then he already was. Alas, I was too late. By the time I got to Tom's boat, he had three huge stripers laid out in the bottom of his boat that he had just dip-netted. Whacked-in-the-head and dead-as-a-stone stripers, to be exact! Pulling up alongside, I said, "Tom, what the heck are you doing?"

"Terry, can you believe it? These fish came right up into the wake of my propeller spawning and I was able to dip net three of them." At least he stayed within the limit. "Look at those hogs lying in the bottom of my boat. Aren't they beauties?" he exulted.

Yeah, they certainly were. Two were in the forty-pound class and one weighed about fifty to fifty-five pounds! I grimaced as I shook my head in disbelief at my larger than life and really innocent, to his way of thinking, friend. "Tom, you knot head! You can't take stripers with a dip net unless you have them hooked and are in the process of lawfully landing them," I said in utter consternation over the legal issues my dear friend was soon to be confronting.

"Yeah, you can. Look here. I already did it three times," he proudly announced.

I just shook my head. Here was a gentle giant of a man and a hardworking one at that. I had let him go earlier in my career for using an "A" deer tag in a ' ' deer tag district, but this fishnet dipping episode was a horse of a different color. Damn, here is a man without much money and now he has gone and done this. And dip-netting fish out from the river is a serious and expensive offense, I thought sadly. Additionally, I had recently gone to work on my local judge, successfully I might add, to increase the fish and game related fines in Colusa County's judicial district. There is no way Tom is going to skate on this one, I once again thought sadly. Not if I was to do my job correctly and treat everyone the same no matter what.

Seizing the three dead stripers after explaining the law, I issued Tom a citation for Taking Fish By Illegal Means, To Wit, dip netting. Issuing that citation broke my heart! We were close friends and I highly respected him for the tough, hardscrabble life he had already lived. He was always a gentleman around my wife, my kids and me and was one of the most generous people I ever met. And he was also as poor as a church mouse and seriously busted up in the lower back from all his previous hard work as a farm laborer. Plus, he was my best informant in the county!

The following Monday found me filing my recent river citations with the Clerk of the Court and they totaled, as I said earlier, into the thousands of dollars. But I had saved one for last. Asking Judge Weyand if I could see him privately in his chambers and, sensing I had some unusual concerns, he agreed.

Moments later in the privacy of his chambers, I said, "Your Honor, I have a problem. I caught a man who truly did not realize catching free-swimming stripers with the use and aid of a dip net was illegal. As you know, it is, and I wrote him anyway because that is my job. I must leave judging a person for his crimes up to you and our system of justice. But if it's all the same to you, Your Honor, I need to intercede in this one. I realize the bail for such an offense is $250. And I think that is the correct amount to have any deterrent effect on our fisherman in such a matter. But in this case, it is just not right because this man truly did not know what he was doing was illegal, is a good community citizen and is as poor as a church mouse. The only work he is capable of doing because of his bad back is as a farm laborer driving a tractor. I would like to make a suggestion. This man will come in and pay his fine with no questions asked. That is just his good nature and the ethics of the man because of his upbringing and Asian culture. I don't know how he plans on coming up with that amount of money but his honor and ethics won't let him try to skate away from this one. So whatever it takes, Tom will pay his fine. As I said, I know the bail for this offense is $250. But I would like to request that you only fine this man $25 and suspend it because of his financial situation and his lack of understanding regarding this particular fish and game law."

With those words out and before the judge could say anything other than wince over my unusual request after all the work I had done with him on increasing the bail schedule, I made my next previously calculated move. Reaching into my wallet, I took out a check previously made out to the Colusa Justice Court in the amount of $250.1 handed the check to the judge with the question hanging heavily in the air, "Paid in full, Your Honor, for this man and his offense?"

"Let me see the citation," said Judge Weyand quietly.

Handing the judge the citation, I watched closely for any emotion or reaction as he read through the identifiers on the citation.

For the longest time he read the citation quietly. It was almost as if he was trying to decide what the appropriate decision should be. Then he quietly reached out and took my check. "The matter is closed, Officer Grosz. Now, don't you ever do this to me again over such an issue." With those words, he turned and left me standing there thankfully in his chambers over his thoughtful and generous decision in the matter at hand.

One week later, Tom was found guilty, fined $25, and the fine was suspended, but not before receiving a damn good hind-end chewing from the judge as it was told to me later by the Bailiff. The next morning, there was a pail of some of the finest homegrown jumbo beefsteak tomatoes quietly laid on the back doorstep at my home where I resided out in the countryside. The generous donor was nowhere to be seen...

The bounty realized on those series of Sacramento River patrols was unbelievable. Most of the fishermen I checked were as right as rain. But there were a number of bad apples, and I saw to it that all the rotten ones I ran across were removed from the bottom of the barrel.

Folks need to realize and pretty damn soon that our natural resources are limited. And those who walk on the dark side of Mother Nature are doing nothing more than stealing from our kids and others yet to come. Someday we will pay for these days of reckless abuse of our wildlife resources in more ways than we will ever realize. I already cry in my heart over never again being able to see flocks of passenger pigeons flying overhead from one of the most numerous bird species ever to inhabit this planet! Martha, the last of the billions of passenger pigeons from those great flocks, died in the Cincinnati Zoological Garden in 1917 ... and I would bet those of you reading these lines never ever got to see a live one! Not even one that had been mounted by a taxidermist. Then look at what happened to the blue fin tuna, sea turtle species, Pacific sardines, Pacific species of salmon, Atlantic cod, wild stocks of Atlantic salmon, Aleutian Canada goose, heath hen, Carolina parakeet, ivory-billed woodpecker and the like. Need I say any more?

Tom died several years after this case was adjudicated under the skilled hands of a San Francisco surgeon during a back operation gone badly wrong. May the good Lord take a liking to Tom Yamamoto and see to it that he is currently fishing on a good striper river wherever he is. And hopefully, it is legal to use a dip net up there if the occasion arises... As I remember, only his wife, the mortician and several other men attended his funeral. Two of those men who were there were his lifelong fishing partner and the other man, his game warden friend, who had written him a citation for illegally dip netting stripers from the Sacramento River... Never again have I ever feasted on such wonderful, home grown by a skilled gardener, beefsteak tomatoes as I did that day so long ago that had been left on my back porch. God, please make sure Tom has plenty of water both to fish in and for caring for his garden. If You do, You are soon in for a treat from this gentle giant of a man. A treat better than any of Your Angels can grow...

THE HOUNDSMEN

Working the Butte Creek area late one morning on the eastern side of my patrol district, I spied a circling murder of crows near at hand. They were circling a dozen or so turkey vultures already on the ground feasting on something. Something good eating to that mess of critters sure has their undivided attention, I thought. Like all experienced wildlife officers, when something is spotted that is out of place from the natural scheme of things, it warranted a second look.

Running off the birds as I drove up and looking out the window of my patrol truck at their previous spot of interest alongside the muddy farm road on which I sat, I observed the partially butchered remains of a female mule deer in the weeds! Not normal remains, mind you, but something even more sinister. It was a freshly killed mule deer all right, but it was minus its hind legs and back straps! Looking on in disgust, I said to myself, Terry, we now have a problem on our hands of unusual proportions. Normally a deer poacher would take everything of value on a. freshly killed deer. Take everything of value because any mule deer feeding off the valley's nearby crops was tender and of excellent eating quality. Additionally, by removing any evidence of an illegal kill not only served to hide the insidious fact but throw any nosy game warden off his feed. Only a sinister son-of-a-bitch would go and do something like this! Whoever killed that deer only took the best parts of the animal—steaks and roasts—and left the rest of the deer to rot!

Looking all around for any clues as to my poachers, I found little that was evidentiary in nature that truly caught my eye. There were the usual muddy tire tracks, smudged footprints in the dampened earth immediately around the dead deer, and a really old empty pouch of Red Man Chewing Tobacco lying on the ground off to one side some ten yards or so distant from the kill site. The empty tobacco pouch was more than likely that left by some Mexican farmhand alongside the dirt road near where my patrol truck sat I quickly surmised. Other than that, nada! Grabbing my binoculars, I took off on foot leaving the deer to the hungry murder of crows and now once again circling turkey vultures. For the next mile or so, I plodded along following the suspect tire tracks in the muddy farm access road looking for any other signs of evidence until they went further off road and onto the soft, heavily farmed soils in the area. Those tracks eventually led to every old nearby oxbow and wet swampy place along the upper Butte Creek drainage area. Probably spotlighting deer in the swampy areas, I surmised. Then the mystery tracks left the soft, off road soils and entered a well-traveled graveled roadway. There, not surprisingly, I lost the suspect tracks. Returning to my patrol truck, I took one more look around the deer's carcass for any clues I may have missed that first go-around. Finding none, I left the area. Left the area because I had a ton of other more pressing work that needed doing but firmly fixed said sorry event in my memory banks for later retrieval. Particularly, if I ever ran across any other like situations or circumstances in the future. Once again, to all my readers out there, remember one of Grosz's Rules. If the bad guys get clean-away with an illegal event, many times they will return and commit the same violation in the same area again. When that happens, hopefully, one of Mother Nature's minions will be out there close at hand to settle things up with the trigger pulling, meat wasting miscreants. And, I knew one such badge-carrying chap who would be more than happy to put the needed medicine on that sickness.

One evening days later, I was working froggers on foot along a large canal just south of one of Terrill Sartain's large rice fields and west of a great warm water game fish fishing area I called Four Corners. Walking along in the darkness in that normally heavily frogged area, I got a whiff of an all-too-familiar sickly sweet smell foretelling the nearby presence of a dead and decaying animal. And from the intense smell, a large sized animal at that. Following my nose and the smell of death along the canal bank, I soon came upon the carcass of a dead mule deer. Closer examination of what was left revealed that it had been dead for a long time. It was also apparent that only its hind legs and back straps had been removed even though it had been severely scavenged upon by numerous critters! Another kill just like the one I had discovered the previous week, I thought with a grimace. Looking around that crime scene for any fresh or obvious clues, I found no signs of any physical evidence left behind because of the age of the kill. However, I had one clue. Both deer carcasses had been dumped along swampy waterways and butchered out in the same wasteful manner. Not much to go on, but at least it was a start and showing the same wasteful pattern of operation.

Faced with such a puzzling situation, I did what experienced game wardens do best. I began mentally cold tracking my problem. First, the carcasses had been dumped in an out of the way deer rich area. Second, they both had been dumped adjacent to remote swampy watered areas, which were normal travel ways for scavengers such as skunks, fox and raccoons. Those critters would quickly make short work of any carcass and, to a manner of speaking, soon dispose of the evidence. Third, they both had been stripped of their best eating parts, namely their hindquarters and back straps. Fourth, both carcasses had been dumped along easy vehicle access routes just off seldom-traveled farm roads. Last, and only possibly with a stretch of one's imagination, at least one member of the deer killing party may have chewed a very popular brand of chew namely Red Man Chewing Tobacco. The tobacco pouch being possibly physical evidence, discovered from my find near the first kill site. That clue in and of itself was a long shot because of the ratty weathered condition and age of the tobacco pouch. But nothing in the way of potential leads was discounted at that point in time. Bottom line, not much to go on, but better than a poke in the eye with a sharp stick. Remember folks, a good game warden is a lot like a cheetah. He always knows where the hyenas are, and, I could now smell the pack...

Thus I began a painstaking inventory of all my local area inhabitants and regular warm water fishermen in the immediate area. In the much used and illegal deer killing Butte Creek area, I had lots of duck clubs and public waterways. First, I contacted all my area duck club gamekeepers to ascertain if they had heard or seen anything unusual. As was standard practice in those days among most commercial duck club gamekeepers, they heard or saw nothing... I guess one couldn't blame them for not speaking openly to me. After all, the local game warden was not their favorite person to be chatting with. Especially in light come duck season when the local game warden would be citing many shooters on their particular clubs, including the gamekeeper, for waterfowl and pheasant related violations. Plus, many of the more crooked duck club members who were prone to routinely committing waterfowl violations, made it quite clear to their resident gamekeeper that they didn't want them talking to that SOB game warden. And if they were found doing so, they could be replaced...

Then I visited with all my regular warm water game fish fishermen along the many canals for any and all information that I could glean. That included not only my regular daytime fishermen but the steady nighttime fishing crowd as well. As expected, I received no new leads from my daytime fishing chaps relative to this illegal deer-killing thing. As for my nighttime fishing chaps, they reported numerous shots being fired at night on weekends in the area. That wasn't unusual though. I had lots of legal coon hunters and illegal nighttime hunters in the valley once dark descended over the land. That was especially true on the weekends when the normal workingman had a few days off in which to pursue the critters of the night. Additionally, using the cover of darkness, those walking on the darker side of the world of wildlife would often come out on the weekends and play. The other scrap of information I had gathered from my nighttime fishermen was that many of them had heard baying hounds accompanying the shooting sounds. A few of them had even seen the dogs and their transport truck several times slowly traveling along the waterways. To my way of thinking, those were the kinds of folks that would normally and legally be found hunting the waterways for the ever-present raccoon because in those areas, that species of critter abounded in large numbers. That was also where the raccoons found the greatest sources of foods like frogs, mice, rats, nesting birds, crawdads, snakes, and fish. And therein abounded plentiful sources of water in which to characteristically wash their freshly caught prey as they often did.

Now to you unwashed, there was a solid reason for those kinds of reports from my nighttime fishermen. Hunting raccoons at night with hounds is both a historic and growing sport in California. Second, raccoons make for some good eats. Now don't you good folks go rolling up your noses over the prospect of eating raccoons. A young raccoon well spiced and oven roasted makes the centerpiece for a wonderful meal. Especially if one were to throw into that mix some baked sweet potatoes smothered in cinnamon and butter, fresh green salad, and piping hot buttermilk biscuits fresh from an oven dripping with gobs of real butter. Then top off that repast with a generous slice of my bride's world famous homemade peach pie. Yum! However, don't try eating the big old boar raccoons which are usually rolling fat and stronger tasting than the younger ones. Plus, the younger ones aren't so greasy.

As an aside, that was the neat thing I discovered about myself. Having an educational background as a trained wildlife biologist in college from the finest wildlife school in the nation, California State University at Humboldt in Areata, California, from the likes of professors Dr. Stan Harris and Dr. Mossman, I made sure I tried everything that God created and threw my way. After all, one only gets to travel this road once in a lifetime. Have any of you ever tried coot stew, a soft-shell crab sandwich, deep fried breaded chunks of nurse shark, smoked rattlesnake, opossum, snapping turtle stew (the best), alligator, muskrat, beaver, mountain lion (wonderful), bobcat (not so good-too damn stringy and dry), dog (eaten on an Indian reservation where I was the guest of honor for helping a dying Native American chief prepare for his trip to the Happy Hunting Grounds with the officially permitted gift of golden eagle tail feathers), monkey (in Thailand before I got ambushed by Burmese insurgents in 1978 while working as a special agent. Read that hair-raising story in my book, Defending Our Wildlife Heritage, in the chapter titled "Asia, 1978"), spider (while I was in Indonesia) or other like delicacies? If you haven't, you are missing some of the spices of life. Get with it, folks, time is a wastin'. But, once again I flew off the handle and digressed...

And during the late fall and winter months, raccoon pelts in their prime were worth a few bucks in the fur markets. So, nothing terribly unusual there about hearing and seeing that kind of hounds men's hunting activity along the waterways after hours, especially on the weekends. Drawing so many dead ends, I figured I was just going to have to spend more time at night along my eastern patrol district waterways. Not that I wanted to, mind you, because I was already swamped—no pun intended—with a massive workload. In fact, I was already working seven days a week and running about sixteen to eighteen hour days in my busy, wildlife resource and poacher rich patrol district. But I was young, full of get up and go, had (and still have) a great supportive wife who let me run, an area holding lots of critters needing help, and the catching was good. What more would an abnormal human being like a glutton for punishment game warden, whose head was hanging out the window of a redneck's pickup like a happy slobbering dog need, eh?

One weekend evening near Davison's Duck Club on the eastern side of my patrol district, I heard the melodious chorus of baying hounds. Leaving the north end of that district, I headed south on a hunch. Soon, I could see lights shining into the trees alongside a swampy area laced with numerous waterways. I could also now hear the excited dogs baying treed into the humid night air. Turning east down a muddy farm road running without lights, I soon came upon the darkened shape of a vehicle that I suspected belonged to my near at hand hounds men.

Stepping out from my patrol truck, I was confronted with a scene straight out of Dante's Inferno. First, a large pack of baying hounds were singing for all they were worth down the muddy farm road a piece as they looked eagerly high into the adjacent line of willow trees. Second, there were three black men yelling excitedly and,

75

using their handheld spotlight, casting a bright light high into the trees alongside a swampy canal. That crazy scene was soon followed with the sounds of numerous light rifle shots being sprayed wildly into the willows at three large raccoons holding onto the upper limbs for all they were worth.

Walking over to the lads who had yet to see me, remember I had driven into the area without using my lights, I stood quietly nearby watching the unfolding scene of events. Soon, their highly inaccurate shooting began to bear fruit. One by one, the treed raccoons dropped from the safety of their perches high in the willows into the waiting jaws of the excited pack of hounds waiting at the base of the trees. When that happened, instant pandemonium followed every time this dropping raccoon event occurred. Baying, howling dogs, snapping jaws from both the dogs and dying raccoons, followed by yelling men trying to retrieve their prey before it was chomped to pieces by the hounds, greeted my eyes and ears. Like I said earlier, a scene right out of Dante's Inferno. Then quiet more or less reigned as the three men got control of the dead raccoons, walked back down the road and laid them up on top of their truck's dog carrier so their hounds wouldn't continue chewing on them.

Speaking of that, those three lads were loaded for bear equipment wise. They were driving a new Ford one-ton truck with a long bed. In the bed was a homemade built-in set of dog carriers. Their dog carrier being a large box-like contraption containing numerous individual locked cages for each dog. In the middle of the truck bed underneath the dog carrier was an open space. Therein laid ropes, tools, a spare tire, dog watering and feeding pans, and a small mound of freshly killed raccoons. As I said, these lads were prepared for bear, er, raccoons!

Then all of a sudden, I was surrounded by a number of good looking blue tick and redbone hounds that were curious about what this new smelling human was doing there by their truck. It was about then that one of the men spotted me in all of my 6-foot 4- inch, 320-pound, Teutonic glory and magnificence quietly standing there watching them from just a few feet away. When he did, he damned near jumped into the nearby canal out of a combination of fear and surprise.

"Hey! Look out, Guys! There is a man standing there!" he shouted as he launched himself into the air trying to put some distance between the two of us. Hell, his fear and surprise was so great, I thought he just might land on the backside of the moon. And, that fellow man made two of me when it came to poundage. But even in surprise, I would have been a damn-site better looking.

Trying to avoid being shot by a group of surprised and still excited men over my unexpected and sudden appearance, I loudly said, "State fish and game warden, Lads. I am here to check a few hunting licenses and to see what the hell is causing you guys to stir up all this commotion this time of the evening."

That helped settle things down a bit, and soon I was surrounded by my three African-American raccoon hunters. But that quiet lasted for only for a moment. A single hound still on the loose, bayed "treed" about forty yards down the canal and the race was on once again! The remaining dogs and two of the men streamed off toward the rest of the now baying dog, leaving me standing there with a shorter, heavyset chap and a cloud of Colusa County's B-52 sized mosquitoes.

"Good evening, Sir. Terry Grosz, State Fish and Game Warden. I heard all the noise and commotion from up the road a piece, and thought I would come over for a look-see," I said.

"Ben Rogers, Mr. Game Warden. Glad to meet you," he said as he stuck out his hand in what I considered as a genuine greeting of friendship.

Shaking his hand, I said, "You guys sure have a nice rig and set up here in this rolling dog kennel."

"Yeah, it is nice. The three of us work in Vallejo at the Navy shipyard. We made this thing during our lunch hours from all the odds and ends of scrap metal just lying around from the ship building and repair docks," said Ben proudly.

Then he proceeded walking me around and showing off his work of art to the night sounds of bellowing bullfrogs, baying hounds, wild shooting, hum of a zillion mosquitoes and two excited yelling men from off in a distance down the canal.

Finally with the sounds of more shooting, Ben said, "I had better get down there. My partners are terrible shots and, if I don't, they will waste any profits we make on this trip off the raccoons by shooting up all our ammunition." With that, Ben excused himself and took off running to where all the baying sounds and shooting commotion were roaring forth in their entire nightly splendor. Just imagine, that was when .22 ammunition was only fifty cents per box of fifty cartridges. Under the current Obama administration, one can't even find any .22 ammunition in 2012 for sale. And if you do, it will cost a fortune. I knew it was just a matter of time before the liberal Democrats found a way to circumvent the Second Amendment to the Constitution through the control of the availability and sale of ammunition. Oh well, there will always be an England...

When Ben left me alone, I took those moments to look more closely over their truck for anything out of line or illegal. The truck was as clean as a hound's tooth, no pun intended. They had eleven dead raccoons in the back and that was about it. There weren't any spent shells on the front floorboards of the truck, possibly signifying shooting from inside the motor vehicle, although they did have a spotlight in the cab hooked up to the cigarette lighter. The spotlight was not out of line however when hunting raccoons at night or looking to retrieve one's lost dogs in the darkness. Checking some of the now empty dog boxes, I only found evidence of dogs occupying those spaces. So much for the earlier hunch that brought me down here thinking these lads were my deer killing bad guys, I thought.

Then I was once again surrounded by a pack of hounds as my raccoon hunters returned from their latest escapade. When they did, I noticed each dog had proper tags on his collar with his name along with the owner's phone number and address. I couldn't help but thinking this was really a top notch, well run operation. Plus, they had a pack of fine looking and obviously expensive, well-kept and cared-for hounds.

As the men returned, I noticed they were carrying two more recently killed raccoons. Back at the truck, they tossed the dead raccoons into the bed. Then they removed those raccoons tossed up on the top of the dog carrier, and they now joined their dead brethren in the bed of the truck as well. Finally, each man whipped out his hunting license for me to inspect. Everything checked out, even down to the permission slip from the landowners for the lands on which the lads were now doing their hunting. Like I said earlier, these lads were locked and loaded for bear and doing everything all legal-like according to Hoyle.

Relaxing since everything appeared to be all legal-like, I began doing what I loved doing most with my sportsmen. That of gabbing, discussing new hunting areas, explaining regulation changes, and teasing different members of the group in a good natured sort of way. I especially enjoyed visiting with my black sportsmen because they could be a good-natured hoot. And having nothing better to do that time of the evening, the four of us visited for about thirty minutes. During that time, I gave them directions to raccoon population-rich areas where they would have even better hunting successes and, as always, we discussed the popular topic regarding the best breeds of hounds.

Getting ready to leave, one of the chaps named David Souls reached into his pocket and took out a pouch of Red Man Chewing Tobacco. As he was grumbling about it being almost empty and now being friends with the lads, I took out my pouch of fresh Levi Garrett Chewing Tobacco. "I know it isn't Red Man," I teased, "but this is a real man's chewing tobacco, unlike that wimpy stuff you have been chewing. It is Levi Garrett and I find it a pretty damn good chew." With that, I handed him my pouch of chewing tobacco and he took out a big cud and plopped it into his mouth rewarding me with a big, toothy grin. Thanking me, he handed it back. I remember that man even to this day. He was as big as a house and had huge hands to match his monster-sized carcass. Hell, he was even taller than me! And like most big men, he was a lot of fun to jawbone with and tease. However, what had been an almost full pouch of chew when I had handed it to him because his tobacco was almost gone, was returned to me with just the nubbins! Like I said, he had monster-sized hands. Laughing over my almost empty pouch, I told him that the next time we met, he owed me a chew in return, big time. All of us laughed and I then prepared to leave. But before I did, I asked the lads what they did with all the raccoons they had killed. Ben responded that in the winter they sold the hides to fur buyers in the Bay Area. All the rest of the year, they supplied raccoon meat to their neighbors and some Chinese friends. Taking that as my cue, I requested from the men their favorite raccoon recipes. I did so because I am sort of a cook and was always looking to learn new ways of cooking old favorites when it came to chow. Boy, you talk about a dam breaking. The cooking ideas just flew between us four cooks standing on the canal bank until around one in the morning. Brother, you talk about a bunch of us "recipe-discussing, tobacco-chewing dingies," but it was fun. And let me tell you, black folks, like Cajuns, are usually pretty damned good cooks. Hence, our extensive chewing the fat over good cooking techniques and culinary secrets, all on government time, of course.

With that, I finally bid the men good-bye, thanked them for their cooperation, wished them luck in their future raccoon-hunting adventures and then headed for my truck. Driving out from that area, I headed for my Four Corners fishing area to see if I had any fishermen needing my attention. Not finding any violating the fish and game laws, I took a shortcut across several rice farms until I hit River Road. From there I went home to get some sleep and maybe spend some quality time with my bride come breakfast time, before she went to work as a schoolmarm in the nearby small Sacramento Valley Town of Williams.

Next morning I lucked out. I was able to sit down and have a quiet breakfast with my hardworking bride before she went off to Williams to teach school. Biting into a piece of fried side pork and shoveling in a heaping amount of fried spuds loaded with caramelized onions, I almost gagged on the grits!

"What is the matter, Honey?" Donna asked thinking it was her cooking.

For the longest time I couldn't respond. Then I choked down the remaining mouthful of food. "Damn," I said. "Finally the sun shines on the manure pile behind the barn," I grumbled out loud over my obvious stupidity.

"Terry, the kids," said my ever-suffering wife over my many times off color verbalizations, which always clashed with her proper Catholic upbringing, other family values, and sensibilities.

"I have got to go," I said as I jumped up and began putting on a clean uniform shirt and slapped on my badge. That was followed with the quick addition of my gun belt and its accessories.

"What is the matter with you? You have hardly eaten anything this morning. Now you sit back down and at least finish your breakfast," sternly warned my beautiful blue-eyed bride.

Smiling, I walked over and gathered her small frame up into my arms. Then I silently thanked the Almighty for giving me the closest thing to an angel and the best wife in the world. Putting her back down, I kissed her good-bye.

"Kiss her again, Dad," said Rich, my older son. So, I did.

"Kiss her again, Dad," said Chris, my younger son (may he rest in peace), so I happily obliged. Then getting a swat from my bride for such, but much appreciated, foolishness, I squirted out the door.

"In the truck," I commanded as I raced for my vehicle, and Shadow, my Labrador and ever-faithful patrol buddy sailed up over the side of the truck and into its bed (may she also rest in peace). No small feat for a large, hundred-pound dog but there was no way she was willing to be left behind. As most of my badge carrying game warden readers with dogs know, one doesn't leave them home. If you do, it breaks their hearts. And ours later on when they are finally lost to the ages as all good dogs eventually are... You know folks, on the ninth day, God created dogs. Dogs who had no egos and could break wind without an afterthought in the cab of a truck on a cold winter day when the windows were all rolled up! Dogs who could tip over the trash, make one hell of a mess and when you walked out to survey the scene, walked toward you with a smile on their faces and wiggling tails on the other end with total innocence written across their happy-to-see-you mugs. Dogs who could bring a family together with genuine love, tolerate all the hair and tail pulling by your children but quietly move away without biting when one of your young children sticks his finger into the dog's hind end to see what that round thing was under the tail... Dogs who always forgave your many flaws, providing you shared part of your venison sandwich with them on a cold fall day out in the duck blind and later gave you that special look of disdain when you missed an easy shot at a Northern pintail sailing into your decoys just thirty-five yards away. Dogs who would love you without any conditions and be under foot if you ever had any thoughts of leaving them behind. Dogs who would let your children dress them up in goofy outfits and still have that look on their faces of pure joy and delight for the attention they were receiving. God, how I miss my dog Shadow and she has been lost to the ages now for over thrirty-nine years as these words are written... Sorry, Folks. Just another one of my almost lost moments and cherished memories in time coming to the forefront of my memory bank from beyond the North Wind...

When I finally return to the prairie sod, buffalo grass and clear nights laced with sparkling necklaces of stars, I hope that moment in time finds Shadow and yours truly on eternal fish and game patrols for The Old Boy upstairs, on patrol chasing those poachers who have slipped under God's ethereal fence and are shooting angels during the closed season. That being the case, there will be a lot of angel-shooting poaching son-of-a-guns hitting the ground back here on earth at a very high rate of speed with the imprint of my boot firmly outlined in their last parts over the fence. And on Shadow's face there will be a grin of pure joy.

Jumping into my patrol truck and starting her up, off we went under a healthy head of steam. Going through the Town of Colusa, I turned east at the end of Main Street, crossed over the Sacramento River Bridge without giving my still numerous boat fishermen a wayward glance and headed north on the River Road. Turning off on Laux Road, I sped east toward a locked gate near the end of the road and then onto another farm road leading toward Davison's Duck Club. Turning east just south of Davison's onto another farm road I had traveled the evening before, I zipped along like a man possessed on a mission...and I was.

Stopping where I had checked and jawboned with my African-American raccoon hunters the evening before, I bailed out from my truck. Throwing a hefty chew of Levi Garrett chewing tobacco into my mouth, I let Shadow out of the truck. After she had taken care of her business, I said on a whim and with a prod from one of my now stirring guardian angels, "Find the duck." That was her standard command to go forth and find any kind of critter, but usually a downed duck. Down along the canal bank she sped, stopping to investigate every dump taken by the blue tick and redbone hounds from the evening before. Then in and out of the brush and road bank weeds she went with her nose to the ground like she was on a mission. Halfway down the road between where the three lads had parked their truck and where they had gotten into the last two raccoons, she abruptly slowed as she picked up a fresh scent. That was when her nose went down and her tail went up as she sped along. Seconds later, she slid to a stop all of a sudden, turned around and faced me. That was her signal to me that she had found something of interest that was too large to retrieve.

Walking over to her, I looked into the brush where she stood. There, bigger than any trout I ever caught in Red Clover Creek in Plumas County with my dad, laid a freshly killed dead doe deer! Both her hindquarters had been removed as well as her back straps! And that wasn't all. Lying just a few feet further away lay another dead deer. It had been there maybe a couple of days and had not started to smell ripe as of yet. Both of its hindquarters and back straps had been removed in characteristic fashion like all the others previously discovered!

Cussing my stupidity from the night before when David, the monster black man, had taken a handful of chew from my pouch of tobacco, I continued looking for more grim evidence. Damn, Terry, I thought, you had your clue and blew right by it after you dropped your guard. When David complained about his tobacco pouch being almost empty, and you wanting to be a good guy and supply him with some of yours, you missed the clue! Albeit a slim one because a lot of farm lads in the area also chewed Red Man, but you blew it just the same. What better cover than coon hunting with the dogs and all for their illegal deer killing forays. You had your deer killers right under your nose and had missed them! Talk about a rookie stunt. But, by damn, I had quickly searched their rig and hadn't seen hide or hair of a deer anywhere, I thought, trying to smooth over my concerns for being a damn poor criminal investigator. So much for a good game warden is like a cheetah. He always knows where the hyenas are thing! The only place I hadn't searched was behind the seat of their truck. And to do so, would have been an illegal search without their permission, continued my rapidly streaming string of thoughts as my eyes continued searching the kill and dump site area for any other clues that would strengthen my budding case against my coon hunters.

Then it dawned on me! My three lads had nine dogs. The dog carrier had slots for twelve dogs! Damn, Terry, I thought, maybe they were hiding the deer parts high up in the top extra dog carrier slots! That would be easy to do, hide and overlook if one was only taking and keeping the hams and back straps off the illegal deer! Besides, David, the monster black man of the group, could have easily swung those illegal parts up into the highest row of dog carriers.

Slowly looking the freshly killed doe over and with a little careful digging with my knife, I managed to pick up several more clues. The animals had been shot with a .22-caliber weapon, if the 50-grain, badly deformed lead bullets in my hands told me any kind of a story. Unlike the first deer of this escapade I had investigated. My coon hunting chaps were all carrying .22s! Then the final piece of the puzzle came into play. Whoever had killed and parted out that freshly killed deer had left a big spew of fresh tobacco juice slopped across the side of the animal where it had lain in the tall grasses after he had finished his butchering task!

After taking several pictures of the deer showing the parts removal areas, I left the scene. I could only hope I hadn't spooked my lads the evening before because, sure as crispy fried grasshoppers are good to eat, I was finally hot on the trail of my now, more than likely, identified deer killers. Then the last clue popped into place from my memory banks. I had only discovered fresh deer leavings on Saturday nights. You could bet your sweet bippy there would be a local game warden out all night now come the following Saturday in the east side of my patrol district! And you could damn well bet, I would not be sharing any of my chewing tobacco with anyone I happened to catch doing to Mother Nature what they shouldn't be doing...

Come the following Saturday, I had crawled my vehicle into a dense stand of brush and weeds off to one side of Putnam Road. Over its top went my camouflage parachute leaving just a peek hole from which I could sit and watch out through the front window. Sitting there hoping for my raccoon hunters to show themselves, I thought over my clues once again. There was one still loose end. The first time I had discovered the dead deer, I noticed my culprits' tire tracks led all around marshy wet spots and several old oxbows. Makes sense, now that I know my lads were using raccoon hunting as a cover, I thought. That kind of an environment would be a natural in which to find their furry, frog eating, food washing prey. It also made for mighty fine, secluded, deer killing and disposal habitat.

Finally the warm sun and my previous many long hours of work began taking their toll on my carcass during the stakeout. Soon I fell asleep in the cab of my truck. Sometime later in the back recesses of my mind, I could hear a vehicle rumbling its way south on the nearby graveled road surface of Putnam Road. Quickly coming back from la-la land, I observed a pickup going by. Damn, it is only Walter Opum. A three-time pinched wildlife outlaw thorn-in-the-side of mine for sure but not the one I was currently looking for, I thought. Half an hour later, another vehicle rumbled its way south on Putnam Road. This time, guess who? Yep, sure as angleworms make good German brown trout bait, there went my suspect deer killers posing as legit raccoon hunters. I could even hear their dogs whining in the back of their specialized truck in anticipation of the hunt to come as they drove by. Little did they know, the real hunt was now on and I wouldn't need any dogs for that kind of hunting activity.

Letting them go on by, I was once again reminded of one of Grosz's Rules. If the bad guys aren't disturbed when doing their dirty deeds, they many times will return to their original killing fields confident that they are home free to do as they please. Sure as when a walleye bites you must bow to the fish so it takes in the bait and then moments later set your hook, there my lads went. And I bowed (that is South-Dakota-John-Cooper-walleye-fisherman-par-excellence talk). Only this time, they were now the ones being hunted and this type of badge-carrying critter on the hunt, unlike the deer and raccoons, could fight back.

Waiting until it got good and dark before removing my vehicle's covering parachute, I finally slid out from my hiding place and began quietly driving south on Putnam Road. Turning off onto the levee road leading up to the White Mallard Duck Club, I parked, waited and listened. Farther south and to the southeast, I could hear a pack of hounds baying their heads off. Then faintly, I could hear light rifle fire, like that from a .22 caliber. That was soon followed by abject silence except for the bullfrogs roaring forth in nearby Drumheller Slough.

Now in those days, I was like a marshal of the Old West. I believed in letting a lad doing the illegal killing, take all the rope he needed to get the deed done. You know, to hang himself with ... and in that practice, I always gave all my bad guys enough rope to hang themselves in fine style. But not so much that their feet touched the ground when they got to the end of the rope once they had dropped through the doors of the trap.

From my position by the White Mallard Duck Club, I later heard several more barrages of shots. Still holding my dead man's hand of cards—you know, aces and eights, the same hand that Wild Bill Hickok held on that fateful day in Deadwood, South Dakota—I patiently waited because where they were, there was only one way out. That was unless they blew through a locked steel gate at the other end of the road while being chased by yours truly. Finally figuring I had given my lads enough rope in which to hang themselves, I slid away from my hiding place. Running slowly in low gear without using my lights, I headed for the sounds of the once again baying hounds and numerous shots being fired.

Approaching a muddy farm road turn off above the raccoon hunters' position, I shut off my engine. Sitting one last time, I listened to the sounds of night. Sure as my mother's pickled crab apples were a delight to eat, my raccoon hunters were off in the willows on the north end of the Butte Creek Farms Duck Club. Starting up my truck, I quietly idled my way in low gear towards what I hoped was to be a grand surprise for my glad-handing, tobacco-chewing, raccoon- and illegal-deer-killing chaps from the Bay Area.

Then I spotted their parked and darkened truck along the edge of the road in front of me. Gliding to a stop just yards away in the middle of the road—by so doing, blocking the road prevented a runner in a vehicle from escaping—I quietly bailed out and walked up to their rig. That time I did a better job of looking around. And that time, I was rewarded for my efforts. Using my flashlight light through the fingers trick, I searched along the side of the dog carrier. There it was! Bright thin streams of fresh blood spewed on the upper sides of the dog carriers along the top row! And the whisper thin streams of blood led right up the side of the dog carrier to the empty top row of dog carriers. Unable to see into the darkened dog carriers without using a lot more light, I waited figuring that was where the deer meat was being placed when transported after the fact.

Soon I could hear hushed voices coming my way. Moments later I was surrounded by a pack of hounds, all smelling me up like there was no tomorrow. But thank the Lord, no warning barks came from them. As the dogs milled around the truck, three darkened figures dimly loomed from out of the darkness walking down the road coming my way without the use and aid of any light from their flashlights. That action alone, one of walking in the dark without the use and aid of a flashlight, sure got up my suspicions. Waiting until they had gotten within grabbing distance, I lit them up with my five-cell flashlight. Man, you talk about three surprised chaps, especially the two lads carrying the hindquarters and back straps from two recently killed deer!

The two carrying the deer parts flung them off to one side into the weeds and started to run! "I know who you chaps are and if you keep running in that direction, you will find that black bear I saw earlier in the evening down that road a piece!" I yelled. Not really, just a foot-stopping ruse if one is afraid of bears—an old game warden trick when runners are at hand. Man, you talk about quick reactions to those words! I saw nothing but taillights coming on from my two fleeing chaps the instant those threatening black bear words reached their ears. Especially in light of the fact that their partner back at the truck was carrying their entire .22 caliber artillery and he was now in my clutches.

Continuing, I said, "Hand me all your rifles, Ben," as I watched my two runners out of the corner of my eyes in the beam of my flashlight slowly returning to their truck.

Still in shock at being confronted by the game warden once again, Ben complied. I unloaded all of their rifles and, since they were single-shot bolt-action rifles, I removed their bolts for good measure. Sticking the bolts from their rifles into the pocket of my jacket, I ordered Ben to sit down. About then, the two remaining chaps sheepishly arrived back at their truck. They, too, were commanded to sit down and they did. Then using another trick I had learned earlier in my career, I advised the lads that the sheriff's office was en route and there was no other way out for them to escape. I lied but the trick was a good force multiplier. It was then I noticed one of the dogs up on his hind legs licking the suspect blood from the side of the truck. You know, the small streams of spilled blood, which had dripped out when I surmised the lads, had loaded the first killed deer's parts high into the top dog carriers from earlier in the evening.

Advising my lads that they were under arrest for possessing closed season deer and taking the same with the use and aid of an artificial light, I searched them for any personal weapons they might be carrying. Finding none, I handcuffed two of the larger men of the three together by their right wrists, which made it harder to escape when so cuffed. To my non-law enforcement readers, cuffing two folks in such a manner makes it very difficult to sprint away because it causes those so handcuffed to run off balance; hence, each man being handcuffed by the right wrist. With everything more or less under control, I crawled up and shined my flashlight beam into the top dog carriers. Two of them held parts of two additional freshly killed deer! The others were full of old dried swatches of smeared blood and telltale signs of what appeared to me to be deer hair. Turning, I said, "Well, Gentlemen, it looks like the three of you had a good night." There was no reply from my seated chaps. Crawling up closer to the highest dog carriers, I began dragging out the deer parts, throwing them into a pile on the ground alongside their truck. Picking up the other parts the lads had just brought with them and then had thrown into the weeds when I had announced myself in surprise, I put those into the pile as well. Then I had Ben kennel all the dogs so I wouldn't have to worry about them taking off and running down another raccoon or eating some of my evidence deer meat.

Finally, the four of us walked back to my close-at-hand patrol truck. Seating my three lads in the bed of my truck, I called the Colusa County Sheriff's Office. Giving the dispatcher the names of my lads, I requested that he contact Joe Willow and have him come out with his wrecker and tow my prisoners' seized vehicle back to the sheriff's impound lot. Driving back to my lads' truck, I noticed a flash of furred irony in my headlights. A large boar raccoon had discovered the deer meat lying in a pile on the ground alongside my culprits' vehicle. Thinking he had died and gone to Heaven," he was helping himself. Running him off with the headlights from my approaching vehicle, I loaded the deer parts into the bed of my truck. Forty minutes later, Joe arrived and hooked up Ben's truck and towed it to the impound yard at the sheriff's office. As he did, I followed him into town with my prisoners. Usually I didn't transport prisoners in the back of my patrol truck because of the possibility of escape or injury if there was a wreck. However, that evening all the sheriff's office units were busy and, as a consequence, I brought my prisoners into the Colusa jail in the back of my patrol truck. A move that was somewhat unorthodox but effective for the short haul during good weather.

After booking my chaps, I later called a veterinarian from Yuba City and had the dogs impounded at his facility. The reason I went to Yuba City for that kind of help was because that vet had the required needed space and the dogs were very valuable. I wanted them well cared for and properly contained so if something bad had happened to the dogs, the State of California would not get stuck with the bill for my inattention.

Judge Weyand later fined my three lads $500 each for taking closed season deer and spotlighting. Later upon payment, he returned their vehicle and dogs. However, their rifles were forfeited to the State of California and later used by hunter safety instructor Angelo Jaconetti in local hunter-safety training programs for the Colusa County kids.

With that kind of financial nick being taken out of my three lads' hides, I wondered if Ben would get concerned over the low cost of ammunition his partners sprayed all over the willows at any treed raccoons in the future. Also, I never again bought any of that Red Man Chewing Tobacco when I couldn't find any of my favorite kind because, it reminded me of being dumber than a stick in the instance of that case. Especially when the Red Man clue was more or less laid in front of me and I ran right by it because I was too damn busy discussing dopey raccoon recipes with the deer-killing culprits. Kind of like the cartoon character the Roadrunner when being chased by Willie Coyote, who was all speed and no brains... Oh well, the last perfect person we had on this planet we hung on a board some two thousand years ago. Ever since then, all the rest of us have been somewhat imperfect, flawed and, in some circumstances, dumber than a stick... Yeah, this was one cheetah that got eaten by the hyenas... I never made that "Coyote chasing the Roadrunner" mistake ever again! Well, maybe not intentionally...

WEST SIDE FOLLIES

It was December in the northern Sacramento Valley and typically, I was physically running on fumes. Working my duck hunters and waterfowl hunting clubs by day and the duck draggers and commercial market hunters in the rice fields at night, had taken its toll on the physiology of my miserable carcass. True, I was a young man full of piss and vinegar on a mission holding vision quest status and raring to go, but the energy tank was now almost empty as I found my hind end dragging. Backside dragging to such a degree that I had to tie a roller skate to my hind end to keep from wearing out the rear end of my jeans... A constant stream of sixteen- to-eighteen-hour days, seven days a week had about laid me lower than whale droppings in the Marianas Trench. It was a given at that time of the year during the height of waterfowl season, that I would have a terrible cold, and my energy levels would be bumping along on the bottom of the marsh along with the catfish and crawdads. But the catchin' was good, my critters were in need of a lot of law enforcement help and like a good catch-dog of the day, I always seemed to find the energy needed to keep on truckin' and baggin' up the lawless.

Then with the winter rains slathering sideways, tule fogs flowing into the valley that were thicker than a bowl of oatmeal with no milk and howling winds from the northwest splattering the entire Sacramento Valley, my ducks had decided it was time to feed out west of Interstate 5. They historically did so because, that is what they did once they had eaten out all their rice grits east of the interstate and closest to the protection offered by the close-at-hand Sacramento and Delevan National Wildlife Refuges. And with those readily observed streams of hundreds of thousands of waterfowl heading to the west side of my district every evening, came a whole new crop of deadly human problems and dangers for my winged, night-feeding critters.

It seemed once the ducks fed out west of the interstate, my wildlife outlaws from the small valley towns of Maxwell, Williams, Delevan, and Willows crawled out from under their rocks and leaf litter in anticipation of the historically easy waterfowl killing to come, especially now that the birds were in the gunner's backyards. Loading up their shooting sticks and waiting for the darkness to conceal their soon-to-be evil efforts, that class of gunners illegally shot hell out of the night feeding ducks in the thousands of acres of recently harvested rice fields. With that change in waterfowl feeding and flight patterns, the serious shooting began for the humans on both sides of the law. And sick and run down or not, the clarion call of those in the winged world of waterfowl, emanated forth in their quiet, nature made pleadings for help from The Thin Green Line...

During those times, I would position myself in such locations where I could watch my ducks when they lifted off from their safe zones on the Delevan or Sacramento National Wildlife Refuges. Those were the two largest and most important of the northern Sacramento Valley's waterfowl refuges, which were located smack dab in the heart of California's rice country and my law enforcement district. When the hungry waterfowl left those safe areas shortly after dusk, they would leave in long, dark, telltale, magnificent strings numbering in the hundreds of thousands! Lifting up off the refuges in cloud like tornados, they would quickly ascend upward and out of shotgun range of the hopeful shooters positioned around the refuges external boundaries. With that little chore out of the way, they headed for that night's distant chosen rice field feeding grounds. Once overhead those selected feeding areas in the freshly harvested rice fields on the western side of my patrol district, the hungry birds would come down in huge, living, dark cyclonic tornadoes. Those living tornadoes were so large and densely packed with swirling masses of ducks and geese of all kinds, that many times I just watched such living biomass magnificence in awe. Especially when the living tornados of waterfowl became so densely packed that even the huge competing flocks of aggressive, soon to be rice-field feeding blackbirds numbering in the tens of thousands themselves, could not aerially penetrate such masses of hungry waterfowl! However, if I could see such miracles of nature in the air, so could those walking on the dark side of Mother Nature. And when the lawless saw, they came like a skulking pack of spotted hyenas with an evil glint in their eyes. That, plus an itching trigger finger lay on the sides of their smoke sticks, and a killing desire in their black souls was all the driving force they needed. And for a law enforcement officer trying to stop such grossly illegal night shooting rampages in the rice fields by himself, was like trying to get your cat to bark. Hell, it was like trying to get your cat to do anything you wanted it to do for that matter. Can all my trusting readers out there tell I am not a cat fancier? Hell, I like cats. One inch high at two hundred yards when one's rifle is zeroed at one hundred is just the recipe for success... Sorry to all you cat lovers out there, but the devil made me do it!

During that particular December evening of this story's remembrance, my ducks chose as a major feeding site a large area holding many thousands of acres of freshly harvested rice fields. That soon-to-be market hunter's, duck-dragger's and run-of-the- mill late shooter's dream of a killing field across the interstate, was located south of Lurline Road, west of Gibson Road, north of Freshwater Road, and east of Danley Road in Colusa County. Once that soon-to-be-killing-field was covered by the dark of night, it was almost impossible to control all those humankind forces of darkness moving around therein like maggots on a long bloated cow on that huge chunk of real estate. However, most of the time there was at least one voice in the wilderness in that killing field no matter where it was located. And that voice didn't have a bag limit or season restriction on the numbers of bad guys that he could run to ground and happily capture. Plus, that voice in the wilderness, when it came to protecting those winged critters, was always a loud mouth...

Running without lights on my patrol vehicle, I turned south off Lurline Road onto a muddy, deeply potholed road called Road G or H. It has been over forty years since those days so my readers will just have to forgive my memory lapses as to exactly which road of the two close-at-hand roads it was. Besides, the exact location of the road didn't make much difference. At the end of both of those roads it seemed with such occurring winter weather events now manifesting itself, I historically always had shooters doing to Mother Nature what they shouldn't be doing. Slowly moving down the mud puddle covered road in order to keep my vehicle's arriving noise down, I finally spotted about ten parked vehicles looming out from the early evening's darkness at road's end. Oozing in among them for the cover they offered in that darkness, I exited my patrol truck knowing that shortly, if history was my teacher, the late shooting crap was to hit the fan.

The wind was blowing strongly from the northwest by then and a light rain was following. I also had the lights phenomenon from the City of Williams to the south manifesting itself. That was the effect of the town's lights shining upward into the low-base hanging rainclouds only to be reflected back downward to the ground. When that happened, it slightly lit up the immediate area in which those choosing to violate the shooting-times regulations, were aided in their endeavors by having the low flying birds partially illuminated, thereby increasing the chances of a sure-fire kill.

Listening carefully in the darkness, I could hear the wing beats and calls from thousands of ducks flying back and forth overhead. All were looking and calling for their buddies on the ground to indicate a safe place to land in the harvested rice fields below in which to feast. I could also hear a number of shotguns shooting immediately to the south of me even though legal shooting hours had ended some thirty minutes earlier! Grabbing my binoculars, flashlight, and Dog from the truck, we moved south to the booming sounds of the guns. Walking briskly about one hundred yards into the semi-darkened rice fields, I quickly became aware of the telltale crunching sounds my hip boots were loudly making in the rice stubble. Not wanting to give my now close-at-hand slinking presence away because of the rice stubble crunching foot noise, I decided I would dig in alongside a close-at-hand rice check. That way, I could easily cut off my illegal late shooters from their vehicles when they exited the field after they had late shot the hell out of the dense overhead flocks of my feathered critters. Plus from that location, I would still be able to observe their activities up to their last late shooting moments with my high light gathering optics.

Glassing the area from where the majority of late shooting was coming from with my 7x50 binoculars, I observed a group of five hunters not fifty yards from my position heading back toward their vehicles. They were legal and not shooting so I focused on the remaining lads of interest who were still shooting further to my south like there was no tomorrow. Through my binoculars, I counted the darkened shapes of ten men still remaining in the field. I could clearly see in the binoculars that they were also now slowly moving from the partially rain-flooded fields back toward their vehicles as well. However, all of them would stop and look skyward every time any flocks of ducks flew closely overhead as if wanting to continue shooting if the opportunity clearly presented itself. And many times, falling to the siren song of the low-flying airborne temptations, they did shoot at the darkened fleeting duck forms moving overhead.

Especially those in the larger, more easily observed and denser flocks. Digging out my notebook and No. 2 lead pencil—ink pens don't work well on dampened paper in the rain—I began recording my shooters and their

99

activities. I did so by recording the shooter's differences in the semi-darkness. The tallest, the shortest, the one with a dog, the ones without, the one with a pump shotgun, the ones without, the ones with a 12-gauge shotgun, or the ones with smaller gauges (judged by the sounds they made when fired: louder for a 12- gauge, quieter for a 20- gauge), and on it went. To record such data, I would lie down in the tall grasses of the rice check, cover the beam of my laid down flashlight with my hat letting just a sliver of light out and record my different shooter's activities in my notebook. As my shooters got closer, my dog Shadow would rumble growl their arrivals. Then as my now known late shooters came by my hidden location, I would quietly ambush them with a voice command and identifier. Once I had their attention, I had them unload their shotguns, and sit down on the backside of the rice check with me where they were out of sight of the remaining late shooters still in the field. That capture procedure was repeated until all my late shooting chaps were sitting on or alongside my wet rice check like a string of German sausages. In fact, that evening I had run out of pages in my notebook and had to resort to writing on my hands and fingers when my shooters continued breaking the law with their extensive late shooting activities—yes, recording the illegal events on my hands and fingers to all you potential conservation officer readers out there. Even if wet, your skin will record information if a ballpoint pen is used, which was also routinely carried in my pocket. You can make ten entries on your fingers and another eight to ten on your palms. Even in the wet of the rain, your entries will remain until you later vigorously wash your hands with soap and water. Just another damn good and old-time game-warden trick of the trade for you readers' edification. Particularly if any of you go on to become game wardens or protectors of those in the world of wildlife who have little or no voice.

Finally having captured all my late shooting lads in that area, we quietly walked en masse back to where our vehicles were parked. There they were checked for their hunting licenses, duck stamps, numbers of birds, and for plugged shotguns. Then the paperwork began. As it turned out, none of my captures that evening were locals but were shooters from the nearby Bay Area who were staying in a nearby duck club, with local farmer friends, or other valley family members—not an uncommon practice in the northern Sacramento Valley in those days when wintering waterfowl were in the valley by the millions. And in those days, many rice farmers did not have a problem with duck hunters hunting in their fields without permission. As a result, it seemed like, especially during the dense tule fogs oftentimes present during the winter months, I had hunters and waterfowl underfoot by the millions... Of that bunch apprehended in the field that evening, the earliest late shooter I captured had shot forty-four minutes late, and the worst late shooter of the lot had shot sixty-eight minutes late. When it was all said and done, my late shooting lads had collectively amassed a total of 545 minutes of late shooting times for that evening's shoot! The local bail schedule called for a $25 fine for the late shooting offense plus an additional $2 for every minute shot early or late. So the total fines for my gaggle of late shooters came to $1,340! Not bad for a guy who was so darn sick that he should have stayed home in bed that evening. However, wildlife dies without making a sound unless someone is out there speaking for them. And like I said earlier, I always did have a big mouth...

Then came the drag that set the hair on my last part over the fence! I had no more than finished with my lads when the winter winds brought me the sounds of a long rattle of about ten shots from drag shooters north of me a mile or so away. For you unwashed, when a mess of drag shooters lets loose into a massed flock of close-at-hand feeding ducks, the multiple string of rapidly firing shotguns sounds a little like one ripping a bed sheet. Quickly turning, I figured my shooters were in the possible vicinity of Wells Road. Drag shooters were folks, usually locals, who knew where the ducks were night feeding, had crawled up onto the feeding birds, and, at close quarters, rapidly shot into the amassed flocks numerous times. In so doing, they were killing anywhere from one hundred to three hundred unsuspecting birds at such a duck slaughtering illegal event. That type of activity was more commonly carried out on feeding ducks than geese, because of the better eating qualities of ducks and the existence of an illegal commercial market. Those birds would then many times be hauled off and sold in the Bay Area to restaurants, shared locally with friends, or stored in the shooters' freezers for subsequent excellent eating rice-fed duck dinners throughout the rest of the year.

"Those are the bastards you ought to be going after instead of us real sportsmen," said one disgruntled fellow who had just received the last citation in the bunch of captured shooters for late shooting some sixty-eight minutes late!

"Count on it," I said as I had Dog quickly load up into the bed of the truck. Then hopping in, I started her up and boiled out from my parking area. Running without lights once again, I slid out onto Danley Road and headed north. By now, the rain was really coming down in sheets, and I could feel the winds buffeting my truck as we moved down the road. A good night for late shooting and an even better one for any duck dragging activity, I thought grimly to myself. It sure would have been nicer to have had a little help from some of my other "Thin Green Line" compatriots that evening. But as it turned out, most of them were just as run down and sick as was yours truly and had wisely decided to stay at home that fine rainy and windy evening with their families. You know, like most normal people would do. Who said good game wardens were normal, eh?

Approaching Finks Road, I turned east and slowed down. Nothing but abject blackness greeted my eyes due to the cast shadows from the now dense, low based rain clouds, and soon I was just creeping along to avoid running off the road and slamming headfirst into a road-bordering drainage ditch. Slowly moving up onto Wells Road leading to the south, I stopped and got out so I could hear better. Petting my dog, I just stood there in the wind and rain, listening. The sad thing was if one was not right on top of suspected drag shooting chaps, your chances were just about nil when it came to catching them. Bottom line, most drag shooters were like child molesters. They didn't advertise their trade or stick around to see the consequences of their lethal actions. Standing there quietly in the elements for another two hours on the now deserted back road, I heard nothing else suspicious such as strings of shooting or the like. I also did not see any vehicular movement in that area or on Fair View Road exiting further to my south. Finally getting back into my vehicle, I thought, Just like ghosts. Only the worst killing kind of ghosts because of all the cripples they leave behind in the fields after the shoot to slowly die or be run down and eaten by avian or quadruped predators.

The next morning way before daylight, found Dog and me setting near Wells Road where we could see and yet not be seen by anyone passing by. Dog and I were sitting there because if my lads that had shot the area and fled the night before had not picked up all their birds, they might just come creeping back the next morning like the maggots they were to glean the remaining duck sheaves from the deadly scene. If that were the case, they would at that time pick up the rest of their ill-gotten booty and then scoot off under the leaf litter once again. If they did return and pick up the cripples and dead birds, hopefully Dog and I would welcome them with open arms and a pair of shiny, stainless steel, Smith and Wesson handcuffs to further celebrate the moment at hand. Because, more than likely, they would be in possession of large over limits of ducks. Large over limits of ducks because of the normal high crippling rate associated with such illegal night shooting actions.

Alas, no such luck. The area in question was as quiet as is the arrival of the Angel of Death. However, I did find muddy tire tracks coming onto Wells Road from a series of suspect harvested rice fields that later led onto Finks Road. Those tracks may have been made by my drag shooters. But again, they may have been made earlier by another duck hunter leaving the muddy rice field or the land owner- farmer just as easily, I thought grimly.

When no one who had illegally shot from the evening before arrived, I relented. Alone, I spent the rest of that morning on foot walking those suspect rice fields in a foggy drizzle. Dog and I finally found the location from whence the drag had originated. There were ten freshly fired, 12-gauge shotgun shells lying behind a rice check, along with numerous knee and footprints in that same muddy area. Additionally, the killing field to the front of the spent shells was covered with oodles of loose feathers, numerous footprints in the mud, splashes of bright red blood not yet washed away by the foggy drizzle, and numerous squirts of dark colored duck poop. No matter how one looked at it, those were the sure signs of a night shooting ambush perpetrated on unsuspecting feeding ducks. Figuring my chaps might return that evening if not bothered by the long arm of the law, especially if the birds piled back into the same area the following evening, I finally got the heck out of there. But not before Dog and I had collected sixty-seven Northern pintail and mallards crippled from the previous night's illegal and wasteful duck shoot. Birds that had been wounded had crawled off into the grasses along the numerous rice checks and were eventually overlooked by the shooters!

Later that day after making a special phone call, I pulled into a prearranged spot known to me for not attracting unwanted attention from the locals. There I met with Dave (not his real name) who came from a long line of previously convicted and federally-incarcerated commercial market hunters and a man who was one of my excellent local Town of Princeton informants. He advised that Roger Long and Fred Davis (not their real names because they still have kin living locally and I try not to embarrass the innocents) from the Town of Willows, had blown up the ducks on the previous night in my area of concern. He also advised they had killed and collected 306 ducks and were now en route to Vallejo in the Bay Area of California to sell them to their middleman. He did not know the name of the middleman, which historically was a very closely guarded secret among market hunters or drag shooters, but he did say the shooters bragged to him about their getting paid $2.25 per gutted duck! Dave also said the shooters would not shoot that area for at least another week so that it might cool off and settle down. Then if the ducks returned so would they. With that and a few other pleasantries, Dave and I parted company. To all my readers out there, help from the general public in the world of wildlife law enforcement is vital! Without the help of concerned citizens, the job will never get done because of the limited numbers of law enforcement officers and the magnitude of the problems. For example, I am told that California has only 207 game wardens employed as of 2013! That is for a resource- rich state of over 30 million people! That should put into perspective why we need help from the general public. I rest my case...

Dave was very concerned about such illegal shoots because he was the father of four boys and wanted to make sure they got to see and enjoy what their dad had enjoyed as a young man when hunting in the valley. Hence, Dave's willingness to get involved. And let me tell you, Dave's information, like that of Tom Yamamoto's, was always spot on. Dave is dead now having been killed by a massive heart attack. However, his boys still hunt ducks, geese and pheasants today. So, I guess one could say, through his efforts, Dave left the wildlife and historical legacy he so wanted for his sons to experience and enjoy. Rest in peace my friend.

Since it was now a scheduled shoot day on a part of each of the Sacramento Valley's four national wildlife refuges administered under agreement between the Department of the Interior's U.S. Fish and Wildlife Service and the California Department of Fish and Game, I headed for the Sacramento National Wildlife Refuge's public shooting area. There in its major parking lot full of hopeful duck hunters waiting their turn to hunt on the controlled shooting zone, I had a ball. Rounding up the small kids belonging to the hopeful hunters for that day's shoot, I gave away the ducks Dog and I had picked up from the previous night's drag site. That made for a hatful of happy kids. Plus, that way the ducks didn't go to waste. Many times that meant the non-hunting kids had a limit of great eating, rice fed ducks, and their dads and older brothers might just come back from the state managed hunting area with just a "spoonie." A spoonie is a common name given to a northern shoveler. A medium-sized duck and, because of its filter feeding habits, was not considered the best of eating birds when it came to waterfowl. Man, I was not only built like Santa Clause but enjoyed giving away Mother Nature's gifts as well.

Later that evening, found Dog and me watching the exodus of thousands of ducks pouring off the closed zone of the Delevan National Wildlife Refuge on a typical feeding flight. Following that massive flight of birds stretching for well over a mile in the air, soon found us at the end of Bowen Road in among another mess of hunters' parked vehicles. Moments later, Dog and I were heading out into the darkening rice fields toward a group of shooters unwilling to leave their hunting areas at the end of legal shooting hours. In the winter winds and rain, Dog and I once again rounded up a pickle barrel full of late shooters. Late shooting chaps who just could not resist the temptation to late shoot into the clouds of low flying flocks of hungry ducks. This local tule creeper just couldn't resist apprehending those walking on the wrong side of the law and good common sense due to their illegal late shooting activities either...

Before all was said and done that evening, nine late shooters had been rounded up and between the group, had accounted for 602 minutes of late shooting! That, and a number of other violations running from no duck stamps in possession to unplugged shotguns, which ultimately resulted in the county gathering in an additional $1,580 in fines. Eight other fellows hunting in the same fields that obeyed the law and had quit on time, had the pleasure of jawboning at my citation-receiving recipients later back at the parking area. There were lots of "I told you so's" coming from the legal group, as they stood around watching me doing my paperwork on those just apprehended chaps with heavy, late shooting trigger fingers. Additionally, I had seized forty-one ducks from my late shooters because they had been taken illegally after legal shooting hours. As such, they could not be lawfully possessed. The following morning, those ducks went to a happy crowd of kids on the state run shooting area on the Delevan National Wildlife Refuge. Done so in accordance with the previous disposal recommendations from the Colusa County Attorney's Office. That procedure of releasing the seized evidence before one had his day in court always made me a little nervous. However, the county attorney had been there long enough and had seen hundreds of like cases cross his doorstep without any problems in such a pre-trial disposal procedure. To my way of thinking and contrary to all the Rules of Evidence training I had received, such a procedure was a legal no-no since I had to prove my case "beyond a reasonable doubt" in any criminal matter. And to my way of thinking, that meant entering as evidence any and all wildlife property seized to support my claims of an illegal action. The county attorney just figured once the seized birds were frozen guts, hide, fur and all, they wouldn't be safe to eat and would just go to waste once any forthcoming legal action was terminated. Hence, his pre-trial release orders to the two Colusa County game wardens so the birds would not go to waste. That procedure only applied to wildlife cases though! All other criminal matters involving seized evidence was held until the case was adjudicated and the judge had ordered disposition. Now that I think back on it, in the three-plus years I worked the waterfowl scene in the Sacramento Valley as a state officer, I never had anyone contest the charges laid against them for such violations. Guess the county attorney knew what he was doing. People were sure different in that day and age... However, once I became a federal officer, this procedure was prohibited by the Federal Rules of Evidence procedures. Evidence was evidence, and an officer had better not screw around with it in any way, shape or form! But, once again, I digressed so you legal beagles reading these lines could rest your concerns involving release of evidence prior to trial. Back to the story at hand.

For the rest of that week, I worked the duck clubs just off San Jose Road. Aside from a few minor violations, they were pretty much law abiding. Then I managed to smack six shooters from Jess Cave's Duck Club for shooting over bait. In that case, those chaps had openly baited the area around their deep-water blind and had shot the hell out of the ducks. That was until I got suspicious and spoiled their little party. Additionally, there was the issue involving possession of over limits of ducks, and two of the six for killing hen pheasants as well.

All in all, it was a very productive week except for those illegally taken critters on the lethal ends of a stream of lead shot. As an aside, use of lead shot was legal in those days. Today one must use steel or other kinds of non-toxic shot when taking waterfowl. That changeover to non-toxic shot was because lead shot, when inadvertently ingested by feeding waterfowl as grit, was many times lethal. And in the case of many of the nation's historic duck clubs, some of which had been shot over for a hundred years, the lead shot build-up was at the level, that truth be known, those most frequently shot over duck ponds probably could have been considered a superfund site for all the deposited lead they contained!

As a further aside, several years later in 1974 as a Special Agent for the U.S. Fish and Wildlife Service stationed in Bismarck, North Dakota, I ran across three of those same six guys from Jess Cave's Duck Club while on a commercial airliner going to Canada. That's right, the same three that had illegally shot over a baited area on Jess Cave's Duck Club in California years earlier! At the time, yours truly was headed to lecture at an RCMP Academy and do other guest lecturing to national conservation organizations in Canada. To listen to those three lads tell it, they had just shot one hell of an over limit of ducks over a baited area in North Dakota and were now on their way to Canada for a moose hunt. Recognizing my three California outlaws as I sat behind them on that plane holding up a newspaper in front of my face so they would not inadvertently recognize me, I quietly listened to their next planned illegal duck shooting event upon their subsequent return to North Dakota from Canada. All I had to go on was the last name of a farmer somewhere in North Dakota as to where their most recent waterfowl violations had occurred. As it turned out, that farmer was the father to one of my previous Jess Cave Duck Club violators. Plus, they were coming back after the moose hunt to kill the hell out of another mess of ducks over the same baited area. My readers will just have to read my book titled, No Safe Refuge, Chapter 7, "It's a Very Small World", to see how the rest of that adventure played out. You don't want to miss that one! It took some real doing and a ton of sleuthing on my part, plus sleeping out on the prairie in a rock pile before I ran those trigger heavy chaps to ground. Ran them to ground with only the last name of a farmer to go on. And that farmer's last name was Germanic and a very common handle in North Dakota I might add. But, I digress.

The next Saturday night, based on the information I had earlier received from my Princeton informant, I was back in country in the vicinity of the area reportedly to be dragged near Wells Road. And right on time, so were my hordes of hungry ducks! This time, Dog and I had walked in about a quarter of a mile from where I had hidden my patrol truck so I would be area-central to the swarms of feeding birds. Then moving carefully so as not to spook the numerous bunches of nearby feeding ducks already in the fields, we pulled a classic sneak on a centrally located mess of the noisy critters in the darkness. In so doing, Dog and I avoided staking out the larger bunches of already feeding ducks. We did so because the local outlaw gunners considered it unwise and bad for one's kilts to shoot the largest flocks. That concern was historically rooted in the local outlaws psyche. A psyche based on ugly apprehension experiences from the early days of market gunning, in which the feds used to routinely stake out the largest bunches of feeding waterfowl. And one sure as hell didn't want to shoot up a mess of ducks and then have the dreaded feds, who had been staking out that same bunch of birds, hot on your trail. That law enforcement method of operation staking out the larger bunches of feeding waterfowl, was based widely on the history that many of the commercial market hunters in the days of old, shot the bigger flocks of waterfowl in order to increase their kills. And more dead ducks in hand, meant more money in their pockets. During my time in the '60s, I faced fewer insidious commercial market hunters but still had a high number of duck draggers crawling around in the leaf litter. The common thinking of the day by my local outlaws was, that since smaller bunches of ducks would be more widely dispersed and numerous, those were the ones to safely shoot. Wiser, because the feds would be less likely to be sitting on the same bunch of birds you wished to shoot. That was because of all the choices the federal officers had to make as to which feeding flock to guard and protect on any given night. And since there were only 178 U.S. Game Management Agents in the Fish and Wildlife Service in the entire United States in the late '60s, and only four assigned to the entire Sacramento Valley, well... Hence, Dog and I staked out a sizeable mess of feeding ducks that were central to the overall feeding area. Then if someone shot birds from other than our staked out flock, Dog and I could quietly move to the fading echoes of the guns and fresh smells of burnt powder, while our shooters were now preoccupied in the act of picking up their kills. And in so doing, hopefully nab a shooter or two.

Shortly thereafter, we were in among about forty thousand madly feeding ducks, which soon totally surrounded us as they fed! Lying motionless against the backside of a damp rice check, Dog and I enjoyed Mother Nature up close and personal like in a way most folks will never get to experience. Ducks were everywhere but they were exceptionally spooky. It was apparent to me that these ducks had been previously night shot elsewhere and were nervous as a house cat in a room full of mean-assed, pit bulls. But even with that, hordes of the critters would feed right up to our rice check where we laid motionless and then flood over us like a living feathered carpet as they fed into the rice field beyond. In the process, I had ducks walking over Dog and me all the while making contented feeding sounds and leaving poop everywhere. That was one of the greatest thrills of my life, one that I will carry to my grave. Sadly, my great dog and constant partner, Shadow, has already made that trip without me. One of my most cherished hopes is that she is up There waiting for me with a wiggling body out of happiness and an expression on her face that reads, "Where to now, Boss? What is our next adventure?" Boy, wouldn't that be cool...

Around three in the morning with me almost asleep from fatigue over my seven days a week, sixteen-to-eighteen-hour days work schedule, my ever-faithful dog softly rumble-growled her knowledge of something suspicious nearby. Quickly snapping back into the world of the living without making any sudden moves, like a Mountain Man trapper of old in hostile Indian country would have done, I slowly began looking all around our position for what had concerned Shadow. For the longest time, no matter how hard I looked, I saw nothing. Then, there it was! Two darkened shapes were slowly creeping across the rice field toward a nearby rice check just to my north. The two shapes finally arrived at the rice check and, for what seemed like a lifetime, they hid in the tall water grasses covering the check, appeared to be surveying the hordes of feeding ducks and never moved a muscle.

Then I realized why. Directly in front of my two crawlers was a mass of happily feeding ducks. That mass of ducks was slowly feeding toward them like a giant living carpet. As ducks would do in such situations, they were a swirl of movement in the front of the flock. In fact, out of hungry greed for fresh rice kernels, many ducks would lift off from the back of the living carpet and swirl just over the bodies of those feeding in front of them. This they did in order to get on the ground not fed over by the ducks in front of them, so they could get at the better eats. The closest thing I could compare that swirling mass of ducks to was what locals of old used to call a grind. And for those of you who can remember, that would be akin to a dust storm of the Dirty Thirties rolling your way. Only instead of a storm of dust, it would be a feathered cloud of waterfowl rolling your way. Just imagine, a solid clump of winged waterfowl biomass swirling like a giant cloud moving toward you. I am sorry that my readers will more than likely never in their lifetimes experience such a phenomenon of living things. Living things that were so densely packed together, that one couldn't quack without blowing the feathers off the hind end of his nearest kin. Sorry because for the most part, ducks in those numbers and behavior, are severely reduced in the Sacramento Valley in 2012, as compared to my memories from those heady days of the '60s.

Absent in such numbers and behavioral patterns, as told to me in current discussions with officers who worked the valley on such details after I had been promoted and left for North Dakota to work for a different conservation law enforcement agency.

That grind of ducks was slowly moving towards where my two earlier crawling humans, had positioned themselves on the backside of a rice check. Slowly and quietly stretching my legs to get the blood moving back into them for the chase that was sure to follow once my lads discovered I was hot on their trail, I waited. Silently and expectantly, I waited for the explosion of shot and shell soon to lethally fall upon my happily feeding ducks. Some of you readers might just be wondering why I would let those chaps shoot into those masses of ducks instead of stopping them straightaway before they pulled the trigger. There was no violation of the law by my two chaps for just being there in that rice field that time of the morning with evil on their minds and shotguns in hand. One had to shoot into the critters for it to be in violation of state waterfowl regulations or the federal Migratory Bird Treaty Act. Hence why the carnage was soon to follow, and there wasn't much I could do about it prosecution-wise unless I caught my shooters bloody red-handed, no pun intended.

After the shoot, one could plan on hearing the roar of eighty thousand frantically beating wings once the killing became a reality. Wings that would create a forceful burst of wind that would carry the immediate pungent smell of rotting rice straw, sour mud, duck poop, burnt powder, and dead crawdads back to where I lay hidden. That is if the Sacramento Valley history of such an ugly moment in time was any kind of a teacher. Dang, I can already see the questions rising in many of you reader's eyes over the above descriptions. Crawdads? You got that right. When the rice fields were flooded and the rice was growing during the hot summer months, the fields were a haven for zillions of happy crawdads. However, once the fields were drained prior to harvesting, many of the crawdads that couldn't escape to a more permanent body of water nearby, perished. Hence, the often times smells of rotting crawdads in the freshly harvested rice fields when I was crawling around in the mud in the darkness, trying to put those in the business of extinction, out of business...

It is amazing to me that after so many years, I can still remember sensory events like I just described. It is for those memories from the fields of battle protecting those voiceless ones in the world of wildlife that I am extremely grateful to the Old Boy upstairs to have in the waning days of my life. Those were experiences that many in the modern day conservation law enforcement community will more than likely never experience in today's world of wildlife. Especially those working grade officers of modern times, when wildlife no longer exists in such abundance or magnitude, as to create such vivid memories. Or because many of those who work for conservation agencies, that are now led by those who have never been there and experienced such wonders themselves. And as a result of those field experience deficiencies, such supervisors many times do not support their minions getting deeply involved in ways in which they need to be in the world of wildlife. Supervisors who don't readily sanction such field endeavors because they themselves cannot sense, understand, or feel the special needs of nature. Or because of heavy administrative workloads mandated by those who have never been there and done that, or have forgotten what it was like in their younger days, that they now bury all those around them with the same trivial paperwork crap. Lastly, because many senior managers are more comfortable with the administrative process instead of the challenging field of battle, they tend to ignore the obvious and pass that ethic down to their minions. When that happens, that paperwork ethic is forced upon one's subordinates many times in today's world of wildlife. In part, that inaction is because many of those current members of the Thin Green Line are not of the land's history and soil. I have found that numerous conservation officers in today's world do not have the real heart and soul that normally comes from a life nurtured in their younger years in close association with the environment. Many of today's officers are academically very bright but a goodly number lack the heart, soul and understanding of the land and its critters. In short, if senior management or the agency leaders haven't been there, they can't be expected to lead real warriors into the field of battle in today's world of wildlife law enforcement endeavors! These ailments are all too frequently found in many modern day natural resource organizations, especially at the senior levels of management. Sorry, Folks, it is hard not to get caught up in those marvelous events of a lifetime now long past, without addressing the history of the very real world values of today. Particularly when I see such basic enforcement problems not being addressed through good solid field law enforcement in today's world of wildlife, because many in senior management can't see the forest for the trees. I have never found that leading from behind is very good medicine for what ails the world of wildlife. When that happens, I get a bit grumpy. I guess it is because wildlife dies without making a sound. And if one is not squalling like a smashed cat trying to stop such lawlessness, then they are part of the problem as I see it. Damn, I can still almost smell the rotting rice straw, sour mud, dead crawdads, and burnt shot shell powder smells wafting my way through the damp air after the deadly hail of shot had found its way into the hordes of feeding ducks in the Northern Sacramento Valley as I write these lines...

The Native Americans of the plains used to say, "There are always echoes beneath your feet and in the air placed there by Wakan Tanka or the Creator. You just have to be silent in order for your heart to hear. But when the whispers in the wind and the echoes of the land are heard, still your mind, listen and follow your heart." To my way of thinking, much of modern day wildlife law enforcement needs to talk less and silently listen to those echoes from the land and times past. For in that, the listener will understand that which needs doing. But, once again I digress.

Then it happened! The ducks madly feeding just moments before, rose into the air in one giant, wing-slapping, thunderclap! Something had spooked them from putting on the feedbag, and now they were madly getting the hell out of Dodge. As the ducks roared their ways to safety, caught by surprise, my two still crawling lads looking for a better shooting position, did not get their shots off in time or while in close range to the masses of feeding ducks. Then almost as an afterthought, they shot anyway into the rapidly disappearing airborne masses of ducks madly fleeing the area. Fortunately, by then the ducks were at the edge of the effective killing range of the lethal streams of lead shot coming their way from the shooters below. As a result, only seventy-three ducks, as discovered later, dropped from the huge fleeing flocks. If something had not scared the ducks, I imagine my lads would have killed several hundred easily! But that time, the duck goddess had interceded which precluded a mass slaughter of her kin. Note the gender, for you non-believers as to who is really in charge up there in the clouds...

After they had shot, my two shooters remained motionless at their positions behind the covering grasses on their rice check. I was sure they were looking around to see if anyone had heard them shoot. And, more than likely, to see if anyone like the areas game wardens or federal agents had heard their shots and were coming their way at a dead run to capture the shooters. However, like my shooters, I lay as still as death on my rice check as did the dead in the nearest cemetery. Checking my watch, I saw my lads had shot ten times at 3:28 in the morning!

Satisfied that no one was hot on their trail, my two lads suddenly jumped up from their hiding places from behind their positions on the rice check. Running across the field in front of their rice check, they commenced picking up the dead and biting across the heads of the wounded ducks. A quick bite across the head of a wounded duck precluded any further struggles and was a favorite method of the local duck draggers in the Sacramento Valley when it came to killing struggling, night shot waterfowl as opposed to just wringing their necks. The reason for not wringing the necks of the dying was that sometimes in the emotion of the wringing moment, the birds' heads would separate from their necks. Without the head still attached, it became more difficult to lug the ducks out from the field on the duck straps or to carry them by hand. In their haste, neither of my shooters saw a darkened figure and a dog moving quietly across the rice field to their previous hiding spot from which they had just shot. Upon seeing the lads scurrying around in the field picking up the ducks, I realized one very important thing. They were not carrying their shotguns! They had left them behind on the rice check in order not to be encumbered when picking up the fruits of their shoot!

That suited me just fine. Because now, I would not have to deal with the safety issue of an accidental discharge if they were carrying when they noticed they were being pursued. Or, were of a mind to shoot at what was pursuing them just for the hell of it ... plus, this would make my captures rather easy. They had to come back to their old hiding places on the rice check to get their shotguns when they had finished gathering up their kills in the field. And when they did, guess what they would get instead? It sure as hell wouldn't be their shotguns but a face full of the world's largest, and many would say the most beautiful, Teutonic game warden around. All right, all right! Beautiful to a cannibal maybe because of my size... How is that for a duck shooting outlaws biggest, no pun intended, nightmare?

Peering through the water grass from my new rice check place of hiding, I saw my lads had completed their gathering and piling of the duck sheaves along the rice check. Then they did another once over on the shooting area to see if they had overlooked any dead or dying ducks. That chore over, here they came at a dead run for the safety their rice check offered as they attempted to hide once again. Plunging over the top of the rice check, my two laughing out of relief duck shooters began bailing back into their previous hiding places. That was when the wheels came off their wagon...

"Hold it right there! Game warden, and if either of you move, I will sic my dog on you!" I yelled. Then reaching over, I grabbed the closest man and jerked him to his feet. Still in shock, my second man had not moved since I bellowed out the presence and nearness of my magnificent Teutonic, without my spiked helmet of course, carcass.

Taking advantage of the momentary shock my current captive was in, I reached over and grabbed his partner by his stacking swivel as well so that fleeing was not an option for either of my night shooting, duck killing gunners.

"Don't shoot me," my stacking swivel yelled. "Don't shoot me, Mister."

"Both of you sit down right here," I said, as I unceremoniously plopped their bottoms into the mud and dead crawdads of the rice field at a somewhat high rate of speed for the effect it would have on any future fight or flight intentions.

Both lads, still surprised at the turn of events and having their hind ends mashed into the mud at a high rate of speed, just cowered. "Watch them, Shadow," I growled. With that, she sat down alongside the lads. Then turning on my flashlight, I splashed the beam of light across their eyes. I didn't recognize the faces of either man but that made no matter. They were captured after illegally shooting my ducks, and I had possession of their shotguns. So for the moment, all was good in "Mudville" that fine morning...

"Hand me your driver's licenses," I growled.

"We don't have them," said a young man named Roger, as I was soon to learn.

"Where are they?" I asked.

"We left them in our truck so we wouldn't lose them in the field," he responded.

"I take it you two are Mr. Long and Mr. Davis from Willows?" I asked.

"Yes, sir," they both replied. But in the tone and tenor of their replies, you could tell they were baffled as to how I knew their names. That information had been forthcoming earlier courtesy of and thanks to my trusty Princeton informant as you readers may remember.

"All right, Lads. Gather up these loose birds and your duck straps so we can head for your rig. Keep in mind if either of you decide to run, I will have Shadow take the closest one and I will collar the other," I said in my meanest sounding tone of voice. Boy, if they only realized I was a powder-puff wimp. "Then if running is in your agenda, both of you will be going to Federal Court in Sacramento. And that means automatic time in the bucket. Do you lads understand what I just said and the consequences of any escape actions?" I asked.

"Yes, Sir," came their dual worried sounding responses.

"All right, grab a load of birds, then let's head 'em up and start for your rig," I said firmly, now coming down from my emotional high of grabbing my two duck draggers caught in their deadly act of butchery.

As I was soon to discover, my two fellows had hidden their truck beautifully in a small line of trees on a dead end, seldom used farm road. Damn, Terry! This is a great place to hide, I thought. I will have to keep this spot in mind for later use.

Once back at their truck, my two men dug out their wallets from the glove box and I commenced writing out their citations. I saw no real reason for booking them since they had not been able to really kill the hell out of the ducks. However, they were in for a real financial ride once I finished. Each lad received a state citation for early shooting ducks, using unplugged shotguns, no hunting license in possession, taking an over limit of ducks, and not having a federal duck stamp in their immediate possession. The last violation involving the federal duck stamp charge was processed later in Federal Court in Sacramento. In the end, both men, who were 24 years of age at that time, paid fines totaling $1,500 each in the Williams Justice Court and an additional $100 apiece in federal court for the duck stamp violations. Additionally, both forfeited their new Browning AL-5 shotguns to the State of California. I never again ran into my two lads from Willows messin' around out and about with my ducks during the dark of the night. I guess one bad experience didn't deserve another, eh?

Several weeks later, I hooked up with another of my informants from the small Town of Princeton on a different matter. Once that business was finished, we talked about my two recently captured Willows duck draggers. My informant advised I had scared the hell out of Long and Davis. Apparently when I rose out from the weeds that fateful morning, I had scared both of them half to death, hence, their lack of running off into the darkness. They had heard that I was a fairly large individual. But when I had risen from the rice check, Long later told my informant, "That son-of-a-bitch was so huge he blotted out what little moon we had." They also advised that henceforth they would only blow up the ducks in Glenn County and leave Colusa County "the hell alone," as Long had put it.

Colusa County, in its day, was a place I will long remember. Its people were some of the best salt of the earth folks I have ever run across in my many years as a wildlife officer. Even a lot of the local outlaws were pretty good human beings, truth be known. And as for the wildlife that county contained, its numbers and species were something to behold! I saw more wildlife in that seven-year period of my life in that county than I ever saw again in such a small area. Everywhere I turned there were wildlife resources beyond compare. Where else could you find an area where the first 167 pheasant hunters I checked one year all had their limits? Or, on one long opening day of the waterfowl season, check two hundred straight limits of ducks on the storied Butte Sink duck clubs when the limit was eight per day before I ran across a hunter who didn't have a limit? Or, check boat after boat with catches of striped bass, salmon and sturgeon on the Sacramento River when the runs were full on? Then take the lowly bullfrog. Have any of you ever checked seventeen gunnysacks full of bullfrogs belonging to commercial froggers? I have and more than once! To my way of thinking, those commercial froggers were in large part responsible for that frog population's demise in the Sacramento Valley. Or, harvested rice fields so full of feeding lesser snow geese, that the whole area was frosty white with their bodies and they made so much happy noise, that one could hardly be heard above the din when talking to another nearby person in a normal tone of voice? And then when spooked, made such a noisy racket as they arose into the air that it would shame the sounds any self- respecting thunderstorm could ever make. And on it went...

Then throw into that mix a young game warden on a vision quest to hold the line in the world of wildlife. Particularly, against those taking more than their fair share of wild things, so there would be something left for those yet to come. After seven hard years, that game warden came to realize that no matter how hard one tried, many of the above-described resources would eventually be severely depleted or mostly disappear because of man and his thoughtlessness.

Colusa County and her people taught me a lot about life, as it actually was. I truly learned how to read wildlife and its needs. I also learned how to read people. And how to cut those out from the pack who needed to be run to ground for the error of their ways in the world of wildlife. I also learned that no matter how big I was, I could only be spread just so thin and then the wildlife losses would start occurring once I ran out of energy. God gave me the heart and soul to look out for His critters. But damn it, He just didn't give me enough mass or many times at the right time or energy levels to carry forth in fine style...

Please put on my tombstone when it is all over, "God was there for me when the fists and bullets were flying. And I was there for Him when His critters were dying."

Chapter Two: Spotlighters and the Andreotti Ranch

TWO BELGIAN BROWNING RIFLES

L eaving my home in the Sacramento Valley of California one hot and humid summer afternoon, I struck out for the Town of Maxwell on the western side of my assigned patrol district in Colusa County. Stopping in at Maxwell, I had a cold Coke with my long-time dear friend, Deputy Sheriff Fred Pilgrim. Fred was a Sacramento Valley boy born, bred and raised in Maxwell. In fact, he had step-kin who were not only duck draggers but also members of the old-time commercial market hunter fraternity. At least that is how the local stories went ... and one of his step-kin tangled with the law for commercial market hunting and feloniously selling migratory waterfowl to an undercover federal agent, or as

125

the story goes once again. That aside, Fred was one hell of an outstanding officer. In fact, many a night when I was working the valley's harvested rice fields trying to catch duck draggers or the few remaining, insidious commercial market hunters in Fred's assigned law-enforcement patrol district, often times by myself, he would be on hand nearby almost every time backing me up if the need arose. Like I said, Fred was a damn fine officer regardless of his step-kin's background. He was a totally professional officer and one of the very best I ever knew and worked with! In fact, I soon discovered one important thing about my buddy. If one ever tangled swords with him over any illegal issue, that person had better bring a lunch. Bring a lunch, because when Fred was finished with you over the illegal matter at hand, he would be hungry. Hence, the need for the miscreant to bring a lunch and a damn good one at that...

Realizing I was going into my backcountry to work the sometimes-dangerous spotlighters (illegal night deer shooters) by myself once again, he put in a call to the Stonyford Deputy Sheriff Carter Bowman. He let that resident officer know I would be out and about in his area and gave him the location of my specific stake out area. Now the Stonyford Deputy Sheriff was another hell of a good man. Carter Bowman (may God rest his soul) was as cowboy- tough as a horseshoe nail and if you messed with him, he would tear off your lips and feed them to the nearest turkey vulture, and that was after he had killed you! Even though Carter was an older man, he was another one who would always be by your side no matter what the odds. In fact, I backed him up one afternoon when Fred and I went with him to investigate the reported location of twelve heavily armed Black Panthers during the late '60s. To Carter's way of thinking, facing the three of us, the twelve mean-as-a-car-hit- owl Black Panthers from the Bay Area, heavily armed with semiautomatic assault rifles, would be over their heads and in deep doo-doo when we arrived. But, that is a wild and wooly adventure story for another time. By the way, just for the record, the three of us should have been killed during that incident! Once again, my old saying that God loves little children, fools and game wardens came to pass that day and fit all three of us country bumpkins. Besides, if God would have had me killed, He would have had to feed me after all the smoke had cleared. And, being the eager eater I was, I think that would have shot the hell out of His monthly food bill. Course now that I think about that, didn't He feed one hell of a mess of folks with just a few loaves and fishes that He conjured up on the spot? I best let that parable and the food bill thing lie...

Thanking Fred for giving Carter a heads-up as to my whereabouts and planned activities, I headed out for my planned stakeout. Leaving Maxwell in the late afternoon, I traveled down the Maxwell to Sites Road. In so doing, I left the humid rice fields of Colusa County for the hot, dry western mountains and foothills of my district. A part of my district that was historically rich in mule deer, black bear, wild turkeys, band-tailed pigeons, feral hogs and numerous deer night-shooting outlaws from every point on the compass. After a few more hot, dry miles, I turned left onto the Sites to Lodoga Road. What a change in not only geography but also the farms and ranches I passed by as well. I had gone from the well-kept, rich fertile farms of the Sacramento Valley into the perpetually arid, cheat grass and oak tree covered foothills of the county. There to be found were hardscrabble ranches, cheatgrass, stunted oak trees, more cheatgrass, star thistle, and even more almost useless as forage except in the spring, cheatgrass. No two ways about it, the country I was now looking at was what I would call "20-40 country." In other words, a cow would need a mouth twenty-feet wide and have to run forty miles per hour to get enough to eat... A short time later, I turned onto the Leesville to Lodoga Road. Just passing the turn off to Cooks Spring Road, I came upon the old Andreotti Ranch. The ranch house itself had seen better days around the turn of the century and was now basically abandoned except when the Andreotti clan and their friends from the Colusa area arrived. Then they used the old ranch house as a sporting lodge while hunting dove or deer during the regular hunting seasons. Other than that, the old ranch was mute testimony to better times now long past.

On the east side of the Leesville to Lodoga Road just past the ranch house was my lonely destination for the evening. Therein lay a small, way past its prime alfalfa field. In fact in those days, it was really the only alfalfa field in the immediate vicinity possessing some green and succulent vegetation for miles around! Bordering this small field to the north and east was a small intermittent creek. That is, sometimes it more or less decided to have a little water in it. Bottom line, this country was so hot and dry that any type of watered area or eatable vegetation was a welcome home to just about every California mule deer in the county. This little alfalfa patch of deer Heaven met all those requirements and I had discovered it quite by accident one fine evening months earlier while out on another lonely backcountry patrol.

First of all, that location was so far out in the backcountry that all the chickens I ran across in that area had square faces! For all my slower readers, that meant I was pretty far back in the bush... Second, the only county road in the area ran right alongside the entire western

Terry Grosz

fenced portion of that alfalfa field. On the southern end of that patch of green, the county road turned in such a manner that one's headlights at night would normally sweep across a major portion of the field. When that occurred, one would see dozens of feeding deer in that area, including many times a goodly number of large, heavily-antlered mule deer bucks. The presence of such animals, especially the heavily antlered bucks, always seemed to lure the kind of folks who had recently crawled out from under a rock pile with an itchy trigger finger, a taste for some illegal venison, a black heart, and a total disregard for the wildlife laws of the land. Particularly during what I called the long season or the lengthy closed big game hunting season, or whenever daylight turned to the dark of the night.

Opening the gate into the northern end of the alfalfa field a little after dusk, I quickly drove in and hid my patrol vehicle back out of the way in a small ravine adjacent to the field. That way, I could still see the entire area of the field in question and yet not be seen even under the glare of a searching-spotlight or the casual sweep of a set of headlights. However, when I came through the gate into my stake out position, I had left it open. Since there were no cattle in the area, it was safe to do so and if I needed to exit the area in a hurry after an outlaw, I didn't have to stop and mess around with opening a gate.

Getting out from my truck, I stretched my cramped legs and let the sweat begin drying off from the back of my uniform shirt because in those days, the fish and game department bought us the cheapest vehicles it could purchase. That meant vinyl seats and no air conditioning. And the temperature, even at that time of the evening where I was, had to still be in the high '90s! Taking a lawn chair out from the bed of my vehicle, I placed it twenty feet in front of my truck at the lip of my covering ravine where I wouldn't be seen or attract a stray bullet meant for a critter. Also, that little trick of the trade of moving away from my vehicle, made sure I wasn't distracted by the sounds the engine made as it cooled down. Sometimes as it clanked and clunked while cooling down, those engine noises would frequently sound like someone night shooting a long ways off. Hence I moved away from my vehicle so I wouldn't be distracted or confused by the sounds it made. Then I walked back and retrieved my binoculars and Stanley Thermos full of cool tea. Notice I didn't say the thermos contained iced tea. It was so darned hot that time of the year in that area, that iced tea kept in an insulated thermos soon turned into cool tea. Tiredly sliding into the comforts of the lawn chair in the now inky darkness, I was ready for bear. Well, not really. More like illegal deer spotlighters and any other kind of night shooters, if you get my drift. To all my readers out there, pitting one's self against an armed individual knowingly breaking the law and one who many times has been nipping on a bottle of 86-proof Old Crow® whiskey, can quickly place the situation into the format of hunting the most dangerous game. Anything can and many times does go wrong during such situations. Particularly if your bad guy realizes he is trapped in his wrongdoing and is about to be apprehended. That dangerous situation can even further escalate if the outlaw or outlaws felt the officer making the apprehension was under-gunned or out manned, which for the most part was generally every time during such night-shooting instances. Then there were those situations when those outlaws being stopped were wanted for more serious crimes elsewhere of which the approaching wildlife officer was unaware. Those kinds of patrols and what ultimately happened were usually those situations we didn't discuss with our loved ones back home for obvious reasons...

Later, about ten in the evening, the full dark of the night was long since upon me. I really didn't expect any action until the local town bars had closed, but I enjoyed the sounds of a living night and tonight was no different. I could hear nighthawks off in the distance, an insect-eating, largely nocturnal migratory bird, wing-booming in their stoops as they pursued their winged insect meals. Then there was a great horned owl, a fierce and small mammal eating, mainly nocturnal migratory bird of prey, hooting from one of the tall oak trees to the rear of my seated location. Occasionally I could even hear the mule deer snorting alarm when my scent sometimes wafted out across the airways, reaching them in the field to my front. And off to the west on the nearby brush covered hillsides, a pack of coyotes let the rest of the world know they had just made a kill and were in full song-dog verbal celebration. There is just something good for the soul of those hunters of humans, when one lets the dark of the night settle down around him like a heavy, living, velvet blanket. Many years earlier as a youngster growing up, I had learned that the earth is always speaking to us. You just have to be silent to hear. That is even more so if one is a hunter of humans. With sharpening primal senses, those ancient whispers now translated into instincts, let the hunter know he is truly on the hunt for the most dangerous game...

For the next hour or so only a few vehicles drove down my lonesome county back road. That was not unusual, though. There weren't many folks living in that remote area anymore, so, it was not only a quiet but also a somewhat lonely night's vigil as I sat there relaxing and listening. Several of the cars that came by had slowed and one had even stopped to look over the number of deer feeding in the field in the light of its headlights. But there was no business for the lone game warden back at the north end of the field lounging in his lawn chair like a potbellied, Walt Disney Cheshire cat character ready to pounce.

Finally, traffic picked up a bit as the bars in Stonyford and Sites closed for the morning. About half a dozen cars rumbled by, but I had no takers for what fed in my nighttime field of dreams. Dreams of spotlighters, many shots being fired, and a game warden around every bush that is. Or at least one beautiful Teutonic knight such as the one relaxing at the end of the field. Relaxed but spring-steel coiled if the bullets began flying about... About three in the morning, a pickup slowly drove down my road in such a manner as to perk up my senses a bit. When that vehicle hit the south end of the fenced alfalfa field, its headlights partially illuminated a mess of feeding deer. Slowing just a bit as its occupants eyeballed the feeding deer, it soon moved on past that end of the field and out of sight from my hidden stakeout position to the north. Fifteen minutes later, that same truck returned and that quickly got my undivided attention! Through my binoculars, I could see two individuals in the vehicle. However, my suspicious vehicle just continued on driving toward the south end of the valley. Coming back from the south twenty minutes later, this time the suspect vehicle's headlights fully illuminated the feeding deer because of the slight angle of the road in relation to the lay of the alfalfa field. Shadow, my ever-faithful Labrador, was now sitting up alongside me and quietly watching the lighted vehicle as if to let me know, "Be on your toes, Boss." Through my binoculars, I saw the truck stop and observed a door quietly opening. Out from the driver's side stepped a man with something in his hand. Then that something was laid over the hood of the vehicle and instantly lit up the field like the German searchlights did when our bomber streams approached Berlin during the "big war" as it has been called or WWII. *Bing!* went a sharp, bright blue-white, pencil-thin beam of a spotlight as it searched across the field of feeding deer. That got the feeding deer's attention, especially when it lit up a nice five-point buck by western count or five antler points to a side. Having been unsuccessfully spotlighted before, that big buck lowered its head and tried to walk away from the intense beam of light. However, that walking away maneuver didn't work this time. That big buck had just taken his second or third step when a huge fireball erupted from the passenger's side of the truck followed by a loud boom! That five-point buck instantly folded like a deck of cards! Then the spotlight quickly went out as did the truck's headlights seconds later. Next, I heard the truck's door slam and off like a shot went my spotlighters vehicle speeding back along the county road without using any headlights to illuminate his way of escape.

Moments later, the truck quickly disappeared from view from my hidden position at the north end of the field. Once it had gone, I had Dog load up as I picked up and casually folded up my lawn chair. Walking back to my truck, I loaded my equipment inside. *I* had been to this rodeo numerous times before so no use getting my crankshaft in an uproar, especially with a dead deer laying in the field and a really nice buck at that.

Turning on my radio, I called the Colusa County Sheriff's Office. When they responded, I asked if they would call and see if Deputy Bowman was still out and about. Soon the sheriff's office radioed back advising he had gone out of service several hours earlier. Calling them back, I requested a backup and the need for a possible prisoner transport vehicle. They advised they would get Carter out of bed and have him standing by for when I needed him. Then Dog and I patiently waited, for as I said earlier, I had been this route many times before and now had the capture routine down pat.

Twenty minutes later, I could hear a vehicle quietly coming from behind my position to the north on the county road that paralleled my alfalfa field. Looking hard with my binoculars from my standing position alongside the patrol truck, I finally spotted my darkened spotlighter's vehicle slowly approaching. Soon it entered into clear view and slowly headed for that portion of the road from where the deer had been shot. Then the brake lights came on and I saw one chap hurriedly exit the vehicle and run to the fence surrounding the alfalfa field. Then even from the distance where I stood, I heard a series of metallic sounding pings. The next thing I saw was my suspect's vehicle driving down off the county road through what had moments before been a four-strand barbed wire fence and out into the alfalfa field. Damn, that is a new one, I thought. Those chaps had just cut the four strands of barbed wire bordering the alfalfa field! That must have been the pings I heard when the tightly stretched barbed wire had been cut with a pair of wire cutters. That way they could drive right up to the deer they had just shot, quickly load him into their truck, and be gone in a flash with no one any the wiser. Pretty slick move but not slick enough.

Watching my lads, I waited. It now became apparent from what I was seeing in my binoculars that the shooters were now stupidly dressing out the deer in the field! That action sure as hell precluded any quick escape action on their part to my way of thinking. Then I thought I heard the sounds of another vehicle quietly coming down the county road from the north or behind my stake out position. Not seeing any headlights, I stepped away from my truck and glassed the road behind me for a better look. Sure as God made hellgrammites good fishing bait for trout, here quietly moving down the road came an all-white sedan! Laughing silently to myself, I got back into my patrol truck. The white vehicle was none other than a sheriff's patrol car. It was Carter Bowman quietly coming my way. He knew where I would be staked out and just couldn't wait for my call for a backup so he could get into the action. Good old Carter, I thought. He just couldn't wait to get into the action and now here he comes. Good. I can use his early arrival to my benefit.

Getting quietly back on my radio, I called the sheriff's office on their radio frequency. I could call the sheriff's office, but I could not directly call the sheriff's deputies in their patrol cars with my fish and game radio. The sheriff's office had to relay any messages from the fish and game units to their mobile patrols. Once the sheriff's office was on the radio, I explained what I wanted done and then got off the air. In turn, they radioed Carter with my battle plan. Moments later, I heard Carter's patrol slow and then stop in the middle of the county road. Then seeing my shooters' vehicle starting back across the field toward where they had cut the fence, I quietly started driving their way out my open gate and down the county road without the use of lights. When my shooters, driving without using their headlights, got to within about twenty yards from the cut they had made in the fence, I started driving off the county road and into the cut to block their avenue of escape. Then on went my headlights, siren and red light. You talk about a surprised explosion in the cab of my shooters' truck! Man, my shooters just erupted!

They were so surprised, I don't think either of them could have passed gas if they had to. The driver quickly turned on his headlights and realizing I had their planned escape route through the hole previously cut in the fence blocked, slammed on his brakes! Then without missing a beat, my spotlighter roared off to the north in the alfalfa field running along the fence like a chicken being run around in the coop by a hungry fox, as he looked for another escape avenue from the field. Barreling completely off the county road through the break in the fence and driving into a huge cloud of dust made by my fleeing shooters, I kept up the pressure as my lads sped along the fence looking for another way out. Coming to my still-open gate at the north end of the field, my panicked outlaw's power slid through the opening. Misjudging the width of the opening and driving too fast, they took out about ten feet of fence with the side of their sliding truck! Finally barreling out onto the county highway, they almost rolled their truck over the berm on the opposite side of the road. However, the driver somehow regained control and began speeding down the highway... speeding down the highway right to my friend and deputy sheriff, carter bowman! On went Carter's headlights, red light and siren and, since his vehicle was sitting smack-dab in the middle of the road, my bad guys had several choices as I saw it. Ram the patrol car and try to get away that way, stop and be apprehended by the deputy, or turn around and ram me. None was a really very good option, especially when Carter stepped out from his patrol car in plain view of the fleeing vehicle's headlights and blasted a round from his 12-gauge shotgun into the air! At that point, in light of the 12-gauge shotgun's explosive blast, I don't think either of my fleeing chaps would have been able to pass a whiff of gas for a week, even if they had both just eaten two dozen hardboiled eggs!

Skidding to a stop in the middle of the county road directly behind my now dead stopped, terror-stricken spotlighters, I was on their tail ends in a flash. Jumping from my truck, I yelled at my chaps, "Game warden! You lads are under arrest!" With that and Deputy Bowman to their front with a leveled shotgun, both sets of their hands flew out their open windows and just like in old time Western movies, they reached for the sky.

Walking up to the driver's door, I opened it and escorted my lad out, and had him spread eagle on the roadway in less time than it takes a rattlesnake to strike. Some of my more liberal and gentler reader types are probably puzzled as to why an officer treats their captures in such a rough way under the circumstances. Well, it is a little more difficult if one is of an inclination to go for a hidden weapon when he is flying through the air without a sufficient number of primary wing feathers needed for flight if you get my drift... By then, Carter had done the same to the passenger. While Carter glowered over the two men, I quickly searched the cab of their truck for any weapons. Two loaded rifles, a spotlight and a set of wire cutters later, I was more than satisfied with my discoveries. Finally taking a look into the back of their truck now that I had more time, I got the surprise of my evening. Therein lay three freshly killed, large mule deer bucks! My goodness, these two lads have certainly been busy elsewhere, I thought with a surprised grin that had now quickly turned into a great evening's heartfelt capture of several lads who really needed my attention.

As if that wasn't enough excitement for the morning, here came round two. Down the road toward our blocked road came a speeding car. I thought for a moment it would hit Carter's parked patrol car before the driver finally got his vehicle under control and stopped. Inside were two men as drunk as British Lords! And from the happy sounds of their whooping and hollering, they didn't care if hell froze over at that very moment in time because they were loaded to the gills with at least 100 proof of good Jack Daniels® whiskey or their own preferred type of anti-freeze...

One fine fellow, the driver, ill-advisedly got out from his vehicle and yelled at Carter to get his damn car out of the middle of the road or he would kick the stuffing out of the deputy. That was the last thing he said as he hit the pavement with a resounding Carter Bowman induced ka-thump on the loudmouth's head as a result of the deputy's accurately swung five-cell anodized aluminum flashlight! Watching closely my two deer shooters still spread eagle on the highway, I kept a cocked eye on my friend and deputy to make sure he was all right in his dealing-with-the-drunk's endeavors. However, there was no need. As stated earlier in this narrative, Carter was an old school law enforcement officer who took no guff from anyone! In short, he was as tough as any old time cow town sheriff in Kansas full of Texas drovers fresh off the trail during the heyday of the late 1800s cattle drives. Both drunks were soon put in their places, arrested, searched, handcuffed and hustled into the backseat of Carter's patrol car for driving under the influence of alcohol and drunk and disorderly.

Letting Shadow out from my truck, I put her on guard over my two lads. Then I hauled the now seized, three closed-season mule deer bucks from the back of my spotlighter's truck and placed them into mine. After being searched and handcuffed, my two shooters were crowded into the backseat of Carter's patrol car along with the two drunks. I guess that was some ride down the mountain and its twisty roads according to Carter when we laughed about it later on. Both drunks got carsick and puked all over the backseat of his patrol car and on my two deer shooters. That influenced my deer shooters' gag reflexes, and along with their concerns over being apprehended with the three illegal deer, they joined the puke party as well... By the time Carter and I got our lads to the Colusa County Jail, his patrol car was a thorough mess with at least two inches of vomit sloshing back and forth over his rear seat floorboards every time the patrol car went around a sharp corner. Thank God it was now daylight and we were at the Colusa County Jail. There, Carter got several prisoners from the jail to clean up the mess in his patrol car. The prisoners each had a week's incarceration later removed from their overall sentences in light of the crappy mess they had cleaned up in the back of Carter's patrol vehicle.

By the time the Williams Justice Court and Judge Gibson had taken care of my two spotlighters later that same morning, they were really sick. After their guilty pleas had been entered, he fined both lads for the possession of three illegal deer, loaded rifles in a motor vehicle on a way open to the public, use and aid of a light to take a big game animal, and trespassing all in the same whack! That came to a $1,300 fine for each shooter, and they both forfeited their beautiful, expensive Belgium made, Browning semi-automatic, 7mm Remington magnum rifles and their spotlight. Then the judge arranged with the landowner to bill the two lads for the cut and torn down fence and gate back at the scene of the crime. Who says crime pays?

By the way, my two lads from the San Francisco Bay Area had just celebrated their birthdays several days apart.

Their happy wives had gotten their heads together and had just purchased, in celebration of the event, each spouse a new Browning semi-automatic, .7mm Remington magnum, Belgian made rifle with brand new Leopold 3x9 power scopes. As I later discovered, one rifle had been fired just three times killing all three of their illegal deer and nary a shot had been fired from the other rifle as of yet! Losing such a fine set of rifles to the State of California had to make both husbands physically sick. But not as sick as they were going to be when they got back to the Bay Area and had to tell their wives what had happened to their fine birthday rifles and now considerably flattened out wallets.

As an aside, I had a very similar case in which my two miscreants had used brand new Browning semi-automatic rifles—only in .243 caliber—doing pretty much the same thing in the same alfalfa field a year earlier. Upon conviction, my shooters lost their brand new rifles as well and if I remember correctly, their wives had purchased the two close friends those rifles as an anniversary gift. At least my four shooters from two different time periods had married young ladies who had impeccable taste in firearms and scopes...

Carter and I never did find out where they had taken the other two large deer. That didn't really matter much though since deer season was closed and I had my two shooters for illegal possession of those extra two deer as well. That series of events was made even better later in the day when those rolling fat bucks were donated to three very deserving and needy Colusa County Mexican farm worker families from the east side of my patrol district. That always made my heart glad, especially when the families had numerous little children and when I delivered them, they were eyeing the deer in a way that spoke of deer steak and spuds for dinner that evening instead of beans and tortillas once again...

KILLING DEER THE OLD FASHIONED WAY

While working early season deer hunters on the western side of my patrol district, I once again chanced passing Art Andreotti's alfalfa field. Giving it only a quick glance because deer were generally not in the field feeding during the hot mid-day hours, I got surprised! Standing at the edge of the intermittent stream bordering the eastern side of the alfalfa field stood a lone deer. It was so abnormally statuesque that I slowed my vehicle and then stopped. Stopping and looking was nothing but normal behavior for a game warden if something was out of place in his district and he is observant. For the longest time, I stared across the alfalfa field at the motionless deer standing still as death in the hot sun. Finally reaching over and picking up my binoculars off the front seat, I gave the motionless deer a closer look. What I saw deeply saddened and maddened me all at the same time! Its entire body was terribly emaciated! Through the binoculars, I could see an angular hind end instead of a normally, healthy rounded rump. Then moving my binoculars forward, I could count every rib on what appeared to be a terribly emaciated and starving animal. Moving my binocular examination to the front of the deer shocked me even more deeply! There was an arrow protruding through both sides of its neck! Where the arrow was lodged in its neck, there was a huge abscess that was swollen almost as large as a football! The deer's eyes were almost closed with what appeared to be a mucous covering, its nose was running small rivulets of a cloudy liquid, and its tongue was swollen black and hanging limply from its open mouth. From all its looks, the animal had suffered horribly since it had crossed paths with the flight of that arrow! And since the deer was a female, it had been illegally shot because no doe season existed in my district in those days!

Sadly realizing what must be done, I quietly stepped from my truck so as not to spook the long-suffering animal and slowly walked over to the highway side of the fence surrounding the western side of the alfalfa field. Steadying my .44 magnum handgun with both hands on top of the nearest fence post—I never packed a long gun in those days—I took a long and careful aim at the still non-moving animal. *Boom!* went the big magnum which lifted my hands slightly into the air from the heavy recoil of the 255-grain Keith-Thompson, semiwad cutter, hand-loaded bullet being fired. As an aside, because of the high cost of commercial grade ammunition for the .44 magnum in those days and my low pay, I cast my own bullets and reloaded all my ammunition; hence the reloaded cartridge being used to kill the deer. Hell, I even carried my own reloaded bullets in the big magnum during my routine law enforcement duties. Such actions were allowed in the days of old. However, probably not allowed in today's law enforcement operations because of subsequent litigation and new agency policies if one was involved in a shootout while using reloads and things went down the wrong road. But, I never had a misfire in over three hundred thousand rounds being shot through that big magnum during my thirty-two years of state and federal law enforcement service!

Looking over the end of the 61/2-inch gun barrel when the handgun had settled back down on top of the fence post from the recoil, I observed that the deer had disappeared. Walking the seventy or so yards across the alfalfa field, my nose was then struck with the fetid sweet smell of rotting flesh! Going over to where the doe had last stood, I found her lying there once and for all out of her misery. The football-sized swelling next to the arrow in her neck was nothing but a putrid pus sac! Looking down, I could see pus was still pouring out from the hole the big magnum's bullet had made in the deer's neck. In fact, the hole was so close to the arrow that all I had to do to retrieve the arrow for future evidence was give it an easy jerk backwards.

Wiping the gunk off the arrow's shaft on the side of the deer, I continued smelling more death in the air from what appeared to be coming from other than that of my recently killed animal. Walking upstream thirty yards or so, I discovered two more doe deer lying where they had died after they had been struck with poorly placed arrows as both had been paunched or hit in the stomach area! The type of wounds that would have led to massive infection and a lingering, painful death for both of the critters! And from the looks of their state of deterioration and scavenging by other critters, they had died at different but earlier times in the week. Grimly looking on, the thought once again crossed my mind of the lingering and painful deaths those animals had suffered! I was not a happy camper.

What the hell is going on here? I disgustedly thought as I got angrier by each passing second. I knew the rancher personally and was sure he did not condone such illegal behavior on his property. Walking back across the alfalfa field, I picked up two more arrows of the same type that I had just discovered in my two dead and the one recently killed deer alongside the creek. Those arrows had been apparently shot at the feeding deer during another time, had missed and then been lost by my shooter as they laid partially covered up in the dirt. This sure has the looks of one poacher's handiwork, I grimly thought. Then I discovered where several more deer had thrashed their last in the soft dirt of the field and had been dragged off back toward the county road. Whoever is doing this appears to he a repeat offender and a damn good one at that, I angrily surmised, based on the sameness of arrow types and the numbers of apparently recently shot-up critters. Now, I was really getting browned off!

Bucks-only deer season in my district had just opened. And the hunters could take them with either a bow and arrow or a rifle. That made it very convenient for a disgruntled bowman on his way home without having killed a legal animal, to silently kill a deer in my alfalfa field in the dark of the night and then be gone before anyone was any the wiser. Unfortunately for that person or persons, a rather large someone was now the wiser, pissed off to say the least. And, now the hunt was once again on and in deadly earnest for what I considered the most dangerous game. Especially one or several men,—I caught very few women doing the above in my day—who apparently killed at will with silent killers, namely arrows. And in so doing, leaving the wounded results of their illegal actions to die a slow, agonizing death. And to those overlooked or just plain not retrieved, to rot where they finally fell! As I have said many times in my other wildlife law enforcement books, it is not nice to mess with Mother Nature. And, that went the same for her minions wearing the green uniforms and the silver badges of their office. Look closely outlaws. The cheetah always knows where the hyenas lurk...

That long weekend, Friday into early Monday morning, I sat quietly in the dark on the backside of my alfalfa field hoping for a return of my modern day Robin Hood. As far as I was concerned, Robin could take the King's game back in England but not mine in California! However, I had no luck in running anyone to ground during that long first stake out period for using a bow and arrow around my alfalfa field. The following week, I would work my constant stream of legal deer hunters during the day in my mountainous backcountry and then stake out my alfalfa-killing field at night. That made for twenty-hour exhausting days but I was now a man on a mission. Once again, I did not bag any bow shooters sniping my deer in the alfalfa field. Notice I didn't call them bow hunters, which connotes fair and legal chase. By now, I was running on fumes having worked my deer hunting public for mostly twenty- hour days for the previous two weeks. Eating out of cans and bags and getting maybe only four hours of sleep a night on the ground in a sleeping bag or in the front seat of my patrol truck was certainly not cutting it. I didn't imagine my bride and two young sons back at home appreciated the long absences of their husband and father, either. As for my dog, Shadow, she loved it. She got to do what she loved and as long as she got fed and could sleep in the back of my patrol truck, life was dog gone good, no pun intended.

But then I got a break! A few miles south of my normally staked out alfalfa field location, the one now holding the remains of all the arrow-shot dead deer, stood an old ranch house in Bear Valley that had been built in the late 1800s. It originally had been built by a cattleman who ranched in the area until he wore out and went to ground. Sometime later after his passing, the ranch had been purchased by my friend and wealthy Sacramento Valley rice farmer, Terrill Sartain. He, in turn, had hired a now retired from his normal job but still active California Reserve Deputy Fish and Game Warden Captain named Cliff Fulton to ride herd on his property. As an aside, as I have been told, California no longer has such unpaid positions because of the liability in California's idiotic lawsuit crazy society.

Cliff was a tall, semi-retired, World War II veteran, a heavyset drink of water, and a dear friend. His job was to patrol the many thousands of acres of western Colusa County land Terrill had purchased as a working hunting ranch keeping trespassers and poachers at bay. Terrill had turned this many thousand acre empire in the Bear Valley area into a wealthy hunters' paradise for mule deer, dove, and recently, feral hogs. In turn, Terrill had to provide some kind of protection from the run of the mill poachers happy to hop his fences and blaze away at any critter crazy enough to show itself. Hence, the entry of Cliff Fulton into the present adventure and a friendship and partnership whose history I have come to cherish long after Cliff's subsequent passing years later.

Once Cliff came on board as Terrill's patrolman, trouble for the bad guys came in double doses. Cliff was a lot like me. He had a great wife named Shirley, who let him run chasing bad guys until his tongue dragged on the ground, and that was good for me. Being located so close together as we worked much of the same backcountry, and both of us being almost rabid catch-dogs when it came to catching wildlife outlaws, it was only natural we close friends teamed up. I would work the western portion of my patrol district checking deer and dove hunters during legal shooting hours and when Cliff was finished with the work in his area of responsibility, he would work the upper end of Bear Valley off of Terrill's ranch lands chasing wildlife outlaws at night with me. Cliff could do this because his reserve deputy state fish and game credentials allowed him to enforce the California fish and wildlife laws statewide. Suffice to say, that teaming up was a hidden benefit for me and a curse for the wildlife outlaws. Since I was already in the remote back country, I was able to stay at the old ranch house in Bear Valley along with Cliff instead of driving the many miles back to my home numerous times when my work was done. Hot dog! That arrangement allowed me more staying time in my outback and less time for my poachers to slip in between the sheets during my absences. Along with that, I now had an extremely capable friend and fellow officer as a very reliable partner. And catch the bad guys who squirted out from under the cabbage leaves we did! Oh my, did we ever... Man, I tell you, my ever-patient readers, the catchin' was great and the subsequent prosecutions were even better. How does one hundred percent prosecution of over one hundred chaps that first summer we teamed up grab you tax payers and hunting license purchasers? There is nothing quite like hunting the most dangerous game when they have their hands in Mother Nature's cookie, er, critter jar. Plainly and simply, there is just nothing else like hunting your fellow man. That is unless you count as a bonus catching those rascals in the act of breaking the law as well...

After teaming up with Cliff one day, I mentioned my bow and arrow killing problems at the several miles distant Andreotti Ranch. Sensing a "catching of a real outlaw needing our attention" in the works, Cliff said he would like to be in on that action. For you see, Cliff was also a zero-tolerance guy when it came to catching chaps breaking the wildlife laws of the land. The following

Friday night found us two crazies staked out in my cherry patch alfalfa field. As in the case of most planned law enforcement stake out operations, not a damn thing happened! So, at the end of that failed detail, home to the ranch and our honeybees at the end of the night's patrol we went. No, you darn suspicious readers, stop it! Cliff and yours truly were committed husbands both lasting in over fifty years of marriage with our also equally committed spouses. That "honey bee" reference was not our code for having some "honeys" stashed on the side at the ranch. The old ranch house's walls were clear full of wild, American variety honeybees! One could always be lulled to sleep with the soft humming sounds they emitted with their wings as they air-conditioned their between-the-walls hive in the oppressive summer heat in western Colusa County. Many years later after Cliff finally retired, the old ranch house mysteriously burned down and the honeybees living in those walls went into history. Daylight the following morning found Cliff and me out and about checking the swarms of city slickers that flooded the western mountainous portion of my district during the mule deer, dove and feral hog hunting seasons.

However, come Friday night after working all day on our deer hunters, Cliff and yours truly were quietly sitting in front of my patrol truck in lawn chairs at my usual alfalfa field stakeout hidey-hole. We were both smoking my wicked little Italian Toscani Cigars and had thermoses of cool tea at our sides. What more could one want except maybe a spotlighter or two showing up and doing something goofy that was contrary to the state's fish and game laws. As it turned out, we sat through another long and silent night. As it turned out, Saturday night also turned out to be as quiet as a graveyard. As the wheel turned, Sunday night was as dead as General Custer as well. However, the deer season was in full bloom and we continued working our deer hunters in the stifling California summer heat during the daylight hours and were damn glad for the night and the somewhat cooler temperatures come the darkness. Well, the 80s at night were far better than the oppressive high 90s and low 100s during the day. Then back to our alfalfa field to set up in the ambush mode we two happy warriors faithfully strode, looking for any spotlighter who sauntered our way once the dark of night was upon us once again. Like I have mentioned many times in my previous works, it is not nice to piss off Mother Nature or her minions. To do so just lets us members of The Thin Green Line creep within grabbing distance and then the apprehension deed will be done up in fine style to my way of thinking.

Around 1:30 in the morning on another quiet stake out, I began feeling maybe we had struck out again. Then along came a Dodge ¾-ton pickup, with what appeared in our binoculars to be three lads riding in the cab. They slowly passed our alfalfa field but kept moving on like they were going to a nearby deer-hunting campsite down the road. Twenty minutes later, our same dodge truck came back! That sure as all get out made Cliff and me sit up in our lawn chairs and take notice like a great horned owl does watching a close at hand, out in the open, fleeing deer mouse. But our three lads did nothing other than slowly drive by our alfalfa field like it was nothing out of the ordinary. Kind of like they were lost in the darkness and just driving by looking for a semi-hidden turnoff road leading to their hunting camp. But then again...

"Cliff," I said, "I wonder if they are driving by the field on both ends of the county road scouting out the area for any signs of a near at hand landowner or the law?"

"That would be what I would do if it were me and I was hunting illegally," he said quietly.

"Me, too," I said, hoping the both of us had our hunting the lawless thinking caps on correctly and were of a clear shooting eye.

Thirty minutes passed and no more Dodge truck. Then I thought I heard a vehicle coming down the county road that eventually ran alongside our hidden stake out position. Turning in my lawn chair so I could see better to our north, I saw nothing in the way of a vehicle or headlights coming down the road toward our staked out position. But by damn, I sure as all get out could hear the quiet running motor of a near-at-hand oncoming vehicle. And let me tell all you good readers out there, good game wardens have the hearing abilities of a cross between a California brown bat and that of a kit fox when they are on the hunt...

"What's up, Chief?" asked Cliff, who had been a machine gunner during the Battle of the Bulge in the Second World War. In that battle, Cliff had lost part of his hearing from having fired so many rounds through his .50-caliber Browning machine gun at the onrushing Germans. Cliff once told me that when that fight was over, there were ninety-two dead Germans in front of his machine gun after that first encounter! He was one tough old man, a patriot in my eyes and a good one to have on your side if and when things got a little out of hand...

"Cliff, I think I can hear a vehicle quietly coming down the road behind us but I don't see any lights," I said still looking to the rear of where we sat from whence the suspicious sounds were emanating.

Then the both of us saw what had captured my sense of hearing. Running without lights, our suspicious looking Dodge truck slowly drove by on the nearby county road adjacent from where we were hiding. Grabbing my high light gathering binoculars, I took a gander at our suspect, slow moving vehicle. In the back of the truck stood two men! One had a bow and arrow strung and at the ready. The other chap held what appeared to be a handheld spotlight!

"Cliff," I whispered, "I'll bet those are our doe killing lads, bow, arrow, spotlight, and all!"

About then the truck stopped and the lad with the spotlight turned it on and began sweeping the field for nearby targets with its bright beam! He didn't have to look far. That evening the field was literally alive with deer. Included in that mess of mule deer biomass were at least four good-sized antlered bucks. Then the light found and froze a fair sized buck. At that very instant I heard the bow shooter release his arrow. Micro seconds later, that recently spotlighted buck jumped like a bug on a hot rock. In my binoculars, I saw a poof of dust rising just under the animal where the arrow had struck low under the belly of the buck. The buck spooked and started to slowly move off with difficulty, semi-blinded from the light's intense beam still intently fixed on the animal's head. But that movement was to no avail. The powerful light stayed right on its head effectively blinding the deer. Then I heard a quiet thump as another arrow was loosed. That time, it wasn't low. Our buck jumped high into the air as the arrow struck and then gave a violent aerial kick backwards with its hind legs indicating a vital hit! That animal began running crazily and soon toppled over in a large poof of dust in the harvested, dry as a bone, alfalfa field, some forty yards distant from the initial point of impact from the arrow!

"I got him!" excitedly yelled a voice from the back of the truck.

"My turn," said another voice from the back of the truck. Then the man holding the spotlight handed it to the previous bow shooter, as they quickly traded the tools of their ill begotten trade.

The bright pencil thin beam of light once again fastened on another nearby and now alerted deer. That time it was a very large five-point buck. But that deer had been shot at before by a spotlighter and quickly took off like a scalded ape. The light tried to follow and blind that deer but he was having none of that, quickly running out of bow range. The light then refocused onto a large fat doe, which it held in utter, blinded confusion. Thump went the sound of a loosed arrow from the shooter and man, could that fellow shoot! For just an instant through my binoculars, I saw the silvery glint of the flight of an arrow in the light of the spotlight. Then it sank deeply into the side of the doe just behind her right front shoulder. The doe staggered under the impact of the arrow, ran a dozen floundering steps and then keeled over like a well-hit pepper-popper target on a pistol range! The truck moved forward a few more yards as our lads traded the tools of their evil trade once again for yet another go around. The lad holding the spotlight fastened it onto another deer as the other feeding deer in the area were now beginning to move off from the alfalfa field in alarm. Thump went the now faint sound of the bow shooting another arrow. Once more, I briefly saw the flight of the arrow in the light of the spotlight. This time the shooter had pulled his shot and the arrow sank deeply and painfully into that targeted deer's hindquarters! That deer lurched and, since the arrow had gone clear through both hams, found it painful and extremely difficult, if at all, to walk! The second arrow flew truer and after a few struggling steps, that deer went down in a poof of alfalfa field dust. Then it somehow regained its feet and began awkwardly trying to walk off. A dozen steps or so later, that deer keeled over and began kicking its last.

"That's enough!" I said quietly, as I tossed my chair out of the way so my patrol truck would have smooth sailing out through gate that I purposely had left open. Cliff did the same and we ran for my hidden vehicle parked a few yards distant. Jumping into the front seat, I saw my dog, Shadow, lie down in the bed of the truck as she expected some rather fast, furious, and erratic driving if history was any kind of a teacher. Not wanting to be spilled out on a wild turn, she had learned her lessons well when it came to many of my high-speed pursuits. Now, some of my readers who are dog people can see why I still grieve today over the loss of that dog. She was almost human in her instincts and thinking.

Before we could fire up the truck, my two lads in the bed of the shooter's truck bailed out, quickly loaded up in the cab of their truck, and sped off. My mind was now racing since I was sure they didn't know I was even in the same county, much less just a hundred yards away. So, why the rush to escape?

"Cliff," I said. "There is no way I can catch that powerhouse ¾-ton Dodge which is probably running a 383-cubic-inch mill. This damn Chevy truck I am driving only has a one-mouse power engine. Plus, we don't have a deputy sheriff currently on duty for a backup within thirty miles to intercept those lads. Now they have killed several nice deer. My guardian angels are now telling me to hold and let them come back for their ill-gotten gains, especially that nice buck. What do you think? You want to gamble that they were trying to fill their deer tags and will return? Or do you think they are just abject killers and will not return?" I asked hurriedly.

"If I was still in Germany during the war fighting Germans and they ran off, I always knew they would return and counterattack. Let's chance it and hope they are like those damn thick-headed Germans," he said quietly.

"Good! My way of thinking precisely. Now here is what I propose we do. I am going to split the difference and head down the road on foot. Once I get to where I feel I should be for a surprise intercept if they stop their vehicle on the road prior to a deer pick up, I am going to hide in the nearby roadside ditch. That way when their truck stops to retrieve their deer, I will be close enough to grab the driver by his stacking swivel and toss him from the rig. In the meantime, I suggest you go into the field, find that big five-point buck and lie down behind it. When they come to get the deer, you rise up and grab the closest one of them. I am sure there will be two chaps coming out because that is a big, heavy deer and two men will be needed in order to drag it quickly from the field. The other man will run off after you announce your presence with a capture of his buddy. He will run for the truck. Hopefully by then, I will quietly have the driver under control. Then when your runner gets back to the truck, I will lay a tackle on him that should knock him into the middle of next week. What do you think, Cliff?"

At first, he never said a word, as if quickly mulling the battle plan over in his head. Then grabbing his five-cell flashlight, he headed out into the field in the dark at a trot running for where we last saw the five-point buck go down. As he ambled off out of sight in the darkness, I heard him say, "I have killed German soldiers meaner than that guy who killed my deer. I will get my man, Terry. You just make damn sure you get yours." God, he was a tough old man. I only hope when I pass over the Great Divide, Cliff and I are teamed up once again. If we are, the devil better stay the hell out of Dodge and away from the rest of us "Cloud People" or we will have his damned ole horned carcass in handcuffs and heading for the Almighty's Court to pass judgment on our devilishly ethereal capture...

Running down the county road in the dark and having to leap over a surprised and pissed off rattlesnake crossing the warm highway asphalt in the process, I finally got to the place where I figured our shooter's Dodge would stop upon its return in order to retrieve that big five-point buck. Then I lumbered off the road and into the weeds in the ditch. Damn it! I yelled inside as I dove blindly into a thick stand of star thistle! To you unwashed readers, diving into a mess of star thistle is like slamming into a pincushion, a porcupine, and a nest of upset yellow jackets—winged critters that can bite and sting all at the same time! Brother, did I ever get prickled!

Sweating there in the summer heat, I waited. Another car came by down the road on its way home but, other than that, nothing but the quiet of the night and my madly thumping heart from the sprint down the road greeted me. Then, I thought I heard a vehicle coming my way. Trying to control the heavy breathing from my hundred- yard dash and my now madly beating heart in the excitement of the moment, I listened intently. There it was again! Only that time I was sure I heard the sounds a quietly running vehicle engine and tires running on the pavement! Then there it was! A darkened vehicle was slowly coming down the road toward me. As it got closer, it really slowed and finally seemed to just creep along. As it passed me, through their open windows I could hear the men in the truck excitedly talking about where to stop in order to retrieve their just killed monster buck deer.

"How about right here, Ernie?" came a voice.

"No. I think that last buck was a little farther down the road," said another voice. Then they were gone from earshot as they continued moving slowly down the road away from my position in the prickle patch of that damn star thistle. A star thistle patch made all the more uncomfortable because of the salt from my sweat running into the holes made in my skin when I initially crashed into the spiny weeds alongside the road. Zuh!

Suddenly the vehicle's brake lights came on. Following that, I heard the truck's parking brake being set and then all the taillights giving their position away went out. Looking down the road with my binoculars, I saw two men running from the cab of the truck, hop the fence and, using a small flashlight, begin looking for that big buck they had shot earlier.

That's my clue, I said to myself as I heaved my miserable carcass out from the damn sticking star thistle patch and began silently trotting on the balls of my feet toward the truck. For all you unwashed, that is an old game warden trick because one can run more quietly that way. Especially if one is running on size 14EEEE feet as I was. Running quietly to the rear of the truck on the driver's side, I paused. As for my lad remaining in the truck, he never heard or saw me approaching because he was so intently watching his guys and their small beam of light moving hurriedly across the field. God, it seemed like it took my two lads in the field an eternity to find their deer but they finally did.

"Hey-hey-hey—run!" went a surprised voice yelling from the field.

"What the hell?" said a surprised voice from inside the truck.

That was the last word he uttered as I stepped forward, jerked open his door, grabbed him by his left arm and neck and hissed out the words, "Game warden, you are under arrest!" He was then lobbed into the ditch alongside the vehicle at a rather high rate of speed! When he hit the ground, all I hear was a loud ummmph! Particularly since, as I was later to discover, my just airborne-ejected lad had hit face first in the gravel just off the roadbed at a fairly high rate of speed and then rolled into the roadside ditch...

Jumping in the ditch beside him, I hissed loudly in his ear one more time to make sure he knew what the hell was happening, "Game warden, you are under arrest! Now, don't you say a word!" Then I could smell the strong smell of fear in the essence of his spraying hot urine. I had scared my chap so badly, he had just wetted himself! Hell, I would have probably done the same if some big damn galoot had grabbed me unannounced by the nape of my neck in the dark of the night and hurled my surprised carcass from my truck into a rocky ditch at a high rate of speed...

Then I heard a loud *scbreech-ooof!* as my single runner from the field, without the aid of his just tossed flashlight, had run full bore into the barbed wire fence surrounding the field. Quickly recovering and fueled with adrenalin, my lad jumped back up from the field where the tightly strung barbed wire fence had flung him backwards. Then he began hurriedly climbing over the fence. But the fence's wire barbs were of a different mindset. Hanging up in the madly fleeing man's jean crotch, the grabbing barbs helped topple him over the top of the fence and hung him face down in the dirt on the other side just a clawing and a scratching! Man, let me tell all you non-believers out there reading these lines, there truly is a God for all the critters. Especially when one takes His critters by means other than legal and tries to escape. And in that ill-fated escape attempt, is rewarded by hanging up one's privates in the biting top strand of a barbed wire fence! All in the name of an ill-fated attempt to clear a four-foot high obstacle in the dark of the night at a high rate of speed, racked by the emotion of the moment!

Guess which meanest son of a bitch in the valley was on that hanging upside down, struggling chap like a hungry coyote on a wing-broke sage grouse? Yep, you guessed right. Dragging my previously apprehended driver by his shirt collar from the ditch, across the road, and down into the opposite roadside ditch with me, we jumped the still struggling fence held chap. Well, to be truthful, I jumped on my fence hanging chap. The driver of the truck was just along for the somewhat rough ride as he was bounced along into the far roadside ditch at a high rate of speed by a somewhat fired up game warden tule creeper type.

"Game warden, hold it right there. You are under arrest!" I bellowed. Those harsh words had little quieting effect on my fence hanger. Maybe it had something to do with the fact that the wire barbs were hanging up tightly and somewhat deeply into his rather sensitive crouch area. Either way, he was having one hell of a time if his hollering and thrashing about levels said anything about his surprise and discomfort...Especially with a huge guy yelling at him in one ear and the fence biting him at the same time in a very sensitive location every time he wiggled ever so slightly.

I finally got some law and order established on my side of the fence. Looking up, I saw Cliff coming across the field holding a smallish sized lad by the back of the neck and seat of the pants. I don't think that little chap hit but only one out of every three steps my 6-foot 4-inch partner was taking. A fitting end to an illegal deer-killing son of a gun, I thought smugly.

Finally sitting all our lads down in the middle of the road, we splashed the sorry lot with our flashlights. "We both are game wardens, Gentlemen," I said. "We will need to see some driver's licenses or other forms of identification from all of you."

Man, you talk about three chaps becoming all ass holes, eyeballs, and false teeth. They couldn't dig out the requested documents fast enough. Sometimes having the be-Jesus scared completely out of one's self seems to have that kind of speeding up the body's physical movement. Once collected, I saw we had two brothers and a third unrelated chap from the City of Sacramento. All three of the men worked for the City of Sacramento as firemen. Man, I sure couldn't figure what it was all about folks in that particular profession but I sure had caught a boat-load of them in the past and more were to come in later years in my wildlife outlaw dip net from that professional field of endeavor.

Holding their driver's licenses, I said, "All right. Mr. Bartleson and Mr. Dale Adams, you are going back into the field and will help Officer Fulton with the deer. I want those deer dragged over to the gate on the north end of the field. There, you will gut those animals before they spoil in this damn heat. Mr. Jack Adams, you and I, after moving your vehicle off the road so other vehicles can get by, will join them. Now, let's get cracking."

"Cliff," I said, "I want those two lads to drag the deer, not you. I don't want you tearing up your back again." Cliff's back was already a mess. He had fallen off a speeding M-4 Sherman Tank during the war in the numerous battles in the Normandy hedgerows and, as a result of that inadvertent fall, had a pretty bad back. But he was still one tough old man. To his way of thinking, his back pain could go to hell in a hand basket when he was on the hunt...

Then I moved Adam's truck off the road, but not before seizing a compound bow, a mess of arrows, a spotlight, and a loaded rifle from the front seat. With that chore out of the way, the two of us walked back to my patrol truck. There I had Adams take a seat where I could keep an eye on him. Shortly thereafter, here came Cliff with his two charges dragging the two recently killed deer. Then the three of them returned to the field for the last deer they had also killed that evening. Finally all the deer were dragged into the nearby draw behind my patrol truck and gutted to avoid spoilage. In the meantime, I had the Colusa County Sheriff's Office call my trusty deputy, Carter Bowman, who lived a short distance away in Stonyford and got him out of bed. He later arrived on the scene and, after a thorough search of their persons, all three men were loaded into his patrol car for transport to the Colusa County Jail. Then Cliff, Carter, and I loaded the three evidence deer into the back of my one mouse powered patrol truck. Boy, did my dog, Shadow, like that, especially with those new smells and all.

After a trip to the lockup and the booking process, Cliff, Carter, and I headed over to my nearby home. There, we had a lumberjack breakfast of hot biscuits, fried spuds, and my world-famous seafood and cream cheese omelet. Yum!

Here I must digress. To all my reader-cooks, including fellow cook Emeritus Guy Sommerville from Illinois, if you want to embark on a touch of Heaven, try this recipe on for size:

TERRY'S WORLD-FAMOUS SEAFOOD AND CREAM CHEESE OMELET

Feeds several eager eaters or lumberjacks.

Ingredients:
Celery, 4 stalks
Mild onions, 3 large. Texas Sweets are great.
Canned mushrooms, drained, 6 oz. drained weight
So   Han "Sonny" Park's homegrown garlic, to taste, freshly minced. Other fresh garlic will do.
Tomatoes, chopped, 3 cups
Crabmeat, any kind, freshly chopped, previously cooked. 1 cup Peeled shrimp, small- to medium-size, 6 oz.
Farm-fresh eggs, scrambled, 1 dozen
Sour cream, to taste
Cream cheese, 4 bricks
Parsley, freshly chopped
Salt
Ground black pepper

Chop up a mess of celery, mild onions, canned mushrooms and freshly minced garlic, then sauté in butter. Add chopped tomatoes to the mixture and sauté all the vegetables once again lightly. Finally, add a mound of crabmeat and another mound of peeled shrimp. Cook for about three to four minutes under medium high heat until the shrimp "pink up." Then add a mess of thoroughly messed up farm-fresh eggs loaded with small gobs of sour cream to taste and numerous small chunks of cream cheese. I usually use at least a dozen eggs, more of everything if you are feeding eager eaters or lumberjacks. Into that heavenly mixture, add freshly chopped parsley, salt, and pepper to taste. Cook up the mess until it meets your culinary specifications.

Serve hot with some buttermilk or beer biscuits (use beer in your Bisquick® mix). You will love it! Calories galore and it will mess up your cholesterol levels, but oh my, what a great way to die. And to be frank with all of you, we are all just waiting to die anyway because death is just a continuation of life, so hit the deck a-running and enjoy!

Man, you talk about several satiated bears after we had finished our breakfast. All three of us could have used a long snooze. Those were some grits if I must say so myself. However, there was still work to be done. I then called Joe Willow and had him tow in Adam's truck to the sheriff's office impound lot. There were citations to file in the Williams Justice Court and the judge to brief on the details of my latest dark-of-the-night adventure. Then, it was back to my house for some long draws on tall glasses of ice tea while I whipped up a great tuna salad, loaded with scads of drained, sea turtle/dolphin friendly, albacore tuna, fresh tomatoes (grown by my friend, Tom Yamamoto, may he rest in peace), lettuce, lite mayonnaise, and to taste, chopped mild red torpedo onions along with an ample mess of chopped avocado. That was accompanied by hot, garlic and butter slathered sourdough French bread, San Francisco style, for our lunches. After that and just barely able to waddle, Cliff and I disposed of the deer to a mess of Mexican farmhands and their families. Then it was back to our ranch house in Bear Valley, showers under a garden hose that ran from a nearby cold-as-a-Nun's-heart spring, fresh uniforms; and back out Cliff and I went to do battle in the world of wildlife. Can any of my readers believe I got paid to do all that?

Two weeks later, our three shooters entered guilty pleas in the Williams Justice Court. Judge Gibson, after hearing their stories as to why they did what they did, rendered his verdict. Each lad was to pay $1,500 in fines for use and aid of an artificial light in the taking a game animal, trespassing on private lands, taking game animals from a motor vehicle, and taking a closed season species (doe deer). Then he ordered that each man forfeit his hunting license for a period of one year, one year in jail with one year suspended, and forfeiture of his bow, arrows, rifle, and spotlight. The good judge also advised my three chaps that if they ever were apprehended in Colusa County for any other fish and game violations in the future, they could expect to serve six months in the Colusa County jail for the error of their ways.

Judge Gibson was a lot like Mother Nature. It was not nice to fool with Mother Nature or, for that matter, Judge Gibson (may God rest his soul) as our three lads painfully discovered. As for my deer-with-the-arrows-in-their-bodies problems, they disappeared with the apprehension of my firefighting chaps from Sacramento. However, the arrows used by my Sacramento chaps did not match those arrows I had discovered earlier in the deer and field that had started my stake out for such killers in the first place... The arrows discovered the first time, were of colors, lengths and broad heads that were all different. Damn! Oh well. As I have said many times in my previous writings, sometimes you eat the bear and sometimes he eats you...

AN ENCHANTED EVENING,
THEN A POKE IN THE MOUTH

Quietly, without using headlights to give my presence away to any poachers lurking in the immediate area, I sailed down the darkened county highway and ducked into my favorite hiding spot at the edge of the alfalfa field on the Art Andreotti Ranch. It was a typical Colusa County summer evening in the western portion of my patrol district. That is to say, hotter than a much-fired pistol and dryer than a popcorn fart. My early deer season was in full swing and I had more than my full share of sportsmen city slickers during daylight hours trying to add venison to their menus. Then if that was not enough of a problem, my deer-poaching spotlighters were also in full bloom once the sun had set and the backcountry roads had pretty much emptied of their usual traffic. Nothing like a typical daily dose of game-warden poison. You could work all day, work all night or as in my case, do both as long as my miserable carcass held together. But the hunting was good and the catching of my violators was excellent so, with those collaterally derived energies, man could do without one whole hell of a lot of sleep. Besides, anything worth doing is worth overdoing... Plus, I still had the world's best wife and she let me run wild within my world of wildlife law enforcement vision quest to my heart's content. Man, no two ways about it, my wife was and still is the sterling force that held our lives and family together throughout those many trying wildlife-law-enforcement years! She is one gal who pulled more than her fair share of the wagon throughout the wonderful years of our marriage...

Parking my patrol truck out of sight in a nearby shallow ravine as I always did, I covered it up with a camouflaged patterned parachute for good measure. No use wasting my time only to have some wildlife outlaw's illegal spotlighting activity accidentally expose my patrol truck's shiny parts and give away my presence before I was ready to spring the trap, I thought. Taking my trusty lawn chair out from the back of my truck, I placed it twenty yards in front of my truck alongside a stand of covering brush. That way, I could plainly see and hear anyone foolish enough to spotlight deer in my cherry patch of an alfalfa field and, illegally pull a trigger or loose an arrow. Returning to my truck, I grabbed my binoculars and a Stanley Thermos full of more or less iced tea. Plopping my tired, last part over the fence into the bottom of the lawn chair, I was now more than ready for whatever the good Lord brought me in the way of deer spotlighting miscreants. Or, anything else that came my way with an adventurous bent, or so I confidently thought. You know, just about the time one gets the big head and thinks he has the world in a downhill pull, the Old Boy upstairs has a sure fire way of quickly diminishing one's head size ... and, that diminution from the world of Mother Nature's little people was not long in coming. Remember what I just said and stay tuned my patient readers...

The inky darkness of that evening was just perfect. It was so dark out, that it would make for any excellent spotlighting activity. Too much moonlight and the spotlight wouldn't have the desired blinding effect of holding the deer in a stand, which made for an easy killing shot. If there was more moonlight, the critters would just up and move off if one spotlighted them because of all the other available light in which to see. In short, my evening was darker than the inside of a dead cow. To my way of thinking, that made it perfect for a deer poacher using a spotlight to exercise his trade and for me, to exercise mine...

As my eyes slowly adjusted into their night vision mode, I tuned up my listening for any sounds that were nature-normal or human- caused and out of place. Off in the distance, I heard two short and one long hoot from a great horned owl high up in a tree. Way far up at the head of the valley, I heard a pack of coyotes happily celebrating a kill. Probably one of the many black-tailed jackrabbits in the area, I thought. Finally, almost nothing but total silence reigned in the remaining inky velvety darkness. That was when I had to chuckle to myself. Behind me in the back of my patrol truck, I could hear the faint snoring of my faithful companion and dog aptly named Shadow. She had been a gift to me from my bride, Donna, several years earlier. Donna knew she couldn't go with me on my many wildlife wars adventures so she substituted my dog, Shadow, as her faithful stand in. What a great team Dog and I made over the years. Especially when she kept me from being stabbed one night by an unseen Indian spotlighter just off the Hoopa Indian Reservation in northern California . And she did so when she was just an eight- month-old pup! If you readers are interested in that almost fatal adventure, you will find that story in my book, The Thin Green Line, under the chapter titled, "Dogs." It is well worth the read. But be cautious in so doing. Some of those stories about other folks' dogs I met in the field or knew of and what happened to them, will bring tears to one's eyes. That will be especially so to you dog lovers, so I urge some caution for the soft of heart.

Presently, my daydreaming was interrupted with the passing of a car on the county road bordering the west side of my staked out alfalfa field. However, it didn't even slow down or fit the profile of a deer spotlighter. Yes, many successful officers profile, to you uninitiated ultra-liberal chaps from the San Francisco Bay Area. Many officers do so because it is an integral part of the internal workings of those of us who make a living hunting the most dangerous game, namely humans. Whether one likes it or not, it is an innate instinct in the badge carrying fraternity of hunters of humans to routinely profile in order to reduce the odds or chances of such an officer getting injured or killed. And just as long as the profiling is within the Bill of Rights, the U.S. Constitution, levels of common sense, and any other judicial constraints, what is the problem? PC. can be damned. I like being alive to greet the next sunrise! In short, if an officer does not master the art and science of profiling, they more than likely will not make it to retirement age unless it is as a medical... But, I digress once again.

After the passing of that last vehicle, quiet reigned once again in my velvety black world. Reaching into my uniform shirt pocket, I withdrew one of my ever-present nicotine-strong, nasty little Italian Toscani Cigars. Moments later, its acrid smoke swirled around me in the stifling hot and stillness of the night air. Within moments of that first drag, I could feel the intense dose of nicotine starting to ramble through my circulatory system like a freight train run amuck. Those little cigars were nasty little devils loaded with buckets of nicotine but they sure made it easy for a tired game warden to put in a twenty-eight-hour day, if you get my drift... Stretching out my tired legs while sitting in my lawn chair after a long day checking and herding my early season deer hunters around, I now settled in for the long haul and whatever illegal came my way in the dark of the night.

Moments later, a pickup came down the road from the south side of the alfalfa field. The road at that end of the field took a jog, allowing any passing vehicle's headlights to casually sweep the field. That pickup did so in a very slow and deliberate manner, which immediately aroused my suspicions as to the possibility of a potential spotlighter. As its headlights slowly swept the field, I could see through my binoculars about a dozen feeding deer scattered about. In that bunch of animals was one medium sized buck and the rest were does. Speeding up, the pickup continued traveling toward my off to one side location as it proceeded down the county road. When that vehicle got alongside my position of hiding parallel to the county road, I could see through my binoculars that it contained only one individual. Other than that, everything appeared normal to the casual eye. Following that, the vehicle disappeared down the road as if on another mission and quietly disappeared into the darkness.

Silence once again reigned around me and my deserted position at the north end of the alfalfa field. Then I heard my dog stirring in the back of my patrol truck like she sensed something was nearby and amiss. Turning around slowly like a Mountain Man of old deep in Indian country and listening intently, I saw or heard nothing out of the ordinary. But my dog's quiet and familiar rumble-growl told me otherwise. Slowly, very slowly, sitting up in my chair as if that repositioning movement would help me look and listen better, I discovered the object of my dog's interest. Boy, did I ever, as I quickly discovered I was not alone! Directly under my feet walked a striped skunk in all its glory! Holding my breath and obviously not wanting to move my now trapped carcass in any alarming manner, I froze. In the meantime, the skunk made itself right at home alongside my feet! Then I remembered why. Earlier in the day, I had seized an illegally taken deer from a sport that had shot the wrong type of critter, namely a spike buck or one possessing an unbranched antler. To be legal, a sport had to take a male deer possessing at least a branched antler or better. While loading that freshly gutted deer into the back of my truck for a trip to a nearby locker plant so it could be cooled out and not spoil in the summer heat, I had gotten some of its blood and fat on the front of my pant legs and boots. That blood-and-fat transfer had occurred when I hefted the deer up into the back of my truck after giving it a boost upward with my knee. The skunk, smelling the dried deer blood and smears of fat on my person, had been attracted to where I now very quietly sat as still as a granite tombstone in a long deserted pioneer cemetery. Once there, the animal commenced licking the dried blood and swatches of fat off my boots. Then standing up on its hind legs and using its paws on my leg to steady itself, it began licking the dried blood and fat stains off my pant legs. At that point, I was sure hoping I hadn't gotten any blood on the crotch of my pants as well... Finally, Mr. Skunk, tired of licking the deer's dried bodily remains from my miserable carcass, dropped onto all fours, and wandered off in its usual shuffle like walk. Man, that was such a close call I hadn't even dared to take a drag off my still smoldering cigar! Truth be known, I was not sure at that moment which smelled worse, my recent visitor or my mean-smelling little Italian cigar. Remember what I told all you good folks earlier about Mother Nature's little people? Don't fall asleep on me now my patient readers because Mother Nature isn't through messing with me as of yet...

With the skunk gone, Shadow and I got back to the evening's business at hand. She to her interrupted sleeping as evidenced by her snoring sounds commencing once again, and me to my looking and listening to the sights and sounds Mother Earth makes when she is at peace with herself. Around midnight, I reached for my Stanley Thermos of iced tea. With that move, I was immediately greeted with the warning rattle of a too damn close-at-hand rattlesnake! In fact, the snake appeared to be very close to my thermos when I had reached for it. Sensing my hand movement and the shifting of my weight in the lawn chair, the deadly snake had sounded off instead of striking! Freezing my hand movement in midair, my eyes searched for my nearby friend in the inky blackness. The damn thing was almost impossible to see in the darkness but I thought I could see, from the echolocation of its close-at-hand rattling, where it was coiled. Then a second warning buzz of its rattles pinpointed its exact position. It was coiled right next to my left boot! For the longest time neither of us moved and finally, the warning sound of the snake's rattles slowed and then died away in the darkness. Finally, I saw what I thought was the snake uncoiling and moving off in the direction the skunk had exited earlier. Boy, I was more than ready for a cold drink from my thermos at that point in time. Too bad the damn thermos didn't contain something a little stronger than iced tea! Like I said previously, I had thought earlier in the evening that I was more than ready for whatever the good Lord threw my way that evening. It always amazed me just how quickly I came down from my high horse, especially when the Chief Game Warden in the sky handed me a dose of reality, along with a healthy serving of the quiet nearness of my mortality...

Over the next hour, I had several more vehicles drive by but none showed any interest in my field now full of feeding deer. However, around two in the morning as Mother Nature had more than settled down around me, I got a wakeup call. The same pickup that had driven by my position earlier in the evening with the one chap inside, came by slowly once again! This time, when he was center to my alfalfa field on the now totally deserted county road, he stopped. Zing, out from the driver's side of the pickup came the blue-white beam of a powerful spotlight! It swung from one end of the field to the other as if looking for something. Then off went the light and the pickup drifted slowly down the road like nothing out of the ordinary had just occurred.

In those days, the State of California had a fish and game regulation that stated: "It is illegal to cast an artificial light upon a game animal and have in one's possession a weapon capable of taking that game animal." In short, we game wardens had just shortened that regulatory phraseology to simply, spotlighting. At that point, I could have bailed from my hiding spot and stopped that vehicle hoping he was carrying a weapon capable of taking a game animal. If that had been the case, under the law, I would have had a solid spotlighting case. However, my judge in the Williams Justice Court preferred that, if I used that particular regulation, my spotlighter had better have an illegal deer in his or her possession or at least had spotlighted and shot at one. His reasoning being was that California had a lot of deer and they were somewhat numerically expendable. To his way of thinking, it was a lot easier to prove a violation of that regulation if a chap had a deer in his possession or at least had shot at one. And in enforcing the regulation in the manner he suggested, that would preclude many expensive and time-consuming jury or court trials. Especially, if an illegal critter had been entered into evidence at said trial. Additionally, Judge Gibson felt better administering a larger fine for such a serious violation if an overt act such as shooting or killing of the spotlighted game animal had occurred. Regardless of which way I thought the regulation should have been enforced, an officer of the law does not mess with any judge who sits at the right hand of God. Especially if he is strongly on the side of the one carrying the badge, if you get my drift. Whatever Judge Gibson wanted, he got as far as I was concerned. When one has a good, fair, and knowledgeable judge, he keeps it that way. To my way of thinking, that was being what I called "judicially judicious" on my part...

Leaning back in my lawn chair again, I lit up another cigar and took in a hefty chew of Levi Garrett Chewing Tobacco all at the same time to settle down the hunting instinct storming around within my miserable carcass at that moment in time. Dang, I hope that last chap returns and does something foolish, I thought. I haven't apprehended a spotlighter all this week and this moment in time would be just as good as any to close that ring of fire. Plus, that meant if my chap returned and shot a deer, after his apprehension and trip to the Colusa County jail, I could go home thereafter and sleep in a bed instead of resting in a lawn chair out in the bush.

During the next hour for entertainment, I had to comfort myself with the howling of a nearby pack of coyotes, the snoring of my dog, and a talkative, lone great horned owl now perched high in an oak tree directly behind me. Then my world really came to life! Back down the road came my earlier suspect pickup with just the one occupant. This time, when his headlights swept the alfalfa field, there was a monster mule deer buck quietly feeding out in the field! Man, with that revelation, my driver sped down the road and quickly disappeared behind me. Ten minutes later, here came a darkened vehicle running without using any headlights, as it moved slowly down the road that ran alongside my alfalfa field. Hot diggity, I thought. Someone running without lights on a remote county road at this time in the morning is up to no damn good and I am just the chap to find out what his level of intentions were when it came to dealing with Mother Nature.

Sure as my style of mashed potatoes is the world's best because I use a pint of sour cream, stick of butter, an eight ounce chunk of cream cheese and numerous spices in the recipe, the darkened vehicle drove by my position and stopped about where the middle of the field would be. Zing out from the vehicle's window zipped a characteristic blue-white pencil-thin spotlight beam. For a fraction of time, the light surveyed the field until it fastened onto the monster buck previously observed in his headlights. In an instant, a bright orange fireball erupted from the driver's side window followed by a loud and ear shattering boom!

Watching through my binoculars, I saw the monster buck's entire body spin completely around from the energy's impact of the bullet and hit the ground in a huge puff of dust in the bone-dry alfalfa field! With that, the spotlight went out, and then I heard a vehicle door slam. Next, I heard the barbed wire fence by the side of the shooter's vehicle complaining as the weight of a rather heavy human crawled over it. Then with flashlight in hand, my deer-shooting chap moved out into my alfalfa field on foot. Taking that as my cue, I came out of my lawn chair. Grabbing my flashlight and with my binoculars hanging around my neck banging on my chest, I took off running. Running quietly along the inside of the alfalfa field fence in the darkness, I hustled over to where my chap's pickup sat directly behind me, darkened and in the middle of the county road. Once there, I took up my ambush station. Since my shooter was still out in the middle of the field, I figured that when my lad came back to his truck, he would be dragging that heavy, monster-sized buck. He had about a forty-yard drag so, by the time he got back to me, he would be more than winded. When my shooter got within grabbing distance, I would flip on my flashlight and let him know the tooth fairy had come early. Little did I realize at that time that the tooth fairy would be badly needed before that morning's events had subsided and the dust had settled!

Kneeling down alongside the fence to reduce my silhouette, I quietly waited for the arrival of my deer-shooting chap. Then the most God-awful, hell-raising noises from the center of the field reached my ears. They were of such a loud and desperate nature, that they caused my hair to stand straight up!

"Yeow, umpff, ackkk, help me, oh god, help me, umpff, kapoof, owwwh, no, don't do that!" screamed a voice from the dark of the night in the middle of the alfalfa field! Jumping up from my kneeling position in alarm, I turned on my five-cell flashlight toward the source of the God-awful noises coming from the center of the field. All I saw was a huge dust cloud rising into the still night air, punctuated with the occasional glimpses of a dust-shrouded deer and a human whirling about within! With that, I took off running in the direction of the dust cloud, the scene of such violent howling, hell raising, screams of terror, and wild thrashings about.

Getting closer, I saw through the dust the spotlighter and the monster deer locked in mortal combat! My shooter had hold of the deer's antler for all he was worth. In that action, the buck was hopping, jumping, thrashing, and kicking out with his front feet all in one motion at the human object hanging onto the critter's antler. Round and round the two combatants flew in a dusty circle. As I moved in even closer, I could see my shooter was holding onto only one antler! The antler on the other side of the buck's head had been shot clean away just inches above the animal's skull. Then it dawned on me as to what had happened. My shooter had tried for a head shot on the big buck but, in the process, had miscalculated with his aim, pulled his shot, and had shot off one antler near its base on the skull. With that, the deer had been knocked down and rendered goofy as all get out for a moment from the energy of the bullet's impact on his antler. When my chap got to the deer and had grabbed it moments later, thinking the animal was dead, the deer came back to life in his world. Getting to its feet, the animal began thrashing about trying to get away from the grasp of the shooter. The man, now realizing he had a tiger by the tail, was hanging onto the remaining antler for dear life since he was unarmed. To let go at that moment in time and have the now very angry buck deer take a lethal swipe at him with that remaining antler, just would not do well in the man's survival department. Therefore, my shooter was hanging on for dear life, no pun intended! In the meantime, the deer was now super pissed, had fully regained his wits, was highly energized, and ready for battle. It was pretty obvious the enraged animal was flat kicking the stuffin' out of my madly-hanging-on-for-dear-life shooter. Then the deer charged the man, head down, trying to gore him with his remaining good antler. Either way, it appeared my shooter was coming out second or third best in that alfalfa field's life and death struggle with the critter.

As for me, well, I was in a quandary. I didn't want to shoot a perfectly good deer, even though he was kind of funny looking with his one antler. On the other hand, I couldn't very well shoot my poacher and put him out of his misery either. He was looking pretty damn funny as well with a still surprised look of terror splashed all over his face. And lastly, my .44 magnum could go clean through the deer and the man at that range if I was to shoot poorly, so you see my quandary. And I, for damn sure, was not going to grab that pissed off monster deer and give my illegal shooter a hand! Being the size I was, I had a lot more stuffin' to lose if the deer then chose to square off and kick the dickens out of me for messing with him during a perfectly good fight. A fight in which the buck was clearly winning...

Then the deer gave a monster lunge forward. Raising up on its hind legs and lifting my shooter clear off the ground, the deer kicked out violently with both front feet! You could have heard that whack! on the carcass of my bad guy clear to the Town of Colusa some fifty miles away when that deer's front hooves connected! With that, my shooter folded like a rag doll and hit the ground in a knocked-colder-than-a-cucumber heap. The buck, now free of his antagonist, fell over backwards. Then, regaining his balance along with his footing, turned and lowered his head, shaking its lone antler menacingly at me. Wrong thing to do, lad, I thought, as the .44 magnum cleared leather and leveled off at the base of the angry deer's neck now just scant feet away. "Make a dumb-assed move at me and it is all over," I said loudly to the deer, as if he would understand a nervous but serious-as-all-get-out warning from the local tule creeper.

The buck pawed the ground with its front feet then calmly raised its head, turned and sauntered away as if he had more than proven his point. Me, I breathed a sigh of relief. There was no way I wanted to kill such a magnificent animal. But if he had advanced or charged me with his lowered deadly antler...well...

A groan brought me back to the spotlighting, deer shooting lump lying at the bottom of my feet. Looking down with my flashlight, I saw a huge pool of blood forming in the dirt around his head! He was lying face down in the dirt at that moment and when I rolled him over and sat him up, I got the surprise of the moment. The buck, in his final lunge of anger, had violently kicked my shooter squarely in the face with both his front set of cloven hooves. My lad's face was now an absolute mess as a result of that last hoof strike. As nearly as I could tell with my flashlight, through all the gushing blood and blood-muddy dirt on his face, my shooter had a broken nose and his upper and lower lips were split wide open to the gum lines! The damage was so bad, I could even see his bloody teeth and gums behind the splits! Then when my injured shooter tried to speak, he began gagging and violently vomiting. Reaching down to help my shooter get to his feet, I saw what the man had been apparently gagging on. It was three of his four front incisors! The deer had kicked out three of the man's four front teeth and he had just gagged as he swallowed them along with a sizeable chunk of his gums! Brother, what a mess that deer's hooves had made of my chap's face in general and mouth in particular!

Getting my man unsteadily to his feet, I walked and he stumbled back to his truck. There I retrieved his rifle and spotlight after the two of us had climbed over the fence. Seeing my suffering lad was going nowhere, I moved his truck off the road and locked it up. Then the two of us walked back to my truck as I explained to him that I was a game warden and that he was under arrest for spotlighting deer in violation of the fish and game regulations. All my fellow did was spit, gag and drool blood all the way back to my truck as he continually groaned in the agony of defeat.

Once in my truck, I gave him a handful of paper towels to stem the blood flow and we headed back to Colusa. Arriving later in Colusa, I got Doctor Palmer out of bed and had him patch up my lad as best as he could. In the doctor's office, he had his nose reset and received forty-three stitches for the splits on his lips and face placed there earlier by the deer's deadly flying hooves. However, there was nothing Doctor Palmer could do for the man's missing front teeth, which had been broken off at the base of the man's gum line and inadvertently swallowed! From there, it was off to the Colusa County Jail and booking for his earlier fish and game violations.

What was really neat was that I got home that morning in time to have breakfast with my bride and kids. While eating, my bride asked if I had any luck catching spotlighters the evening before. Between forks full of her great home cooking, I nodded. Once my mouth was empty—she hated it when I spoke with food in my mouth—I told her I had caught one chap spotlighting deer. Then without missing a beat, I told her that I had a little help. She asked if my help was from Deputy Bowman, and I told her as I took another bite of her world's best homemade bread, "No, Honey, it was an assist from Mr. Buck." With the utterance of those joking words, I could at least happily smile with a full set of teeth...

Two weeks later, my chap appeared in front of Judge Gibson in the Williams Justice Court. Man, he was still a mess. His face was still pretty swollen, bruised like all get out and exhibited a purplish- yellowish-brown in color facial look where he had been struck numerous times by the buck's flying front hooves during their battle in the alfalfa field. All that facial damage was seconded by two beautifully blackened eyes. When asked how he pled, he mumbled, "Guilty to all the charges, Your Honor." Without a moment's hesitation, Judge Gibson advised that he found him guilty of using an artificial light to take a game animal, fined him $500, and forfeited his rifle and spotlight to the State of California. By that time, the judge was also aware of the earlier battle between the winning-buck and the losing-shooter. Taking that Mother Nature thumping of the shooter into consideration, he let the rest of the possible fines slide (trespassing, shooting from a motor vehicle, loaded rifle in a motor vehicle on a way open to the public) with an admonishment never to appear in his court again unless he wanted to do serious time in the Colusa County Jail.

So, I guess one could say that evening was one of enchantment, especially in light of the close calls with the rattlesnake and the skunk. And I would also have to admit, that was one of the best fights I had seen in a long time. I would imagine my shooter paid a hell of a lot more than the $500 fine to get his front teeth replaced with false teeth though. Those were in the days when the science of dental implants were not yet in vogue like they are today in 2012, hence the false teeth routine that was sure to follow.

Oh, by the way. I saw that one antlered buck several times after that during the remaining deer season in the alfalfa field once darkness overcame the light of day. He was still wearing a large patch of my spotlighter's shirt on that one good antler. I guess that was the buck's red badge of courage, eh?

THE McVEYS

Shortly after arriving in Colusa County as a resident game warden during the early summer of 1967, among many other outlaws so named in local stories, I heard about the alleged notorious, wildlife laws violating, McVey Clan. As I came to discover among the law enforcement fraternity within the sheriff's office and the towns of Williams and Colusa's police departments, those agency officers would often share intelligence with me about which wildlife outlaws in the county I needed to keep an eye on. Especially those walking on the dark side of Mother Nature in the rice fields at night killing ducks, poaching deer and pheasants, or, those who had a historically dangerous mean streak and liked to fight when confronted by any member of the law enforcement community. As it turned out, soon there were dozens of names of local wildlife outlaws, duck-club operators and run-of-the-mill poachers whirling around in my head that I needed to keep track of as a result of my informational sources. And, for the most part they were of a duke's mixture to say the least. Those so identified ran the gamut: illegal fishermen; duck draggers; a few left-over commercial market hunters mostly dealing with the sale of ducks; farmers killing rice-field-depredating ducks during the summer months; live trappers of pheasants of the year, which were considered the most tender and best eating; those running illegal set lines in the numerous waterways; illegal froggers; individuals who liked to open the dove season early; those who never ran across a buck deer that they couldn't resist killing, be it daylight or dark, open season or not; and all the way down the list of seriousness to numerous duck-club game keepers catching too many black bass while using illegal live bait such as mice! Those serious revelations were soon followed with information on those duck clubs in my assigned patrol district, who had reputations for taking too many ducks and geese if given the right opportunity. It wasn't long before my cup was spilling over with potential wildlife outlaws of every ilk. Wildlife outlaws whose life histories seemed to be intertwined with every kind of fish and game violation known to man and even some laws they had made up themselves just so they would have something to break! With such good intelligence information, I soon went from a twelve to an eighteen-hour day, many times seven days a week operation in my new resource rich patrol district. I quickly discovered this I had to do just to hold open the lid of life for all those things naturally occurring in the world of wildlife! However, one family or clan name that kept coming up, from friend and foe alike, regarding every kind of wildlife violation under the sun, was that of the McVeys from the small Town of Olivehurst in the Sacramento Valley. Always eager to stay one step ahead of my poachers, I catalogued this McVey clan information into the "need to catch quickly" annals of my mind. However as most things wild worked out, it was a good year before I ran across a single storied member from the McVey clan. One fine summer morning, I finally got to put into law enforcement practice that which I had previously heard so much about.

Sitting in my lawn chairs at the edge of the Andreotti alfalfa field in the darkness with Reserve Deputy Fish and Game Officer Cliff Fulton, we were shooting the bull as we usually did during slow times. As far as any spotlighting activity was concerned, it had so far been a quiet night into the early morning hours in our little spot of the world. We were just about ready to leave and get a few hours' sleep so we could also work the day shift of legal deer hunters since that season was open, when I told Cliff, "Let's wait just ten more minutes. Then if nothing happens, we can go back to the ranch and get some sleep." For all you game warden type readers out there, remember one of Grosz's Rules. When you finally get ready to leave whatever stakeout you are running, wait just ten more minutes, then leave. During my career, it was amazing the number of people I caught during that ten-minute waiting period. By the way, so has my special agent son who, as of 2012, is the U.S. Fish and Wildlife Service's Resident Agent in Charge stationed in Bismarck, North Dakota. He has used many of his dad's tricks-of-the-trade teachings, including the "wait just ten more minutes" trick, and has enriched the state and federal coffers several times over as a result. Bottom line, by using that little trick of the trade, Rich has put a lot of those in the States of North and South Dakota who are in the business of extinction, out of business...

I had no more than uttered those words of waiting a few more minutes when around the southern corner of our staked-out alfalfa field came a vehicle. It was moving very slowly, like most night hunting poachers will do, and caught our attention in a heartbeat! Then, if the slow-moving vehicle didn't do enough to get our blood pumping, what they did next—just as sure as a ten-pound sack of flour makes a big biscuit—sure as hell did!

The vehicle stopped and then zing, out from its passenger window came the bright thin beam of a spotlight! The light raced across the alfalfa field illuminating numerous quietly-feeding mule deer. Just as fast as it came on, it went out. Seconds later, the driver gunned the vehicle's engine and raced by on the county road near the location where we were sitting and out of sight like the law was hot on his tail.

As it did, Cliff turned and said, "That is odd. Why didn't he shoot? He sure as hell had lots of targets including that damn nice buck at the south end of the field he illuminated in his spotlight when it first went on."

"I don't know why that chap didn't shoot. He sure as hell can't see where we or the patrol truck are hidden," I answered. Then my guardian angels kicked in! I got the strongest feeling to just hold our position and remain patient. You know, almost as if there was a boatload of illegal action to come just as long as I was patient. In fact, that feeling to hold was so strong that it was almost physical in nature. And remembering past history, which included previously experiencing numerous such sixth senses, I resisted the desire to run down my just-observed chap working a spotlight. "Cliff, let's just hold our position and wait and see what happens. If we hear shooting to the north of us in the direction they have gone, we can call Deputy Bowman and he can cut off those chaps with his patrol car down the road a piece. Then we can slide in behind them and we will have the lads in our pinchers," I suggested with a grin having been to that type of rodeo numerous times before, especially in my previous law-enforcement district as a game warden along the coastal counties of northern California. And in particular, working the out-of-work loggers who were notorious for spotlighting and shooting the grand Roosevelt elk and Columbian black-tailed deer once the dark of the night was on the scene.

"Sounds good to me, Chief," said Fulton. With that, we relaxed a bit, but not too much... To all my unwashed readers out there reading these lines, when hunting humans, patience is a much- needed virtue. In order to be good at your work as a wildlife officer, one must be as patient as an alligator snapping turtle at the bottom of a pond waiting for a fish to be attracted to its gaping mouth by the turtle's wiggling-worm like tongue... Just to put this situation into perspective, especially for all my non-law enforcement and questioning snapping turtle life history chaps out there, that is pretty damn patient!

Ten minutes later, we heard another vehicle coming from the southern end of our staked out alfalfa field. It, too, was moving slowly and stopped alongside the southern end of our alfalfa field. Within seconds, out from that vehicle's passenger window came the beam of a spotlight! That light raced around the field, fastened onto a couple of nice-sized buck deer, and then moved on. In so doing, off went the light, just like the earlier vehicle had done. Following that, the suspect vehicle quickly raced by us as if trying to escape any game wardens who might be watching since it was illegal under the California Fish and Game Code to spotlight a game animal and have a weapon capable of taking that game animal in one's possession...

Now really perplexed, I said to Cliff, "What the hell is going on?"

"Don't know, Chief, but it sure is weird," he responded. Again, we decided to sit and wait to see what the dickens was going on. That decision was strongly seconded by my now really fired up guardian angels fluttering around inside me like fallen aspen leaves in the face of a fierce winter wind in November in the Rocky Mountains of Colorado.

About ten minutes later, we heard a third vehicle approaching our stakeout position from the south. That vehicle also stopped and ran a spotlight across the field as if looking for that certain buck! Then, its spotlight went out off as it sped down the road and by our stakeout position like if its tail was on fire just like the previous two vehicles had done...

"Cliff, have we stepped off into the Twilight Zone?" I questioned.

"Chief, I am going to walk back and see if the parachute came off our vehicle and they are somehow seeing and keying off it," he said as he got up and left. Pretty soon he returned. "Nope, all is well with our rig still being out of sight," he told me as he slid his large frame back down into the comfort of his lawn chair. "Damned all to hell if I know what the dickens is going on," he slowly continued.

Not hearing any shooting to our north where the three vehicles had driven, we began to relax. Then I heard a vehicle approaching our position from the north or from behind us. Pretty soon, one of those same spotlighting vehicles we had seen earlier through our binoculars returned. Again, that vehicle stopped, spotlighted the field and then left in great haste fleeing to the south. Ten minutes later, here came another vehicle from our north. Looking it over through my binoculars, I determined it was one of the earlier vehicles we had seen as well. It also stopped, spotlighted the alfalfa field and then left in great haste just like the preceding vehicle.

"What the hell is going on, Mr. Fulton? It is almost as if these vehicles are decoys and are trying to draw out any game wardens staking out this field," I finally said slowly.

"I agree," said Cliff as he drew his revolver, opened up his cylinder, and checked to make sure all his chambers were loaded. I promptly did the same thing figuring if someone wanted a "hoorah" from this mess of weird acting vehicles, come and get it!

Then, a third vehicle coming from the north did the same goofy maneuver as the previous two had done. It, too, was a vehicle we had seen earlier. And just like the others, it raced off into the morning's darkness heading south. The next half hour passed as quietly as a well-irrigated stalk of corn growing on an Iowa farm in the July heat.

Then once again, here came one of the same vehicles from the south. Arriving at the alfalfa field, it spotlighted the field and then sped off to the north as if not wanting to get caught for its actions. Right on schedule moments later, here came the same second vehicle in their string. It stopped alongside the alfalfa field and zing,, out came the beam of their spotlight. That light looked the quietly-feeding deer over, including one large, heavy antlered buck just like before. All of a sudden, *boom!* went a heavy rifle being fired from the passenger window of that vehicle!

"Holy crap, Cliff. They just shot! " I said in amazement, expecting that vehicle to spotlight the field as they had done before and then just quickly move on.

By then, Cliff was up and out from his chair looking intently with his binoculars. "Terry, that big buck on the south end of the field is down," he hissed.

Then the lights on the vehicle from whence the shot had just come went out and I heard the alfalfa field's barbed wire fence objecting moments later as if someone heavy had just gone over the top wires in a big hurry.

"Cliff, I can see two lads in my binoculars running across the field toward where we last saw that big buck," I whispered in excitement over the fast-paced rodeo events now taking place and in anticipation of those reactions on our part soon to follow...

"Gotcha, Chief," he said. "They have the deer they just shot and are dragging it like all thunder back toward their vehicle," he continued in a low voice.

In my binoculars, I saw the two remaining chaps back at the vehicle race for the fence. Once there, they helped the two in the field boost and pull the large buck over the top of the fence. Into that vehicle's trunk went the big buck followed by a loud slamming of its lid. Within moments, down the road toward us came the shooter's vehicle running without lights. Passing our position as they sped by, I could hear a lot of excited talking among the vehicle's occupants through their open windows in the summer's heat.

Tossing our lawn chairs out of the way so we wouldn't run over them once we exited the field, Cliff and I headed for my patrol truck. Waiting until our shooters were out of eyesight and hearing, I started up the truck and we pulled out from under the parachute. That was easily done because we had placed large rocks on the parachute's backside, which was laying past the end of the bed on my truck on the ground. When we drove out from under it, the chute just slid away from our vehicle slicker than cow slobbers. Rolling out onto the county road, I called the sheriff's office and requested that Deputy Bowman cut off our shooter on his end of the road. The sheriff's office soon confirmed Deputy Bowman was on his way rolling toward our position. Speeding up and running down the deserted county road without the use of my headlights, I soon approached our suspect vehicle from the rear. By now, our shooter's vehicle was using its headlights and casually going down the county road just like they were leaving a church social. It was obvious they were driving in such a manner so as not to draw any unwanted attention their way. Well, that dog wasn't going to hunt...

Slipping up behind them, I turned on my headlights, red light, and siren. Brother, you never saw such surprised activity in a sedan as you did in that one at that moment in time! They slowly pulled over after they had taken the time to unload their rifle and tried hiding their spotlight—actions observed looking through the back window of their sedan. Once their vehicle had stopped, Cliff removed the lads from the passenger side and I took out those on the driver's side of the car.

Moments later, we had four very surprised chaps sitting down in the middle of the road. But, boy, were they mouthy! Denials of any wrongdoing filled the morning air like a swarm of irate honeybees, African variety. That was until we pulled out the recently fired rifle, spotlight, and moments later, one large, freshly killed specimen of a mule deer buck from the trunk of their car! That deer had not been gutted, the blood around the wound channel had not yet coagulated, rigor had not yet set in and the animal's eyes had yet to dilate, all keys as to a most recent kill! Plus, there was still sticky blood and snot smeared across their dusty back bumper. Remember that trick of the trade, all you budding game warden readers out there. Fresh blood and snot smeared across the back bumper of a vehicle from a just recently loaded big game animal will give you some damn good probable cause to think about when conducting a warrantless search. Even the F.B.I. would say that was pretty fresh evidence and a damn good probable cause clue. That is if they were up at that time of the morning...

Then the crap hit the fan! From the north screamed a vehicle running down the county road at a high rate of speed, then skidding into our car stop area. Out piled two lads loudly demanding to know what the hell were we doing. Coincidentally, the vehicle just driven up from the north was the first car that had driven by, as if acting as a decoy, shortly before the deer was shot. Moments later, here came another vehicle, only this time from the south, just a-poopin' and a-scootin'! It also skidded to a stop into the area of our car-stop activity. And coincidentally, it just so happened to be the other car in what I was now figuring was part of a well-planned decoy and "if all clear then shoot" operation. A planned, elaborate scheme designed to draw out any staked-out game wardens before anyone had shot any deer or other critter governed by the fish and game laws. A scheme that I thought was pretty damn slick. But to be truthful, not slicker than a mess of good old-fashioned cow slobbers or two pretty damn dedicated game warden types that had ridden most every bronc in the remuda. That is if you readers get my drift...

Out from the last arriving vehicle bailed a real mouthy chap named Charlie McVey III. "Who is in charge here?" he bellowed into the morning air like an Alaskan bull moose deep in rut.

"I am," I said, as Cliff and I were in the process of handcuffing our four spotlighting, deer killing suspects in the middle of the road.

"The hell you say. Take those handcuffs off my kin or I will have your ass thrown so far back into the slammer, you will grow moldy before you get out. I am an attorney. And if you don't do as I say, I will sue your ass clear off," he continued bellowing like a gored ox just two feet away from my face.

Well, I had worked a lot of long, hot days previous to this encounter and without a whole hell of a lot of sleep. But you, my dear readers, would have been proud of me. I held my Germanic cool and didn't rip his lips off and feed them to the nearest magpie. Ignoring the mouth, Cliff and I continued searching our now handcuffed prisoners for any concealed weapons.

"Didn't you hear me, Asshole? Take those handcuffs off my kin or I will have your collective hind ends in a heartbeat." And with those words, he grabbed the front of my shirt. Big time mistake! Using a martial arts move I had learned at the fish and game academy, I soon had Mr. Big Mouth Attorney marrying his last part over the fence to the highway asphalt at a high rate of speed with a rather resounding ka-thump! That impact was immediately followed by his rather loud and surprised utterance of "Oof!"

"Don't ever grab me again, Mister, or you will be the one resting in the slammer covered with mold before anyone discovers your miserable carcass," I quietly advised as I stood over him.

About then Deputy Bowman slid to a stop and happily joined the morning's party. Soon our four poachers, McVeys all or kin thereof, were in the back seat of his patrol car. The deer, spotlight, and rifle went into my patrol truck. However, as I was soon to discover, not all was said or done in the moment at hand. I soon had the mouth once again squarely stuck in my face.

"I want your name and badge number, Mister," he bellowed. "No sweat," I said. "My Fish and Game badge number is 221. It is right there on the front of my shirt if you care to look. My name is Terry Grosz, and I am stationed in Colusa."

"Good," he said. "You won't have a job when I get through with you after this goes to trial and my kin are found not guilty by reason of an illegal search and seizure."

"Be my guest," I said, trying very hard not to reach out and squeeze his neck until his eyes squirted out from his head and then popped.

By then, we had a list of all the names of everyone involved and a subsequent search of their vehicles revealed no other firearms present. If they had any firearms, since they had illuminated numerous game animals earlier, their hind ends would have been en route the Colusa County Jail as well. However, as reported earlier to me by the deputies, these chaps were outlaw smart and one wouldn't catch them napping or making a dumb-assed mistake such as having a rifle in the decoy car's possession. As it turned out, we were confronted with nothing but a nest of in-laws and outlaws from Olivehurst, whose last names mostly all ended with McVey or were friends thereof. When Charlie McVey III got into my face one more time, and having had a gutful of such antics, I made a point abundantly clear: "Mr. McVey, the wildlife in Colusa County is here for those resident folks and their kin. And if you or any members of your clan want to illegally kill wildlife, do it elsewhere. Because if you don't and choose to violate the fish and game laws here in this county, I will throw you and your violating kind in jail every time I run across your stinking carcasses! Do I make myself clear?"

With that, we departed the scene with four of their deer poaching kin in bracelets en route to the lock up in Colusa. As expected later after they posted bail and were released, the four poachers pled not guilty and demanded a jury trial in the Williams Justice Court.

That is when the wheels almost came clear off my wagon. In those days, there wasn't a bucket full of guts or a thimble full of brains in the Colusa County District Attorney's Office. To my way of thinking, if any attorney type couldn't get a decent job anywhere else, they could go to work for the Colusa County Attorney's Office, and join the rest of the half-wits ensconced therein. And talk about pissin' backwards, especially when they discovered they were going to have a jury trial on four spotlighters for spotlighting and the illegal possession of a deer. Brother, that county attorney's office skedaddled faster than the Union Army did after the First Battle of Bull Run during the opening moments of America's Civil War.

Anyway, I finally got the Colusa County District Attorney to gather up his skirts and supply me with a deputy county prosecutor. However, I could have done better during that trial with a dead man as a prosecutor! One who had been dead for at least a month...The prosecutor assigned to that case had not an ounce of brains, even less guts, and zero, fresh-out-of-law-school prosecutorial experience! Anyway, I had a tough but good judge in Judge Gibson in the Williams Justice Court so off to trial we went like a gaggle of geese.

A week later after the state had presented our case in open court, I sat there for almost an hour listening to my outlaws defense attorney rant, harangue and rave about everything under the sun that was wrong with the closed-season deer-killing case and its arresting officers. The counties gutless prosecutor never objected one time to anything the defense brought up! Then came what was to be their final blow against the government's case. Charlie McVey III, the mouthy one, testified that I had threatened him scaring him half to death. He told the jury in lurid language that I had threatened him, telling him never to come to Colusa County ever again unless he and all the rest of his kind wanted to go to jail and grow moldy in the process.

My gutless county attorney turned to me in panic and quietly whispered, "Did you say that?" I could tell by the way he asked the question that he more than likely, figuratively speaking, was in the process of wetting all over himself and onto the courtroom floor. Man, no two ways about it, I had a standing invertebrate for a prosecutor...

"Damn right I said that," I whispered. "Put me back on the stand for rebuttal," I demanded quietly.

"No! God, no! I can't do that," my weak fish county attorney advised.

Standing up at our table, I just stood there looking down at my wimpy, lack-of-guts, wet-legged prosecutor. Being backed into a corner with me just standing there in open court waiting for him to act, he finally requested I be allowed to respond to the defense's accusations to which the judge agreed. It was at that point that I caught the judge smiling. Not much of a smile mind you, but just a little. Kind of like the spider does to a nearby fly.

Taking the stand once again, I looked right at the jury. Right off the bat as I had done earlier, I recognized one avowed, previously- convicted commercial market hunter who had been captured by game wardens of old; six alleged local duck-dragging outlaws I had yet to catch; and one previously-apprehended-by-me deer spotlighter sitting in the jury box! Serious game-warden-hating outlaws, one and all. In fact, of that bunch, I had already caught and prosecuted three other of my peers sitting on that jury for various other less-serious wildlife violations. Like I said, my prosecutor didn't even have the backbone to toss those folks off the jury with his earlier challenges after I had quietly identified them as problem jurors for the prosecution! Anyway, I took the stand and my attorney asked in a quivering voice, "Officer Grosz, did you tell Mr. McVey to stay out of Colusa County or you would throw him into jail until he got moldy?"

Looking hard at the jury members, I said, "Sure did. I made it very plain to all the McVeys and their kin, that the fish and game in this county is limited. And to my way of thinking, it was reserved for the folks of Colusa County and their kids. Then I told Mr. McVey if he ever wanted to violate the fish and game laws again, do it elsewhere. Otherwise, if I ever caught him or any of his clan in my county again breaking the state fish and game laws, I would throw their hind ends so far back into the clink that they would grow moldy before anyone discovered their miserable carcasses therein." Man, with the utterance of those words, you could have heard a small spider racing across a wet lawn.

With that and no further questions from the prosecution or the defense and still in a stone cold and quiet courtroom, I got up, walked over and sat back down at the prosecutor's table. The jury was given their instructions after the attorneys' concluding remarks, and then they left to deliberate. They were gone just eight minutes by my watch when they announced they had arrived at a verdict! With that, everybody scrambled back into the courtroom and quietly prepared to listen to the jury foreman, the one I caught and had previously prosecuted for spotlighting a deer himself sometime earlier, for his or her verdict.

When the judge asked if they had reached a verdict, the foreman advised that they had. I looked right at him and he looked right back at me with hardened eyes showing little or no emotion, or love for that matter, for his local, sitting-in-the-courtroom fish and game warden. "Your Honor, We the Jury find the defendants guilty as charged. And we wish to compliment Officer Grosz for protecting the resources of this county from the likes of the defendants and their kin sitting in this here courtroom! The game warden was correct in his assertions that the game of this county belongs to the people of Colusa County and their kids. And anyone taking our game illegally needs to go to jail and the key needs to be thrown away." Then my deer spotlighting, previously-convicted jury foreman sat back down. But, not before giving me a slight smile. But, just a slight smile that I doubt anyone else in the courtroom caught...

With those remarks, Judge Gibson found the deer-killing McVeys and their kin guilty on four counts of violating the fish and game code. Guilty for the use and aid of an artificial light to take a game animal, possession of a loaded rifle in a motor vehicle on a way open to the public, trespassing, and illegal possession of a game animal. He then pronounced sentence and fined each of the four culprits $750! He also sentenced them to a year in jail and then suspended that sentence, providing none of them ever got caught for any fish and game violations in Colusa County again. The rifle, spotlight and the deer were forfeited to the state as well.

Then my wet-legged, gutless prosecutor was all proud of himself over his win. Hell, it was handed to him. I never again encountered the McVeys or their kin in my western back county breaking the fish and game laws involving mule deer. Elsewhere, yes. Especially in adjoining Butte and Sutter counties when the Sacramento River flooded over its banks in the winter, inundating hundreds of square miles of the valley's floor and, in so doing, blurring county lines and private property boundaries, especially as it related to waterfowl over limits and other related fish and game violations. But never in my backcountry in Judge Gibson's Judicial District ever again. Like I said, members of that clan were some very cagey outlaws. And the judge's words of warning about jail time, especially if ever apprehended and found guilty in his judicial district again, did not go unheard or unheeded.

For those next three years as a state fish and game warden assigned to Colusa County, I worked my night shooting deer poachers every lick I could. Using an artificial light to take a big game animal I considered a very serious wildlife offense. Hence, the many long hours I spent working in addressing such issues during the summer months of the year. It always amazed me as to the ingenuity many of my outlaws exhibited to duck a swipe from the long arm of the law. And to be frank, many more than I caught got away through ingenious or lucky means. Be it a locked gate they got behind before I could put the snatch on them, going to ground, or just "pure-dee" stinking luck, vanishing from sight on one of the areas' many back roads. But I knew for a fact, many I missed on the first go round, I ran to ground later. After all, hunting the lawless was the name of that deadly serious game. Catching on the other hand, well, that was a bonus!

When I was a game warden for the State of California, its statewide officer corps averaged six deer spotlighters per officer per year statewide. My average per year was thirty-eight with no losses in a court of law! I would say I caught my fair share of those who were heavy on their trigger fingers taking a big game animal while using an artificial light and were slow of step...

Cliff Fulton, my dear friend and longtime deputy game warden sidekick, has long since crossed over the Great Divide. So have other dear friends like, Deputy Sheriff Carter Bowman and Judge Gibson. All those men were not only great public servants but American Patriots as well. Rest in peace, my brothers, I will be along shortly. Then if the good Lord needs some great catch dogs for those outlaws who have somehow slipped under the good Lord's heavenly fence and are shooting His angels during the closed season, He will have four of the best badge carrying hunters of violators on hand. My guess, if that is the case, our first catches of those outlaws shooting angels during the closed season with the use and aid of an artificial light, will be someone from the McVey Clan...

Chapter Three: Butte Creek

In the eastern portion of my assigned fish and game law enforcement patrol district running between Colusa, Butte and Sutter Counties in the Northern Sacramento Valley, runs a rather large natural waterway named Butte Creek. Historically, that waterway has been very well utilized by day and night fishermen because of its excellent warm water game fish fishery. Several species of catfish, along with crappie, carp, largemouth bass, bullfrogs, and even the occasional lost migrating, summer run, king salmon from the Sacramento River are found therein. After my arrival as the local Colusa game warden, I discovered numerous county residents and Bay Area fishermen frequented that fishery throughout the year because of its great producing fishery and its excellent public access. Therein came the rub. Anytime you mix an area rich in wildlife related resources and human beings, many times bad things will happen to the critters. In the attendant situation, the occasional use of gill nets, frogging over limits, drop, set, and twig lines were just a few of the frequent illegal evil visitors to the area. Not so much during the daylight hours but when darkness fell, out from under the rocks came the bad guys, or what I called the creepers, to do in the critters. Oh, and I might mention, one onto-their-little game tule creeper, or game warden type, who was many times found lurking in the bushes as a constant visitor as well. But, a most beautiful and amply configured game warden by anyone's highest of standards, of course...

THE UNUSED BOAT

Dropping south one evening late onto Butte Creek from the Gridley Highway, I began checking my numerous warm water game fishermen. At first, no big deal. I had a ton of Bay Area fishermen that Saturday hoping for the big catfish and a number of locals fishing for the excellent eating crappie. Those were the times I loved the most when I got to visit and chew the fat with the variety of members from my fishing community. They were a good-natured lot of human beings unto themselves and generally honest as Old Abe when it came to their sport. Oh, there were always those who didn't have a fishing license, couldn't count past the one pole restriction, or flunked Mrs. Wilson's third grade math class when it came to counting their catch to make sure they didn't exceed their bag limits, but those were generally small potatoes. Overall, we all had a good time, as did the always happily present, Colusa County, B-52-bomber-sized mosquitoes when it came to visiting all us slow moving warm-blooded targets.

About six in the evening on that particular Saturday, I chanced upon two lads who, from the sounds of their drawl, were from the Deep South (clue No. 1). They had a nice camp set up alongside Butte Creek, had a smoky fire going for the mosquitoes' benefit and, as it turned out, were out of chewing tobacco. I saw to it they got a pouch of chew from my stash since I always carried extra in my patrol truck and then the three of us had a nice, laid back visit. As I made ready to leave, I walked by their four large tackle boxes (clue No. 2). Two were wide open and I noticed one was clear full of used spark plugs and the other loaded with several large spools of heavy monofilament fishing line (clue No. 3). Walking by their vehicle, I noticed it was licensed in Arkansas (clue No. 4). Remember me writing in an earlier chapter about the common use and great value of profiling done by many of us law enforcement officers? Well... Getting back into my vehicle, I continued my patrol downstream after a friendly wave of my hand to the Southern fishermen. They waved back and it was about then that I passed a small wooden boat tied to the shore some thirty yards or so below their camp as I drove downstream to continue my patrol (clue No. 5). To all my readers, once again, notice the type of profiling I am using. Is there anything wrong or illegal to your way of thinking, political correctness or whatever, for what I have done as of yet? I ask because there is such an uproar in our weak-kneed society in 2013 among the liberal Democrats about law enforcement officers profiling. Especially among those politicals residing in the major cities strung along the west and east coasts of the United States. And, I sure as hell don't want to offend anyone's sensibilities because that and a five dollar bill will get you a cup of coffee in this damn day and age in our society...

After driving downstream about half a mile on an old farm road that paralleled Butte Creek, I stopped. Sitting there, I began running through my mind the profiling problem indicators I had just stumbled upon at my last fishermen's camp. My lads were from the Deep South, the land where the use of drop, twig, or setlines is often officially condoned. Fishing with such techniques weren't legal in California in those days but in some parts of the South, as I said, it was legal and allowed. Additionally, there really was no need or use for four large tackle boxes full of gear on Butte Creek. All one needed was essentially a gob of worms and a package of Eagle Claw® No. 4 sized hooks and you were set for whatever swam in Butte Creek. To my way of thinking, all those used spark plugs in the one tackle box I had observed were a dead giveaway for a common crime found on my warm water game fish waterways. Many times previously, I had discovered drop or twig lines being illegally used along Butte Creek that commonly utilized old spark plugs for sinkers. The reason being, they were cheaper to lose than commercially purchased, heavy lead sinkers when you snagged and lost your terminal gear on an underwater obstruction. The large spools of heavy monofilament line observed in the other open tackle box rang another profiling bell as well. Previously when I discovered other chaps running illegal setlines, or tied-off lines running from bank to bank, they needed large spools of heavy monofilament line to be used as their main, bank-to-bank line. In this current situation, Butte Creek was anywhere from forty to seventy feet wide. Hence, trailing downstream off a proper setline attached at appropriate intervals running from the heavy main line would be lighter, baited fishing lines that were individually weighted with single old spark plugs. Next, I noticed the lads had oodles and oodles of bait on hand, yet they were only running two fishing poles in camp. So, with only two poles, there was no need for the small mountains of bait they openly possessed. But on a setline or a series of setlines, all trailing numerous individual fishing lines and hooks, a great amount of bait would be required. Lastly, they had a small boat with a motor. The best fishing was midstream from a boat tied to a log or a partially sunken tree limb out in Butte Creek. Why were they only bank fishing when I first met them? My guess was the lads had set lines out and only used the boat to run those lines, which would have been anchored from bank to bank. Hence the need for a boat in order to set the original set lines, bait numerous hooks, check those lines periodically, retrieve fish taken in such a manner and if that particular line was not producing, move said line in its entirety to a more promising fish-catching location.

I realize that many of you readers are now thinking I had stereotyped my Southern fishermen. And in a sense, I guess one could say I was using a form of wildlife related, culturally based, human profiling. However, conservation laws are just that. They are meant to conserve our vanishing natural resources, which, by the way, are truly limited. Remember, we always had more buffalo or passenger pigeons just over the next ridge in the days of old. That was until we had run out of ridges... My feelings regarding the above profiling political correctness nonsense crap rift throughout our current day society is this. Get the job done, just as long as your actions conform to the laws of the land, the U.S. Bill of Rights, and the U.S. Constitution. Other than that, damn the torpedoes and full steam ahead. Remember, there are hawks and doves culturally scattered throughout our society. Well, folks, as you can clearly tell, these words you are reading are being written by a human being who considers himself an eagle! Especially when it came to enforcing the wildlife laws of the land for those folks yet to come. That is, if you get my politically incorrect drift!

With all those potential indicator factors and a subsequent battle plan fast forming in my mind, I got on my fish and game radio and called the Colusa County Sheriff's Office. There I requested they call my bride and let her know I wouldn't be home any time soon. I did so because when one is going to work a possible set line case, that officer best plan on spending many long hours on a continuous stakeout in order to gather the evidence needed to successfully prosecute such a major criminal investigation. With that housekeeping chore under my belt, I hotfooted it down a mess of farm roads to Laux Road. From there I headed east and was able to cross over Butte Creek into Butte County. Taking a number of smaller farm roads once again, I headed back north toward my suspect Southern fishermen's camp. Only this time, I was on the opposite side of Butte Creek and hoped to sneak in and take up a hidden stake out position just across from my suspect fishermen's camp. That way, I could run or sneak unencumbered alongside brushy Butte Creek on the opposite side when they traversed it in their boat and lessened my chances in the darkness of being discovered. If they ran any set, drop, or twig lines, I would be almost on top of the action and would have the evidence needed in a court of law regarding any regulatory wrongdoing. Remember, in a criminal court action, which this had the potential to become, the officer has to be able to prove his case beyond a reasonable doubt. You do that by exhibiting the best evidence in a court of law. That means presenting personal knowledge or observations of the illegal act being performed by the accused, along with the physical objects used in the violation of the law. Lastly, that also included any fruits of the crime or critters they may have illegally captured.

Parking my patrol truck in an out of view location, I grabbed my notebook, binoculars, chewing tobacco, flashlight, fingernail clippers (I knew you unwashed would inquire about the inclusion of that item), canteen full of drinking water (before commercially available bottled drinking water), and a full can of Off™ Mosquito Spray. Then I trotted a quarter mile north until I was quietly hidden just across from my two suspicious, to my way of thinking, Southern lads. If I didn't catch these chaps doing what I think they will be doing, I am going to look pretty damn silly in the eyes of you more liberal politically-correct readers, am I not? Well, just remember, a guy doesn't get as big as I am by being last in the chow line...

For the longest time, nothing out of the ordinary or illegal happened. My chaps smoked, fished, and chewed the fat. About nine at night, as I watched through my binoculars, they retrieved their boat from below their camp, put two tackle boxes into it and a bucket holding a ton of stink bait. With that, they slowly motored their ways downstream. As they moved downstream, I followed out of sight on foot along the east bank of Butte Creek keeping my distance a short ways behind them. About a hundred yards below their camp, they swung their boat over to my side of Butte Creek. When they did, I soon found myself laying in a dense stand of willows as my chaps nosed their boat into shore right below where I now lay hidden by the cloak of darkness. With one chap running the motor holding the boat in place against the slow moving current, the bow lad leaned over the bow, reached deeply into the water and lifted up a long, heavy, monofilament set line. That line was attached to a large, heavy root at the base of the willows. Hanging onto the line, the bow lad slowly pulled the boat across Butte Creek as he checked his numerous individual illegal drop lines attached to and running off the main line. That action was facilitated by the motorman keeping the boat and motor slowly running just below the main line pushing gently against the current. That was necessary so the bow man could easily work the individual drop lines without putting too much of a strain on the main line with the dragging-weight of the boat wanting to drift downstream. It was pretty obvious from the men's smoothly rehearsed actions, that they had done this type of illegal endeavor many times before.

The main set line was composed of a very heavy monofilament line. Every few feet or so there would be a lighter line attached to a loop in the main line. As my chaps moved their boat slowly across the creek, the bowman would pull up each individual drop line checking for a fish. If he had a good eating fish on the line, it was removed and placed into a gunnysack laying in the bottom of their boat. Then the hook was baited and dropped back into the water. On the end of that line tied below the hook was a used spark plug acting as a sinker. That line checking action was to be repeated all the way across Butte Creek. In so doing, I counted the bowman working twenty drop lines and hooks off that main line. Once that action was completed, my lad in the bow let go of the line and the boat drifted slowly downstream a short distance. Then the stern man turned the boat around and motored slowly downstream once again. As they did, they stayed in the middle of Butte Creek where, if one was running a setline, it would be the deepest under water at that point. That way, their prop would not cut their main line on the next set line below them which, as I soon discovered, was another major line running from bank to bank.

About forty yards farther downstream, the lads nosed their boat over to the bank on my side of Butte Creek once again. Another submerged setline was lifted from underneath the water where it had been tied to a large tree root. The earlier line-checking process was repeated. This action was repeated several more times until the lads had run all of their set lines. Observing all of this, I had counted at least one hundred twenty drop lines running off those seven main set lines being used in the light of their on board lantern! And by now, they had taken a huge load of fish of all species. Those the lads considered eatable, they kept. The poorer eating carp and suckers were tossed back into the creek after being unhooked. Finished, my lads quietly motored upstream as I followed trotting behind them out of sight in the dark along a farm road running on the opposite creek bank. When they motored upstream, they were careful to stay in the middle of the creek and up on step. That way they rode over the deepest part of their setlines once again and avoided cutting the numerous main lines with their propeller. About thirty yards downstream below their camp they nosed their boat quietly into the bank. With that, the bow lad got out and slowly ambled back to their camp. Once there, he took a long look around making sure the coast was clear. Satisfied all was clear, with a flashlight he signaled his buddy in the boat who then motored quietly into their camp. There they unloaded a gunnysack partially full of fish and the rest of their gear. Then the lad running the boat took it back downstream so it wouldn't attract any undue attention and anchored it once again below their campsite.

Back at camp, the two men hurriedly filleted out their fish, tossing the filet meat into an ice chest which had been recently removed from the back of their camper. Once done, that ice chest of fillets quickly went back into their camper like nobody's business. Then the bucket of fish offal was taken a short ways downstream and dumped into Butte Creek from the bank for the other fish and crawdads to eat and enjoy. And in so doing, cleverly the men had rid themselves of any damning over the limit evidence as could have been indicated by a large gut pile at or near their campsite.

Pretty damn slick operation, I thought. That was, except for one small thing. There is a tule creeper on the opposite side of Butte Creek watching and recording your whole illegal operation. Then I waited. During that wait time, I discovered my lads were running their lines every hour on the hour. After establishing that fact, I set into motion my Plan B. Walking back downstream to the first setline's location, I stripped down until I was as naked as a baby jaybird, much to the delight of the always-present mosquitoes. With that, I carefully slipped down the muddy bank and into the dark water of the creek just below that first set line. Knowing it had been fishing the longest, I figured it had the best opportunity to catch fish during that hourly period of time between being tended. Careful to avoid the trailing hooks attached to the main line running from bank to bank, I slowly worked my way across that line pulling myself hand over hand as I paddled my feet against the slow moving current. Stopping at each hooked line, I checked for any fish. Those lines holding any fish were brought up. Then looping my arm over the main line as I paddled with my feet vigorously to reduce the current's drag against my most magnificent body, I took the fingernail clippers from my mouth and clipped that hooked evidence fish's caudal fin. Now you readers can see why I brought those darn fingernail clippers along. That way with marked fish on the line and later in their catch bag, I had a much stronger case, especially when I finally dropped the hammer on my Southern friends. I got fish clipped on two more trailing setlines before I was interrupted in my work by the quiet sound of my Southern lads outboard motor coming slowly downstream. Hearing that defining sound, I had to quickly scramble back ashore on my side of the creek to avoid detection from my boatmen who had returned to check their lines just upstream from my position downstream checking for any more fish on the next following line of the series.

Lying there on the bank all bare naked and not being able to move because my illegal fishermen were so close at hand, the mosquitoes had a field day working over the backside of my fairly large but most beautiful carcass. However, I got more firsthand illegal-fishing information that just further corroborated and strengthened my case as my outlaws continued their activity working their illegal set lines directly to my front.

Figuring I had enough evidence, I waited until my lads had checked their last setline in the series and returned back to their camp. Then I thankfully dressed as I cussed a million mosquitoes buzzing around me, who by now had put out the word to their kin that a rather large and defenseless warm-blooded carcass of monstrous proportions was close at hand... Following that, I trotted back to my patrol truck. Speeding south, then across Butte Creek and back to a hiding place just below my chaps' fishing camp, I lurked in the bushes ready to execute the rest of my Plan B ambush. When they finally returned from checking their set lines the next time, I let them go through their little check out their camp first routine. When my boatman arrived with their burlap bag partially full of fish, I let him bring it ashore. That chore finished, my one boatman left to go and hide the boat. When he returned and the two of them began filleting out that last sackful of fish, I made my grand "Robert Redford the beautiful" entrance. You know, it is really hell being so beautiful and wonderfully bountiful in size all at the same time...

Well, you talk about being the one at the party finding the dead frog in the senior prom punch bowl. I was that critter. Stepping out from the bushes as quiet as a mouse, well, maybe a rather large meadow mouse, I said, "Good morning, Lads. How is the fishing?" Man, from their reactions to my voice, you would have thought I had just gut-shot the pair! One man damned near jumped back into Butte Creek, and the other hurriedly rose, stumbled on the ring of rocks around their fire and then fell over backwards from his filleting duties butt first into their campfire with a loud "Oof!" Realizing where his bottom was located and now smelling it cooking, my testing the heat of the campfire chap went airborne from a flat sitting position. That had to be the only time I ever saw a human being go from zero-to-sixty in one fluid motion and then defy gravity by flying straight up into the air from a sitting position! However, his aerial trajectory was poor and he once again dropped straight back into the fire with a resounding crump! He managed on the second try to quit frying his backside and got the hell out from that fire in a rather ungraceful rolling move. But from the amount of smoke coming from his backside, I would say he lingered in the fire longer than he probably should have...

When the lads finally regained their composure, they both started eating out my last part over the fence for sneaking up and scaring the hell out of them. As they did that bit of hollering at me, I could see one of the men regaining his composure and quietly trying to scoot the partially full gunnysack of recently caught, illegal fish with his foot back into Butte Creek so they would be out of sight and out of mind. Quickly stepping between that man and the bag of fish before he compounded their evening's troubles, I scooped up the sack half full of still flopping warm water game fish.

Hauling the sackful of fish up onto a safer place, I said, "Well, well, well. It looks like you lads have done quite well fishing here this evening. Let me see what you lads have caught," as I emptied out their sack of flopping fish. When the quick count was over, they had exceeded the bag limit for crappie and largemouth bass. The fish were then quickly returned to the bag, a rope tied around the opening so the fish could not escape and then tied to a nearby tree. Finished with that chore, the tied-off bag was returned to Butte Creek so that many of the fish could live until I had finished with my guys. "Well, Gentlemen," I continued. "We have a slight problem here. You have a few too many species of fish for what the law allows. May I see some driver's and fishing licenses, please?" Without a sound other than the one man continuing to beat out the hot spots on his still smoking hind end, the two men hastily dug into their overalls as they got out their wallets. Surprisingly, they were all too happy to show me their licenses. Gee, I wonder why f I thought, with a knowing smile. Anytime anyone is all too eager to comply with an officer of the law, that law dog should more than be on his toes. That kind of behavior usually signals that there is something else wrong. Hell, even my retired FBI friends, Bill and Tony in Bismarck, North Dakota, would call that a clue.

Taking my two chaps and their driver's licenses, we walked back to my patrol truck. A quick call to the Colusa County Sheriff's Office was later to produce one Deputy Del Garrison, dear friend and a lad equally as large as me, if not a tad bigger. But, I was still the prettier of the two or us in comparison... With my call into the sheriff's office for prisoner transport finished, I took my crestfallen lads back to their camper.

All at once, the devil got into me, which was pretty easy in those days of my youth, and I got a crazy idea. I figured I would pull my super nose trick guaranteed to get their tongues wagging once they were both back at work as to the sharp sensed prowess of California game wardens.

"Say, Lads. Do you smell that?" I asked.

"Smell what?" both of my fellows asked in unison.

"I can't figure it out. I can clearly smell freshly filleted fish. You know, like ones that are in an ice chest, iced down and all," I said with a very serious, wrinkled up, still sniffing nose. And, what a magnificent looking Romanesque nose it was, I might add.

The skinny one of the two said, "I don't smell no damn fish. Hell, I couldn't even smell those in the gunnysack earlier because of all the mosquito spray we are using."

"Me neither," said his partner but with just a touch of worry creeping into the tone and tenor of his voice.

Then I made a big deal of smelling loudly all around their camp like I was trying to find those mystery-filleted fish. Man, to an outsider, I sure had to look like a damn fool walking bent over and sniffing all around like a blue-tick hound hot on the fresh trail of a black bear. Finishing those crazy but necessary antics for the next move I had in mind, I abruptly walked to the back of their camper and took a deep whiff with my rather large, but extremely handsome, Romanesque nose. "Damn, Boys. Those fish I am smelling must be in this camper. Man, can't you guys smell them? Those mystery fish are smelling stronger than all get out when I get next to this camper," I continued, trying hard not to laugh, especially after looking at the disbelief written all over my lad's collective faces. Especially as I continued making a darned fool of myself through my exaggerated sniffing actions with my more than handsome proboscis.

The skinny one, realizing I must be smelling the fish in the ice chest inside the camper, responded hopefully trying to throw me off the trail by saying, "I cain't smell a damn thing, Officer. Maybe what you smell is dried fish slime on the door handle to my camper." He knew that if I ever got into that ice chest in the camper, they were going to be up to their gills in the proverbial brown stuff normally found on the bottom of one's shoes in a public park where everyone is walking their dogs without a pooper-scooper. Especially when it came to their huge over limits contained in the ice chest therein.

Then the larger of my two chaps said, "Officer, I ain't trying to be a smart ass, but how the hell can you smell fish that you think have been filleted? Especially with all the smoke from our campfire, the Off! mosquito spray we have been using by the gallon and the fact we two ain't bathed in several days."

"No offenses taken, my friend," I said. "In answer to your question, we are taught at the fish and game academy to smell out contraband like too many fish, especially those fish that have been radically altered, like being filleted. Because once filleted, the fish's cell tissues are damaged and they lose some of their life giving fluids. Once that happens, those fluids deteriorate very rapidly and give off that unusual smell that I am now smelling. They teach us that technique because illegal filleted fish can be more easily hidden. And as I said earlier, fish that have been filleted out have a unique smell because of the cell tissues being ruptured with their life's juices leaking out, which soon starts the deterioration process."

How was that explanation for being nothing more than a bucket of horse pucky? Brother, you should have seen the looks of disbelief flying back and forth between those two men. They were priceless! Then came the hammer. "Lads, I need you to open up that camper so I can take a better smell." Then I just looked long and hard at the skinny one who had earlier hidden the ice chest full of previously filleted fish in the camper. Finally, he opened up the camper door, all the while looking like a cottontail rabbit with no place to run after being set upon by a hungry long tailed weasel in the dead of winter with no warren close at hand. As he stood back from the open door, I stepped forward and took another deeply exaggerated smelling whiff.

"Whew-ee! That's it!" I yelled. When I yelled, both men jumped like the proverbial June bug just spotted by a hungry chicken. "That is where the smell of fillets is coming from," I hissed loudly. "Drag out that ice chest," I barked to the skinny one. To those of you from San Francisco still smarting over my earlier profiling tendencies, getting into that camper with a voice command was not an illegal search under the Fourth Amendment to the U.S. Constitution. Remember when I had observed the lads earlier filleting out their catch, putting them into the ice chest, and then placing the chest back into the camper? That visual evidence was all I needed for a legal warrantless search conducted within the Fourth Amendment guidelines to occur. Brother, it was a good thing I wasn't standing in the doorway when I gave that command to open up the door to the camper. By now, I had my guys convinced about my super powers of smell and the skinny one couldn't drag out that ice chest fast enough.

Once out on the ground, I slowly opened the lid on the ice chest for the effect it had to be having on the two guilty men. Once open, there lay about eighty fillets from various assorted species and sizes of warm water game fish! With that revelation, you could have heard a pigmy shrew passing gas in a Type 5 tornado in eastern Oklahoma in April at a thousand yards as it tore through a farmyard full of loudly objecting Rhode Island Red chickens who were in the process of losing all their feathers in the high cyclonic winds...

About then, my buddy, Deputy Sheriff Del Garrison, pulled into the fish camp. Extracting his huge frame from the patrol car, he walked over to me saying, "What kind of business do you have for me this fine morning, Little Buddy?" Many of you regular readers will remember this often-used deputy's name. Del had a large family and found it necessary to work every available shift he could in order to make ends meet. Therefore, he was almost always the one on the east side of my patrol district responding to my calls for backup or prisoner transport. Del later died of complications from diabetes. He was my dear friend and a good Christian man. And to this day, I am still saddened because I never got to tell him good-bye before they drugged him to ease his pain during his final moments. I called Del in the hospital the following morning when I had gotten up enough backbone to tell a dear friend I would meet him on the other side. But, I was too late. I was informed by a nurse that he had just passed... I sure hoped the good Lord took a liking to him because I sure as hell thought the world of him.

"Gentlemen," I said. "This is Deputy Sheriff Del Garrison. I asked him to provide some support to me this morning."

"Del," I said, "Here is the picture. These two chaps have been running a series of seven setlines across Butte Creek. I have been watching them for several hours and have all the evidence I need pertaining to this case. That is why I called for some backup. I need you to watch over one of these lads, my evidence sack of fish in the water and cooler full of previously fillet fish. In the meantime, I will take the other man and their boat back downstream. There I will pull those seven setlines and return. In the meantime, would you call Joe Willow and ask him to come up here and tow their camper into the impound lot because these lads are going to be booked for their fish and game violations. But have him wait until I return so he can take their boat and motor also."

"I think I can handle that," said Garrison with a big grin.

Then as an afterthought, I retrieved the sack of the most recently caught fish. In it were my eleven fin-clipped catfish and largemouth bass. Once identified from all the rest of the fish, I showed the now very quiet fishermen the clipped caudal fins on my evidence fish. Then I explained how I had swum along the lines fin clipping the fish so I could have marked evidence in their catch bag. More silence followed that telling revelation. Then the sack of fish was returned to the water for safekeeping.

Asking the heavyset set man to come along with me and run their boat, we began walking downstream to where it was anchored. On the way down the man remarked, "You have us, Officer. We was runnin' the lines in the hopes of catching enough fish to sell to the Chinamen in Yuba City to be used in their restaurant business. Then we would have enough money to pay for gas and food to get us back home. We was here lookin' fer jobs at the Navy shipyard at Alameda. But there wasn't none. So, all we could find in the way of work was nothing but odd jobs. Now it looks like getting home may take us awhile longer."

"Well, that is up to the judge. And the fine in this county is pretty steep for running set lines because it is such a serious offense," I said.

"How much do ya think that will be?" he asked with a worried look.

"Well, the minimum bail is $25 for the violation and $10 per hook," I responded.

"Whoo-ee!" he said. "It may be a spell afore we are able to git home," he quietly uttered in a subdued tone of voice.

With that, we boarded the boat and headed downstream. I just let him guide me into the lines to add to my evidence gathering, particularly when it came to showing his culpability or knowledge of the violation and of the individual locations of each and every set line.

Then the two of us tended the seven setlines. First, I removed all the live fish and returned them back to Butte Creek after recording their numbers and species in my notebook. Then I wrapped up each setline into a separate bundle after recording the numbers of hooks per line in my notebook. When finished, we headed back upstream to my lad's fish camp.

Once there, it was like old home week. Garrison and Joe Willow were there as well as Joel McDermott, the Colusa County Under Sheriff. Together we counted out the hooks on the setlines again just to make sure of their numbers. They came to 123 hooks! Then we counted out all the fish and fillets as best as we could. My fellows from Arkansas certainly knew what they were doing when it came to running a setline. Between the fillets and whole fish, they had

51 assorted catfish, 22 largemouth bass, some up to five pounds or more, 36 crappie, and one monster-sized rainbow trout! Those fish still alive from the sack that looked like they would make it were returned back to Butte Creek so they could live another day. Those in worse shape, looking like they would not live because they had been too deeply hooked and roughly handled, were kept as evidence.

While Joe hooked up my lads' camper plus their boat and Del searched and handcuffed the prisoners, I tended to my evidence. We then caravanned back to Colusa where the prisoners were booked in the county jail. The following day, my prisoners were arraigned in the Colusa Justice Court, entered their guilty pleas, and were found guilty by the judge. Bail was set at $1,000 each, and the courts arranged for a payment schedule so my lads could make bail and go out and find work in order to pay off their fines. Their boat and motor, being held by the court as collateral, were eventually returned after they paid their fines. As for the mess of fish, I gave them to four needy families in towns of Colusa and Williams.

I am told that by 2010, that was still the largest set line case ever made in Colusa County to the present. Not bad for a broken down ol' tule creeper who spotted some tackle boxes with a suspicious looking mess of used spark plugs, spools of heavy monofilament line, buckets of stink bait, a raft full of fishing hooks and a little politically incorrect profiling—to some folks way of thinking—of a couple of Southern fishermen. They called that particular case: Lions 2 and Christians Nothing...

FROGS AND A WHOLE LOT MORE

One late spring morning, yours truly and the ever present Colusa County B-52 bomber sized mosquitoes were patrolling the east side of my law enforcement district. While there, I chanced upon a trio of African American lads running raccoons with their hounds. Stopping to check the lads for their hunting licenses and see how they were doing, my time with them soon progressed into a rather unique moment. That was except for the high-speed deadly incident with Mr. Raccoon that soon followed. After checking my lads for their hunting licenses, they pointed out their dilemma as they stood around the edge of a thirty-yards-wide and ten-feet- deep, brush-filled canal. They had an exceptionally large, madder- than-a-wet-hen boar raccoon trapped twenty yards out on a log in a deep and brushy portion of a canal named Drumheller Slough. The lads were afraid to let their valuable dogs go into the deep water after the raccoon for fear he would drown them in the ensuing battle. Based on my life-history knowledge of raccoons and their fighting temperament when aroused or cornered, especially in deep water by dogs, that decision to not loose the hounds was great survival thinking on the part of their owners. For you unwashed folks from San Francisco, a madder-than-all-get-out boar raccoon is nothing more than a cross between a hungry tiger shark and a mess of aroused Africanized bees. Plus, boar raccoons of the size and temperament of the one they had trapped on that log had a time-honored fighting technique learned from an early age that was almost genetic in nature. Any pursuing dog foolish enough to tackle such a predator in deep water, would soon find himself in the process of being drowned in fine style—drowned in fine style, because the raccoon's tried and true battle technique was to wait until a dog swam within grabbing distance, then jump onto its head and hold it under water until it drowned. That way, the raccoon could drown one dog, while fighting off the others from its position on the drowning dog's head. Plain and simple, raccoon one, dogs zero! Additionally, all my sports were too damned scared to strip down and swim out in the dark canal waters in order to physically dislodge the cornered beast from behind his protective log so their dogs could have another go at the raccoon on better fighting ground. Further discussion with my chaps revealed that the plan after killing and recovering the raccoon, was to eat the beast and sell his hide to a fur buyer for the few dollars it would bring. Walking down to the water's edge, I could see why they had a problem. The raccoon was huge and pissed! He was hanging onto the back side of a big floating log and peering over the top just daring the houndsmen to let loose their dogs into his environment. All one could see twenty yards out into the dark canal with the aid of a flashlight was the log, a flashing set of eyes, and a mouth full of bared teeth that would have made a great white shark proud. Not to be denied, my lads had been shooting at the small target of the head of the raccoon for the last ten minutes using up about fifty rounds of .22 ammunition. As I soon discovered, all that shooting had been to no avail. It turned out, there wasn't an accurate shooter in the bunch. No Buffalo Bill Cody in that modern day bunch of shooters. Hence, the still pissed off raccoon hanging onto the floating log for dear life, a pack of hounds along the shoreline howling like all get out wanting to be let loose so they could continue the fight, and a floating log full of .22 caliber bullet holes.

"Misser Game Warden, would you shoot that damn ole coon for us? Them is good eats and we'uns jus hates to leave him there after runnin' him so hard," said one of the men to me in his deep, hard to understand Southern drawl over the baying of the hounds.

Well, I was a pretty damn good shot with a handgun, but man, that damn raccoon didn't leave me much of a target. Twenty yards away and just the top part of his head sticking up over that big ol' log was my target, if I chose to show the lads that I was not Little Miss Sure Shot or Annie Oakley of Buffalo Bill's Wild West Circus fame. "Well, let me try," I finally said, after several more good-natured requests for my official assistance. With that, I unlimbered my Colt Commander .45 ACP club. Now the sights on those old Colts were not that good. I had factory sights on that gun which made it essentially a close range, point-and-shoot weapon at best. It was not like my Smith and Wesson, Model 29, 6 1/2-inch .44 magnum that I usually carried. Hell, I could kill a running human at one hundred yards with that magnum hand cannon while using full house factory loads! In fact, during all my required handgun qualifications, I always shot Distinguished Expert with that artillery piece. But alas, my Dirty Harry was in the shop having a cylinder realignment since I had shot so many rounds through it that it was now uncomfortably shaving and spitting lead every time I pulled the trigger. With that cannon, all I had to do was hit the log and its concussion would kill every living creature within a mile...well, maybe half a mile.

Taking careful aim over the sounds of their still madly baying hounds, I squeezed my club-sighted .45 off.

Boom, and with that, the raccoon disappeared from behind his log! Immediately into the water went three of the men's pack of hounds, all wound up and mad with excitement at seeing the raccoon disappear! Moments later, they brought the huge, deader than a hammer, boar raccoon ashore. Brother, you talk about a bunch of happy Black Americans. They were flat beside themselves over finally having that monster raccoon, which must have weighed about thirty five pounds, in their possession! Then the men who had gathered around the dead raccoon looking happily on at their prize moments earlier, went suddenly silent as Count Dracula's graveyard during a full moon on Halloween in Transylvania.

"What is the matter?" I finally asked over their collective silent as death reactions.

Every one of my houndsmen just stood there looking at me like I was a ghost saying nothing. Not being able to figure out the reason for their goofy damn behavior followed by their abject silence, I walked over to the man standing nearest to the dead raccoon. Looking to see where I had hit the animal, I saw I had hit the beast squarely between the eyes! I swear, that .45-caliber round hole was not one millimeter off dead center from between that critter's eyes! I couldn't have done any better if I had taken a bench rest and used a rifle with a scope! But for those houndsmen from the Bay Area, I could just see what was going through their minds, especially since there was so much unrest in the larger California cities in the 1960s between the law enforcement folks and some of the more radical members of the black communities. Unrest in the form of a lot of cracked heads and people shot when messing with the law during those trying and turbulent periods. "Here is an officer, boys, you do not want to mess with. For if you do, he will put a bullet squarely right between your eyes just as sure as he did this here raccoon," finally said one of the men quietly for the others benefit...

Hearing those words and realizing what they had to be thinking, I had to laugh to myself. There is no way in the world I could have duplicated that shot with my Colt club. But those guys didn't know that! From then on when I ran across this trio of hounds' men hunting in my area, they were always perfect gentlemen. Maybe that was because when I saw the bullet hole in the raccoon, I had casually commented that I was a little off dead center and would try to do better the next time we met under like circumstances...

Leaving my now very happy, good-natured trio of raccoon hunters with meat in the pot and a mangy hide to sell, I headed south wanting to take a look at some of my warm water fishermen along the nearby Butte Creek public fishing areas. I had hardly gotten going when I noticed some bright lights flashing high into the air behind the old California Duck Club. Froggers, ran through my mind having seen that kind of massive light reflection off the water many times before. Trying to figure out how to get to my froggers so I could check them out for licenses and such, I began running down every muddy farm road leading in the direction of the suspect lights. Still no luck. Whoever they were, they were sure as the dickens off the beaten path. They weren't in Butte Creek proper but appeared to be off in some adjacent remote feeder waterway. Finally dead-ending on another muddy farm road, I saw I was going to have to hit shank's mare if I wanted to get to and check those folks suspected of frogging.

Calling Warden Bob Hawks on my radio because my lads of interest were at the edge of his law enforcement patrol district in Butte County, I didn't get any response. Calling ahead when in another officer's district was a common courtesy among game wardens so one wouldn't mess up anything that officer might have going. What did you expect? I asked myself. After all, it was 2:30 in the morning. Skirting a last year's muddy lima bean field, I headed out toward my lads last observed general location on foot. Anyone messing around so far out in the hush that the chickens out there had square faces at this time in the morning always deserved another look-see, I thought as I slogged along in the now calf deep mud and water. Before long, I was breathing hard with the weight of all the mud clinging to my hip boots and breaking out into a mosquito attracting sweat. But I kept slogging along, especially since I had just now heard a single shot! Not the booming sound a heavy rifle makes but the light, sharp cracking sound like a .22-caliber firearm would make. There sure as hell would be no need for shooting anything this time of the year in the location they are in unless it is another raccoon hunter or a trapper killing a beaver in a leg-hold trap, I thought. Now the mud was getting deeper as was the sheet water. Soon I found myself blocked by a larger marshy area. No way through that mess without swimming, I thought, and I sure as hell am in no mood for doing that this time of the year and at o-dark thirty in the morning out in the damn middle of nowhere.

Then I noticed my lights were now moving off in another direction. Now they were heading westerly back toward Butte Creek in Colusa County, the edge of my assigned law enforcement district. Stopping to get my breath and make doubly sure of their directional change, I continued watching the movement of the flashing lights. Sure as biscuits and gravy makes for a great breakfast, especially if the gravy is thick and heavy with sausage like

I usually made, my lights and the lads using them are probably now back in my district, I thought. Being able to move that fast means they are likely in some kind of a boat, I surmised as I once again changed my direction of travel to match theirs.

Retracing my steps, I headed back for my patrol truck. Once there, I kicked most of the mud off my hip boots, piled in, and headed back towards the White Mallard Duck Club. Later stopping and parking up onto that duck club's high levee, I got out and with my binoculars looked again for my flashing mystery lights. For the longest time I saw nothing. Then I began thinking maybe they had turned south and gone back down Butte Creek. With that thought in mind, I bailed into my truck and was just starting to leave when I once again saw my suspect lights dancing high into the heavens. The dancing lights were now in Drumheller Slough on the Colusa County side of my patrol district. You know, the same slough where I had made the lucky shot on that poor damn old raccoon earlier that morning.

Heading out and later parking my truck on another close-at-hand farm road, I took off toward my wildly flashing lights on shank's mare once again. Finally getting closer to my mystery lights, through my binoculars I saw one lad poling a small boat along the edge of the slough. Lying in the bow of the boat was another lad working a strong light along the northern bank of that slough. Creeping along (Yes, a guy my size can creep with the best of them. Darn you, Readers... Just because I am shaped like a pitcher's mound doesn't mean I move like one!), I was soon just yards away and directly behind my unsuspecting lads. Using my binoculars once again, I could see several gunnysacks laying in the bottom of their boat. And one gunnysack was really moving all around with something alive and wiggling inside like crazy! For the life of me, I couldn't figure out what would be in that moving sack. My frogger had a sack alongside his position in the bow of the boat for the just caught frogs, and there was another semi-full, tied-off burlap bag laying in the bottom of the boat probably full of frogs, but neither of those bags were moving around like the suspect sack. Moving in as close as I dared, I continued quietly walking out of sight just behind my chaps in the boat. Finally the lad working the pole in the stern of the boat headed for shore. Pulling the boat up onto the shoreline, he stepped out and began taking care of a call of nature. Figuring that was my cue to get my carcass into gear, I silently moved into their personal space.

"Good morning, Lads, state fish and game warden," I boomed out.

With that, my surprised man with his back towards me taking care of the call of nature, bolted, stumbled, and fell face first into the dirt. Jumping back up like a scalded cat, he started hollering at the top of his lungs! What the hell? I thought. Did he impale himself on a sharp stick when he fell or what?

Then my fellow wiggled all crazy like as he hopped around like a wounded jackrabbit, all the while hollering as if there was no tomorrow. Finally, he did something with the front of his pants and quit yelling as loudly as he had been earlier. But now he was loudly moaning. What the dickens is the matter with this chap? I thought as I began walking into their immediate area.

"You all right, Mister?" I inquired as I approached.

The man was holding the front of his jeans with both of his hands. And from the looks of it in the light of my flashlight, it was apparent he had wet all over himself when I had surprised him earlier in the act of urinating.

Then in his surprise and confusion of the moment, he tried to quickly zip up his fly. However, everything was not clear of the zipper. Jerking up his zipper at a high rate of speed because of my surprise entry, he had apparently taken a lot of skin along with it from that which had wetted him and was hanging out just moments earlier! Now he was a slightly bloody mess as well.

"State fish and game warden," I said again lamely. "Sorry for causing you to have an accident," I continued. By now, my chap was just doing the hop around dance. Damn, that must really hurt, catching himself in the zipper and all, I mused.

"When you quit hopping around, I would like to check your fishing license," I stated. "And that goes for you as well," I said to my man still in the boat. It was then I saw that he was trying to oddly maneuver one of the gunnysacks around in the bottom of the boat. From where I stood, it appeared like whatever it was, he wanted to dump its contents overboard into the canal, sight unseen in the darkness off the far side of their boat, if at all possible.

"Hold it right there!" I barked. "Don't touch that sack unless you want to go to jail," I commanded. With that, the man recoiled from the moving sack like a snake bit dog. Continuing, I said, "You in the boat. Get your carcass up here." Then in a flash my Colt .45 was in my hand as I saw my lad in the bow quickly reach for an almost sight unseen .22 pistol lying in the bottom of their boat next to where he had been sitting!

"Don't even think about touching that pistol, Lad. If you do, it will be your last remembrance of what it is like here on this planet," I growled! No idle threat. As I said earlier, I consistently shot Distinguished Expert with my .44 magnum. With the .45 at that distance, it was anyone's guess where the bullet would end up, but I had to growl like a smashed cat anyway!

With that, the lad dropped the pistol saying, "I was just going to put it up on the seat where it wouldn't get so wet," he said meekly.

Then, he exited the boat and walked up onto the levee where I stood. "You never ever reach for a gun when an officer is talking to you," I admonished. "Now, let's see some form of identification and a fishing license."

By now, my lad with the wet pants was through hopping around and produced a fishing license. Boy, my chaps' luck was all bad with the zipper incident and all. His fishing license was expired. My other lad did the same and his fishing license was not current either. As in the case at hand, when frogging, a current fishing license was required under California law.

"Lads, it seems you forgot to buy current fishing licenses," I said as I looked at both of my chaps. They said nothing and just balefully looked back at me. "Well, let's go and see what you have in the burlap sacks," I said. Just for an instant, I saw concern fly across my lads' eyes. Not a lot but enough to put me on high alert. "Either of you two packing any other heat?" I queried.

"No, Sir," came their two instant replies. Their quick responses were such and in a tone and tenor of voice, that I believed my two lads. Dang it. There I go again using some of my tricks of the trade when it came to profiling. As I said earlier in the book, profiling is a common trick of the trade used by many officers in the law enforcement profession. Bottom line, many times it serves in keeping one alive. In the current affair, a quick response to a question many times will validate the honesty of an answer. Hence, another trick of the trade put to good use when profiling an individual under stress.

"All right, let's go and look in those sacks. And while we are at it, don't either of you get near that pistol laying in the boat," I ordered.

Walking down the side of the levee to the boat, I could still see my one sack of interest moving around in the bottom of the boat like crazy. "Hand me that moving sack first," I said. Then holding the side of the boat so my lad could safely get back in, I picked up his pistol, unloaded it, and stuck it into the back of my belt with my free hand. My lad handed me the moving sack without saying a word. Well, well, well, another profiling trick of the trade. When one hands you some evidence of wrongdoing and has nothing to say, his silence relative to his level of guilt is many times deafening. Opening up the burlap bag and looking inside, I saw ten live, wiggling like all get out, wild ducks! Closer examination revealed that they had been crippled during the previous hunting season and were now just living along the canals and off the land as best as they could. Man, you talk about a bunch of sorrowful-looking quackers. It became apparent to me that my lads had caught such wounded and crippled ducks by hand, as they had frogged along the waterways. Opening the bag and laying it on the bank, the ducks quickly funneled out and waddled back into the slough to whatever life they could eke out. No two ways about it, they had a rough row to hoe ahead of them. Not being able to fly and with the area full of predators, both aerial and mammalian, their futures were bleak. But it was either that or I could wring their necks and give them to a poor family to eat. And my bad guys were going to eat them, that was for sure, once they got them home anyway. So either way, there wasn't much light at the end of those ducks' tunnels when it came to a future happy life. But for the moment, they appeared to be a lot happier back in the canal instead of being roughed around in the bottom of a burlap sack.

"Hand me your bag of frogs," I instructed. Therein were twenty-three live frogs. They, like the ducks, didn't look any too happy either. And since they had been caught live by hand and were uninjured, they went back into the wilds of the canal as well. That was because the lads had expired fishing licenses and couldn't lawfully possess any of them. And, there was no purpose served by destroying such a resource for evidentiary purposes, to my way of thinking, under the present "no valid fishing license in possession circumstances."

"Now, hand me that last bloody sack," I once again instructed. The lad hesitated for a moment, then, picking it up with difficulty, handed me the heavy bag. Opening it up and looking inside, I could make out what appeared to be freshly skinned out and quartered deer parts! Dumping it out into the bottom of their boat, I counted two front shoulders, two hindquarters, two back straps, the heart and the liver from what appeared to be the remains of a freshly killed, illegal mule deer!

"Well, Lads. I don't think those items are anything even closely resembling frogs. Anyone care to tell me what the dickens is going on here with this bag full of critter?"

Finally "Zipper," a man named O'Brian from Marysville, said, "We were froggin' and spotted the deer on the bank in our spotlight. I took a shot with my pistol and made a lucky hit in its head. Then the deer damn near tumbled down the bank and into our boat. So we took that as a good sign and kept the best parts to take home and eat since we have been a little down on our luck as of recent."

"Well, it might have been a lucky shot, but I don't think the judge will find it so lucky," I said, shaking my head in disbelief at my lads' evening's take.

Walking the lads back to my patrol truck, I made a call to the sheriff's office and this time they sent out an even bigger man than Deputy Del Garrison as my prisoner transport officer. That deputy's name was Vern Swanson and he was one big dude! My two men were then transported to the jail forthwith for illegal possession of a closed season big game animal. The next day at their arraignment in the Colusa Justice Court, they pled guilty to illegal possession of a deer and no fishing license charges. I didn't file on them for being in illegal possession of the ten ducks. I just figured they had enough trouble without me stacking additional charges onto their miserable carcasses. They were later found guilty and assessed a fine to be paid over time in the amount of $550 each. The deer parts were later forfeited to a Mexican family who lived out on the east side of my district, a poor family that had thirteen kids! A Mexican family whose dedicated and loving father worked double shifts every day, seven days a week, for rice farmer Terrill Sartain and managed to send every one of his children through college on a farm laborer's salary. A family that I frequently donated seized and forfeited game to on a regular basis. Who says America isn't a great land full of opportunity...?

The Smith and Wesson Model 41, .22-caliber semi-automatic pistol used in illegally taking the deer was forfeited to the State of California. Colusa Hunter Safety Training Instructor Angelo Jaconetti later used it in required state sponsored hunter safety- training programs. Required safety-training programs if one wanted to lawfully acquire a hunting license so they could participate in the sport of hunting. That safety-training program was originally proposed by the National Rifle Association (NRA) and later universally accepted by state governments nationwide. Today it is a nationally accepted program provided in order to reduce accidental injuries and deaths caused by the unsafe handling of firearms while sport shooting or hunting. As a result of those NRA proposed and many times sponsored programs, the injuries caused by the unsafe handling of firearms nationally have been drastically reduced over the years. Boy, those NRA folks who are always supporting one's right to keep and bear arms under the Second Amendment to our Constitution are really evil and miserable people aren't they...?

As far as being a HST Instructor, Angelo was one of the best. I remember one time he told me a story that exemplified the soul of the man and his conservation ethic line of thinking. On a Hunter Safety final exam, Angelo had a question about what one does when they see a game warden approaching. One student from a known family of wildlife violators responded with the words, "Shoot him!" Angelo promptly flunked that student. Yeah, Angelo was a good man.

I have often wondered if getting caught in one's zipper hurt any worse than a $550 fine and the loss of a damn fine handgun. But I guess that is a moot point. Especially since one of my lads got to experience both ends of that painful spectrum all in the same touch.

COLD-TRACKING A DROP LINE FISHERMAN ON BUTTE CREEK

Just off Laux Road near the Butte Creek Gun Club lie several public access fishing areas along Butte Creek.

Early one morning I was checking my warm water fishermen along that stretch of waterway. I had previously checked about twenty fishermen scattered along Butte Creek further upstream and, surprisingly, none of them were doing very well in the catching department. That time of the year fishing along that high yielding biomass waterway was historically well worth the effort. But as I was quickly discovering, my fishermen were basically coming away empty-handed due in part to the abnormally cold and windy weather portending an incoming storm. A few of my fishermen had a catfish, carp or two, but that was about it. Then I chanced upon a fishing site just above the Butte Creek Gun Club with only one older African American fisherman wetting his line. He, like all the others that morning, was sitting alongside the creek quietly fishing. Pulling into his parking area, I unlimbered my miserable carcass from the patrol truck and walked into his campsite. He had a small tent set up containing a laid out sleeping bag fronted by a pint-sized campfire. Nearby sat a five-gallon pail nearly full of nice pan fish, a couple of tackle boxes, a closed ice chest, and one fishing pole. I also noticed he had several closed quart jars of stink bait, two canisters of worms, several cans of whole kernel corn, and a small open jar of some sort of homemade stink bait that was so putrid that it stunk to the high heavens even clear over from where I was standing. How the hell someone could put their hands into such a stink-bait concoction and then slap it onto a fishhook was beyond me. If it had been me fishing in that area, I would have stuck to an Eagle Claw No. 4 sized hook and a gob of worms hoping for a great eating, freshwater trout instead of what he was after. But what the hell did I know being a "stink bait using wimp" and all.

Then the tired game warden from working many previous long hours inside me kicked in like the Coyote in the cartoon when he spotted the Roadrunner near at hand. He had way more bait than even normally for the bite at that time of the year. Plus, he had a large bucket almost full of freshly caught catfish and other good sized warm water game fish! Normal looking to the casual eye, but remember, everyone else I had checked earlier that morning fishing along Butte Creek in other locations had little in the way of a catch of any kind. Something with that scene arrayed around me, like the man's evil smelling stink bait, stunk to high heaven to my now awakening law enforcement senses.

"Good morning, Lad. How you doing this fine morning?" I said as I approached.

"Fine, Mr. Game Warden. I be doin' jus' fine," he politely replied in a low Southern drawl.

"Dang, Man, you are doing very well," I said looking into his almost full pail of fish. "What kind of bait are you finding to be the most successful?"

"My brand of stink bait seems to be doin' the job," he replied with a toothy grin.

"Boy, I guess so," I answered looking into his nice bucket of warm water game fish again. As I looked however, I could see he was still a ways from having a full limit on any of the regulated species in the Butte Creek system. "You have a nice mess of fish here, Lad," I continued, "not to mention some dang fine eating down the road."

"Sure do, Mr. Game Warden," he replied as he dug out his fishing license from his overalls without being asked.

Checking his license, I found all was in order. But my guardian angels were becoming restless. He had a lot of bait and fish from a creek that had basically been producing little in the way of catch, kept spinning through my now getting even more suspicious mind.

Then wanting to look around some more and see if I could find anything else out of the ordinary without pissing him off with my obvious snooping, I got to stalling by talking fish cooking recipes with my fisherman. Even that ruse didn't help me gain any real lingering and looking time. The man was cooperative beyond a fault and now that bothered me as well. It is hell when your interest is piqued, but your leads are taking you nowhere. Realizing I had burned out my nosing-around candle at that moment, I punted. Thanking my chap for his cooperation, I loaded back into my patrol truck with my tail between my legs and exited the area. However, still not satisfied, I put Plan B into effect.

Crossing over Butte Creek on a farm access bridge further down the road with my truck, I parked it out of sight in a stand of willows. Then I walked back upstream and found a place to hide and watch on the opposite side of the creek directly across from my suspicious fisherman's campsite. Sitting down, the ever-present mosquitoes and I quietly watched. The only good thing about that time of the year and the mosquitoes was that they were cold as hell and flew like it. When they landed on me it was in a clumsy sort of way and could readily be felt. So when the mosquitoes made smash landings on my miserable carcass they were felt and got smashed in turn. For once, I had the upper hand and could really get down to the business at hand of watching my chap and not getting distracted by being bitten ten thousand times in the process. Staked out there that morning, it was darker than the inside of a dead cow with no moon being present to aid me in my endeavors. But my fisherman had a Coleman Lantern going which partially allowed me to observe his actions through my binoculars. That was until he rose up from the bank, walked back to his tent and turned the lantern down to just a faint glow. Now it was so damn dark that I couldn't see crap outside the small ring of light around his lantern! Well, maybe he is going to bed, I thought. After all, that is where most people with any common sense would be this time of the morning. About thirty quiet minutes passed without any sign of activity or sounds coming from my suspect fisherman or his camping area.

Tiring of my stakeout, I was just getting ready to leave when I heard the bell attached to the end of the man's fishing pole begin faintly tinkling. He had a fish on his terminal gear if his tinkling bell was any indicator and soon on went the man's Coleman Lantern to full power. With that, the man emerged from his tent, landed a nice catfish, put him into his bucket of water and other fish, baited the hook, and once again cast out his bait. Then he sat there still as death alongside his fishing pole for the next hour. I thought that was pretty strange. Why didn't he just go back to his tent and his sleeping bag? Oh well, no one ever said fishermen were sane... Now really tiring of my non-producing stakeout, I made ready to leave. It was then my fisherman got up, reduced the lantern light again to just a faint glow, and blackness once again swallowed up the morning. Only this time my instincts were telling me something was really amiss. Then I saw it! A very small, almost not seen with the naked eye spot of light was slowly moving down Butte Creek below my chap's camp along its brushy bank! You know, like the light from a small, partially covered penlight. Even with my binoculars, I could see but very little. Twenty minutes later, I saw my man with the tiny beam of light returning to his campsite, and it sounded like he tossed another rather large flopping fish or two into his fish bucket. Then, he turned the Coleman lantern back on to high and light flooded his campsite once again like nothing out of the ordinary had just occurred.

Now I knew something was rotten in the henhouse! Why all the lowering of the light on the lantern? I asked myself. It appeared the chap was up to no good, but damned if I had anything illegal on the man. Then I got my last part over the fence in gear. Sneaking back downstream, then crossing over the bridge, I slipped back upstream closer to the man's campsite on his side of Butte Creek and hid in the brush. From my new vantage point, I could now watch his every action even more closely without his knowledge that I was even in country. Now let him try something outside the law and then I would be all over him like a mess of piss ants on a cube of sugar.

Twenty minutes later, my fisherman arose and once again lowered the light of the lantern. Then I could hear someone quietly walking along the creek bank not far from my position of concealment. I could clearly hear someone moving nearby but couldn't see hardly anything because he was now moving around over the edge of the creek's bank in the cover of the brush! Shortly afterwards, he then walked out of my zone of hearing. Now I found myself in a pickle. It was so damn brushy there along the creek that I couldn't very easily follow my chap as he quietly moved downstream. Long minutes later, back came the sounds of someone quietly moving through the brush and coming my way. Then I saw the shape of my chap moving his way back to camp. Shortly thereafter, the lantern light back at his camp was increased once again.

All right, Terry. This lad is up to something illegal, but what? I asked myself. Why all the lantern manipulation and skulking along the darkened creek bank below his camp? Then the sun finally shone on the manure pile behind the barn. This lad had to be fishing illegally. Maybe he had extra fishing poles strung out all along the creek bank below his campsite out of sight in case the game warden came by, I surmised. No, that didn't really make much sense, I quickly thought, because if a really big fish struck and the rod was unattended, over the bank and into the creek the whole mess would go and be lost forever. Then it hit me! Damn, Terry, your man must be running drop lines! Why else all the extra bait and a bucket of fish when no one else checked earlier had any such success when it came to fishing normally. Finally, that was all followed by a mysterious pattern of movement walking back and forth over the creek bank and out of sight every ten yards or so.

That's great, I thought, you finally figured it out, you damn dummy. But now, how do you prove your case beyond a reasonable doubt when you can't see crap because it is so dark along that brushy creek bank? I asked myself.

Then I came up with Plan C. The next time my lad left his campsite fishing spot, I would quietly head for his camp so I could be in his back pocket in a manner of speaking when he returned. Soon my opportunity arose. As my chap walked by heading downstream once again and disappeared into the creek side brush and darkness, I rose up heading for the far side of his tent for the concealment it offered. Standing by his tent, I quietly waited. Finally he returned. As he walked by me, I turned on my flashlight. That act so startled my chap that he yelled bloody murder and tossed the two large catfish he was carrying skyward all at the same time. When things finally settled down and the man got back his heartbeat, I quietly asked, "Where have you been and what the dickens are you doing going back and forth over the stream bank all the time?"

"I was just going to the bathroom, Mr. Game Warden," he quickly replied. "I have a bad prostate and it makes me go to the bathroom lots of times during the day or night."

"With two catfish in your hand? How the hell did you do that if you were just going to the bathroom? In fact, how the hell did you catch them without using a fishing pole?" I continued. The man was stumped for a quick answer to those last questions and finally just stood there balefully looking at me. Then I knew I had him! Well, I had something anyway...

"Why don't you pick up those fish you just tossed out onto the stream bank and put them into your fish bucket full of water so they will at least have a chance to live. Then you and I are going to take a little walk," I said.

"Yes sir, Mr. Game Warden," he said. But with those words and being from a large city in the Bay Area during those turbulent times in the '60s between the cops and many of the more militant black folks, I could tell from the tone and tenor of his voice that a walk into the dark of night with a white, armed law enforcement officer out in the bush was not high on his Bucket or Christmas Lists.

With that command, he put the two now dirt covered, flopping catfish into the water of his fish bucket. Then I said, "Open up your tackle boxes, please."

"What for, Mr. Game Warden?" he asked.

"I just want to see what kind of tackle you are using," I advised.

The man opened up the tackle boxes and stepped back. They were full of spools of monofilament line, small plastic boxes of gold colored No. 4-sized hooks, and old spark plugs! Way more terminal gear than a chap would need in a lifetime, unless he was running what I now figured were drop lines.

To you unwashed, drop lines are just that. Tie a spark plug on the end of the line, a baited hook somewhere in the middle of that line, and tie off the other end onto any handy limb or sturdy root next to the water. Toss the contraption with a baited hook out into the water. Since many fish move along the stream banks because of the reduced currents which require less swimming energy being expended or are using bank overhangs as cover, you have a deadly fishing combination lying there in wait right in the fishes back yard. Then move on downstream and repeat the process with each set of drop-lines. With increased numbers of fishing lines in the water, you increase your catching successes. Hence, my initial reasoning and further questions over his full bucket of fish when all the other fishermen previously checked on that same body of water had hardly anything in the way of a catch. That, plus his brand of stink bait which seemed to be doing the trick on that cold and blustery, off-fishing morning.

"Sir, I need you to walk in front of me along the creek. I think you are using what I call drop lines. Why else would you be taking walks in the dark along the creek at timed intervals and then returning with fish without a fishing pole in hand? That, coupled with using a hand-shielded small light more than likely to check your lines for fish. So with that in mind, we are going looking along the creek bank," I said to remove any dread he may have had in light of the lawless times in the major cities between a number of inner city blacks and local law enforcement, especially when it came to a lone suspicious black man taking a walk in the dark with a white-armed law enforcement officer out in the boondocks.

"Mr. Game Warden, youse has me all wrong. I has a prostate problem and has to goes to the bathroom lots of the time. That is why I go along the creek so I don't stink ups my camp," he replied to my earlier accusatory statement.

Good answer; I thought, but I still want to take a look. Then if I am wrong, I have lots of time to apologize for being such an inquisitive hind end. Plus, that doesn't explain why one would leave to go to the bathroom and return with a fresh flopping fish just about every time. However, my guardian angels were now working overtime in their sixth sense fluttering department so I figured I had my fisherman hooked and about to be landed.

"First before we go anywhere, I want to see the bottom of your shoes," I said.

"Why is that, Mr. Game Warden?" he asked.

"So I can cold track you as you walked along the bank of the creek. That way I don't get your footprints mixed up in the soft bank soils with those from other fishermen who have fished in the same area at an earlier time," I replied.

"Yes sir, Mr. Game Warden," he quietly replied. With that he showed me the soles of his shoes. They had an unusual pattern, one that would be easy to follow, I smugly thought over being a game warden who was now and finally as slick as a good mess of cow slobbers. And a wonderfully beautiful catch-dog game warden that was now hot on the trail. Well, to be frank, hot on the trail of something...

With my gentleman walking in front of me but off to my right side so he wouldn't mess up my cold tracking efforts, we started back down Butte Creek. His numerous footprints were very evident and easy to follow in the soft dusty creek bank soils because of the pattern on his shoe soles and his rather large foot size. Plus, he had been up and down the creek bank so many times he had left a distinct trail in the soft dust. Following those footprints, we went about twenty yards downstream from his camp. At that point, the footprints turned toward the creek and went over the bank. Looking over the edge with my flashlight, I spotted a monofilament line attached to the root of a tree sticking out from the bank. From there, the line went out of sight into the water. Asking my chap to step further back from the creek so if he decided to rush me I would have time to recover and defend myself, I waited. Moments later, after he had complied with that command, I stepped over the bank and grabbed the suspect line. Pulling it up I discovered what appeared to be some of his brand of stink bait covering a gold No. 4 hook with a used spark plug acting as a sinker... Pulling the contraption out from the water and cutting it loose from the tree root with my buck knife, I walked back up the bank. Holding it out for my lad to see, I said, "This terminal gear is the same as you have in your tackle boxes back at camp and what you are using on your fishing pole there as well."

My fellow just looked at me and said nothing. With those accusatory words ringing in the morning air and no reply from my chap regarding my accusation, we commenced walking downstream once again. Five yards further downstream, his unique set of footprints led off the bank toward the creek once again. There I discovered another drop line matching my first discovery. Only this time, its hook held a nice black bullhead weighing about three pounds. This routine was repeated successfully eight more times until I found no more drop lines or downstream footprints matching the soles of his footwear leading directly to other tied off drop line contraptions matching those previously discovered.

Gathering up my evidence, we walked quietly back to his camp. On the way, we passed where my vehicle was hidden. Stopping, I removed my point-and-shoot camera and then we walked the last forty or so yards back to his campsite. Once at his campsite, I photographed his bait, tackle boxes with the gold No. 4 hooks, and spools of line. Lastly, I photographed the tackle box holding all the spark plugs and finally the bucket load of fish. Taking the bucket of fish, I released all the live ones that looked like they might live back into Butte Creek. The rest of the dead or dying fish that had been hooked too deeply I kept as evidence on a stringer in case this case ever went to a court of law.

Turning over the now empty fish bucket, I flopped it down on the bank and took a seat. Looking hard at my fisherman for a few moments, I said, "Well, do you want to tell me in your own words why you were running a mess of illegal drop lines?" I did so in order to strengthen my case with his own words of guilt if he so chose to talk and admit his illegal involvement in an unlawful fishing activity.

"Mr. Game Warden, I usually don't breaks the fish and game laws. But I had a good reason to do so this time. Youse see, I have two nephews jus' back from the big war in Vietnam. Both have lost parts of their legs in that fight. And when I went to visit them recently, they asked that the next time I came to visit to bring them a mess of Southern fried catfish. Youse see, they are at the Oakland

Veterans Facility and them white folks can't cook a black man's meal if they has to. So's I told them I would try to gets them a mess of fish, return to their hospital, get permission to use their kitchen, and cook them up so's they could have some fine Southern home cookin'. The fish weren't biting, so I jus' used what used to work for me back in Alabama. And it worked here jus' fine, too. So, until youse tossed away most of my mess of fishes, I was on my way to getting some good Southern cookin' to my nephews." With that, he just stopped and looked at me with a sad set of unblinking eyes.

"What are your nephews' names?" I asked. That question under like circumstances will usually produce a moment's hesitation on the part of the miscreant if he or she is lying about the situation at hand. If he or she is lying, they will hesitate as they fish around for a couple of names as they try to alleviate their pain over being apprehended. When that happens, after a flurry of associated conversation, the officer needs to ask the suspect for the names once again of the wounded chaps. Nine times out of ten, your suspects having made up the names in the first place, will stumble trying to repeat those same names when asked moments later. When that happens, you good folks out there reading these lines know what happens next...

"Carol Williams and LeRoy Dobson," he quickly answered without hesitation. Did so, like they were the real thing and not just made up names to avoid receiving a fish and game citation for illegally fishing and the resultant fines to come.

After writing down those two names, I commenced writing out a citation to my fisherman for using eleven lines while fishing in inland waters. He was later assessed a fine of $125 in the Colusa Justice Court, and the remaining fish I had seized as evidence went to a needy family living in the Town of Maxwell.

After my fisherman had settled up with the court a week or so later, I made a call to one of my fish and game warden academy classmates who was at that time a boarding officer on the thirty- five-foot patrol boat named The Bass in the San Joaquin Delta. That call went to one Warden Jim Dixon. Jim was one of the toughest, no-nonsense fish and game officers I ever met. I can even remember at the academy, Jim's actions during the regular evening's five-mile run across the stinking hot San Bernardino countryside in particular. Jim would make the entire run jogging backwards just to piss off our smart-assed, smug, arrogant and highly impressed with himself, local sheriff's office physical-training drill instructor. A man who openly resented the fact that every one of us lowly game warden types possessed one to several college degrees—a hiring requirement in those days—and he didn't have any. So, in part, just to show our physical training instructor that he was not the toughest son-of-a-bitch in the valley, Jim ran backwards the entire five miles and made it look easy. And for Jim it was easy because he was in tremendous physical shape and rawhide tough. However, when Jim did that, the instructor would take his pissed-off attitude out on the rest of us and make all of us run an extra mile or so in the stinking southern California heat and smog. That just made all of us one hell of a tough bunch of a "Band of Brothers" in the end and close friends to this day. That is, those of us that are still alive from that Class of 1966, which as of 2012 isn't many. But Jim and I were very good friends and he was one hell of an ace in the hole when anyone from his academy class needed anything, especially something odd, unusual or out of the ordinary. In short, Jim was a damn good scrounger...

I told Jim of my recent case on my African-American drop-line fisherman and my idea of helping out those wounded Black American Patriots fresh back from the Vietnam conflict and their desire for some good, Southern home cookin'. I had found out after some checking that my black, drop-line fisherman had indeed been telling the truth. He did have two Vietnam War veteran nephews recovering from serious leg wounds at the Oakland Veteran's Hospital Facility. A short time later, after my unusual request to Warden Jim Dixon, he had discovered a friendly, commercial fish farming source and fellow California Patriot. A Patriot who provided free of charge one hundred fifty pounds of fine eating, catfish filets from his fish farming and processing facility. Jim saw to it that my request was answered in spades, and those fish were donated to the Oakland Veterans Facility so all the "Wounded Warriors" in the ward could have a homemade Southern fried catfish dinner. As it worked out after I placed another phone call, my black drop-line fisherman got a bunch of his buddies and fellow cooks together. They, in turn, subsequently provided the expertise needed when it came to cooking a proper black man's Southern fried fish dinner. I figured that was the least I could do for a band of Patriots who had given so much for a country that many times had historically neglected them, their culture, and their contributions toward making this great country of ours what it is today within our complex world community.

Jim passed away in 2011 at the age of 70. I hope the good Lord takes a liking to Jim and turns him loose on some wildlife violators who have sneaked their way up there into the clouds along with the rest of the really good

Cloud People. If He did, there will be some outlaw son-of-a-bitches hitting the ground back here on earth in short order once Jim gets on their trails. Yeah, my friend was a great officer and a good Christian man. I miss him dearly. As I write these words in 2012, there aren't many of us left from that original group of rookies from The Class of 1966. Some of my classmates, I have been told, were shot, drowned trying to rescue others, died in car wrecks, lost their battles with cancer, heart attacks, alcohol, or, like me, just plain wore out.

Honor is a gift only man can give himself... Jim was a very honorable man. As I see it, we are all walking between the two great eternities from our genesis to the exodus of our souls. And as we walk, we are all looking for the extended Hand of God. I hope Jim found that extended Hand of God. If not, I am glad that God loves little children, fools and game wardens. That way, Jim should have all his bases covered. Just don't piss God off, Jim, and run backwards during physical training exercises up there in the clouds just to show Him that you are the meanest-son-of-a-bitch in the Valley. If you do, Partner, that is one race you won't win...

TWO-TIME OFFENDERS

Borrowing a Grumman Sport Canoe from Bob Norris, a U.S. Game Management Agent —akin to a federal game warden—who was stationed in nearby Chico, California, I prepared for another of my goofy nighttime patrols on the much fished and frogged Butte Creek waterway. Only this time instead of being afoot and horseback, I would be innovative and use the navy. I did so because it seemed every time I checked my fishermen along Butte Creek, there were always sizeable numbers of suspect fishermen using boats anchored out in the middle of that heavily utilized recreational waterway. That "out in the middle of the stream" situation many times presented problems. Problems because being on foot when I asked the fishermen to come ashore to be checked, numerous times illegal evidence would be quietly slipped overboard or gotten rid of before I became aware of what was going on and could do anything about it. And, that loss of evidence was even more so at night under the cover of darkness, when I couldn't see every sleight-of-hand activity performed by some of my more clever outlaws preparing to come ashore and be checked. And more than once suspect fish stringers holding over limits were quietly let go into the deep to avoid a well-earned citation. Plus, I was sure it was a pain in the last part over the fence for the honest fishermen to have to reel in, up anchor, interrupt their fishing experience and come ashore to be checked by the local game warden.

Tiring of such tomfoolery (read: tired of losing cases and getting my butt kicked), I decided to take the bit in my teeth and show that sometimes-questionable class of illegal inland fishermen they could run but not hide. Hence the start of a new set of adventures that evening so long ago, when I slipped the borrowed Grumman Sport Canoe into the dark of Butte Creek just south of the Gridley Highway and initiated the patrol actions of the fish and game navy for the first time. On the stern I had a 9.5-horsepower Evinrude outboard motor. I also carried two paddles plus my usual complement of game warden gear for just such a patrol. My plan was to paddle quietly under the cover of darkness downstream, using the gentle current as an assist. That way I could surprise and check my hard to access boat fishermen because that was when many of my violators, feeling safer under the cover of darkness, would illegally do what they did best to squelch the life out of those in the fisheries world of wildlife. When finished with that kind of patrol, my plan was that I would motor back upstream, load the canoe, and head for home for some much needed sleep. Sounded simple enough but little did I realize that the first surprise Butte Creek boat trip would yield outlaw gold by the bucketful for the county's fish and game fine money coffers. In fact, gold beyond my wildest dreams! Not to mention, having the profound surprise effect of gilding the lily on some of my local wildlife outlaws who needed one whole hell of a lot of attention from ye old game warden...

Sliding the canoe into Butte Creek just before midnight, I settled onto the seat with my dog, Shadow, placed in the bow for the proper weight distribution. Once that was done, I adjusted my delicate 320 pounds of Teutonic magnificence accordingly, and began a quiet and memorable trip downstream letting my night vision adjust to the dark of the night conditions as we glided silently along in Butte Creek's gentle current. After about a hundred yards quietly drifting in the current, my eyes had time to adjust and get their night vision mode more or less squared away. Now, I was ready for whatever the good Lord threw my way and hopefully it wasn't a curve ball like a wet unexpected swim from a tipped over canoe or a poke in the eye from an unseen low overhanging limb along that sometimes-brushy waterway.

Quietly drifting another one hundred fifty yards down from my entry point, I floated into my first unsuspecting customers. Rounding a bend in the creek, I spotted the soft glow of a Coleman Lantern dead ahead of me in a small boat. Shipping my paddle, I took up my binoculars and observed three fishermen quietly fishing from their boat.

In the soft light being emitted from their lantern, I counted the monofilament glint of eight fishing lines running overboard! Not bad for a start, I told myself. One line fishing in inland waters per fisherman was the legal limit in those days. These lads with their eight fishing line running overboard, were now in the illegal toilet and it was about to be flushed! Paddling softly once again and using a trick I had learned one summer in Alaska when paddling guaranteed not to make any paddle noise in the water, I approached my unsuspecting chaps. I always enjoyed getting in as closely as possible to my person or persons of interest breaking the law before they discovered I was in country. That way, I would surprise the be-Jesus out of my chaps and be on them before they could cut any lines or release any fish stringers with over limits of fish tied alongside their boat. Plus, there was another method to my madness of sneaking up on my culprits as closely as possible. Being surprised and so easily caught in such a manner usually broke many of my local outlaws from sucking eggs in the future, if you get my drift. Especially being sneaked up on by a guy my size. Being caught in such a manner, usually made for great lessons in conservation ethics being discussed and forwarded at the workplace the following day. Particularly on any potentially like-in-kind violators when discussions were held in the lunchroom with their workmates over what had happened to those just apprehended in the dark of night by the world's largest and most strikingly handsome game warden. Not to mention, in the present circumstance, one who had sneaked up on the errant chaps and had made not a sound.

To my way of thinking, if a law dog could sneak up on someone as quietly as a snake moves across a wet lawn, there is a lesson in that to be learned by those walking on the dark side of the world of wildlife ... and in that lesson, a much-needed trick of the trade force multiplier is exposed to the light of day in the world of wildlife law enforcement, namely, you can run but you can't hide...

In the present case, I was right alongside the fishermen before they knew what had hit them. And in the instant situation, it was always helpful in my sneaking tactics when all my lads were facing the other way and quietly talking up a storm just before the onset of the gathering storm...

"Good morning, Gentlemen. State fish and game warden. How is the fishing?" I quietly asked just as I reached out and gently latched onto the side rail of their boat. Man, you talk about having a handful of surprised chaps! In fact, it took a couple of moments before all of them had settled back down and gotten their hearts started once again over my totally unexpected arrival. Then even more consternation manifested itself within my three miscreants. It quickly dawned on my chaps that they had just been caught with eight lines overboard fishing, when they could legally have only three! With the game warden being only two feet away, that precluded any cutting of fishing lines tomfoolery and my chaps just sat there in quiet "you got me" resignation. Checking fishing licenses, I recognized every one of my chaps. They were from the Town of Chico, and I had pinched all of them previously for large over limits of frogs that they had caught in the backwaters of my Colusa patrol district. At the time of their apprehension for that violation, my lads had 232 frogs or 157 over the legal limit to be exact! And, that little hopping affair had subsequently cost each of those lads $450 in the Colusa Justice Court, not to mention the loss of all their frogs and frogging gear...

By the time I finished with that little event, I had issued three citations for fishing with too many lines with an additional bonus of apprehending my three "two-timers" for fishing without valid fishing licenses. That episode later netted the county $225 in fine monies! Not really big bucks in today's money but forty-five years ago that was a pretty good nick out of one's moldy old hide if they chose to run on the wild side of Mother Nature.

Pulling away from my chaps, I bid them good morning and, like a passing night shadow, quietly slid back into the inky blackness of the early morning on Butte Creek. However if one looked closely enough, one could see my teeth now exposed by a great big smile. If nothing else, I had accomplished what I had originally intended to do, and that was to create uncertainty among my night fishing outlaws. With the possibility of that kind of patrol being out and about, wildlife outlaws never could be assured of hiding anything from the local game warden. He just might be anywhere. That went doubly for those who really deserved my undivided attention like my last three customers. Additionally, my three lads were warned against any further fishing that morning since none possessed a valid fishing license. In short, their morning fish-capade was now a mess thanks to the fellow in green. With that, I escorted my lads downstream to their parked vehicle since they couldn't fish anymore until they had purchased current fishing licenses. Then having been there before, I sat nearby and waited until they left the area so they could not pull a Paul Revere and warn off other nearby like-in kind outlaws that the local tule creeper was in country. I would say I had more than invested myself into that moment in time...

Again moving downstream after the culmination of that little affair, Dog and I began enjoying the early morning coolness and the many sounds of nature associated with such a detail. Feeding deer were often spooked off the creek bank, there was tail-splashing by surprised beaver upon discovering the closeness of my presence, muskrats were startled by the canoe's close-at-hand presence as they quietly swam by, burring sounds came from the darkness made by raccoons happily feeding along the shoreline, and the jug-a-rumming of hundreds of bullfrogs completed the night's symphony for the man in green and his trusty dog, Shadow. God, it was great to be alive! To my way of thinking and according to the Native American's Creator, Wakan Tanka, any questions one might have in life, you will always be able to find the answers in nature. You just have to know where to look. I discovered early on in my life, that the earth and her critters are always speaking to you. You just have to be silent in order to hear. However, great moments in our lives, like I was now experiencing from Mother Nature as I floated quietly along, many times do not return. So, I made sure that I didn't blink...

FROGGING IN THE WRONG PLACE AT THE WRONG TIME

My next mini adventure that morning on Butte Creek was soon upon me. Coming toward me after I had traveled several hundred yards further downstream were two chaps in a boat who my experience and their light set-up told me they were commercially frogging. Looking through my binoculars, it was obvious they were live grabbing a ton of frogs from along the shoreline like there was no tomorrow' grabbing live, blinded-by-the-strong-light frogs by hand. However, if commercial frogging was their case, a small problem existed in that amphibian-catching endeavor. To commercially frog in a game warden's district in those days, those licensed froggers had to call and advise the local conservation officer of their operations and where their activities were geographically to be performed, in advance! I had not received any such notification that evening via landline or by radio from the sheriff's office. If that was the non-notification circumstance and they would be in my county frogging, they were in violation of the fish and game regulations! A violation that I strictly enforced because of the overall damage I perceived being done to the bullfrog populations by that class of state licensed individuals. Even more important to my way of thinking, no prior notification to the local game warden subjected the offenders to not only a steep fine but also the subsequent loss of their commercial frogging licenses upon being apprehended and successfully prosecuted.

Sliding my canoe up alongside the nearest creek bank for the cover it offered, I grabbed an exposed tree root and just sat there waiting in ambush. Using my free hand to hold my binoculars, I watched my chaps live catching the hell out of the frogs lining the banks in their bright lights as they slowly came my way. Soon their strong car battery powered lights lit up Dog and me sitting there quietly in our canoe. By then it was too late to flee and I was on them like stink on the skin-covered head of a turkey vulture after he had stuck it through the side of a long-dead, bloated and juicy rotten cow in the July Colusa County heat. Yes, my readers, that bit of rank avian life history information and biology is a fact. Vultures have a skin covered head and neck. That way the goo from the over ripe chow they are feasting upon does not stick to and muss up their head and neck feathers. A pretty specialized and clever life's adaptation I might add. Plus for your further edification, vultures routinely defecate on their feet after feasting on their overripe selection of roadside chow. Yep, that is correct. Their feces are chemically strongly basic, which cleans and sanitizes their feet, thereby reducing harmful bacteria contained thereon. Lastly, their stomach acids are strong enough to dissolve metal! Those juices being that strong in nature, precludes any type of infection derived from what they are eating. With that bit of off-the wall world-of- wildlife information, I hope it isn't lunchtime in your household. But once again for my readers' edification, I digressed...

"Morning, Gents," I said as I released my hold on the tree root, moved forward and latched onto the side of their boat. "State fish and game warden. How you boys doing?" I cheerfully asked, knowing damn well they were clear up to their eyes, after the fact, in vulture juice...

"We be fine, Officer," said the more than surprised lad in the bow doing all the live frog grabbing by hand so as not to injure his prey. Living frogs were more readily sold to the biological supply houses, which needed live frogs to inject with their red and blue dyes into their veins and arteries for high school and college science class dissection purposes. Living freshness was also a requirement if one was involved with the illegal sale of said critters in the restaurant trade. Hence the necessity of the frogs being caught by hand, live and uninjured, for whatever legal or illegal commercial market they subsequently ended up in.

Looking into the bottom of their boat, I observed two gunnysacks almost full of frogs and another attached to the end of their catch box that was damn near filled. For those unwashed commercial froggers among you readers, a catch box is a small square plywood open-ended tube tied onto the end of the gunny sack that had two spring loaded doors on its front end. The frogger would grab a frog and thrust it through the spring-loaded doors on the catch box leading to the gunnysack tied below. When he let go of the live frog, the critter dropped through the wooden tube and into the sack. Upon withdrawing his hand, the doors sprung back tightly shut. That way, frogs once tossed through the doors could not escape and subsequently be easily bagged up for transport to their final destination.

"You boys frogging commercially?" I asked. Because if they weren't, they had one hell of an over limit of frogs if they were just sport frogging. The sport limit was twenty-five frogs per person per day during that period of time in the 1960s. And, they sure as hell had a lot more frogs then that sacked up in the bottom of their boat...

"Yes, sir," said the man operating their small boat motor.

"May I see some commercial fishing licenses?" I asked.

The two lads handed me their commercial fishing licenses required for such an endeavor, which I duly checked. Then I asked, "You lads contact the local game warden before beginning your frogging activities here in this county?"

"Yes, sir," said the man in the bow. "That's what the law requires."

"Who did you guys contact this evening before you began your commercial frogging activities?" I inquired.

"I don't remember his name but we did contact him," said the bowman.

"Do either of you remember what town that officer lived in?" I asked, knowing damn well they would soon be fumbling for an answer since no one had contacted me.

One man blurted out Yuba City at the same time as the other blurted out the adjacent Sacramento Valley Town of Marysville.

"Lads, let's cut through the chase. You are in Colusa County and I am the resident game warden for this portion of the county. I did not receive any phone calls from either of you chaps and neither did my wife." In those days, the fish and game department considered our home phones as our business phones to be utilized by the public as a source of information or notification. "If you lads had called my wife regarding your commercial frogging activity in my patrol district, she has standing instructions to call the sheriff's office immediately and so advise so they could notify me via radio. It appears to me you lads are in violation of Title 14 of the Administrative Code regarding officer notification of your commercial frogging activities," I quietly advised.

"Aren't we in Sutter County?" asked the stern man.

"No, Sir. The two of you are in Colusa County. And if you were frogging on the other side of this waterway, you would be in Butte County. The two of you are a damn site long ways from Sutter County, the truth be known," I responded. "Gentlemen, I need to see some driver's licenses, if you would, please," I continued. Then it dawned on me when I examined their driver's licenses and read their names. I had previously caught these same two chaps sport frogging on the 2047 canal in the central portion of my patrol district, with 51 frogs over the limit or 101 frogs in their possession a year earlier! With that name-recognition revelation, I just grinned inside. Who says there isn't a God looking out for the poor damn lowly old bullfrog.

Man, you talk about two glum looking chaps. No way in hell did they expect to meet a game warden out in the bush at that time of the morning. As suspected, my two lads were just commercially frogging until they ran out of frogs or gunnysacks, whichever came first. And, county boundaries and the fish and game notification regulations be damned. Notification regulations be damned, because there was so much money to easily be made if one just put their minds and a little bit of capture-per-sale effort into it. That plus Colusa County was a prime rice-producing area in the Northern Sacramento Valley. And the thousands of acres of flooded rice fields seconded as tremendous food sources for resident bullfrog populations (crawdads, water snakes, insects, ducklings, small frogs, etc.). That plus the flooded fields acted as optimum warm-water incubators for frog eggs and young. Then once the fields were drained in preparation for the fall harvest, the frogs just migrated a short distance away into the counties numerous adjacent canals and waterways for the safety and living conditions they offered. Hence, Butte Creek, like many other watered areas, became a favorite frog hunter's paradise.

Both men were then issued citations for failure to notify the county's fish and game officer prior to commencing their commercial frogging activities. To you unwashed, this might look like a "CS" ticket, but that class of chaps, to my way of thinking, along with their subsequent mass frogging harvest endeavors, were severely reducing the bullfrog populations in the Northern Sacramento Valley. They were collectively catching frogs by the tens of thousands on a weekly basis because of some stupid damn hair-brained decision made in Sacramento. A decision made by some high level, desk bound, tweed-backed, idiot-stick bureaucrat in my fish and game agency allowing such dangerous extreme harvest levels of a species to freely occur! A desk bound idiot who had little or no knowledge of how such an excessive harvest of one species, could put a tilt into the rest of the health of an ecosystem! Tell your readers how you really feel, Terry...

The frogs taken under that commercial frogging program were supposed to go to biological supply houses for subsequent educational uses in high school and college science classes. However, from my numerous intelligence sources, many frogs were moving into the Chinese restaurant trade in the larger cities of Marysville, Yuba City, Sacramento, Oakland, and the San Francisco Bay Area because of the higher prices being paid for frog leg dinners in those commercial markets. That, as opposed to the lower profits gained from the sale of said critters to the biological supply houses. You readers need to be aware that this was before the age of lawfully farm-raised bullfrogs moving legally into the commercial markets during today's times in 2013. In 1997, I was told by some of my old California game warden buddies that finding large numbers of bullfrogs in the Northern Sacramento Valley like they used to occur, was now quite rare. Not totally decimated as a result of this commercial trade, but it sure as hell was a major factor in the bullfrog population numbers being so drastically reduced. Add to that the still mostly unknown effects of climate change, excessive use of herbicides and pesticides in the rice fields by some farmers and recent water shortages in California in 2014, all of which makes a thinking person wonder what is next for that unique amphibian resource. But, I digress.

After thirty-two years as a wildlife officer in the field trying my hardest to protect what is your heritage my readers, I have a tendency to get rather ill tempered, wound up and rather short on patience sometimes when it comes to bureaucratic stupidity and intemperance. Especially when I have too often seen critters go into the pipeline at one end and come out as slurry on the other end because of some poorly thought out official human decisions, be they political or otherwise. But, like the caring bonehead I am, I digressed once again...sorry. Back to the story at hand.

Then you should have heard the lads yell when I released all their frogs, read profits, back into the wild. The lads were hopping mad over what I did and the frogs were hopping glad to be back into the environment they loved. Me, I was just plain ole pleased... Both my lads each paid $250 in the Colusa Justice Court for their little geographic and notification error a week later. Plus, it subsequently cost them their commercial fishing licenses once the fish and game department was notified of their prosecution for their failure to notify violation. I would call that, "Lions two, Christians nothing in the Sacramento Valley's Coliseum!"

There were to my recollection twenty-six commercial frogging licenses issued by the State of California during my years as a state fish and game officer in the Northern Sacramento Valley. During my three-year tenure as a game warden in that area before I switched agencies in 1970 and went to work for the U.S. Fish and Wildlife Service as a United States Game Management Agent, I caught twenty-four of those twenty-six commercially licensed rascals and they all lost their licenses. I tried, frogs, I really did. But there just wasn't enough of me to go around to do what needed doing. All that happened was other froggers just stepped forward with dreams of huge profits splashed across their faces, procured their commercial frogging licenses and the ruination of a great resource continued unabated... As I said earlier, today as the words to this story were written in 2012, the bullfrog population in the Northern Sacramento Valley still has not recovered its former numbers of greatness from the 1960s, thanks in part to being over harvested commercially.

THE GAMEKEEPER

Leaving my glum commercial froggers to think over the error of their ways as they left for wherever they had come, I continued my adventures down Butte Creek. But first, I had to stop and let Dog get out of the canoe to answer a call of nature. Then she had to sniff everything to make sure there weren't any California grizzly bears nearby. Unfortunately, the last California grizzly bear had been killed in the late 1930s. Finished with that business, back into the canoe and out onto the creek we headed quietly once again.

Slowly drifting downstream once again, we traveled another half mile in the inky blackness when I saw what I perceived to be a faint fisherman's light ahead on the near shoreline on the backside of the White Mallard Duck Club. Man, I thought to myself, I would never have suspected anyone could get into that area to fish because it is so remote, brushy, roadless and isolated.

Grabbing a tree limb from the trunk of a sunken tree sticking up out in the middle of the creek, I held on with my arm looped around it while I glassed what appeared to be a damn well hidden and brushed-out fishing area. I saw only one fisherman but I could clearly see four fishing poles propped up high up in the air in the garish light of his Coleman lantern on forked sticks which had been driven into the muddy bank. And yes, I could see their glistening monofilament lines going into the water from the ends of each fishing pole as well.

Letting go of the tree limb I was holding, I silently glided toward my unsuspecting illegal fisherman. Coming out of the inky darkness into the light of his lantern in his fishing area, I was on my fisherman before he could pass any amount of gas with enough sufficiency to gain anyone's attention in a crowded church pew at a Sunday mass in Alabama's July heat and humidity in an unconditioned church.

"Morning, state fish and game warden," I said as I slid my canoe up onto the muddy shore. Then danged if at that very moment I almost did a handstand out of my canoe! There sat a very surprised local duck club gamekeeper with eyes as big as garbage can lids over my unexpected creek side early morning arrival. No way had he suspected anyone would ever come calling that time of the morning in that deserted and remote little piece of real estate. Especially at his little, out of the way, fishing hidey-hole. But, sure as God made crab apples for my mom to make into the world's finest pickled crab apples, there stood the game warden in all his Teutonic magnificence, good looks (of course), huge smile and official green, mosquito spray covered uniform, shoulder patch, shiny badge and all!

Hot dog, I thought. This chap has been nothing but a thorn in my side ever since I had worked this valley as a game warden. And specifically, the White Mallard Duck Club, the one he oversaw as its gamekeeper and hired hand in that day and age. He had ratted me out to his outlaw shooters every time I had been discovered afoot, afloat or in a vehicle on his duck club during the duck season when the waterfowl hunting was in full swing. Many times he had stymied my law enforcement efforts by pulling a Paul Revere and warning his other club members of my on-site or in-country presence so they would have time to stash their extra birds. Or, by running and concealing extra birds with his boat for some of his club's bigger high-rolling outlaws so they wouldn't be caught with the over limits in their possession. Now, it looked like he may have a smallproblem on his hands. And I was just the chap to give him a good dose of heartburn over his small fishing transgression for all the heartburn he had given me during the previous waterfowl-hunting season.

"How you doing, Harold," I boomed out like he was a much loved and long lost friend.

Still in shock over my sudden and unexpected appearance, all he could do was acknowledge my presence with a head nod, full-well realizing his old butt was in hot water over his three-out-of-four fishing line violations.

"All these rods yours, Harold?" I asked with a knowing grin as I stepped out from my canoe.

All my lad could do was just nod once again. "Well, it seems we have a small problem here. Since the State of California allows fishing in inland waters with only one pole and you seem to have four out at the moment, that creates a boo-boo," I said with an even bigger grin. It was always nice in the world of wildlife law enforcement to have a twist on someone who really deserved it. And in this instance, Harold was taking on the look of a kosher New York pretzel sold by a Vietnamese vendor in Chinatown during an Irish parade...

"Well, I will tell you what, Harold. Why don't you dig out your driver's and fishing licenses and I will just issue you a citation for fishing with more than one pole and line. Then I can be on my way and you can get back to your fishing with only one line this time or go home and get some sleep," I said with a hard-to-suppress grin.

Harold still hadn't said a single legible word as he handed me his licenses. Long moments later, the paperwork was done and with a friendly wave of my hand, I boarded the canoe. Shoving off into the velvet darkness of the early morning, I had to chuckle. Every time I had met Harold on the White Mallard Duck Club during my previous waterfowl season, he always had a lot to say to me, mostly about my poor sub-human German lineage and questionable genetics. Gee, for some reason he had little to say about my humble background that morning. I guess that kind of silence would come when one is between a rock and a hard spot, eh?

Harold later forfeited $55 in the Colusa Justice Court without an audible whimper for that little error in judgment, but the battle wasn't over... Stay tuned, Readers.

"HEY, YOU STUPID SON OF A BITCH!"

Taking a drink of cold ice tea from my thermos as I drifted further downstream, I strained my eyes looking for any more signs of lights that might indicate I had another night-fishing customer close at hand. To all you unwashed folks out there, the human eye is a remarkable organ. The human eye is so beautifully constructed that it can discern the light from a single flickering candle at a distance of ten miles in the dark of the night! That is right! That is a distance of over one hundred forty football fields away! Pretty remarkable isn't it. Protect your eyes folks, especially all you budding game warden type readers out there... Seeing no further indications of artificial light in the distance, I kept my canoe close to the Butte County side of the creek bank for the lack of overhanging and troublesome brush it offered along that stretch of the waterway. Rounding a bend in Butte Creek almost opposite the old California Duck Club, I heard some thunking sounds my canoe was making as it glided over something unseen floating in the water.

What the hell? I thought. The thunking continued as it passed beneath the entire length of my canoe. Reaching down with the tip of my oar, I snagged it on something with a rope running through it. Then there was more thunking alongside my canoe as I lifted up a rope with floats attached at intervals! It took me a second to realize I had just run over an illegal gill net and the floats on its float line! That was followed with another rather unique surprise of the evening.

"Hey, you stupid son of a bitch! Watch out where you are going!" said a loud Hispanic sounding voice. Then on came a flashlight from the creek bank illuminating Dog, the canoe, and me in all our glory.

Quickly paddling to shore once I overcame my surprise, I beached the boat and instructing Shadow to "Come," we literally ran out of our beached boat. Up onto the high bank portion of Butte Creek in Butte County were the glowing remains of an almost out campfire. Lying around it were two chaps in ragged old blankets who had been sleeping just moments before I had awakened them, when my boat had thunked loudly as it had moved over the float line of their illegal gill net. Getting the two lads up to full attention, I quickly recognized one of the men. That lad was a Hispanic fellow who worked for a farmer friend of mine as a farm laborer. As it turned out, a lad I had caught the previous hunting season with two illegal hen pheasants he had popped with his .22 rifle for dinner.

"Jose, what the hell is the meaning of running an illegal gill net in the creek?" I asked.

"Terry, I didn't know it was you, otherwise, I wouldn't have called you that bad name. I just thought you were another damn Mexican robbing our net of its fish," he said.

By now, the other chap in their camp was standing up shivering in the pre-dawn cool as well. A man and another farm laborer I also knew named Lito Garcia. Lito I had caught just a month earlier fishing illegally with three poles.

Here I had two poor as a church mouse, Mexican farmhands trying to make a living so they could send some money to their kin back in the old country. Somehow, somewhere, they had found a gill net and were running it in Butte Creek hoping to catch some fish.

Stepping away from my surprised lads, I dragged in their 20-foot gill net, wrapped it up into a ball and threw it disgustedly into the bottom of my canoe as evidence. Then both men received citations for fishing with an illegal gill net. Man, you talk about two guys who were dumber than a box of rocks. Hell, they didn't even have any fish in the net because the mesh size was too large and meant for salmon sized fish.

When I finished, Jose quietly came up to me asking if I was going to tell their Patron about what they had done. Their Patron was also a Mexican Butte County lima-bean-ranch foreman, a friend of mine whom I used to hunt feral house cats with at night and one who was as honest as the day was long. I told him, "No, but you had better pay your fine or else! Besides, Jose, why on God's green earth were you lads running an illegal gill net in Butte Creek anyway?"

"Terry, it was a way to make some extra money. We figured if we caught some fish, we could sell them to the Chinamen in Marysville. That way we could send more money home to our families in Mexico," he quietly replied.

"Best stick to making an honest living, Jose, or you and Lito (who spoke little or only halting English) will end up in jail," I warned my friend. "And make sure you tell Lito to quit this illegal crap as well. Besides, you both know damned good and well, you can call on me for some money if you or your families need something extra during the tough times of the year." Jose just hung his head and nodded. Poor old Lito. It was all he could do to just breathe in light of their situation for fear of being deported as he was in the United States illegally.

My two lads later pled guilty and were fined $150 each in the Colusa Justice Court. However, for some reason, the judge suspended all but $25 of the fine for each man... In that case, instead of filing in the nearest Butte County Justice Court, which held a no-nonsense hanging judge—read "high fines being routinely administered" —I swung the tickets into my court in Colusa. I was able to do so because being on a jurisdictional boundary such as I was currently, an officer of the law in those days could swing the citation into either court's jurisdiction. That way I figured maybe I could influence my judge and the fines would be lowered for a couple of misguided, but hardworking, poor Mexican church mice just trying to make a go of life in America. Suffice to say, my little judicial sleight of hand worked beautifully! However, Lito shortly thereafter returned to the old country never to be seen by me ever again. I guess he had enough of running from the law and always being found out by the resident game warden.

Shoving off, I left Lito and Jose thinking over their situation and their impending dreaded appearance in a court of law. However, the morning was still young, I had more creek to cover and I still felt pretty good over my enforcement efforts so far. I had checked eight chaps and written every one of them! This canoe patrol needs to be run more often in the future, I thought, especially in light of my catch per unit of work effort.

As a roaring-funny aside to the above story, in my book The Thin Green Line, Chapter 8, titled "Dogs", there is a sub-story titled, "Big Jake, The Owl, And The Scalped Cook" involving Jose and Lito's much feared Patron. The Patron was a Mexican ranch foreman named Joe, who like me, liked to kill the valley's zillions of feral house cats. Feral house cats that, because of their extreme numbers in the valley, killed and ate every ground nesting species of wildlife they could lay their paws on. And to my unwashed cat- loving readers out there reading these lines in horror, cats left to roam in the wild are very efficient killers of everything small that makes a wrong move in their presence. Hence, my pursuit of such critters with a 12-gauge shotgun and No. 4-sized shot... Joe, the Patron, had a monster-sized, mean-assed dog named "Big Jake." Big Jake also liked to kill feral house cats when Joe and yours truly went out into the darkness to hunt such ground-nesting-species killers. If you readers want to read a story that is guaranteed to put you on the ground in a laughing fit, I suggest you read that one. When you get through, your sides will hurt from all the laughing you just experienced in reading that adventurous tale of woe. Especially when you get to that part of the story where the world's toughest great-horned owl got involved, uninvited mind you, in our nighttime cat killing escapade...

THE FROG GIG AND THE WORTH OF A GUARDIAN ANGEL

Drifting further downstream, Dog and I began enjoying the soft sounds of darkness once again. We had drifted about another half mile when I saw a faint light on the Colusa County side of Butte Creek. As I got closer, I could see a small boat with two fishermen fishing right under an overhanging embankment. They had a small lantern in the bottom of their boat and would have been almost impossible to see if I hadn't been in a boat looking directly at them.

Silently gliding toward my chaps, I came up with a funny. I thought this time I would drift right up onto my two fishermen, reach out and quietly grab a hold of the side of their boat before I announced my magnificent Robert Redford presence. One, to scare the pants off them since I could see through my binoculars the extra glistening monofilament fishing lines being used in violation of the law, and two, to give them a tall tale to tell at work on how quietly this huge monstrosity of a game warden had sneaked up on them from out of nowhere. Sneaked up on them sight unseen and sound unheard, to put the grab on their miserable carcasses for fishing with too many fishing lines. And in so doing, maybe scare off a few other like in kind chaps from breaking the same law when they fished at night. Especially after hearing this tale of woe from their recently apprehended buddies at the workplace.

However, as I slowly and silently glided up on my two unsuspecting chaps who were facing the creek bank and not looking in my direction, my two guardian angels began stirring. Then as I got closer, my guardian angels quietly told me to duck. Ignoring the "duck" command, I kept concentrating on the detail at hand as I silently glided even closer up on my two unaware fishermen in their darkened pocket of the creek. "Duck," came the command one more time from my guardian angels as I continued my stealthy and highly focused approach. However, this time the warning was issued more forcefully. However, knowing everything about the earth, sun, moon, stars, and all its forces (read: "bull-headed"), I ignored the warning and kept silently moving in on my now very close-at-hand fishermen. Then my guardian angels said, "Duck!"

That time the command was so strong, it was almost physical in nature. Duck from what? Hell, I was still a good fifteen feet away from my chaps! So to humor the old feathered lads assigned to me as my guardians, I ducked my head off to one side but just slightly because I was on a mission of surprise, extremely focused and didn't want to be bothered at that close-at-hand moment in time. Ducked slightly, because I was now so close to my unsuspecting lads that to make any kind of movement in the canoe, would give away my now very close-at-hand presence and the wonderful surprise I had planned for my fishing miscreants that was sure to follow. Well, talk about a surprise...

Whifff! sailed a three-pronged, heretofore unseen frog gig so close to the side of my forehead that it smacked into the felt edge of my baseball cap and removed it from my head slicker than cow slobbers! That long handled frog gig had been sticking out from my chaps' boat into the dark of the morning, prongs and all! In the dark, coming head on to the pole with the three-pronged, barbed frog gig sticking out into its Butte Creek side, I had not seen the danger it represented. If I had kept going the way I had been positioned previously, it would have struck me squarely in the face and, more than likely, would have taken out one or both of my eyes!

The slight shifting of my weight in the canoe to humor my guardian angels, which allowed me to ultimately duck the unseen frog gig, quickly alerted my two fishermen. It scared them half to death because I was now just a scant few feet from them. Well, by the time things had settled down and my heartbeat was once again that of a human being instead of that of a hummingbird, I had my two chaps fishing with an illegal pole apiece. And, my set of healthy eyes was still intact as well! A set of eyes that went on during the next thirty years to help me catch a lot of bad-guys and assist my miserable carcass in ducking a lot flying fists and other high speed projectiles coming my way. Those eyes also enabled me to see and enjoy many of God's creations laid out for those of us who were lucky enough to be looking. They also enabled me to enjoy many of my family's related pleasures over the years. Thinking about it now, it is amazing what impact a little ole frog gig can have on one's life... Like many folks who have come before me have said, "Sometimes life is just a series of inches..."

Now extremely humbled and thankful over my narrow escape, I took care of the paperwork, thankfully tucked my tail between my legs and left. My two chaps each posted $35 bail somewhat later in the Colusa Justice Court. As it turned out, I had apprehended these same chaps, twice, doing the same thing months earlier! Then after paying their fine and remembering the evening's events that went along with that court action, they went to the Chung Sun Market in Colusa and purchased several rolls of toilet paper for the next time they went fishing on Butte Creek in the dark of the early morning hours... Suffice to say, God had been my co-pilot on that sneak-up-on-my-fishermen detail. Thank goodness He had and carried a current pilot's license!

Having had enough of the night patrol and running out of the most heavily utilized fishing waters, I lowered my motor, cranked it up and headed back upstream in the profound knowledge that if I hadn't listened to my guardian angels, I would have lost at least one eye, if not two, to the unseen frog gig! And, I would have lost the opportunity of the wonderful career still lying ahead of me, not to mention all the other facets of life. That was the last damn time I seriously ignored any warnings received from my guardian angels. Fact was, those angels were to test me shortly thereafter, very shortly...

THE GAMEKEEPER, ROUND TWO

Quietly motoring slowly back upstream toward my launch site just south of the Gridley Highway, I hadn't been running long when I got another angelic warning! This time my guardian angels were telling me to shut off the motor and just drift. Figuring they were warning me in advance of a collision with an unforeseen limb sticking out over the water or a sunken log in Butte Creek, I shut the motor off and quietly drifted in the velvety darkness. Once again, the feeling from my guardian angels was pretty strong. This time, after the nearness of the frog gig incident, I was all asshole, eyeballs, and false teeth in the alertness department when they began fluttering around inside my miserable carcass. Resorting to my paddle and now slowly moving upstream, moments later I rounded a brushy bend in the waterway and quickly observed a muted light near the White Mallard Duck Club. You know, the same exact same spot where I had caught

Harold, the duck club gamekeeper, with too many fishing rods and lines angling earlier.

Quietly approaching the lighted area, I got another great surprise of the morning! There was Harold still fishing! Feeling I would not be back anymore that morning, he was arrogantly fishing once again using his same four fishing poles! Talk about the height of arrogance! Well, I have a sure fire cure for such behavior, I thought as I silently slid up into the lantern light of his now not so secret fishing area and beached my canoe. Man, you talk about a chap being more than surprised! Flabbergasted and pissed was more like it! And this time, unlike the last, he had a lot more to say to me about my lineage, genetics, lack of beauty—those last comments really hurt, especially about my most beautiful and ample waistline—and the like. Since he had not learned his lesson the first time, I seized all his fishing rods on that second go-around and then wrote him another citation for fishing in inland waters with more than one line. By now, he was fit to be tied! Not me. I was having one hell of a good time! Especially when it came time for Harold to sign another citation promising to appear on or before the court date listed on the citation for breaking the same law, the same day, in the same place, within just a few hours of time between violations... In the end, all he could do was mutter out loud to himself and foam spittle at the corners of his mouth he was so pissed off. Finishing with the pleasant business at hand, I got back into my canoe and shoved off once again into the inky darkness. However, this time I had a Cheshire Cat grin like that critter did in the old Walt Disney animated work from the film, Cinderella. Harold may have given me fits on his duck club during the previous waterfowl-hunting season when I was trying to enforce the fish and game laws but this time, the cat had caught the King Rat.

Harold later forfeited $75 for that second violation and the judge ordered his fishing poles that I had seized that morning forfeited to the state. That really gave Harold a major case of the vapors! Especially since one of the seized fishing rods was a very old and valuable split-bamboo fly-fishing rod that had originally belonged to his now long-past father. Oh well, sometimes you eat the bear and sometimes he eats you.

Leaving my fishing fool friend, I continued heading upstream back to my original launch point. This time, my guardian angels let me know it was all right to use the motor. You talk about a lesson in life, well, I got one that morning. Henceforth, I listened to my guardian angels and their voices from inside my miserable carcass the rest of my career. I can think of at least sixty times those angelic warnings probably saved my life, kept me from getting seriously injured, or led me into solving a major wildlife investigation. You know, folks, God really does love fools, little children, and game wardens...

That Butte Creek canoe patrol, aside from the inner voices of my guardian angels, produced ten—eleven if you count me catching Harold the game keeper twice—chaps stepping over the lines of legality. As a result of those law enforcement efforts, it produced $975 in fines, not to mention a number of dang good conservation ethic lessons learned by those in the sport fishing public who chose to walk on the dark side in the fisheries world of wildlife. That was not a bad return for a few hours of work. That was especially so for the very good lesson I had learned when it came to listening to my feathered instincts. That aside, Bob Norris, the U.S. Game Management Agent and my friend who had loaned me his

Grumman Sport Canoe for my Butte Creek patrol and for many other subsequent adventures, has since stepped over the Great Divide. May he rest in peace. Man, I am sure getting old. Lord, I am just too young to be this damn old...

Chapter Four: The Elder Lake Basin Adventures

Because of California's moderate numbers of overworked fish and game officers in the 1960s, it was not unusual for adjoining game warden squads to share officers during periods of high recreational use by sportsmen in another game warden's district. For example, during the heavily utilized spring and early summer trout fishing months in the Sierra Nevada Mountains, our Sacramento Valley Squads used to assist those assigned high country officers with their hordes of trout fishermen. This mutual assistance program was also carried out in the early fall in the Sierra's during their heavy use mule deer hunting seasons as well. Then when the late fall and winter months arrived along with the Sacramento Valley's tremendous waterfowl and pheasant hunting seasons and its collateral high hunting pressure from tens of thousands of devoted duck, goose and pheasant hunters, the high country officers responded like in kind with their assistance. With that historic high sportsmen's use, the mountain wardens, many now hampered by deep Sierra winter snows, periodically headed for the Sacramento Valley. And in so doing, giving those of us locally assigned valley officers the extra needed law enforcement coverage. It was a shared duties system that worked fairly well with the officer corps and provided the critters some much needed relief from the unusually high numbers of sportsmen and just plain run-of-the-mill game hog outlaw gunners.

Once that shared officer program was in operation, it allowed the warden force to keep up the enforcement pressure on historic and problematic, periodic high use hunting and fishing areas. Collaterally, it gave all of us officers a good look and a mess of subsequent wildlife law enforcement learning experiences relative to the other geographic officers' problems and issues. In short, the California fish and game license buyers got more than their moneys' worth when it came to our combined and shared law enforcement efforts. And through the effectiveness of many of those combined law enforcement efforts, the critters got a little more breathing space, allowing many to live to see another day in their world of wildlife. Lastly, many times such fish and game warden exchange programs were a form of pure poison for the local outlaws. Particularly those observant outlaws who were more or less familiar with their resident officers usual patrol patterns and enforcement programs. That being said, those local outlaws would react accordingly when they got a wild hair to do something illegal and stupid in the world of wildlife. However, throw into that enforcement mix a different officer from another squad not used to the usual ebb and flow of another officer's district and it ended up numerous times when the dust had settled, with "hells-a-poppin'." Local outlaws doing what they did best predicated on the resident officer's routine patrol patterns, many times discovered to their chagrin, that a visiting warden using different patrol techniques and patterns caught them with their pants down. So, all in all, a great time was had by all except by many of those walking on the dark side of man. Especially outlaws who were surprised by those of us wearing the game warden green, when surprised with their hands illegally in Mother Nature's cookie jar...

One morning early my phone rang and it was my squad's fish and game captain, Jim Leamon. His counterpart stationed in Paradise, a great captain named Dave Nelson, had requested extra trout patrol assistance from our valley squad for some of his squad's overworked high Sierra officers. My captain knew I had been raised in Plumas County, which is situated in the northeastern high Sierras of California. And as it just so happened, a county that was smack dab in the center of Captain Nelson's patrol district. A county known for its excellent trout fishing, game bird and big game hunting opportunities— opportunities of which I had availed myself numerous times as a young man growing up in the area. Leamon also knew I was particularly familiar with the Sierra Nevada Mountains work area in question that Captain Nelson had described to him as needing extra patrol assistance. And with that intimate background knowledge, figured I would more than likely be his best-suited officer for just such a requested, out of squad patrol assignment.

"Terry, I need you to give a call to Warden Clyde Shehorn in Blairsden. According to Captain Nelson, our airplanes are currently dropping large numbers of trout in the Elder Lake Basin." For my readers' edification, because of the high fishing pressure in the Elder Lake Basin and the hard-to-reach-because-of-no-roads lakes, the fish and game department used airplanes to restock the lakes with fingerling and catchable sized rainbow trout on an annual basis. Continuing, Leamon advised, "According to Captain Nelson's intelligence sources in the U.S. Forest Service, the deep snows [forty feet deep in some places] have receded and now the really serious back country fishermen are flocking into that great fishing area in very high numbers. Dave further advised that the pilots air-dropping the trout are also seeing high numbers of fishermen around many of the more accessible lakes when they are making their release passes. Dave also reported that a wealth of information from the public is coming in about game-hogs taking numerous over limits of trout as a result of the ice-out bite being so hot. He further advised they need someone familiar with the Elder Lake Basin to run an undercover foot patrol to corral some of those folks breaking the law and show the flag. It seems that Shehorn is now also busy in the eastern part of his district working Frenchman and Davis Lakes' numerous trout brood stock feeder stream spawning areas (some holding spawning trout up to seven pounds) and their related closed season fishing zones. In short, Clyde has a number of poachers fishing in the closed fish spawning zones (small, highly accessible spawning creeks and streams running into his two major eastern district lakes) who are also taking large over limits of his monster sized, valuable spawners. Clyde is swamped with work in two far apart, geographic locations in his district and can't efficiently work both areas at the same time. According to Captain Nelson, Clyde needs the assistance of an officer unknown to the locals and familiar with the Elder Lake Basin, to work one side of his district while he works his major lakes feeder streams on the far eastern side of his district for the poachers taking his closed season spawning trout. Clyde has requested through Nelson, that you come up and give him a hand if you have the time since you are so familiar with the trout-fishing situation in the Elder Lake Basin. Any problems with a week or so of back country covert foot patrols and camping out in that neck of the woods this time of the year?" my captain asked as he finally ran down on the details of the assignment that Captain Nelson had requested of him. For my California readers' edification, this assignment came before the later establishment of the game warden position in Portola. Once that position had been established, the Portola officer could assist the adjacent Blairsden warden position with such backcountry and trout lake spawning details.

"No, Sir, Captain. No problem. I would be glad to get out of the Sacramento Valley's heat and mosquitoes for the cool of the Sierra Nevada Mountains. Besides, a change of pace would do me a whole lot of good. Plus, Clyde is a damn good officer and wouldn't ask for assistance unless he really needed it. When do you want me to leave?" I asked with a grin of anticipation spreading across my mug.

"Why don't you call Clyde and work that out with him. In the meantime, I will let Dave know you will be coming up to help Shehorn just as soon as you can get free from your most pressing duties here in the valley."

With little more to say, the captain quickly hung up. From that abrupt action on his part and the lack of any greeting or salutation earlier in that phone call, one could probably deduce I was not one of his favorites. I was the squad's best pistol shot and carried the highest caseload, as well as the highest successful prosecution rates—one hundred percent. Therein lay the problem. The captain and I didn't get along very well because every time he came into my resource- rich patrol district in the Northern Sacramento Valley, all he wanted me to do was to take him hunting or fishing... However, I was too damn busy doing my job to put up with that kind of foolishness. Besides, getting the right to trespass and hunt or fish on the valley's extensive private lands and many times landlocked waterways was a pain. The whole Sacramento Valley was prime hunting, frogging and fishing habitat. Therefore, many of the landowners, and rightly so, often kept such resources for paying customers, their friends, family members or themselves. Plus, I was catching a lot of the local landowners breaking many of the state's fish and game laws, which, surprise, surprise, didn't seem to endear many of them to me. It would have been difficult, to say the least, to write a landowner a citation for a fish and game violation one week, then turn around the next and ask him for hunting or fishing privileges on his properties so my captain could have a good time. Besides, hunting or fishing on private lands under such circumstances, was unethical to my way of thinking. That was because soon one would find himself in the position of having to grant in turn the landowner a break or favors as well. And to my way of thinking, everyone should be treated the same, especially when it came to enforcing the laws of the land. So, I always found excuses not to take the captain hunting or fishing in a resources rich county within his patrol squad's assigned boundaries. As a result, he got pissed at my intransigence when it came to not providing him recreational opportunities, or never being available to do so. So, we weren't exactly what I would call the best of friends. Especially when he could get the other assigned Colusa County game warden located in

Williams, the one in charge of the southern half of the county, to do his bidding in that department and I didn't. However, since the Williams game warden liked to hunt and fish every opportunity he got just like my captain, instead of working his last part over the fence off as the needs of the district dictated, they got along famously in the recreational arena. So those two peas made a great pod. Don't get me wrong. I would hunt with the best of them, especially for waterfowl with my 10-gauge double-barrel shotgun but only on the private lands of my closest friends and with the understanding that if they ever crossed the line of legality, they could expect a ticket just like everyone else. And with that philosophy, I more or less got along famously with everyone except for my illustrious captain. Well, I can't really say that. I didn't get along very well with most of the plethora of hard case wildlife outlaws in the valley either ... and believe you me, there were a plethora of wildlife outlaws running around in the county, both day and night!

After that phone call, I let my bride know I was going to be on the road for a week or so and out of touch in the High Sierra wilderness since I was going to be on foot and out of radio contact.

Hell, we were so backwards in the fish and game department in that day and age, we didn't even have any reliable hand held radios for high country wilderness use anyway. And then if I needed any assistance, who the hell would come running within moments, since I would be so far back in the brush that the chickens out there had square faces. Besides, the bears had to eat... Now my dear readers, you can see just one of the many reasons why fish and game wardens have a mortality rate that is nine times higher than the next form of law enforcement officers in the United States! Bet you folks didn't know that, did

283

you? And, those are FBI figures I refer too, not mine! When one is enforcing the laws against many folks who are armed and you are out there alone, many times outnumbered and out gunned, bad things can and do happen. Then you have the adverse weather events to deal with plus, numerous bad-assed critters that don't cotton to being handled or helped by humans, making their physicality know on one's soft body parts. With those thoughts in mind, one can get a taste of what the wildlife professional law enforcement officer actually experiences on a daily basis. And, that doesn't include those times when you have to risk your life to rescue someone else doing something careless. Careless like rafting in the mountain waterways during the high and dangerous spring run offs and the like. One just has to hope the good Lord takes a liking to the one carrying the badge. That and the fish and game officer had better be physically, mentally and tactically prepared for any kind of eventuality. However, I would take my dog, Shadow, along with me and that gave my bride some comfort when it came to my safety on such a lonely back-country assignment. Plus, she knew damned well that I lived for sleeping out with the black bears, wood ticks, dirt, eating crappy meals, using the calls of the areas birds for my morning wake up, swimming in the icy cold mountain lakes for my daily bath, all among the vicious, dinky in size with big stabbers, ever-biting mountain mosquitoes... Regarding that last issue, all you high mountain fishermen know of what I speak when it comes to the biting abilities of those dinky, winged critters with those big stabbers. She also knew, scattered among those many Heaven sent adventures, would be a jerk on my fishing line leading to fresh trout for my breakfast (one of my very favorites still to this day); cool, clean smelling mountain air; remnants of California's mining and gold rush histories from the gold rush days of '49 scattered about at every turn in the trail (I am also a history buff); starlit nights; great heaven-sent sunrises; and the always welcome smoke of a campfire. Damn, life sure could be tough for some of us poor damn old game warden types... Dang it! I once again let the wheels fall off my wagon and digressed. Sorry folks, let's get back once again to the upcoming adventure at hand.

Then I placed a phone call to my good and lifelong friend, the Blairsden District Fish and Game Warden, Clyde Shehorn. Now, that man was not only a damn good game warden but a true gentleman as well. He was thirty-five years older than me and came from the old school of game wardens who settled everything with a cool head, gentle tone of voice and if that didn't work, a pistol barrel was laid alongside one's head to emphasize the point Clyde was peddling. No better chap ever crapped between a pair of boots than that man, to my way of thinking. I had known Clyde since my boyhood days, as I hunted, fished, explored old mining camps, crawled around in abandoned gold mines and looked for arrowheads in the backwater areas of the Sierra Nevada Mountains in Plumas County. In my later years, it seemed he was always the one who checked out our family mule deer hunting party in Clover Valley every September at our usual camping spot at historic Bird Springs. And a wild group of family deer hunters and some outlaws I ran with was an understatement. Those family members were of pioneer stock and didn't cotton much when it came to obeying all the tenets of the long arm of the law and the fish and game code. The family's genetic stock originally came from a population of western Tennessee Irish moonshiners, crossed the plains in wagon trains, settled in northern

California during the fabled Gold Rush days of '49 and when they arrived, hewed out an existence on a land that was as rough and tough as a wild mustang. And in that process, bowed their heads to no one other than God. However, when it came to the official presence of Clyde Shehorn enforcing the fish and game laws in the area during the annual deer-hunting season, he was very highly respected by our bunch and was always welcome in our family's hunting camp. And no one in our group broke the law when that man was in country. That is, unless he wanted to go down the road kicking rocks because of stupid illegal behavior in the presence of such a good guy and friend of the family. Bottom line, what Clyde didn't finish with the issuance of a citation or a set of handcuffs, my stepfamily of rock hard Irish Americans did in short order...Sadly, Clyde has long since stepped over the Great Divide. I only hope when my time comes to do the same, I get a chance to strike up our friendship once again. And together, maybe cast a fishing line in some quiet high mountain creek among the clouds and share some good ol' pan fried trout, fried spuds mixed in with freshly dug wild onions from a rocky hillside, topped off with some fresh beer batter, Dutch oven biscuits slathered with my mother's thick homemade apricot jam. Clyde was a great man and a tremendously good human being. I respect and miss him to this day as these words are written some thirty-five or so years after his passing. Please take kindly to him, Lord, for he was a great man and protected your critters with the best of them when they needed it the most.

By the second ring of the telephone, I had my dear friend Clyde Shehorn on the other end of the line. "Clyde, you old scudder, how the hell are you doing? And by damn it, what the hell are you doing answering the phone.

A good game warden would be out and about this time of the morning catching those doing to Mother Nature that which they shouldn't be doing," I bellowed.

"Well, I'll be damned. Don't tell me they scraped the bottom of the barrel from that useless Captain Leamon's squad and are going to send me your scraggy ass up here to help control my high lakes local outlaw fishermen?" he barked right back upon recognizing my voice.

"Sure as God made little green apples. I guess the powers to be figured you are doing such a crappy job, they would send someone to teach you how to get the job done," I bellowed right back at my dear friend with a grin in the tone and tenor of my voice.

"Well, hell fire. When can you get here? I have at least a million fishermen up here this time of the year in my backcountry. Hell, they are breaking every law in the book and where they can't find one to break, they invent one," he grumbled.

"Well, if they had any kind of a game warden in that neck of the woods, that wouldn't be happening," I shot right back, knowing that would drag him out from his hole like a giant spawning carp after a big gob of worms on an Eagle Claw No. 6 hook that had just sailed right by the front of its nose.

"You keep that up and I will tell Barnes [Otis Barnes, my step dad and Clyde's longtime friend] that he needs to take a razor strap to your damned mangy big ol' hide," he threatened right back with a grin in the tone and tenor of his voice as well.

With that, the two of us laughed easily at the antics of two very close friends. Then Clyde got down to the business at hand. "Terry," he said, "you up to some damned ol' tough foot patrol around some of my high country lakes this time of the year?" he asked.

"Sure am, Clyde. What do you have in mind?" I asked.

"I need someone who knows the Grass, Rock, and Jamison Lake areas in the Elder Lake Basin. As you know, they are the first of my lakes in the basin to ice out and the fish historically are hungry as hell when that happens. The word I am getting back from some of my better quality back-country fishermen, is that there are some folks casting a line in those particular lakes who don't give a damn about the limits of fish allowed. And by damn it, I can't be in two places at once. The Nevada fishermen and a bunch of my local outlaws are now cleaning out my big trout in the shallow closed zone spawning streams around Frenchman and Davis Lakes like there is no tomorrow. And as you well know, I can't be there doing a good job near the Nevada border and in the Elder Lake Basin on the other side of my district all at the same time. Now I know you, your dad, and uncle used to fish all three of those lakes and know the best spots for fishing like the back of your hand. I hear tell that a lot of over limits are coming out from those three lakes as we speak and that is the area where I most need your attention. I also heard there is a lot of littering and night fishing going on up there as well." (Night fishing was illegal in inland waters in those days for all species of the family Salmonidae which included salmon, trout and white-fish.) "I damn sure could use some good old-fashioned undercover footwork by an experienced officer in those areas. And for someone your size to crawl up on those rascals and scare the hell out of them for breaking the law, would be just to my way of thinking, the sure fire ticket along with the right kind of local outlaw medicine needed. Now for the most part, those folks breaking the laws are many of my dyed-in-the-wool, game-hog locals.

And every damned man-jack one of them knows I am having to work my eastern lakes this time of the year because of the need to patrol by horseback my spawning areas in the closed to fishing creeks feeding into Frenchman and Davis Lakes. Knowing that, they also know I won't be in the Elder Lake Basin until my eastern lakes spawning protection patrol work is done and my big spawners have returned to the safety of the deeper waters of their respective lakes. So, that is the kind of patrol help I sure could use if you are of a mind," he hopefully advised, knowing he already had my big ole mangy, adventure loving hide hooked. Plus, Clyde knew my bride, Donna, very well. Donna, being an understanding game warden's wife, who had an excellent agency reputation for taking the job in stride when it came to understanding the unusual fish and game job requirements, along with the many associated lonely patrols and dangers inherent therein, which was not unlike many of the better wives in those days that had married those of us wearing the game warden greens. She basically held a reputation of understanding the need to let her man run loose in his world of the wildlife protection vision quest, a vision quest to save every darn critter he could and pinch every wildlife-violating miscreant in between. If the bad guys only knew that the best game wardens had the world's best wives. And because of that and the wives' temperament, grace and understanding, many a mangy bad guy fell to the ladies' fellas. So, in essence, the bad guys by abstraction, had been caught by the ladies... Man, if that word got out, that real life information would surely put a stain on a wildlife outlaw's kilts. Especially, if they only knew the whole truth behind the how and why they were run to ground so many times by those of us in The Thin Green Line...

"I think I can give you a hand up there. I haven't been to any of those lakes since I was a young man but that country will come back to me once I get my feet on the ground. What kind of time frame are you looking at for those foot patrols?" I asked.

"If I could get a week of back country work out of you as soon as possible, that would be one hell of a help," he said. "Knowing you and your style of work, that would cause many of my local outlaws to lay low for a while once you got into them and the word got out. Then just about the time they figured you had left the country, I will be back from my eastern patrol duties, both afoot and on horseback. And like you, I damn sure know how to scratch their illegal damn game-hog itches and desires to slide around on the wild side of Mother Nature."

"I don't mind spending a week in that back country you want worked, but how the hell do I keep my seized evidence trout from spoiling?" I asked. "As you well know, trout just don't keep for a week without some kind of refrigeration. And I just can't hide them in a handy snow bank because your black bear, raccoons, and mink will soon find them, dig them out, and eat them in a heartbeat when I am not looking or keeping an eye on my evidence cache. And I sure as hell can't walk out those many miles every time I make a case back to town and to your freezers just to preserve my evidence. If I end up doing that, I don't think I will have much of a deterrent effect on your outlaws, especially since I will be spending all my time walking those many miles back and forth from the Elder Lake Basin to your home in Blairsden so I can put my seizures of fish into your evidence freezers so they don't go to waste."

"Simple," he responded, "I have a handle on that problem as well. I want you to cite those breaking the law, with special emphases on those taking over limits. Now, since I will more than likely know most of them because they are from around here, this is what I want you to do. After citing them, send them out of the backcountry with their over limits of fish. Do so with the warning that they are to come straightaway to my home and drop off their illegal fish with my wife before they spoil." Truth be known, a game warden's wife's work was never done. In my day, I was not aware of any female game wardens working for the State of California, hence the use of the term "wife" in my narratives. And in those days, the wife never got paid for all the free work she did as the public's local fish and game information source in the absence of her husband, for the state in which he worked. "As expected, I won't be there. But my wife, Virginia, will be and she knows what to do. Tell the violators that I have worked this out with the local Justice of the Peace in Portola and if they don't do as you tell them, he will smack every one of them into the county jail for three days for contempt of court in addition to their fines. And most of those local folks know what a cantankerous old buzz saw my judge can be. So I figure they will mind and do as you say. And as far as catching my non-locals, treat them the same way. Just send them to my place with the same set of instructions. That, plus you putting the fear of God into them if they don't comply, ought to do the trick. I don't expect many out of state chaps to be fishing so far up there in that neck of the woods this time of the year, so, that shouldn't be much of a problem. However, if by chance you run across any of those out of state scamps back there breaking the law, just seize all their gear. That ought to make them appear in my court later on because to do otherwise will cost them their fishing equipment not to mention a huge fine with an arrest warrant and jail time to follow."

"So you want me to write them up and send them to your home in Blairsden with their over limits? And I am to instruct them that if they don't, when I come out with copies of their citations, they are going to jail once the judge discovers they are playing games and the seizure figures don't jibe. Particularly if the illegal fish count does not add up in accordance with what it says on my citations. Is that correct?"

For my readers' edification, especially you non-law enforcement types, many old-time game wardens in the '50s and '60s had very good relationships with their local justice court judges. And keep in mind, in those days many of the judges were also the well-known town barber, mortician, local cattleman, or shop owners. So, there was more than just a professional relationship in existence between the local game warden and his judge. It might seem a little strange to you readers having violators bring in their own evidence to be used against them. Especially since that endeavor is at the very least, a little off the wall. But that was the way it was done in many backwater districts in the old days. Kind of like a vestige of the Old West. They were just simpler times compared to the boar's nest and subsequent judicial activism present in many of today's legal communities. Activism like what I just heard about on a local news channel. A recent judge's ruling giving a member of the politically powerful DuPont family in Massachusetts, probation for many years of sexually molesting his children numerous times ... and for some of my older badge carrying, tule creeping readers, you know of what I say about how things were done in the good old, simpler days of yesteryear. Days of yesteryear when your handshake was as good as any contract and your word was your bond of honor.

"Yep, my local folks know the old judge and are aware that he doesn't mess around. If they do decide to play games, he will take a nick out of their hind ends," he continued, followed with an easy cowboy's laugh. His easy laugh reminded me once again that Clyde was raised as a young man and a real life, down to earth cowboy on a Colorado ranch. As an aside, I have often wondered in 2014, how Clyde would feel about his once beautiful birth state now. One that is over run with a mess of "potheads and druggies," all "lawfully" skating under the federal law of the land prohibiting the use of such drugs. Skating under the federal laws of the land while classified as those individuals needing medical marijuana in order to survive. That medical marijuana thing is nothing more, for the most part, then a horse-crap excuse to get a controlled substance to further one's drug habits to my way of thinking! Well, Obama did tell all those eager voting Americans he was going to fundamentally transform America...

"Got you covered, Clyde. That warning to those cited for taking over limits of trout, will take care of my long-range concerns about losing my evidence. Plus it also frees me up to roam at will, not having to mess with a ton of spoiling fish at the end of the week. Especially with every hungry, just out from hibernation, black bear in the country smelling them and following me around hoping for an easy meal," I answered. "I will come up in the undercover truck so your lads won't recognize who I am at the trail head and will use a Nevada license plate to complete my cover. That way, with first blush and all, anyone coming in behind me will just figure I am another of those damn out of state Nevada fishermen and won't give my vehicle a second glance or be suspicious. When are your court dates and am I allowed to let the lads know what the minimum bail is for each of their violations?" I asked.

Clyde filled me in on the court dates for his justice court and gave me the most common bails one could expect for routine fishing and littering related violations. With that, we exchanged several other pleasantries and left with the understanding I would arrive on site in three days. Once there, I would work his three most pressing problem lakes on foot patrol, camping out wherever darkness or opportunity found me. Then at the end of a week's footwork in the backcountry with his fishermen, I would exit the area. The final plan was to hook up with Clyde at his home on the following Sunday at the end of my undercover foot patrol detail. There I would have a hot shower, a home cooked dinner, pass on my citations and any case particulars to him so he could file them in his court and thus advise his judge as per citation circumstances. Then I would return home for more of the same chasing wildlife violating outlaws in my own patrol district. God, what a great life, just as long as one doesn't weaken and sprain his face from grinning too much over having such fortunes and blessings!

But to all you mothers out there reading these lines with sons or daughters with a wildlife law enforcement bent, just remember, there is a dark and deadly side to that profession as well. All is not biscuits and cowboy songs as one of my Wyoming game warden friends used to remind me while afoot or horseback on the trail in grizzly bear country hunting the most dangerous game, namely illegal bear shooters. Sometimes the specter of flying fists, speeding bullets, high speed car crashes, horse wrecks, drownings, dangerous winter weather, generally being outnumbered by armed individuals, mean assed critters, crooked politicians, and the like, can sometimes accompany the unwary wearer of the game warden greens...

With that, we hung up and I thoughtfully slipped back into the comfort of my kitchen chair. My mind and its selected memories ran hog wild around in my head like a mad Africanized honeybee trapped in a glass jar. I had fished the Elder Lake Basin with my step dad, Otis Barnes, and my uncle, Lanoie Dresden, as a young man. My uncle and dad worked in the lumbering and logging industries in Plumas County during the weekdays. However, on the weekends, they would get together and go trout fishing somewhere in the backcountry of the High Sierras. In the process, they dragged along a 13-year-old, snot-nosed kid, namely me, who was nuts about trout fishing and learning about the early pioneer history of the area. And boy, did I learn the history of the land and its people from the two of them in the process. Especially from my step dad whose ancestors had arrived in the area by wagon train in the 1850s and had settled down in Plumas County. And in those family adventures, I got to do a lot of fishing. Fishing in places where an eighteen to twenty-inch fish was a common catch and six trout would more than fill a fishing creel! And talk about excellent eating... My mouth is watering as I write these lines over those tasty memories of pink-meated trout frying away along with some spuds and eggs all done in the wide open spaces while smelling the wood smoke from a nearby campfire and hearing the birds welcoming me to a new day. All that accompanied with a curious Steller's jay flying into camp to eat a piece of proffered fried trout left on a nearby log for the critter to enjoy for his breakfast. In fact, many times the Steller's jay, especially in the wilderness areas where humankind visits were infrequent, would land on one's hands and take a piece of food from your fingers. And, do so without a care or worry in the world. Those were some of my fondest of days and memories! Little did I realize that those and many other world of wildlife memories illustrating the need for defending our wildlife heritage, were the genesis of my thirty-two-year career to follow in the state and federal wildlife law enforcement arenas. Well, those memories, plus courting and eventually marrying the love of my life that still is with me some fifty-two-plus years later as these words are being edited in 2015...

In addition to my looking-back, the Elder Lake Basin memories were of a historic area rugged beyond compare with its massive granite bluffs, densely snowbrush-covered ridges, crystal clear, High Sierra lakes, trout fishing beyond belief and wildlife of every sort close at hand. I guess to my way of thinking in its simplest of forms, the Elder Lake Basin was a necklace of sparkling lakes, enjoyed by human kind and watched over by God. It had been home to the California Indians first, followed by early Spanish explorers, the hardy Mountain Men fur trappers a few years later, then the hard drinking, strap steel tough placer, monitor and hard rock miners of '49 during the fabled California Gold Rush days. Cluttered throughout the basin was evidence of the miners' past legacy: old abandoned mines; historic relics of campsites and broken down, slowly rotting cabins; yellowed tailing piles; wagon trails chiseled out of solid rock; old mining machinery in their rusted, silent beauty abandoned to the elements; a few old overgrown stamp mills; old, now sun-colored purple whiskey bottles dropped along the trails; and the occasional broken pick or worn out shovel head spoke to the history of this rugged landscape. That, plus the many ghosts of yesteryear, who had ventured into such country as young men with hopeful hearts and for whatever deadly event's occurrence, were never allowed to leave...

Twice as a young man fishing in the area, I came across numerous grave-sized mounds of rocks heaped knee high, deep in the snow brush fields, that for the most part, were lost to the casual glance of the untrained human eye or the loved ones of those lying now unknown underground and waiting. These rock piles placed there to keep the grizzly bear and wolves from digging up and eating the mortal remains, were more than likely the final resting places of some poor, unknown unfortunates who had not survived the rigors of the heady days of the California Gold Rush. Individuals who were forever lost in the annals of time but not forgotten by the One above. And sadly, even the California grizzly bear and the wolves that used to dig up the less-tended graves have disappeared into the musty pages of natural history as well. In the summer, days seldom were above sixty degrees at that altitude and at night, frosts and sometimes snow in mid-July were commonplace. The winter snows in the high Sierras during the historic days of '49 were heavy with moisture and many times twenty to sixty feet deep! Snows as such during those hard times, requiring most everything to be brought in on pack boards on one's back, by sled, or by mules wearing snow boots so they wouldn't sink so deeply into the snows while pulling heavy loads. It was a hard life to be sure and a short one for man and animal alike, especially when one took into account the accidents, freezing to death, explosions, cave-ins, starvation, muck trains colliding with powder trains, coming out second best after tangling with a California grizzly bear, horse wrecks, and other such life threatening events normally occurring on a daily basis to the unwary or unlucky miner. And the reward—gold! Hundreds of millions of dollars' worth were extracted from the massive mountains and high Sierra valleys in the Elder Lake Basin during its hell-roaring days! Some of the mines in the basin produced over one hundred million dollars' worth of gold and that was at the 1850s prices of twelve to sixteen dollars per ounce—golden wealth that filled few miners' pockets but in total, helped to build the greatest nation in the world.

Today's "wealth" in that area is not mineral but the fishing, hunting, hiking and other outdoor recreational values that are now found in the Elder Lake Basin. The entire area is dotted with numerous deep mountain lakes. Lakes that are full of brook, German brown, and rainbow trout. And still many big ones waiting to be caught at that! The scenery that accompanies such fishing adventures into that area is beautifully rugged beyond description. Throw into that mix numerous resident blue grouse, black bears, mountain lions, yellow-bellied marmots, the rare wolverine and monster mule deer, and you get a slight taste of what awaits one venturing into such a piece of Heaven located right here on earth. And the real beauty surrounding such beautiful natural heritage in my days in the '50s and '60s, was that there were few roads into the area. And on those that were more or less present, you had better travel with one hell- for-stout four wheel drive because the last wheeled vehicles that had traveled such roads were drawn by straining yokes of oxen, teams of hardy mules or spans of stout draft horses. If you wanted to see the crown jewels of the High Sierras like those within the Elder Lake Basin, you had better plan on doing so by shank's mare. And if you do, what a natural treasure awaits your eyes, heart and soul... I couldn't wait to get back into those lands of adventure, history, hope, historical despair, all over laid with gold fever and the soft *ker-flop* of trout on the rise on an unspoiled, deep and rocky, High Sierra lake, not to mention the smell of pan-fried trout and spuds for breakfast over an open campfire! Forty-five years later as these words are written, I can still feel the thrill and anticipation of those periodic High Sierra patrol and fishing adventures in this burned out and broken down old carcass that I now call myself. However, I still smile over those long ago, wonderful adventures that in part, brought my miserable carcass to such a worn out physical state. But let me tell you, the brightness of those adventures will burn in my heart and soul until all my other lights go out. Oh well, you cannot make history unless you are a part of it... and in the above case, great moments in one's life usually do not return. So, they are to be cherished as well as enjoyed during those rare moments and kept as memories to be retrieved during one's rainy days of age and life...

GRASS LAKE

Kissing my long-suffering bride and two young sons good-bye, Dog and I headed out for the Elder Lake Basin undercover foot patrol in Plumas County. Through the Northern Sacramento Valley of greening up rice fields into the Town of Oroville I headed for lunch at a favorite Chinese restaurant of mine named "Charlie's." Oroville was another one of those fabled historic mining towns and districts during the California Gold Rush days, an area producing millions in gold from the ore bearing sands, bedrock, and the gravel from the nearby Feather River. Even today from the window of your speeding automobile, if one is sharp eyed and history bent, you can readily see the hardscrabble results from the miners and their labors. Evidence clearly exists where the miners changed the river's channel and then stacked huge piles of river rock along the banks in their efforts to get at the gold bearing bedrock below.

Oroville was also a onetime stopping-off place and sometimes hangout of a famous California stagecoach highwayman and poet named Black Bart. One of the things that made him famous was that after a successful robbery of the stagecoach's strongbox, Bart would leave his taunting poem—he hated the Wells Fargo leadership—and signature poetic calling card signed, PO 8 (poet). Bart had at one time robbed an old personal friend of mine and one-time stagecoach driver named Andy Swingle. Andy had been pressed into service driving a Wells Fargo Stage Coach from my Sierra Nevada Mountain hometown of Quincy to Oroville as a relief driver. Andy was a regular mud-wagon stagecoach driver from Quincy to the gold mining town of La Porte. A mud wagon was nothing more than a very stoutly built stagecoach, that was commonly used in the early California days when traversing the rough and largely undeveloped roads to various communities that sprang up in the Sierra Nevada Mountain gold camps. It seems, according to Andy, that the regular Wells Fargo stage driver from Quincy to Oroville, had developed a bad case of the "trots" after consuming some bad food earlier along the way at one of his previously scheduled stage stops. That driver, being unable to continue, had pressed Andy into finishing out his route to Oroville. Hence, Andy's presence as a relief driver on that fateful and historic day. After walking his three-span of horses up a very long grade from out of the Feather River Canyon onto a level patch of timbered ground, Andy had stopped to let the horses blow. It was at that moment that Black Bart stepped out from behind a convenient boulder wearing a flour sack-like hood over his head with holes cut in it for his eyes and mouth, leveled a double-barreled shotgun at Andy and demanded the strong box! As an aside, if any of you readers care to read about the rest of that remarkable piece of California history, you will have to read about it in one of my books titled Genesis of a Duck Cop, Chapter 7, titled "Andy Swingle." What a wonderful adventure that real-life story turned out to be for me as a result of my visiting a lonely and dying 98-year-old man who had no living relatives or friends. As it turned out, doing so as a wide-eyed teenager growing up in the onetime mining Town of Quincy in the early '50s, at the behest of Medical Technician Howard Larson, a man who would become my future father-in- law ... and in the process, scared to death at the specter of the old man's near-at-hand passing but also held thereby some other force of nature in order to provide him comfort during his last days. Little did I realize at that moment in time as a result of those hospital visits, I would be privileged, figuratively speaking, to have my feet planted in real-life California history from two different centuries! You good folks need to read that story of Andy Swingle. For to do so means that he still lives, if only in the minds of others...

Then my travels took Dog and me up through the rugged Feather River Canyon so aptly named by early Spanish explorers for the many bird feathers discovered floating thereon. The river's namesake feathers had been deposited there by the native California Indians living along that historic waterway from the birds they had killed and picked at the river's edge. Up along the scenery spectacular State Highway 70 Shadow and I continued until we reached the small historic mining and now slumbering lumbering town of Quincy. A location that was an early home in the High Sierras for many of my adventures and memories over my formative years as a boy and a young man. Memories of fishing, hunting and exploring the old, collapsed gold mines and almost forgotten mining camps for colored bottles, pocket "mickies" (whiskey bottles purposely rounded to fit into miner's hip pockets) and any other artifacts from the gold rush days then long past that I could lay my hands upon.

By now, my readers can tell I am a bit of a dreamer and a happy student of American and natural history.

There in Quincy I stayed overnight with my folks, Otis and Alberta Barnes (may they rest in peace). Dad and I had time to chew the fat while Mom fixed her boy one of her world famous dinners. Mom was a North Dakota farm gal and boy could she cook! I still remember so many of her great dishes made for my sister, Nancy, and me as we grew up. Think about that! Those had to be some sorts of meals to be remembered these sixty-five years later. And when it came to her baking of homemade bread, rolls, beer buns, pastries, and sweet rolls, there were none finer. Except those possibly now made by my blue-eyed bride and blessing of fifty-two years of marriage and still counting.

Daylight the next morning found Dog and yours truly traveling eastward on Highway 70 until we arrived at the small mountain town of Blairsden. Then on to the smaller old mining, then lumbering, and now recreational town of Graeagle. Finally down the road a piece past the Gray Eagle Lodge and then onto the turn off for one of the Elder Lake Basin trail heads.

Dressed in grubby clothing like any other fisherman, I shouldered my pack with my necessaries, grabbed my fishing rod, and, with Dog at heel, off we went into the fabled and historic Elder Lake Basin. Taking the trail to Smith Lake, we passed its west end in route to my first area of interest and Clyde's concern, namely Grass Lake.

The trail into that area was rocky and full of numerous ground seeps and small springs. Rivulets of clear, icy cold water spewed across the trail at every turn and made for a wonderfully refreshing number of drinks as I hiked ever upward. The sun was warm, and soon I was sweating as I climbed higher and higher under the weight of my pack and thinning mountain air. Opening my light jacket, but not enough so passing fishermen could see my .44 magnum in its shoulder holster, I continued up the narrow historic mining trail. I had planned on making Grass Lake by late afternoon so I could set up my camp and catch a mess of its fabled pink-meated trout in time for my supper. Knowing that, I picked up the pace in order to meet my first adventure of the patrol. To my south loomed Mt. Elwell and to my west was equally impressive Mt. Washington. Man, being the dreamer I was, I was soon a miner toting a heavy pack in route to some far off fabled hard rock mine speckled full of golden riches. Then I had to stop my travels and let a female blue grouse and all her little peeping fuzz balls of youngsters cross the trail ahead of me. By quietly stopping, I didn't scatter all those little guys to the four winds and a possible slow death in case they couldn't find their mom again.

After another half hour of climbing ever upward in the thinning mountain air, my living in the lower Sacramento Valley's elevation finally caught up with me. Pausing at a turn in the trail to rest once again, I quietly surveyed the wilderness vistas below and above me. Then I became aware of the abject stillness and silence of the area. Not a bird song rent the air and in the quiet of the moment, I could hear my laboring heart beat and actually feel the blood coursing through the arteries in my neck. God, what a beautiful and special moment in time greeted my being! Not a cloud in the azure blue sky, the sun's warmth glancing off my shoulders, not a breath of air moved, all of which was interlaced with the intense surrounding smells of the turpens heavily scenting the air from the many adjacent ponderosa pines. Then that silence was interrupted when I heard and then observed a rare Clark's nutcracker high up in a recently lightning struck pine, industriously hammering away on a skeletal dead limb. A limb whose golden brown branches were starkly contrasted against the fading dark green of the dying parent tree. Let me tell all you readers out there, to smell the clear, vegetation scented air, walk under a pollution free clear blue sky, drink from any cold running spring I wanted without fear of getting any water borne parasites, and to be surrounded by wildlife in such a vast wilderness, was truly Heaven sent! And could you believe it, I was getting paid for being there and enjoying such pristine surroundings! Plus, I was getting to hunt the most dangerous game, namely Man, doing what he shouldn't be doing to Mother Nature. A hunt in which I was plain and simply born for... Can any of you folks imagine the tremendous heartfelt joy in all of that?

Finally arriving at the north end of Grass Lake, I shut her down for the day. Setting up my camp under several towering, sweetly scented Douglas fir trees, I commenced gathering together enough rocks to make a fire ring. Then I laid out my sleeping bag after gathering a mess of soft, green Douglas fir and snowbrush boughs for my backcountry mattress. Finishing, I eagerly rigged up my fishing rod and headed for the nearby lakeshore. Like its name connoted, there was a lot of emergent vegetation and grasses along the lakeshore. Shucking my leather-hiking boots, Dog and I waded out into the knee-deep icy cold lake water. My second cast with a small golden colored Meps spinner was followed by a flash of silver in the water near my lure followed by a strong tug on the end of my fishing line. Soon, a fat fourteen-inch rainbow trout graced my part of the grassy shoreline as it flopped away its last moments. Thirty minutes later, I had six trout from ten to fourteen inches long lying on the lake's grassy bank. In those days, the limit was fifteen trout per day per person or twenty-five pounds of fish per day. But for me, those six fat trout were enough for Dog's and my supper that evening so I quit fishing.

Fishing for the sleek and fat rainbow trout was not my only reason for looking the part of just another fisherman that evening. I was also on the hunt for my fellow man walking on the dark side of Mother Nature. Not forty yards away were a couple of fishermen. They had a small, two-man pump-up, yellow surplus military life- raft anchored on the lakeshore near their campsite. Smoke rose lazily from their campfire as the two fishermen were gutting out a mess of trout by the nearby lakeside. I did the same as I carefully watched my two chaps without making it look too obvious as to what I was doing. They had a large mess of fish from what I could see and, when they finished gutting and washing off all their trout, they put them into several doubled plastic bread bags, tied off the open ends and stuck them into a close-at-hand snow bank next to their campsite. Then they tended to their camp duties as they prepared for supper. On the far side of the lake, I observed four other folks fishing and camping. After gutting my trout, I took the innards into the edge of the timber surrounding the lakeshore near my campsite and laid them on a rock in plain view for the aerial critters to enjoy. Moments later, several Steller's jays who had been intently watching my every move from the safety of a nearby tree, as they are wont to do, flew down and made sure the fish innards did not go to waste.

Well, for starters, I had six fishermen of concern on my little lake. The two closest ones, if they didn't have limits, were sure close to it from what I could see from my location. As for the others, I was too far away to see much of any fishing activity's exact definition without using my binoculars. And to do so under those circumstances, would have blown my cover with my close at hand, now suspect fishermen. Since this was my first day in country, I figured I would have time later on to watch that bunch of fishermen on the far side of the lake more closely. So with those thoughts, I passed on using my binoculars. I was glad I did as I was soon to discover... Walking back to my camp with my hands full of washed off and gutted fish, I took a closer look at them for the first time. They were beautiful specimens. Very firm, having come from the icy cold lake waters, and the meat was a deep pinkish orange in color signifying they had been living on a high protein rich diet. The outside coloration on their bodies no artist could ever put to canvas as had the Hand of God on the original specimens. Realizing I hadn't eaten anything since breakfast at my folks' house many hours earlier, I was starving, to say the least. Digging around in my pack, I retrieved a large potato and an onion. Both of which had been heavily wrapped in aluminum foil. The spud had earlier been washed, greased with butter, dusted with garlic salt, punched with holes so it wouldn't explode while cooking and then tightly wrapped in foil. The onion, peeled, smeared in butter, and heavily spiced with garlic and seasoning salt, then double wrapped in aluminum foil so it wouldn't burn so easily because of the high sugar content found in an onion, was on deck and ready to go as well.

Building a small campfire from a close-at-hand gathering of dry limbs and branches, I headed for my pack. Digging again through my supplies, I pulled out a sixteen-inch cast-iron skillet. Into that went a generous slab of margarine removed from a plastic bag. Taking four of my trout, with the rest placed into a handy nearby snow bank, I dusted them lightly with seasoning salt, garlic salt, flour, and then a generous sprinkling of pepper. The frying pan was then set by the fire's edge so the margarine would slowly melt. By then, I had sufficient coals in which to lay my potato and onion so they could bake. Soon the heavenly smells of a slowly cooking onion and spud filled the cooling late afternoon air around my camp. Man, you talk about being in one's element, outside of not being with the rest of my family, I was home! As my great little wife used to often say over the crazy antics displayed by her husband when it became obvious that he lived for just such outdoor experiences, "You were born a hundred fifty years too late." Years later in honor of those thoughts, she had purchased a framed print of an old weathered and grizzled fur trapper from those heady and dangerous days when the West was young and unspoiled. When looking at that print, she used to say numerous times during our many subsequent conversations, "That was you a hundred and fifty years ago." I wondered if she realized that is when I had been born, what I really looked like and that was what I did for a living during my first life...

"Hello, the camp," said a husky voice.

Turning, I first looked at my dog, Shadow. Why the hell didn't she warn me about the approaching stranger? I asked a little bit bent out of shape for being caught unawares. Then I spotted my dog. She was buried up to her hind end in a deep hole as she busily attempted to dig out a yellow-bellied marmot from a nearby rocky hillside next to our camp.

Turning back towards the voice, which I figured was from one of the men from the nearby two-man camp with the yellow dinghy, I spotted a large man with a potbelly like mine, approaching my campsite.

"Afternoon," I replied.

"I saw you come in and figured I would be a good neighbor and bring you some fresh trout for your supper in case you hadn't caught very many," he said.

In his hand, he held a Blue Seal Bread bag and it was clear full of freshly cleaned trout! There weren't any big ones, just numerous smaller fish about eight inches long.

"Well, thank you," I said, as I extended my hand in friendship. After shaking his hand, he introduced himself as Jim Duce from Blairsden.

"Who might you be?" he asked, as I caught just for a fleeting moment his eyes carefully looking over my campsite with what appeared to be more than a casual interest. Almost to my way of thinking, as if looking to make sure I wasn't a game warden instead of another fellow fisherman.

"My name is Terry Grosz. I am a schoolteacher from Colusa in the Sacramento Valley. I came up here on my Spring break because I heard there is good fishing in this area," I responded with a dumb-assed look meant to put anyone looking for any evidence of the law completely at ease.

To my quick thinking and cautious readers, you might be asking yourself why I had used my real name when introductions were made. Don't officers use phony names and elaborate background stories when working bad guys undercover like they always show on the television? A good question with a simple answer. When doing light undercover work like I was doing, keep it simple. Using information you are familiar with and can speak or relate to easily is the best way to go. That way, it is harder for you to trip yourself up when being asked numerous additional questions previously asked by the targets of your concern at a later time. In short, it is easier to remember that which is true than a big made-up lie or a fancy phony story. Made-up stories many times when one is working undercover, can get your "tang all toungled up" if one is not careful...

"Well, you got that right. About the good fishing up here, that is. Fishing has been real good. In fact, my partner, Dan, and me have way more than we need. That is why I brought over these little ones. However, they are the best eating, especially when fried. We are keeping the bigger ones we caught earlier over there in that snow bank next to our camp. We figured when we got a big enough slug of fish, we would head out and mosey back down the mountain. When we get them home, we will brine, smoke and freeze them," he continued, as his eyes kept suspiciously and carefully looking over my camp for any signs of a law dog or tule creeper game warden type. Fortunately for me, my light coat was still on concealing the big magnum in the shoulder holster and my badge was snugly tucked away in a buttoned up shirt pocket. Other than that, I looked and smelled just like every other fisherman in the backcountry who had made the long hike into the Elder Lake Basin.

"Well, I sure do thank you and your partner. I caught a few but as you can see, a man of my size can be a real eager eater. And this mess of fish you brought will go a long way towards filling that empty boiler of mine not only for my supper but for my breakfast as well," I said with a friendly grin. Even sharks have grins, don't they?

Satisfied that I wasn't a visiting game warden, he handed me the plastic bread bag full of fish. Then he said, "I have to get back to our camp. Dan probably has our supper ready." With that and a friendly wave of his hand, he was gone into the fast falling darkness. Shadow, in the meantime, kept worrying that damn ol' buried clear out of sight yellow-bellied marmot like there was no tomorrow.

When Jim was out of sight and it was safe to do what I wanted to do, I counted out the bread bag full of trout. There were twenty- nine rainbow and brook trout in that mess! Remember, the daily bag limit of all species of trout per person in those days was fifteen. Putting the fish back into the bag, I set them off to one side. I had brought some evidence bags with me and figured I would just wait until it got good and dark and then transfer the fish just received from Jim into those stronger bags. Then they would go into Mother Nature's refrigerator, namely the nearby snow bank by my camp for safekeeping.

Grinning over my luck at having a potential bad guy come into my camp with the goods on him and his friend, especially with their other bag of fish in their campsite snow bank, they now had to be way over the limit! With that and a happy grin, I tended my fire and soon to be my supper's grits. By now, my spud was feeling finger- soft through the aluminum foil (i.e., baked), and I knew the onion was also done because of its faster cooking qualities. Pulling them both away from the edge of the coals, I set the frying pan on a couple of rocks over the coals and watched the now-melted margarine getting bubbly hot. Into that pan went four of my largest spiced and floured trout that I had caught earlier. Soon the smell of frying trout filled the cooling night air, intermingled with cooked onion and spud smells. Then, of course, here came my dirt covered, watch dog figuring it was dinner time for her as well with all the great cooking smells flooding the air. She hadn't even come close to that damned old marmot, other than picking up a mess of that critter's ever-present fleas from the ground surrounding the entrance to its burrow.

Supper was a touch of Heaven that evening. Dog had the two largest fried trout which were fried extra crispy so there wouldn't be any worry over her choking on the bones because, as most of you know, Labradors wolf down their food without hardly ever tasting a single morsel. Hence, Shadow's fish were basically cremated. That was then followed with a can of dog food because she had a boiler as large as mine and two trout would not have satisfied her appetite or basic daily needs. But, I always made it a point that when I got to eat, so did my faithful dog, Shadow. I still carry that bond made with her so many years ago even to this day. And, what a special bond that was. Me, I delightfully finished off the remaining fish along with my onion and spud. Then it was into the sleeping bag for a sparkling star filled evening around the embers of a dying campfire. And unlike Colusa County, all I had to put up with were the smaller but more vicious snow mosquitoes until I drifted off into the times long past during the fabled gold rush days in the summer of '49...

Just before daylight, I was up with the birds and at the job. After starting my campfire, I opened up a large can of dog food for Shadow. As I scooped out her dog food with a stick onto a nearby flat rock, I got a pleasant surprise. Plunk, went a fair sized bird as it landed on my head! Realizing it was a curious bird and not wanting to spook it off my baseball cap, I slowly continued scrapping out Shadow's dog food, as she patiently drooled a pool on the ground in front of where she had been told to sit in anticipation of her breakfast. Then my unknown aerial visitor moved from off the top of my hat onto its bill. Finally, a Steller's jay's head peeked over the bill of my hat and looked me dead in the eyes from about three inches away! Knowing how intelligent the Corvidae family of birds could be (their taxonomic classification), which included jays, I slowly moved my hand back to the pile of dog food laying on the rock in front of me. Taking a small amount of dog food in my right hand, I slowly raised my hand toward my feathered breakfast visitor. In an instant, the jay was on my hand and eagerly grabbing and gulping down great chunks of dog food with its beak. When the food in my hand was gone, back to the bill of my baseball cap he returned. Two more trips to Shadow's somewhat disappearing pile of dog food and my friend the jay, now once again back on my hand to eat the newest offering, was finally satiated. Then he was gone off my hand as fast as he had appeared... It was a wonderful wilderness moments in time. A wonderful wilderness moment in time that I realized once again, I had been granted as a gift from nature by the Hand of God...

With the jay gone and Shadow being knee keep in her drool, she was released from her sitting position and ate what was left of her breakfast. When finished, back to her hole in the hillside to worry the deep underground marmot she went and to pick up more fleas. Digging out my last two trout from the evening before from the snow bank, I began cooking them for breakfast. For all you chaps who are frothing at the bit for me to get off my dead hind end and catch some bad guys, note the leisurely pace. Well, "Slow her down, Newt, she is rearing for the barn." Even hungry snakes move slowly... Beside me on a rock lay a small notebook. In it were drawn two stick figures fishing from a nearby two man yellow inflatable life raft. One had caught eight fish and the other six since I started watching them when they initially had begun fishing that morning. Where I was sitting was a perfect place for watching without being too obvious in what I was doing, so like Custer, I held the high ground. From that location, I could see my two dinghy fishermen and all four chaps from the distant fishing camp as well. Those four had obviously moved up the lake more closely toward my position to get away from all the emergent vegetation growing along the shoreline more commonly found at their previous campsite, vegetation that had interfered with their normal process of fishing. Now they also were within good eyeball distance and into my potential kill zone, if they were foolish enough to stray across the line of trout fishing legality. Those four were catching fish at a pretty good clip and the notes in my notebook duly recorded their individual trout fishing successes as well.

I took my time having breakfast and since Shadow had lost a portion of her breakfast to the jay, I shared one of the freshly fried trout with her. Having only one fish to eat for my breakfast didn't take much time and then I tended to what few chores I had to do around camp. Chores like burning the dog food can so it could be easily flattened and hauled out with any other trash I had, washing up in the cold lake waters, and slowly rolling up my sleeping bag. All those "make work" chores were for a good reason. It gave me time to count the numbers of fish my dingy fishermen, Jim, and his pal, Dan, had already caught without arousing their suspicions. In fact, by my count, both men now had over limits, and that didn't include the fish they had caught the day before!

Like the true game hogs they were, they didn't show any signs of stopping. And since I was the game warden on scene, I didn't have a daily bag limit either...

Finally grabbing up my fishing gear, I started bank fishing. Catching and releasing several smaller fish, I continued fishing like the best of them. However, I was now slowly moving down the shoreline toward Jim's and Dan's camp in such a fishing manner so as not to arouse any undue suspicion. I figured I would get close enough so when they came in with their dinghy, I would be on them before they could toss any fish. Also, that casual movement towards them put me between them and their snow bank cache of extra fish. That way, I could have my cake, namely the dinghy fishermen, and eat it too, meaning those fish in plastic bread bags stashed in their nearby campsite's snow bank. How is that for being slicker than cow slobbers?

Finally in the catch position where I wanted to be, I casually fished and waited. I didn't have to wait long. Soon, in came Jim and Dan with their two-man dinghy. Dragging it up onto shore, Jim asked how I was doing.

"I got a few and released most of them," I advised. "However, I sure am not catching any big ones like I did yesterday afternoon."

Then Jim hefted up his stringer of trout. There had to be at least thirty fish on that stringer! And his pal, Dan, had another stringer with at least as many!

"Damn!" I said in false amazement. Then I reeled in my line and casually walked over the last few yards to where the two men were unloading their dinghy as if to admire all their fish. "How many fish did you guys catch?" I asked like a rube as I falsely eyeballed their stringers full of fish like any goofy dingbat would in the act of amazement over the moment at hand.

"Don't know," said Jim. "At least fifty or sixty fish in total," he said smugly.

"Is the limit bigger up here on these mountain lakes?" I asked, continuing my act like "Joe, the Dummy."

"Naw," said Dan. "The limit is only fifteen each, but there isn't a game warden within miles so we do as we want," he chortled loudly. "Up here we are the kings," he continued, as both he and Jim laughed heartily. "Especially with that prick Shehorn off holding the hands of his Nevada fishermen catching all his spawning fish in the closed zones on Frenchman and Lake Davis."

With those words, the devil took over my normally meek, lovable, mild, and of course, all sweetness, Robert Redford, the younger, self.

"Well, I will tell you what. Since you guys have so many fish, how about giving me a stringer full?" I asked, like an idiot full-well knowing what was coming next.

A cloud of scorn flew over Jim's face and then he said, "How about you go to hell! Go catch your own fish, you dumb shit. These are our fish and you can go to straight to hell!" Then both men just scowled at me like they were wishing for me to leave and posthaste at that.

"Well, I don't think so, Boys," I said. "Since you won't share, how about I take all the fish?" I said like a goofy rube without a single ounce of common sense and even less brains.

Boy, that sure brought an outright verbal explosion from both men! Right then and there, I was asked to get the hell out of there if I knew what was good for me and in terminology I can't put into print so as not to offend any of my more delicate readers. Still having fun and grinning like a Cheshire cat, I put my fishing rod down, took the fish and game badge from my shirt pocket and quietly made sure the lads knew who I was. Man, you talk about the scene getting as quiet as a mouse pissin' on a ball of cotton. The two game hogs just looked at me in utter disbelief! I always enjoyed those moments in time, especially when the bad guys full- well realized that the bear trap of life has just snapped shut on their last parts over the fence...

Taking their stringers of fish and having the men walk over to their campsite and out of sight from the other four fishermen still fishing below their location, I said, "Boys, I need to see some identification and a couple of fishing licenses if you don't mind. And in the process, please don't make what you are doing too obvious because I still have those four fishermen over there to check as well."

For the longest time both men just stood there like they didn't hear me. It was obvious from their lack of response to my earlier request that they were still in a surprised shock over the unfolding events at hand. Then they began slowly digging for and through their wallets for the requested items. Neither man had a valid fishing license on top of what appeared to be major over limits. I guess they felt they were so far in the outback that they could do as they damn well pleased, eh? And as I said earlier, that moment in time didn't count the fish back in their snow bank or the ones given me from the late afternoon before! Before all was said and done, the fish were counted from that day's catch, their snow bank, and my snow bank holding the fish they had caught and Jim had given to me the afternoon before. In the end, both men were charged with having 124 trout, or 94 fish over the limit! I cautioned the men about taking their fish to Clyde's home in a timely manner and warned them about what would happen if they showed up with a few fish shy of what the citation indicated. They were also advised that their fishing for the day was over, and they had best pack up and skedaddle back down the mountain before their fish spoiled, because if their fish spoiled, they would be facing another charge for wanton waste. Within an hour, my two very good catchers of trout—not called fishermen because of the lack of fair chase and illegality—had left the lake and became backcountry history.

With that, after stashing my seizures, I headed down the lakeshore to check my remaining four fishermen on the lake before the word got out that a tule creeper was on the loose and crapping in all the bad guys' mess kits, especially those who had trouble counting the number of fish caught. Those four fishing lads had several problems as well. They, too, had over limits of fish, but not like Jim and Dan. Their joint overages were only thirty-nine over. That, plus they had been drinking Lucky Lager Beer. When finished, they had tossed or sunken their beer cans into the lake, all within eyesight of a rather large but beautiful-looking visiting game warden. In California, that was considered littering under the fish and game regulations. By now, a number of the tossed beer cans had wind drifted all over the lake. I picked up those that had drifted back onto the shore. For those cans still floating out in the lake, retrieving them was a simple matter. I just had Dog swim out and retrieve them, which she was more than happy to do. Plus, that helped in drowning all the fleas she had picked up around the marmot's burrow. After receiving citations for over limits and littering, my four fishermen decided it was in their best interests to shorten their fishing trip since they couldn't fish anymore because of their current over limits. They, too, left in a grumpy state of mind shortly thereafter as well. They were also given the empty beer cans and trout overages to take back to Clyde's house to be used as evidence against them. In their care also went their copies of the citations for possessing over limits of fish and for littering. As for me, I kept the remaining copies of the citations to give to Clyde for comparison and later filing in his local justice court in Portola. Nothing like everything working out just slicker than cow slobbers or smoother than a schoolmarm's thigh...

Knowing my six disgruntled fishermen would now be telling everyone on their way out and down the trail that a game warden was patrolling Grass Lake, I was prepared to institute my Plan B to counter the above Paul Revere actions on their part. Especially since I had pinched everyone fishing on the lake that morning and because there were no untouched fishermen left on the lake, I made ready to split. Heading back to my camp, I made sure my fire was out. Then Dog and I loaded up our gear and left for other lakes further into the interior where the fishermen who were already there did not know I was in country. And by the time I got back to this lake later in the week, the game warden scare would have worn off and it would be like fresh pickin's once again. With that battle plan in mind, Dog and I headed out for the next lake on Clyde's list of lakes in the high country that he wanted covered.

ROCK LAKE

To my way of thinking, Rock Lake was the family trip down memory lane crown jewel on my undercover assignment that Clyde wanted me to patrol. Don't get me wrong, my earlier fishing trips into the Elder Lake Basin were young man memories of the highest order. In every case of a new fishing lake there was always another new series of adventures with the fishing, the wildlife or the historical remains of the hard rock gold mines from the Gold Rush Days of '49. But what made it even more special to such a young man, was I was there sharing such adventures with my step dad who I considered my dad and my favorite uncle. Those were special times in a special area with special people. I still remember as a boy the first time hiking up to Rock Lake to fish with my dad and uncle. The two men had packed in a seven-man life raft all the way from where we had started at the trailhead miles away to where we would ultimately fish. When we arrived at the lake, they had me pump up the raft with a foot pump and off we went fishing. My uncle rowed the boat initially while Dad and I trolled Ford Fenders, a type of trolling lure, and related terminal gear. Between the three of us changing off regularly so we could all fish, we caught and kept only nineteen rainbow trout. But the smallest one was twenty inches long and the longest was a solid twenty-six inches in length and almost as round as a small beer barrel! It was the only time in my life when I caught a weight limit of trout in California, or twenty-five pounds per person per day, instead of the more commonly and easily accomplished daily possession limit of fifteen trout!

However, enough day dreaming, back to the moment at hand. Walking the quiet trail to Rock Lake with Dog at my side, I reveled in my surroundings. Clean air, clean water, wildlife at every turn on the quiet trail, all scented with the pleasant breath of pines and firs, surrounded by numerous fields of brightly covered blankets of mountain flowers. God, it was great to be alive! Rounding a turn in the trail and almost hearing a Beethoven symphony of beautiful music in my ears with my arrival, there it was! Nestled high up in the Sierras, Rock Lake lay at the base of a massive granite dome. The lake itself was small in size but deeper than all get out. In fact, the local legend was that the lake was move then one thousand feet deep and it sure looked it! Its waters were the deepest blue-black in color I had ever seen and the water temperature out in the middle was as cold as any waters I encountered years later while working in Alaska as a budding wildlife college student. Being that it was nestled below a huge granite cliff out of the way of the elements, its waters were as smooth as a schoolmarm's thigh, even during the windiest of days. After a fairly long and steep uphill but beautiful hike, Dog and I had finally arrived. Slinking into a hidden position on one high cliff side so I could see the entire area below, I carefully peeped over into the lake. It held only two fishermen fishing from a small, two-man rubber life raft. For the rest of that day, I watched my unsuspecting lads as they easily caught fish after fish while they slowly trolled around and around the small lake. However, only one man rowed and the other did all the fishing with two poles off the end of their life raft. In the process, my chap doing all the fishing caught or released fifty-seven fish. However, he kept an even thirty of the largest fish! In other words, he caught a limit of fifteen fish for himself and a limit of fifteen for his friend! The only problem was that California did not allow one person to catch all the fish, or "party fishing" as it is commonly described, in inland waters. In short, my chap was fishing illegally with two poles and had caught an over limit of trout, To Wit, fifteen over the legal limit! Finally having limits, my lads headed for shore where they retrieved the rest of their gear that had been stacked lakeside and set up a small campsite. Continuing to glass their actions, I could see from their activities in the late afternoon that they were staying for the night. With that realization, just before dusk I slid away from my hiding spot and scouted out my evening's campsite to be near the outlet creek just below Rock Lake. That way, if my lads decided to sneak out unannounced later that evening, I would be between their escape route and campsite on the lake.

Turning over a few rocks in the outlet creek after my arrival, I soon found and caught a number of large hellgrammites (salmon fly larva). Onto an Eagle Claw No. 6 hook they individually went and I quickly had a mess of large, rolling fat, brook trout for the supper of Dog and Game Warden Terry. Building a small fire, I soon had my usual spud and onion roasting in the coals. Shortly thereafter, a mess of well-seasoned trout graced the hot margarine in my cast iron skillet, and the air was once again filled with one of the world's greatest outdoor smells. After supper, Dog and I found a flat, grassy knoll next to the creek and settled down for the evening. The evening soon turned to pitch black and the skies overhead were filled with zillions of twinkling diamonds. Laying there in my sleeping bag on that grassy knoll with Dog resting next to my side, I quietly thanked God for my many blessings. Then the quiet darkness of night, effects of the high altitude on my physiology being I was a flat lander, a long hike and fullness of life overcame this happy traveler. With that, sleep was ordered by the Chief Game Warden up in the sky and soon was forthcoming.

Very early the next morning, the deep rumbling growls from Dog told me we had an uninvited visitor in camp. Turning over in my sleeping bag and in the soft light of my dying campfire, I saw one monster sized black bear helping himself to the two trout I had fried the evening before. Trout that I had fried and set aside to cool not ten feet away on a nearby flat rock for my breakfast the following morning! Well, apparently God and my 450-pound bruin intruder had different ideas and the bear gobbled my breakfast down in a flash. Holding Dog in one hand and my .44 magnum at the ready in the other, we laid there on the grassy knoll in the light from my campfire until the bear quietly ambled off looking for more easy pickings. The bear was so close, that I could smell him and hear the rumblings in his stomach as he polished off my hoped for breakfast trout! Sleep after that was rather fitful, even though the soft comforting sounds of the running creek and the body warmth of my dog resting alongside my sleeping bag were near at hand.

Daylight the next morning found me once again overlooking my two lake fishermen from my hidden high vantage point in the snowbrush on the side of the cliff. This time the lads had changed their fishing positions in their life raft. The one rowing the dingy the day before was now fishing with two poles while the other man was now doing all the rowing. That was all right with me though if they duplicated their illegal party fishing actions like they had the day before. If they did, that meant both were now going to get a citation for over limits as well as for angling with more than one hook and line! Sure as I had wished for a double helping of biscuits and gravy for breakfast that morning, my new two-pole fisherman eventually caught a double limit of trout. It was now noon and my lads were looking like they were making ready to leave.

Hustling off my hidden perch, I headed a short distance down the trail below Rock Lake after making sure my lads were breaking up their camp and were getting ready to leave. However, before I left, I noticed one chap had a large backpack that sported a rubber insert. Into that went four limits of freshly gutted trout from their two days of fishing and a mess of snow from a nearby snow bank. Then the smaller of the two men loaded up his backpack. Into that went only one limit of smaller, gutted brook trout recently caught in the lake's shallows that morning. If one is to be a game hog, you might just as well go whole hog appeared to be their demonstrated backcountry philosophy. Then the smaller of the two men with the one limit of trout and carrying the now deflated rubber raft headed out first. Behind him, a moderate distance away, came the second lad carrying the large over limits of trout in his backpack and the rest of their camp gear. It almost appeared to me that one man was a decoy and the other would trail along slowly a short distance behind, making sure he never saw his partner being stopped and checked by a game warden. I surmised that if a game warden checked the first lad, the other would dump his over limit of fish upon seeing the trailside fish and game inspection, then proceed down the trail like nothing out of the ordinary had occurred. However, someone had figured out their little ruse and had a plan of his own in the making.

With that, Dog and I split for a concealed intercept point further down the trail leading away from the lake. Shortly thereafter, down the trail came the first man from the Rock Lake fishing party. From my hidden position, I let him pass carrying the single limit of trout. In so doing, I noticed he was nervously eyeballing the trail down below as if looking for a game warden type. A short time later, my man carrying the large over limits of trout came slowly walking by. However, I also noticed he appeared to be just as alert as is a mountain lion upon hearing a pack of blue tick hounds hot on his trail. Taking that as my cue, I quietly stepped out from behind a dense stand of snowbrush alongside the trail. My sudden appearance surprised the dickens out of my chap and tickled the hell out of me. I always loved that moment in time when I confronted my bad guys and they never had any thought or idea that I was within a country mile of their miserable law-breaking carcasses. Especially when they were caught red-handed with the fruits of their illegal labors and, they knew they were had.

"Afternoon. State fish and game warden. I would like to check your fishing license and your over limits of trout, please!"

Man, you talk about getting a look of utter disbelief! The look I got from that chap was classically priceless. The man couldn't even speak for a moment and just looked at me with a set of goggle-eyes. Here we were out in the middle of damn nowhere and then this huge, but of course terribly handsome and wildly beautiful game warden had just materialized out from behind some tiny twig. Then he demanded to see "your fishing license and your over limits of trout." *Zuh!* was the only thought that must have come to the racing mind of my trout-over-the-limit, game-hog outlaw!

"Yes, sir," came his reply finally, "but I don't have any fish. All the fish I caught were eaten earlier back at camp."

"Don't embarrass yourself, lad," I said. "For the last day or so, I have been watching you and your partner fishing at Rock Lake. I also saw the two of you take an over limit apiece each of those days as well as another limit from the shore a short time just before you left this morning. Additionally, each day you fished, the two of you alternately fished with two rods, which is illegal in inland waters. Since that is what I observed, I will issue both you and your partner, just as soon as he returns, citations for taking as well as possessing over limits of trout and fishing with two poles. Now, your license and a look at the fish, please," I asked once again.

By the time I had issued that first chap from the town of Graeagle his citations, his partner had come back up the trail looking for him as I had suspected he would. Since his trailing partner in crime didn't show up after a while, the lead chap with the one limit of smaller fish figured something bad had happened. With those thoughts in mind, he had doubled back on the trail looking for his partner in crime. Well, he had that right, something bad had happened...

By the time I had finished with the paperwork on the second chap, both lads had settled down a bit and now had an uneasy laugh over the whole matter. They had to laugh because, come to find out, Clyde knew both men very well. In fact, both men were Hunter Safety Instructors for Clyde and had helped him rescue yarded up and deeply snow bound, starving mule deer the previous winter. Both men were totally embarrassed over what they had done and even more so when they realized they had to confront Clyde later on with their more than rather ugly over limit story. Down the mountain they were sent with the same set of instructions the earlier over limit violators from Grass Lake had received. That embarrassed the men even more because Clyde's wife had fixed them several meals in the past when they had worked with Clyde on a public service volunteer basis. Before they left that morning, they also admitted the lead man had in fact been sent out as a decoy. They figured the number two man and partner in crime, in order for their little deception to work, would be walking a ways behind the leader. If the leader was stopped by Clyde or another game warden, and before that officer would see or get to the unseen trailing man, the trailer seeing the action ahead, was to dump their over limits of fish. Then the second man was to proceed down the mountain like nothing out of the ordinary had occurred carrying the rest of their camp gear. I wondered if the bad guys fully realized that game wardens do this watching-the-bad-guys-do-their-thing every day for a living? In fact, this ruse has been seen so many times before by wildlife officers that we have given this little decoy ruse a number instead of a name. Where I came from, we call this "leader-follower- lure-the-game-warden-away" attempt at raiding Mother Nature's Pantry, "Ruse No. 3."

As we sat there discussing the situation before they left for Clyde's and later their homes, two more fishermen walked by in route to nearby Rock Lake. One was an older man, like a father, and the other a young kid. Since I was right there with my bad guys and just visiting at that point in time, the two recently apprehended culprits couldn't say anything about a game warden being in country to the newcomers. And since I looked just like any other fisherman and the recently seized fish were out of sight, the new fishermen said their greetings and continued on their way. When my recently cited chaps had left, I made sure they didn't backtrack to Rock Lake and spill the beans about my presence to my two new fishermen. Finally realizing my two previous chaps had left for good, I headed back towards Rock Lake. Sure as God made really neat grandmothers, there sat my two fishermen. They were bank fishing and catching mostly smaller brook trout weighing up to a pound each that were commonly found in the shallow end of the lake. To all you unwashed out there, those smaller fish, by staying in the lake's shallows, avoided being eaten by the larger trout out in the deep of the lake. Then the older man got mad at the boy over something and the boy got grumpy and quit fishing. Putting up his fishing rod, he just sat there on a rock and pouted. But that didn't stop the older man from continuing his fishing. He just kept fishing, catching his limit and eleven of the boy's as well! He at least quit at the overall limit, and when they came out later in the afternoon, there I sat quietly once again alongside the trail like a big ol' grizzly bear waiting for his share of the piscatorial over limit spoils.

As they approached me sitting along the trail, I identified myself and asked to check their fishing licenses. They both complied and were legal and up to snuff in that department. Then I asked for the adult's driver's license. He got a quizzical look on his face and asked why I requested that particular license. I informed him that I had observed him taking an over limit of fish, "To Wit, eleven over his legal limit of fifteen." With those words, he came unglued, denying emphatically that any such thing had occurred. Sensing his intransigence, I got out my notebook and related back to him the times he had caught the extra fish after the young man had quit fishing. He still denied any wrongdoing in the face of my evidence, trying several times to get his son to lie saying he had caught his own limit of trout as well.

Finally, the embarrassed boy having a gut full over his dad's lies spoke up, saying, "Dad, I am a Boy Scout and you as my scoutmaster have said many times before that lying is ungodly. Being that is what you have said to me many times, I will not lie." Turning to me he said, "I only caught four of those fish, Officer. My dad caught all the rest."

Turning to the older man, I just looked at him like a chicken does when it spots movement on the ground nearby that may be some form of creepy crawler goodies.

"All right, you got me. I caught the extra fish just like you said. Write me the damn ticket and be done with it," he grumbled as he dug out his driver's license.

With that, I issued him a citation and filled him in on what Clyde wanted done with the fish. I also advised they could keep any four of the fish—the ones the boy had legally caught earlier—but the rest would have to go to Clyde's house as part of the over limit. The man never said anything after that and just glowered at me and then the boy. Moments before they left, I complimented the boy on his honesty and shook his hand. I told him how refreshing it was to find an honest young man like him. Finished with the young man, I turned and thanked the father for raising such an outstanding young man and son. I did so because that seemed to be the right thing to do. However, the old man just remained pissed, if the grumpy, tight- lipped look on his face said anything to a casual observer.

Leaving the two since it was getting late in the day, I took another trail and started my trek over to Jamison Lake. The next lake in Clyde's wish list, which was just a short hop away distance- wise. Unfortunately, Dog and I could hear that young man's ungodly howls clear across the canyon as we headed for Jamison Lake. Howls, as the boy's old man beat the living tar out of his son for telling the truth once they were out of sight and a safe distance away from yours truly. However, the dad didn't figure that I would have the ears of a California brown bat or that of a kit fox when it came to discerning and identifying such sounds at a distance... Some scoutmaster he turned out to be, I thought. Later, I made sure that Clyde was aware of the circumstances between the boy and his father on the mountain that day. Shortly thereafter, when Clyde got through with the lying father, the child beater and game hog was no longer the local scoutmaster.

JAMISON LAKE

Dog and I arrived at Jamison Lake later that afternoon. Scurrying around, we set up our meager camp off to one side and away from the close-at-hand prying eyes of the other fishermen on the lake. Hauling in several armloads of limb wood for my campfire, I set out the smaller limbs for a quick fire start once I returned. Then Dog and I headed for the lake with fishing pole in hand. Looking around, I spotted a group of older and younger men camped across the narrow end of the lake. They looked like a bunch of fathers and their sons on a fishing trip. From the looks of it, they were doing fairly well in the trout-catching department. Further along on my side of the shore stood a lone fisherman. His fishing action was pretty slow, so I soon lost interest in that lad. A few yards distant past my lone fisherman, I spotted several more fishermen. Those lads were catching a few fish with nothing else out of the ordinary occurring around them. Finishing that human inventory for my memory bank, I went fishing for my supper. Soon I had eight glistening rainbow and brook trout lying up on the grassy shore. They weren't as big as my earlier Grass Lake fish, but they were natives and plump as all get out. Some damn good eating ahead, I thought in keen anticipation of what was soon to come. Gutting my fish and placing their innards on a nearby rock for the birds, I washed the gutted fish off in the cold lake waters and then headed for my campsite.

Starting a fire as the afternoon shadows lengthened, I opened up my pack. Laying another tinfoil wrapped spud and onion by the ring of rocks surrounding the campfire, I got out my trusty cast iron skillet. Smearing the bottom of the skillet with a generous helping of margarine, I seasoned all eight of my trout with liberal doses of garlic salt, flour and pepper. Sitting there at the edge of the campfire's smoke to discourage any aggressive swarms of hard biting mountain mosquitoes, I let my mind wander as Dog investigated all our camp's nearby unfamiliar smells.

Then surprise of surprises! Dog brought me a live adult female blue grouse! The grouse was firmly in my dog's jaws but didn't appear at first glance to be physically injured in any way. She was all wet from my dog's slobbering, but Shadow was soft-mouthed so the grouse was not really any worse for wear. That poor damned old grouse probably had the heartbeat of a hummingbird being in the mouth of a feared predator but other than that, she would live another day to tell her tall tale if I had my say. Shadow, beside herself with joy over her find, was all wiggles from stem to stern, a typical Labrador. Still surprised, I gently removed the grouse from Shadow's mouth, all the while telling her what a good dog she was. Little did she realize that in the late afternoon light, there were about a dozen little fuzz balls right behind her looking at the thing that had disappeared their mom into its mouth! Not wanting Shadow to step on any of the following chicks, I had her sit. Checking the grouse over carefully to make sure she was uninjured, I gently put her back down on the ground next to her chicks. With a ruffle of all her wet feathers, the gentle bird, who had probably never seen a human being so up close and personal like before, slowly clucked off into the brush with all her little charges none the worse for wear. Shadow was disappointed to say the least as she watched the bird and her young disappear into the brushy surroundings. Here Dog had worked hard and caught her boss a nice plump grouse. Then that damned hardheaded klutz of a boss had let a perfectly good eating bird go. Some boss he was... I think she had visions of a warm grouse gut pile instead of a couple of highly seasoned trout and a can of bland Alpo dog food for her supper that evening.

By then I had a mound of coals in the fire pit so into the edge of those went my previously foil wrapped spud and onion. Shortly thereafter, the heavenly smells of a cooking onion and potato graced the evening air. Down the lakeshore apiece, the excited talk from my fellow campers was dying down as they prepared their suppers as well. With darkness finally setting in, I cleared away all the rocks from under my sleeping area and laid out my sleeping bag. Then back to my campfire I went to turn my onion and spud in the coals so they wouldn't burn. Shortly thereafter, they were removed from the coals and set off to one side to cool since they were now "finger soft," or cooked, to all of you non-cooks. Finally, into my now sizzling frying pan went four freshly-caught, floured and seasoned trout. Again, the cool night air soon smelled Heaven sent. Damn, I thought, if I didn't have a family back home to care for, I could get used to this living out under the stars thing, especially during the warm summer days and soft High Sierra nights. After setting those freshly cooked fish aside to cool on an adjacent flat rock, into the pan went more margarine to melt and four more floured and seasoned trout. Then Dog and I shared those first four crispy fried trout. Were they ever good, fins and all; the fried fins ate like potato chips. After turning my

331

latest trout in the skillet, I opened up the foil covered spud and onion to cool even further. Then with the still warm trout, spud, and onion, I feasted just like those pioneers and hard rock gold miners of old had done decades before in the Elder Lake Basin. Well, maybe not quite like the miners of old with the likes of a fresh spud and onion. I figured they ate more along the lines of beans, Dutch-oven biscuits, and probably old rancid bacon. Especially since fresh vegetables were largely non-existent in the backcountry in that day and age and were too expensive for the average pocketbook even if they were available.

The next morning right at daylight, I was back at the lakeside catching my breakfast after taking an exciting cold bath in the lake's icy and mist-covered waters. Meanwhile, Dog continued snoring as she slept deeply on top of my comfortable sleeping bag. After a superb breakfast of freshly caught trout, I lit up one of my Italian cigars and commenced quietly watching my various groups of Jamison Lake fishermen. Sitting back off a ways hidden in a stand of young firs, I could now watch them with my binoculars without being easily observed. By ten o'clock, many of the fishermen were returning to their camps for either a late breakfast or an early lunch. And up until that time, I had not observed one single violation. That did my heart good not to see anyone violating the conservation laws of the land. By almost day's end, that was the case for all my fishermen. I never saw a single one of them doing anything illegal. In fact, they even picked up any and all trash they found along the lakeshore and made ready to haul it out like good campers do who respected their surroundings.

Realizing I had an ethical bunch of fishermen on that lake that day, I broke camp the next morning and prepared to hike back through my string of lakes to see what else illegal I could stir up. However, as I started walking back toward Rock Lake, I noticed a single lad bank fishing on the far side of Jamison Lake off by himself. He was the same chap I had noticed the evening before from the looks of his dress but now fishing in a different location. Anytime a game warden finds a singleton in the sporting world, it usually deserves another more serious look. Another look, because I had discovered over my years as a game warden that many times a singleton hunting or off fishing by himself, was up to no good. Why else would the lad be off by himself? Setting my gear back down in the brush where it would not be inadvertently discovered, Dog and I crawled back into some snow brush where we could see better but not be seen in order to check things out with my singleton more thoroughly. Soon my dog's snoring just about drowned out all the singing birds in the area. Getting out my binoculars for a closer look, I intently glassed my singleton. He had one rod out and was just sitting back waiting for a fish to find his bait. Then I saw it! Off the end of his pole floated a small red and white bobber. No big deal, I thought, a lot of people fished with a bobber. But, there were also four other small bobbers floating around in front of my fisherman as well! Surprised over what I had observed, I crawled further into my binoculars for a better look. Sure as a slice of onion on a peanut butter sandwich makes for an exceptional eating experience, I confirmed there were a total of five bobbers floating in the water in front of my fisherman but with only one fishing pole in use! What the heck? I thought.

About then, one of the outside bobbers sank quickly out of sight. My fisherman reached over, picked up a monofilament line lying unseen on the ground adjacent to where he was sitting that was tied to a small stake driven deeply into the shoreline. Moments later, he hauled in a brook trout on his makeshift fishing hand line! Taking the fish off his hook, the man looked all around as if looking to see if Johnnie Law or anyone else had seen the illegal event. Seeing none, he took the fish up into the close-at-hand snowbrush, disappeared and then reappeared on the lakeshore shortly thereafter. Baiting the hook, he tossed his heretofore-unseen hand line, anchored to the bank by a limb stuck into the lakeshore, back out into the water adjacent to the other nearby bobbers. Sitting down once again, he watched his five bobbers for any sign of piscatorial action.

That smart son of a gun. He is using monofilament hand lines along with his fishing pole making him look like the Real McCoy as an honest, one-pole fisherman. When a fish struck, he quickly removed it from the hook, and took it back into the dense snowbrush behind him. More than likely, that is where he is keeping his fishing creel (a wicker like basket with shoulder straps for carrying over one's shoulder, used to hold fish and other fishing gear). Having seen enough, I woke up my dog and we began sneaking down toward my lake fisherman. As luck would have it, I got to within about fifteen feet of my chap as I sneaked up from behind, before he realized he had company of the worst kind. When he heard the nearness of my approach, he turned, took a quick look at me, got up, and began moving down the lakeshore like any other fisherman changing one fishing position for one he felt was better. However, I was sure he was trying to lead me away from his telltale extra fishing lines still anchored on the lakeshore where he had been sitting earlier. That sneaky little maneuver and a nickel would get one a cup of coffee in those days. Boy, how long ago was that when one only had to pay a nickel for a cup of coffee and that included unlimited free refills? In other words, that little familiar ruse simply didn't work—hmm, Ruse No. 4? I soon had my chap and his five lines rounded up and was doing the paperwork. Oh, I forgot to mention that he did have his fishing creel secreted back in the shade of the snowbrush in a snow bank. Alas for him, it also contained twenty-three trout, or eight over the limit! Finished with my paperwork and instructions on how to find Clyde Shehorn's house in which to drop off the evidence fish so they wouldn't spoil, I headed back for my stashed camping gear.

Retrieving my previously hidden gear, I continued on my foot patrol. Only this time, it was for a return trip to Rock Lake. When finished taking a second look at Rock Lake, I would head back to Grass Lake to look things over once again as well. With that, my back country trip would be over and I would head out to Clyde's home for a debriefing, well-earned hot shower, change of clothing, a shave, a great home cooked meal and the blessing of being able to spend some time with my bride and two sons once again.

ROCK LAKE REVISITED

Dog and I retraced our steps and once again climbed back toward Rock Lake. There we would camp out for a day and see what kind of devilment we could get into. Well, that hoped for bit of action was coming towards me a lot faster than I had anticipated. On the way up the rocky trail to Rock Lake, I chanced seeing two lads in the snowbrush a few short yards ahead of me. They were off the trail and throwing rocks into the brush with a vengeance. What the heck? I thought. We are up too high for any rattlesnakes to be in this area. What else would they be throwing rocks at with such vigor? I asked myself. Not coming up with any good answers, I picked up my pace so I could take a better look at my rock throwing party. Rounding a turn in the trail above my rock-throwing lads, I saw one of them holding up high for the other to see a still wing fluttering and now dying blue grouse!

Those son-of-a-guns! I thought. Blue grouse season isn't open! Besides, this is the time of the year they will have little ones running around. Being that they had just killed what was probably the female that meant sure death for any of her chicks. To say the least, that really browned me off! Well, they killed that grouse at the right time if there ever was one. Right in front of the game warden who just so happened to like the gentle little blue grouse species. And if anyone was there to put the medicine on that misery, it was me! I thought.

Picking up my pace, I soon rounded the turn and was upon my chaps before they could pass any gas to bring suspicion their way if they had been sitting in a tightly packed church pew during Sunday Services on a hot July day in Alabama, after singing song number 299, "In My Heart There Rings A Melody." Then the lad, who so happily moments before was holding the dead grouse high in the air for his partner and the whole world to see, quickly changed his mind once he saw me rumbling his way. Quickly dropping the grouse in the brush alongside the trail like it was something too hot to hold, my chaps, after exchanging a few hasty words and looks regarding my soon-to-be arrival, continued along their way up the trail as if nothing out of the ordinary had just occurred. Well, lads, I thought, that cow done messed in the clover, to my way of thinking.

"Morning, lads," I boomed out. "How is the closed-season grouse killing?" Man, you talk about the blood draining noticeably from two lads' foreheads in fine style. Within seconds after my arrival, they both had the look of two ashen-faced dead men lying in coffins on display along the main street of Dodge City in the late 1880s, after being caught red-handed robbing the local bank and then were shot all to hell as they tried escaping. In a manner of speaking to my way of thinking, they were dead men. Dead wrong in what they did and now dead in my sights, I grimly thought. With that, I rumbled into their personal space.

"We ain't hunting," the previous dead grouse holder lamely replied.

"If not, then why is there fresh blood and grouse feathers still on your hand?" I asked.

With those accusatory words, my chap quickly looked down at his hand. Seeing the red smears and breast feathers on his hand, he quickly tried to wipe it off on his jeans as if that would take care of his dilemma. Fat chance of that happening any time soon...

"State fish and game warden, gents," I said. "Get the duck, Shadow," I commanded, sending my Labrador ahead of me on the trail. Within moments, she returned with the freshly killed grouse in her mouth. Man, you should have seen the looks of shame creeping across my two lads' faces. And rightfully so, I might add. Blue grouse are also commonly called "Fool Chickens" or "Fool Hens." They are very gentle birds because of their isolation from man, living like recluses in the high stands of coniferous timber, places where they infrequently cross paths with man because of their lifestyle, hence their almost total trust and calmness when around mankind.

That many times accounts for why they may be taken with just a well-thrown rock or stick.

As an aside, I can remember times when as an officer, I would be working elk and deer hunters in the high country making sure they were within the confines of the law. Several times during those patrols I would run across a close-at-hand blue grouse during the open season. Stopping and getting out my handgun to try and collect the critter because they were damn good eating, I would draw a bead on their heads. I did so because body shooting a grouse with a .44 magnum is not a smooth move if one wants to eat the bird. If I missed that first shot, many times the grouse would continue walking away like nothing out of the ordinary had just happened, but usually by the second miss, they would take to flight. Like I said earlier, they were a gentle bird that had well-earned their nickname as a Fool Hen.

Plopping my hind end down on a convenient boulder alongside the trail in plain sight, I took out my badge letting the lads see the silver representation of my office. More gloom and doom on the faces of my ashen faced lads quickly followed.

Then remembering my initial concern, I asked, "Was that grouse a female?" I was met with blank looks on the faces of my two rock slinging, grouse killing experts... Notice that I didn't call their little rock throwing action "hunting." That term connotes legal fair chase and killing a grouse during the closed season surely did not fit that hunter terminology. Getting my tail end off my convenient boulder, I carefully walked past my chaps and into the area where they had been previously throwing rocks at the grouse like Vesuvius did onto Pompeii. Sure as God made a world full of wildlife outlaws for us game wardens to catch, there running around were about a dozen lost fuzz balls peeping loudly for the hen who was no more. Those desperate little actions on their part were now an open invite for anything with an appetite for little fuzz balls and an empty gut to have at it.

"You lads give me a hand in catching these little guys. And by damn it, be careful where you are stepping so you don't squash one of them," I growled. Soon the three of us were grabbing up the gentle little guys right and left. Even Shadow, my soft-mouthed dog, brought me one fuzz ball wet as hell from all the dog slobber but alive and unharmed. Pulling up several hands full of green grass from alongside the trail, I made a bed in the bottom of my empty, carried- just-for-looks, wicker fishing creel. Into my creel went thirteen of those little guys. Another ten minutes of searching produced nary another chick. Even Shadow couldn't find any more, so I figured we had them all. Then I got down to the business at hand. Both men received citations for taking a protected upland game bird during the closed season. Man, you talk about two contrite grouse killers, especially since we had just earlier rounded up the now bewildered and totally helpless little chicks.

Finished with my grouse killers, we split company. Me to continue my trip to Rock Lake, and my two lads to ponder their fate at the hands of the judge as they made their way shamefully back down the trail from whence they had just come. I was sure their trip back to Blairsden was made all the merrier with the addition of the now cooling and drawn-so-it-wouldn't-spoil, evidence female blue grouse in their possession. You know, the one they had to take to Clyde's house for storage in his evidence freezer. Fortunately, for my grouse killing lads, they only had legal limits of trout in their possession.

Arriving later at Rock Lake, I observed two chaps bank fishing. Moving in closer to them on the far side of the small lake to avoid their suspicions as to my real identity, I set up my camp. Fishing for my dinner, I had a chance to watch my lads. They were good fishermen who properly returned most of the fish they caught back into the lake by wetting their hands prior to handling and releasing the fish. Being that they were both fly fishermen, that was what I had come to expect from that usually high-class breed of fishermen when it came to fisheries conservation. For the most part, fly fishermen seldom broke the law and kept few fish caught. That evening, because of the historical conservation ethic of that breed and figuring I would not be making any cases off those two lads, I up and moved my camp closer to theirs. Soon the three of us were visiting like fishermen will do. During that visiting process, I mooched two slices of white bread from my fly fishermen's grub box, along with a fuzz ball explanation, of course. Taking that mooched bread, I laid it alongside my campfire that evening to dry out so it would be crusty hard. Later, Dog and I had our usual dinner of spud, onion, and fresh fried Rock Lake brook trout. In the meantime, my little guys in the creel had balled up for the warmth that closeness offered and were soon quiet as a mouse pissin' on a ball of cotton in the darkness of the bottom of my creel.

The next morning, I took one of my now-hard bread slices and ground the hell out of it in my hands until it was just small crumbs. Then I carefully placed the crumbs into the bottom of my creel on the grass floor with the fuzz balls. Man, did they ever do a number on those breadcrumbs! It was obvious that before their mom had been stoned to death, she had properly instructed her chicks never to pass up any Blue Seal Bread crumbs. Then I got some grass wet and placed it into the far side of my creel so it wouldn't inadvertently get my little guys' down wetted, which would lead to chilling. My fuzz balls were soon thirstily pecking at the water drops on the blades of grass. Feeling better over the welfare of my new family, I bade good-bye to my fly fishermen after asking them not to give away my official presence to any other fishermen they encountered. With that and a "thank you," I headed for Grass Lake on the Elder Lake Basin trail for what that part of my enforcement detail would bring. As for that next adventure to be, it turned out to be a wild one and in much need of the timely arrival of a badge carrier like me who was on the hunt.

Moving down the trail toward Grass Lake, I chanced upon my fishermen and their kids I had observed earlier in the week from Jamison Lake. They were resting along the trail on their way home so I stopped and visited since they were not aware of my true identity. By that little break in the action, I was given the opportunity to look the lads over. Here you readers get a good look at what a game warden does best. He or nowadays, she, is always looking for anything out of place. That is if the officer is worth his or her salt. Not in an obvious sort of way but just looking and listening... During one of those moments, I took a gander at my grouse chicks to make sure they were faring well and soon all the kids were gathered around looking at the fuzz balls in the bottom of my creel as well. Then I got a welcome surprise from clear off the wall from one of the kids. Remember, a good game warden's ears are just as valuable as is his handgun...

"You think that is great, Mister, you ought to see all the fish our dads caught. They have at least a hundred. And to keep them from spoiling, they are carrying them in their hip boots packed with a lot of snow to keep them cool. That way the game wardens won't look inside their boots," the youngster proudly volunteered.

With those telling words ringing off the canyon walls like a close-at-hand rifle shot when in hostile Indian country in 1876, I looked up and over at the dads. I am sure the look I gave the dads upon hearing those damning words probably resembled those same looks which a great horned owl gives a fleeing deer mouse in the dark of the night, who was running like hell was on his tail, across an open snow covered field with no cover in which to hide... They each were casually carrying their hip boots hooked together and slung loosely over their shoulders as they sat around resting on some nearby rocks. I could see that the hip boots were bulging out all over, being that they were partially stuffed with something. But I also noticed the dads never looked back at me after that little kid's off-the-wall revelation of mice and men being hidden in their dads' snow-filled hip boots. Having been in this type of bulging hip boots scenario in outback trout country before, I had planned on checking the lads before we parted company anyway. The reason being that hip boots made a good place to hide smallish extra piscatorial critters taken over the limit. And now that I had a perfectly good reason for being nosy, into that void I ventured forth in all my Teutonic magnificence.

"Gentlemen," I said, "I am a state fish and game warden. Is it true what this lad just said? That you lads are carrying your extra fish in your hip boots stuffed with snow so they won't spoil?" Brother, you talk about guilty looks, especially when I flashed the men my badge just removed from my shirt pocket with my question still hanging heavily in the crisp mountain air.

"We were fishing for a couple of days back at Jamison Lake with the boys," one man finally said lamely, "but we ate most of the fish we caught." However, his statement about eating most of what they caught just didn't really ring true. Particularly, if the look on his face was any indicator as to the truth of his statement. And, what did his statement about eating most of their fish have to do with my question to them anyway?

"Then you lads won't mind if I check your fish, will you?" I asked pointedly. Talk about a lot of glum looks coming from the four men when I asked that question. They all looked like they had just swallowed something that did not taste good and now it was about to come back up with a hot and sour tasting vengeance!

"Well, we have what few fish we haven't eaten left in our hip boots stuffed with snow. If we take them out for you to see, they will spoil before we get them back to the trail head," said the tallest of the lot, somewhat unconvincingly, I might add.

To me, it was obvious the men were trying their best to hide what they had in their hip boots. Unfortunately for the lads, I had been to this hip boot rodeo many times during my career and had managed to always make "the eight-second ride." And being part mink, I knew damn well when the scent of the hunt and fear from those being hunted, was strongly in the air and close at hand. Then the men began getting to their feet, telling the boys, "Let's go, Boys. We have a far piece to travel before we get home today so we had better get moving."

"Well, before you lads leave, I would like to check your fish. As for the snow issue, there is more down the trail near Grass Lake and you can refill your boots there. That way you can get home before your fish spoil," I said, determined now not to let the lads off without me looking at their several pairs of suspicious looking bulging hip boots carelessly slung over their shoulders like sacks of dirty laundry.

The men just stood there looking at each other as if hoping someone had an answer to my request that would get them off the hook, no pun intended. Even up there in the quiet of the High Sierras, the noise of their silence was incredible. No immediate actions were forthcoming as to my earlier request and I persisted like an African meerkat going for a tasty centipede right at daylight on the hot and dusty plains of Africa.

Finally, one of the men sighed and dumped out his hip boots along the trail on a nearby bed of Squaw Carpet (a dense mat of low growing vegetation). Out eventually tumbled fifty-three brook and rainbow trout! As it turned out, that was twenty-three trout over the limit that he and his son could lawfully possess. That was the same situation, other than numbers over the legal limit, for everyone else carrying bulging hip boots except for my last chap of the bunch, a tall lanky fellow. When he dumped out his hip boots, he exposed 103 fish! And since he had no son with him, that little boo-boo found him 88 fish over the limit!

Finishing the paperwork and reporting instructions with that bunch of game hogs took some doing. In the meantime, several bunches of legal fishermen walked by and when they saw what those chaps had done, they just either shook their heads or clucked their tongues in disbelief.

Finishing with my lads citation-wise, I let them take the lead as we all headed down the trail. Soon they were out of sight and probably happy to be so as they headed for Clyde's house and evidence freezer with one hell of a load of illegal fish along with a fist full of well-deserved citations for their little error in the counting department.

GRASS LAKE REVISITED

Later that afternoon, I hiked my way over to Grass Lake. Along the way, Dog and I quietly slipped up on a seven-point mule deer buck (western count), which was still in velvet. That deer had at least a thirty-five-inch spread, a typical Roman nose, and double eye guards as he quietly drank from the small spring along the trail not eight yards distant as he faced away from us! Freezing, Dog and I watched Mother Nature up close and personal like for what seemed to be an eternity but in actuality was probably only a few seconds. Then sensing something out of the ordinary was close-at- hand, that grand old Roman nosed buck with a pure white muzzle flipped his head up from the spring. There he stood statuesque for the longest moment trying to wind or see the perceived danger his ten thousand years of instincts and genetics told him was close at hand. Not moving and having the slight mountain breeze in my face, the animal could not truly sense the closeness of Dog and yours truly as long as we didn't move. Still sensing some sort danger, the monster buck turned and slowly began walking away from the spring where he had been drinking. In so doing, he walked right towards me! Not moving for fear of losing that wonderful moment in time and the critter still being none the wiser, that magnificent animal walked to within eight feet of me! Then he stopped and looked right at me finally realizing I had not been there earlier when he came to drink and now more than likely, this thing standing stone still was not a natural occurrence. It was truly at that microsecond as I looked into his intense dark eyes rimed by his long eyelashes, that again for the umpteenth time, I truly understood my purpose in life as a wildlife officer! By now, Dog and I were utterly frozen in that wonderfully natural moment in time between animal species from two different worlds. Then the softest of changing breezes wafted about my body and, with a snort and a tremendous jump sideways, the huge bodied animal was gone forever leaving only a truly spectacular memory and a slight drift of dust in the air created from his explosive leap away from perceived danger. Man, it was then I realized just how rapidly my heart was beating over such a close-at-hand encounter with the magnificence of wildness in its truest of forms. Reaching down, I gave Dog a big pat because when I had stopped and frozen over the realization of the uniqueness of the moment, she had also stopped and, upon seeing the buck so close at hand, had stood as motionless as death. Following that great experience, Dog and I stopped at what I had now just named "Mulely Spring" in honor of the memory moment in time and took a deep and cool drink ourselves from the same pool like it was nothing out of the ordinary. Standing back up, I noticed the old buck's front hoof prints in the soft earth. His hoof prints were almost five inches in length and the tips of those cloven hooves curled inwardly! And lastly, so as if not to forget the experience, I was reminded of the magnificence of that moment by his slightly pungent essence hanging in the air emitted from his metatarsal glands. What a blessing to experience such a moment in time and not having to share it with any other human! Just the game warden, his trusty dog and a wily old mossback, Roman-nosed buck. For some men, nothing is written unless he writes it! For all intents and purposes, I had just written that experience down with a goose quill pen and free flowing ink into my life history memory banks with a flourish...

With a knowing grin in my heart, a memory firmly affixed in my mind and a lightness of step, Dog and I finished our hike to the Grass Lake shore. Spying several likely looking groups of fishermen that were new to me, I moved into the middle of them but at a reasonable distance from where they were fishing so they could fish in peace. Then Dog and I set up our little camp, which was just a short distance from our original campsite near the lake. Leaving Shadow to guard the fuzz balls in my creel from any hungry, on the prowl mountain critters like mink or weasels, I spent some time gathering up dry limb wood for my evening campfire. Back at my new campsite, I rolled out my sleeping gear and then tended to my charges in the creel. Crushing up my last piece of hard bread, I placed the crumbs into the bottom of my creel. Talk about a happy bunch of chicks. They made short work of my offering. Following that, I once again wetted a handful of grass and placed it on the far side of my creel so the little guys could have a drink from the drops of water hanging on the blades of grass after they had finished eating all the bread crumbs. Finally finished with my chores as Mother Nature's newest dad, out came my spud and onion routine as my fire had now crackled away into ashen coals. Twelve casts later in the lake with my Meps golden-colored spinner and I had dinner. Back to my campsite I meandered after I had gutted the plump brook trout and then out came my trusty frying pan. Into the coals went my last spud and onion as I greased the frying pan with my remaining margarine. Shortly thereafter, freshly caught trout graced my cast iron frying pan like in the days of old. Sitting back, I let the great smells of a cooking onion and rich smells of frying fish flood around me. Man, it was great to be alive, but it was also great to be at the end of my patrol. It would be nice to play again with my two boys back in Colusa and hold my bride, Donna. My love for the great outdoors and the world of wildlife was boundless. But the love for my family was of a higher order and would remain so for as long as the good Lord let me greet every sunrise that He sent my way...

Finishing up my dinner and cleaning up my gear, I spied what appeared to be two fishermen casually walking my way in the early evenings on coming darkness. Walking up to the edges of the light from my campfire, both men just squatted down on their haunches and strangely looked at me like something of extreme importance was sticking in their craws.

"I take it from your size that you are the game warden that has been knocking the hell out of those who needed a little of your attention. Am I right?" asked the larger of the two men.

Sitting there with my back resting up against an old fir tree stump, I was more than surprised at the way they had entered my camp without announcing their presence, squatting down by my fire in my personal space uninvited and then asking straight away if I was the game warden. For the proper manners in those days, acting as they did, took a lot of sand. At that point in time, I figured everyone in the area would have forgotten about me being in country. "What makes you say that?" I casually asked.

"Well, other fishermen passing by have advised that a big game warden with a large black dog is patrolling the fishing areas on foot and pinching the hell out of everyone catching too many fish. You are as big as a horse and look like you could eat hay, plus you have a law enforcement crew cut haircut, so we just figured..." he said, as the rest of his words drifted off into the now cooling night air.

"Yes," I finally said. "I am a game warden. Why do you ask?" I casually asked.

"Please don't make it look too obvious. In fact, that is why we waited until it started getting dark. Those two men just below our camp over there by that finger of trees are game hogs. We have been here two days fishing and so have they. In that period of time, they have caught at least one hundred fish and kept all of them! Me and Mike here have had about had a gut full of that kind of crappy behavior, and were just about ready to go into their camp and take the law into our own hands when you arrived. Thankfully, you arrived when the two of them were napping and they didn't see you come into the lake area and set up your camp. We was hoping you were the law and, now that we know who you are, are damned glad you are here. Those two will catch a limit of fish and take them to that snow bank over behind their campsite, where the fish are bagged and then hidden in the snow. Then they are back at it like nothing is wrong with what they are doing. We resent those kind of fishermen in our neck of the woods, plus they should know better. We also hear tell that both of those game hogs are deputy sheriffs from Reno, Nevada. If they want to take over limits of fish, they can do it in Nevada and not in our own damn backyard," said the larger of the two men.

"Well, I appreciate the heads-up," I said. "I would also appreciate it if the two of you said nothing of your concerns to anyone else about those two chaps and just let me do my job. Lastly, I would appreciate it if the two of you said nothing to anyone else about my official presence here at the lake to any other fishermen so I could do my job as it needs doing."

Both men nodded in the affirmative at my request, then rose. "If you need any help, Officer, me and Mike here will give you a hand. We both pull the green chain at the mill in Delleker and would be all too happy to back up and enforce whatever you say or want done in the situation just described," the big one slowly concluded.

"We was both raised to obey the laws of the land and that goes double for those who are fishing on our favorite lake," the larger of the two men then added as an important afterthought. "We fished here with our dads when we was younger and bring our kids up here every chance we get. As such, we don't cotton to game-hog son-of- a-bitches, especially those from Nevada, taking all our fish. Them trout is for our boys and other good folks fishing in this area."

Starting to smile, I got the feeling those two strap-steel-tough lumbermen meant what they said. And if push came to shove, they would come out on top of any frog-pile, if you readers get the lumberjack essence of my drift, especially if they pulled heavy green lumber off a conveyor belt all day long back at the mill in Delleker.

As an aside: That mill, like many others in Plumas County, is now long gone, just as are many of the county's big virgin stands of sugar pine, Douglas fir, incense cedar and ponderosa pine. Who says, "There are always more buffalo just over the next rise?" As a further aside, when I was a high school lad of 16, I had lied about my age—one had to be 18 to legally work in the woods doing such a dangerous job—in order to work at a better paying job as a logger. Then the money saved went to pay for my future college education. Working in the woods as a logger in northeastern California in Plumas County, I saw lots of thirty-two-foot cuts of timber that took a D-8 cat pulling and a D-9 pushing just to get that single log up to the landing! Thirty-two foot cuts of timber that ran about twelve thousand board feet to that cut of the log! For the most part, those one-log logging truckloads in that geographic area are now history as are most of the lumber mills. There goes that damn "always more buffalo over the next rise" lesson once again...

Dawn was just breaking the next morning when my two suspicious and unsuspecting fishermen rolled out from their sleeping bags. Over the lake a mist was rising and one could hear the noisy quacking of hen mallards from across the way. My two fishermen built a roaring fire and soon had breakfast going. The smells of cooking bacon, eggs, and fried potatoes wafted up into the dark timber and snowbrush right above their camp. Those great smells were also picked up by a rather large fellow secreted in that same covering snowbrush behind them next to their camp. A fellow who had skipped his breakfast so he could be hidden and on station for whatever came his way in his line of work, courtesy of the two lads below him having such a fine breakfast. From my position, I could watch my chaps as they fished and yet not be seen. Dog soon became bored with the stakeout and, typically on such details of little or no activity, began snoring. Watching her sleep, I had to grin. All four of her feet were twitching like she was running in her dream world, and the small whimpering noises she made, indicated she was not catching the rabbit or whatever other type of critter she was now happily chasing. I still miss those little cherished moments in time with that ever-faithful companion... To most folks she would just be a dog. But to me, she was a damn good people.

After finishing their breakfast, my lads set out and began fishing. I quickly observed why they allegedly were catching so many damn fish. Each man opened up a jar of red colored salmon eggs once they got into the water and were soon tossing handfuls of them into the lake where their bobbers, trailing baited hooks below with the same attractant, were located. That action was called chumming and was illegal in California in those days. Soon they were reeling in fish after fish attracted to the salmon egg buffet baited area. After an hour of "catching," note at that point I didn't call it "fishing" which involved fair chase, one of the men with an 1800s era handlebar mustache, waded back out from the lake and headed into their camp with a creel jug full of fish. Without even gutting the fish, they were slid into several plastic bread bags and placed into their nearby snow bank refrigerator. Then back out into the lake the first chap went to start fishing again. A short time later, the other lad of the party waded back to their campsite along the lakeshore and did the same thing. I let this game-hog behavior continue until each man had caught a double limit of fish or fifteen over the limit. I just figured if they were going to be game-hogs, I would let them have all the rope needed to hang themselves high. You know, just enough rope so that when the trap door opened beneath their feet and they dropped to the end of their ropes, their feet wouldn't quite touch the ground...

Waiting until both men were totally absorbed in their catching and had their backs turned to me, I made my move. There was a large Douglas fir tree right next to their camp. There at its base, Dog and I sneaked and quietly sat down so I could continue watching my game-hogs in their dance with the devil up close and personal like. Pretty soon, here came "1800s Mustache" with another creel full of fish. Not suspecting I was even in country and therefore not looking for me in particular, he walked right by me to his snow bank refrigerator. During that moment, I just sat there quietly as a bullfrog on a lily pad with a grin as wide as the mighty Mississippi is long. How I loved hunting the most dangerous game, namely man ... especially those who needed being run to ground for their fish and wildlife transgressions. One of Grosz's Rules learned over the years of law enforcement service is if they aren't looking for you, they won't see you. Man, that rule is sure dead on the money when it came to being true! After hiding his fish, the man moved off to one side of their campsite and attended to a call of nature of the smelliest degree. It was only then as he squatted a short distance away, ridding himself of last night's heavy dinner, that he noticed me quietly sitting at the base of the fir tree not thirty feet away keeping a peeled eye on both he and his still "catching trout like there was no tomorrow" partner!

"Jumping Jesus!" he yelled, as he tried to quickly stand up and finish his business all in the same fluid motion, no pun intended. Have any of my readers ever been in that situation? Major surprise, as your pants are still down around your ankles, then jumping up. It doesn't work that way, trust me. Remember Newton's Third Law of physics. For every action, there is an equal and opposite reaction... Jumping up from his squatting position, my fellow tripped over his tight and low pants, then awkwardly fell backward! "Auggh!" he yelled, as he plopped his tail end unceremoniously squarely onto last night's now-once-used dinner, pine needles and all!

Rising from my position and taking that accident as my cue, I said, "Good morning. State fish and game warden. I would say you have a small problem." Well, that really wasn't totally true. My chap now had a major problem, if squarely sitting down in his rather large-sized dump at a high rate of speed had anything to do with his soon-to-be-special moment in time...

My chap continued to gag and moan about his predicament, especially when the dump fell off his bare last part over the fence as he struggled back to his feet, and then dropped squarely into the inside open bottom of his jeans still hanging down around the man's ankles! It was at that point, I broke out laughing, politely of course. A nicer thing could not have happened to a game-hog better than that. To me it was as if the Brook Trout God had loudly spoken.

It was then I noticed that my chap with the smelly problem and all his crazy antics had alerted his still trout-catching buddy. Seeing me and now realizing a problem may be forming back at camp, he grabbed his creel and began opening up the wicker top. Having seen such actions before by outlaws wishing to do away with their evidence and suspecting what was coming next, I hurriedly bellowed, "State fish and game warden. I want to check your creel. Do not dump out those fish or you will be facing additional charges for 'Failure To Show Upon Demand' under the California Fish and Game Code!"

My chap, regardless of what I had just shouted, did not hesitate one whit. Without a moment's hesitation, my chap grabbed his creel and emptied out its contents of flopping trout back into the lake. And since the wicker creel had been partially submerged in the water at his feet in order to keep the fish alive and fresh until their last moments, my evidence happily swam away. No problem. My chap had clearly heard me telling him to hold the contents of his creel for my inspection. Dumping out his fish after hearing my warning just meant he was now faced with an additional charge. A charge of "Failure To Show Upon Demand" which I would most happily institute once he was within the legal system trying to square away his sails. Plus, I had dutifully recorded in my notebook every trout he had caught, as well as the time he had dropped each fish into his creel after having removed them from his hook. In those days, many of the courts of the land took "Judicial Notice" of an officer's testimony over that of the apprehended and so charged. That meant the court many times weighed the testimony of the officer more heavily than that of a single offender. And I got paid just as much to catch the lads violating as I did testifying in a court of law against them. So, let them dump their fish if they were of such a mind. Since I had previously observed the lad catching and putting an over limit into his creel, I would be filing those charges as well, fish or no fish, as evidence of the illegal deed.

"You might as well come ashore," I advised. With that my chap came ashore, splashing water every which way like he was one pissed-off mother at being disturbed in such a manner by such a lowly human being like a game warden. Me, having been to this type of a rodeo many times before, just calmly waited.

Meanwhile, my other chap back at the campsite was trying to use a small stick to remove the remains of his dump accident from his fanny. As nearly as I could tell, all he was doing was spreading last evening's healthy dinner all around like peanut butter on his slice of bare bottom.

Finally getting the two of them together, I officially identified myself once again with my badge and asked for their fishing licenses. Just as my lumbermen visitors from the evening before had thought, my two lads were from Reno, Nevada. My chap with the messy problem asked to be excused while he took off his pants and washed them and his bottom off in the lake. I allowed him that latitude since he had also just surrendered his driver's license. Sitting my one still glowering lad with the angry fish-dumping attitude down by their camp, I waited for my other lad to clean himself off and wash out his only pair of jeans. Soon he was back at camp wetter than a beaver

355

and colder than the proverbial older teaching nun's heart at a Catholic school when you screwed up or got out of hand in her classroom.

As my one wet chap stood by their now regenerated fire trying to warm up and dry out, I sat down on a log by their fire pit. "Gentlemen, I have been watching the two of you since before daybreak. In that period of time, I watched both of you catch a double limit of trout. Additionally, I watched the two of you hide your extra fish in that snow bank behind us. Then when I announced who I was, you, pointing to the lad who had dumped his creel, dumped your fish back into the lake so I wouldn't catch you with yet another over limit of fish. However, in doing what you did after I warned you not to do so, you just added another fish and game charge to your list of violations. As it now stands, both of you will be charged with taking an over limit of fish. Additionally, when I begin digging into that snow bank behind me, I will bet both of you will also be facing large trout possession over limit charges as well. Then there is the little illegal issue of both of you using red salmon eggs as chum to attract the fish to your terminal gear. Finally, (pointing to my fish dumper), since you dumped your fish on me, as I stated earlier, you will be looking at an additional charge of 'Failure to Show Upon Demand' under the fish and game code. Any questions, lads?" I asked.

The one with an earlier attitude, upon hearing my advisories on their illegal behavior, outwardly softened and said, "Mister, we are both deputy sheriffs in Reno. What about some professional courtesies here since we are fellow officers?"

Fastening my eyes on the fish dumper asking the question, I said, "Being officers of the law, the two of you should have thought of the consequences before you broke the fish and game laws of the State of California."

"Nothing like being an asshole. Hell, you aren't even a real law enforcement officer as far as I am concerned. You are nothing but a dumb-assed game warden," growled "Fish Dumper" with the quickly rejuvenated angry attitude and now getting even more agitated by the moment.

"You can think whatever you want, but I am a California State Peace Officer with all their powers and authorities. If you choose to dispute those facts, you can do so in a court of law," I coldly replied. To my way of thinking, my chap had just crossed the line. And Hell was now going to follow him on a black horse if he continued along the path he had so unwisely chosen.

"Now, are the two of you packing?" I asked.

"Damn right!" said Fish Dumper. "What did you expect?" "Well, Gentlemen, here is the bottom line. Since both of you are non-residents, under California law you are going to be arrested and taken forthwith to the justice court in Portola where you can post bond. The reason being is that both of you have committed several rather serious fish and game misdemeanors. And California usually doesn't issue arrest warrants for fish and game violations for nonresidents if they choose to skip out on our court systems because of extradition problems involving those kinds of misdemeanors. With that in mind, I think it best the two of you go with me so the both of you can enter a plea and post bond. So, I will have those weapons the two of you are possessing before we head off down the hill to the justice court. Once there in Portola, the two of you can post bond. Then if you don't want to return and contest the charges, you are all through with the court system here in California. In short, your posted bond will settle your fine. In turn, your sidearm will be returned to you when the bond has been posted."

Because of the seriousness of the crime, their peace officer status, and the one's angry attitude, I chose to ignore Clyde's earlier suggestion that non-residents just have their gear confiscated and let them come to his house with their illegal evidence by their own free will. I figured these lads would just skate over across the Nevada border and ignore returning to California to take care of their legal obligations. In light of such probable skipping the local court's actions on their parts, I decided I would take them forthwith. Plus, it would more than conveniently fit into my time schedule for departing the area since this was the end of my long foot patrol through the lakes designated earlier by Clyde. And, it would take me a while to walk back out to the trail head, so, I would gather up my two illegal law dogs and we would walk out together.

"Well, no damn piss-anty game warden is going to take my sidearm!" said Fish Dumper. Like I said earlier, his attitude was getting even worse by the moment.

"Come on, Bob. Let's not dig this hole any deeper," said the smelly one. "You can have my pistol," he said, as he headed for his bedroll. Once there, he retrieved a stainless steel .357 Smith and Wesson revolver with a four-inch barrel.

When he handed it to me, I unloaded it and returned his cartridges.

"Well, sir," I said, turning to his partner. "What will it be? Another charge of resisting arrest which will cost you your job back in Nevada, or will you peaceably surrender your sidearm? Either way, you will not be going down the hill with me to the justice court with a sidearm in your possession. What you do next is your call," I coldly advised.

For the longest time, there was nothing but stone cold silence and an angry deadpan stare from Fish Dumper. Then he looked over my shoulder at something of obvious surprise and interest behind me. From the look on his face, I knew whatever was behind me that he was staring at so intently, was not a threat to my personage. If it had been, Shadow would have been growling a warning unless she was digging up another damned old smelly and flea ridden yellow-bellied marmot. With that realization, I continued looking hard at deputy knot head to my front. Then I could see the look of resignation slowly creeping across his eyes.

"Need any help, Officer?" said a familiar voice from the evening before. Soon alongside me stood my two rather sizeable lumbermen from the mill at Delleker. And at that point, neither looked any too friendly-like at my two game-hog Nevada fishermen.

"I think I have it under control, men," I said without taking my eyes off the angry officer still standing in front of me. "This officer was just in the process of surrendering his firearm to me before the three of us headed down off the mountain and to the Portola Justice Court so these two gentlemen can be arraigned and post bond for their fish and game violations," I quietly replied. Damn, I could swear I heard the faint tones of a cavalry bugle dying off in the distance once my burley lumbermen had arrived, if you readers get my drift...

With that matter now obviously settled, I followed Fish Dumper over to his bedroll. There he surrendered his .357 magnum. And once again, I unloaded the weapon and returned his cartridges. Sticking that pistol in the back of my belt along with the other deputy's firearm, I returned to the snow bank. As I did so, my two deputies just sat on the log by their fire looking somewhat forlorn. After a mess of digging, I soon had 206 brook and rainbow trout of various sizes spread out at my feet in the grass. Trout that I had pulled from the numerous bread bags that my two law dogs had caught earlier and stashed!

Sitting down next to the campfire, I began the paperwork. One lad was cited for taking fifteen fish over the limit, joint possession of 206 trout, and Failure to Show. The other lad was cited for taking an over limit of trout, To Wit, fifteen over the limit, and for being in joint possession of 206 trout over the limit. The citations I just hung onto, figuring I would personally issue them once in court. Then while my two game-hogs cleaned up their camp and prepared to leave, my two lumbermen and yours truly cleaned fish until we were blue in the face and smelled like trout.

Swinging by my camp, I gathered up my gear and then received a pleasant surprise. My two lumbermen had earlier folded up their camp and had decided they would escort me down the mountain with my two game-hogs. I guess they figured if my two bad Nevada lawmen tried anything funny on the way down the mountain, they would have their hands full in so doing, that is if my lumbermen happily had their druthers...

My two lads later posted bond to the tune of $1,000 each by certified check for their violations, and the judge kept their sidearms and fishing gear until their checks cleared. The judge also took care of the disposition of the trout to several needy families in the area. I never saw those deputies again.

As it turned out, that latest of several trips taken into the Elder Lake Basin over the year, was a great one and sadly my last. I never again saw that historical and wonderful neck of the woods because of the paths my fish and game and later my new fish and wildlife careers took from that day forward. During that patrol, I had managed to apprehend numerous chaps who really needed the attention of a game warden. The violations from that trip ran the gamut from a number of serious over limits of trout to taking a blue grouse during the closed season. Additionally, that trip was an adventure for me back into the annals of time involving the history of the 1849 California Gold Rush to my early remembrances of family history now long gone like the hard rock miners of old. It was also a trip in which I never again was able to duplicate the number of illegal trout seized on any single detail. In the end, I had seized over seven hundred trout that had been illegally taken! Clyde was right. He really needed some help in patrolling his back country High Sierra Mountain lakes during the spring ice out as did the Elder Lake Basin's storied fish stocks.

Then I got another surprise. When I arrived at Clyde's house to drop off my citations, he was home. It seems he had ridden his horse across a rickety wooden bridge while checking for backcountry poachers on the spawning streams and he and his horse had fallen through the old bridge into the creek below! Apparently the combined weight of Clyde and his horse had been too much for the rickety old wooden bridge. In that fall into the creek below, the horse had also rolled over and flattened poor old Clyde out flatter than a flounder. When I saw him at his home, he was a mess, all gowed up, bruised, and bent over from the horse wreck like there was no tomorrow! However, he still had a good sense of humor and we had a fine visit as well as a wonderful dinner prepared by his bride, Virginia. No two ways about it, Clyde was one tough as a horseshoe nail kind of a game warden. Man, I

361

miss running across tough old men like he was in today's modern world of conservation officers. I really think Clyde's generation were some of the finest human beings this country of ours has ever produced along with those of our Founding Fathers...

Several years later, I resigned my commission as a California Fish and Game Warden and accepted a federal commission with the U.S. Fish and Wildlife Service as a United States Game Management Agent. That new position was a lot like being a federal game warden, only with wider and more varied criminal investigative responsibilities than that of a state fish and game officer. As such, I had a different set of laws and duties to master along with learning a new geographic area in California. With that new position, my area of responsibility went from six hundred square miles as a state fish and game warden in Colusa County to one that encompassed the western half of Northern California! Plus once I became a federal officer, my duties could take me throughout the scope of the entire United States whenever called.

Upon return to my duty station in Colusa after that Elder Lake Basin patrol assignment, I had Chief Fullerton in Sacramento write my two fishermen green-chain-pullers from Delleker nice thank you letters for defending their wildlife heritage and backing me up during a touchy arrest situation involving two less-than-happy Nevada peace officers.

As an aside, all my little blue grouse fuzz balls were taken in by Clyde and his lovely wife. They successfully raised all of them and, when the time came, they were released back into the wilds of the Elder Lake Basin. I have often wondered if those little guys ever got together later at a family reunion and chirped about their wild ride down the mountain in the bottom of a game warden's fishing creel. Well, if nothing else, it had to be a ride in a fishing creel carried by one of the world's prettiest damn game wardens they ever saw and one who had arrived at the right moment in time in their young lives.

After all these years, I can still vividly remember looking into the dark, intense eyes of that surprised monster buck at Muley Springs from just a few feet away. I have often wondered if that magnificent old Roman-nosed buck, had been sent there by Someone to make sure I had the right world of wildlife heart and soul, was made of the right stuff, and would be able to go the distance in His world of wildlife? Yeah, I went the distance and loved every minute of it... When the fists and bullets were flying, He was therefore me and when His critters were dying, I was therefore Him...

THE NORTHERN SACRAMENTO VALLEY

The geography of the Northern Sacramento Valley of California, combined with its temperate climate, has made for ideal ancestral wintering grounds for millions of migratory game and non-game birds for eons. During its day in the sun, it was also utilized by the Ancient Ones, the Mexicans from Old Mexico, the Spanish Conquistadors, Russian sea otter hunters, American fur trappers, western explorers, gold miners in '49, settlers, folks from the distinct market hunting era subculture, and finally, the rest of modern day man with all his warts.

At first, watered, weedy, grassy and other wild areas in the valley lured in the huge flocks of migratory waterfowl as nesting grounds for some and for the many other winged species, as migratory stopovers during the fall and winter migration. Then as the early settlers began breaking the virgin Sacramento Valley soils and farming the rich lands, the variety and sheer volume of food plants changed from natural plants producing vegetative materials and weed seeds to numerous grain rich cultivated crops. With that, the great flocks of winged critters flooded into the valley, only now in even greater numbers, as they moved into the newly discovered and ever expanding food baskets as the tilled acres increased. Years later came one of the greatest changes in the northern valley's habitat with the advent of rice farming and its great advantages for farmer and winged migratory critters alike.

However, as farming methods and its related humanity evolved, so did the lives of the great hordes of hungry migratory birds that soon heralded dark and threatening life history clouds on their horizons. Those historical concentrations, especially of feeding and wintering migratory waterfowl, soon crossed paths with the dark side of Man. Millions of depredating waterfowl were slaughtered as farmers and land owners in those earliest of days attempted to protect their hard won crops from the empty crops of the winged ones. Soon, that slaughter of depredating birds morphed into providing a migratory bird food staple to both struggling agricultural families and protein hungry city slickers alike. Vast sums of money were now to be made as man and his technology, in the forms of advanced modes of wheeled transportation such as motor vehicles and the invention of railroad refrigeration cars, took center stage in the transportation of thousands of pounds of recently slaughtered migratory bird carcasses to the nearby population centers. New firearms technology, such as multi-shot, repeating or auto-loading shotguns, and improved ammunition soon graced the killing fields as well. Following those technological advances, millions of migratory waterfowl were increasingly slaughtered and sold because of the lack of enforceable conservation laws, spotty game law enforcement, lax public attitudes accepting such slaughters as normal events in their lives and huge commercial market hunting profits to be made in the now rapidly growing, protein starved city centers. For the next seventy years, migratory birds by the hundreds of thousands, fell prey to scores of those in the market gunning subculture who were providing wild game to the population centers and other landed masses. Just as those same style of gunners had once done with the vast herds of bison, clouds of passenger pigeons, sea otters, wild turkeys, white-tailed deer and the like. The once blackened skies full of winged creatures soon began to thin and then disappear. Loss of habitat through new, more efficient farming practices, droughts on the northern nesting grounds and increased gunning in all its forms began taking its inevitable toll. Today in part, because of the long reaching deadly stain of humanity, those once historic numbers of migratory birds are but a fraction of their former turn of the century variety of species and greatness.

Because of those great bird losses and the now finally aroused, politically concerned public over the devastating slaughter, the market hunting subculture gradually came under the stricture of many new conservation laws in California, some going into the books as early as the 1850s! A major federal law named the Migratory Bird Treaty Act was passed in 1918 forbidding, among many other activities, the commercial market hunting and sale of migratory game and non-game birds. However, the profits and bloodlust killing stain of market hunting was sub-culturally too deeply ingrained into many resident gunner's souls to be easily removed overnight.

Collaterally, the days of sport hunting migratory waterfowl, due to the fact that many of the landed masses now sporting more money and leisure time, exploded. With greater frequency, numerous and expensive duck clubs began dotting the best ancient migratory bird flyways and wintering landscapes. In just a few short years, the killing from those recreational venues was being strongly felt on the migratory game bird populations as well, particularly in the days when twenty-five ducks and thirty geese per day were legally allowed bag limits per gunner! The mass killings continued but now at a somewhat more subdued pace because of the passage of additional state and federal conservation laws and more aggressive law enforcement efforts by The Thin Green Line. However, once again, many of those early law enforcement efforts failed due to lack of manpower, insufficient judicial prowess by the legal system, crooked political intervention, lack of fiscal resources, and sometimes scant, grass roots conservation support from many of the rural public. A rural public that had been raised on the subcultural enterprise of migratory bird slaughter and sale for many years and saw little need in many quarters for its change. For many reasons, the millions of whistling wings that annually blackened the skies in the Northern Sacramento Valley of California around the turn of the Nineteenth Century, have now for the most part been greatly impacted or reduced. What is yet to come of the once great migratory bird resource is in the hands of modern day man to decide. Remember, honor in the world of wildlife is a gift only man can give himself. And there is honor in providing such a beautiful winged resource for those yet to come. To folks like the author, there is nothing like hearing the clarion call of Canada geese on a frosty cold November morning, having a pair of Northern pintail silently drop unannounced into one's decoys or the loud quacking of a hen mallard from across a mist covered high mountain lake in the morning as a trout tugs on one's fishing line. Sharing such quality times with a youngster are nothing short of life giving moments in the whispers of time. And, being able to pass on such moments to those yet to come, is just one of the blessing from those of us representing The Thin Green Line... Remember, there was always another herd of bison just over the next ridge, another sky-darkening flock of passenger pigeons in the oak forest beyond, more Atlantic salmon in the next watershed over, another pod of bowhead whales behind the trailing waves, more grizzly bears or gray wolves in the next glen, more bighorn sheep on the ridge below, more California condors on the next thermal ... nuff said.

JESS CAVE'S DUCK CLUB

One fall evening during the full swing of the annual waterfowl- hunting season, I had stayed home from working my perennial late shooters and was having a rare supper with my family. Knowing in advance that I planned on taking time off and would be home for the occasion, the love of my life, my bride, made me my favorite dinner. Fried chicken crispy style, mashed potatoes, thick chicken gravy, homemade buttermilk biscuits, garden peas, and a just out from the oven homemade peach pie with a melt-in-your-mouth crust as only she could make. And let me tell you, when my wife made a homemade pie, it was so damned good, especially her mouthwatering, always flaky crusts, even God would take a little time off from His heavenly labors and come down for a piece of her great earthly baking. Now all you readers out there can see just one of the many reasons why I love her so much and will until the day I die! To have such a wonderful woman and mate is truly Heaven sent, especially one who is the sterling force of direction and the author of my life. There is no doubt, I will love her forever and a day...

I had no more than finished supper and was contemplating asking my bride for a second piece of pie when the phone rang. My wife just looked at me with her patented patient look. "Answer it. It is more than likely for you anyway," she quietly said. Getting up from the table, I headed for the phone while my two young sons were arguing once again over who was going to get the last chicken leg from the meat platter. When one has young, always hungry and still growing sons, it is too bad a chicken doesn't have legs like a centipede come suppertime...

Lifting up the phone, I said, "Good evening. This is Terry."

"There is bait on Jess Cave's Duck Club." Click.

"Hello, hello," I said into a now dead phone. Damn! I thought. If that duck club is baited, where? Running through my mental map of the hunting club area, I remembered that particular duck club had two distinct watered shooting areas. One was located just shy of the corner of San Jose and Lurline Roads. The other was secreted out back and behind the Capital Duck Club's property and just to the north of Jess Cave's Lurline Road hunting property.

Turning, I observed my bride standing a few feet away holding up a clean uniform shirt. Removing my duck blood and feathers covered dirty uniform shirt, I slid into my clean one. While she buttoned up the clean one and fastened on my badge, I took that opportunity to fuss over her a bit. As these words are written in 2012, my sweetheart from the eighth grade, and now my bride, have been married for over fifty years! Man sure needs a good woman if he is going to be successful, especially in the world of wildlife law enforcement, and make sense of some of the world's ugly happenings. As it turned out, God gave me one of His very best angels. What a blessing!

Heading out the door into a good stiff and freshening winter wind from the northwest, I could sense the heaviness of the moisture in the air. To my weather-reading practiced mind, there was a major atmospheric event change on the way. Slipping into my well-worn insulated hip boots waiting for me at the edge of the back steps in my garage, I found Shadow, my ever-faithful female black Labrador retriever, at my feet and more than ready to go. Not wanting to be left behind, she made her intentions of going with me very clear that windy evening if excited body wiggling and happy sounding verbalizations as only a lab can make meant anything to the casual eye and dog-practiced hearing ear.

Shadow was a big lab, somewhere in the hundred-pound range. Not fat, mind you, but just a big model of a beautiful block headed Labrador. Reaching down, I took off her heavy chain collar, which made too much noise if the two of us were going to be doing any serious sneaking around in the darkness. Whenever I did that, it meant to her that serious business was at hand. Early on, I had trained her that when wearing her chain collar she was to act like Ferdinand the Bull. In other words, gentle as all get out and take all the lovin' she could get. But take that collar off and she knew it was business time. That meant a full mouthful of teeth and bad attitude, if it was commanded or a dangerous turn of events involving her master called for such behavior.

Loading Dog into the back of my patrol truck, I stood for a second facing and enjoying the freshening wind. The elements will be on my side this evening, I thought with a grin. With a wind like what is now blowing, sneaking around in the dark will be a snap. Plus, it would allow me to sneak closer to any ducks feeding over a baited area without sending them prematurely skyward in alarm over my intrusion. Once I had located the exact feeding concentrations of the ducks that would telegraph to me where the bait had been placed. With that, it would be a piece of cake getting a bait sample, marking out the suspect area in my note book and getting the hell out of Dodge without being caught by those responsible for placing out the bait who might be watching the area. Watching the area to make sure their little illegal action had not been observed by the local hated game warden. Shooting over a baited area in Colusa County in those days would result in a pretty stiff fine if one was apprehended with his kilts down around his ankles if you readers get my drift. The fine for such a serious offense was usually a month's wages and that didn't take into account the extra price tag for the numbers of ducks one killed over that baited area.

Firing up my truck, Dog and I headed down the Princeton Highway toward the northern end of the Sacramento Valley Town of Colusa. Once there, I turned west on Lurline Road. Seeing the road was basically without traffic that time of the evening, I turned off my headlights and flipped on my cut out switches. That way, I could let my eyes adjust to the darkness and brake or backup without any lights coming on to give away my position to those I didn't want to know I was in country. Somewhat later, I slipped down off Lurline Road into a dense stand of eucalyptus trees where my vehicle would not be so easily observed in the dark of the night by the casual sweep of someone's headlights and shut her down. I sat there for a few minutes to see if anyone from the nearby Jess Cave Duck Club and hunting area in general, had seen me arrive. Satisfied I was unseen, I bailed out from my truck and unloaded Dog. Sneaking back north across Lurline Road at a trot, I headed for the first of Jess Cave's Duck Club shooting areas. Running to some high ground on a small levee, I used my binoculars to look over the pond and areas where his commercial duck and goose blinds were located. I saw a few ducks flying by like cannon shot in the darkness but nothing of the characteristic giveaway swirl of ducks swarming over a watered baited area like a living, feathered tornado or a swarm of upset bees around their hive.

Realizing there was no discernible bird evidence of a baited pond discovery in that portion of Cave's duck club, I took off north down a muddy farm access road on shank's mare. The next area I headed for was a weedy duck pond hunted almost exclusively by Jess and some of his closest cronies during recognized Sacramento Valley shoot days (holidays, Wednesdays, Saturdays, and Sundays). The thinking at that time was to regulate the days one shot over a duck club so the ducks would not be burned out due to constant everyday gunning pressure. After walking in about a hundred yards or so along that suspect shooting areas eastern boundary, I stopped and listened. There it is! I thought. The classic sounds of madly feeding ducks over a baited area near a shallow water duck blind just to my north and west. I'll be damned, I grinned. Whoever tipped me off about the Jess Cave Duck Club being baited was spot on. Probably a disgruntled duck club gamekeeper from the adjacent Capital Duck Club. Or, another nearby gamekeeper whose hunters were not killing enough ducks because the baited Jess Cave Duck Club was pulling in all the ducks so other surrounding clubs' shooting went to hell in a hand basket. Good old honor among thieves, I thought with a pleased and experienced grin from having been here in other like situations when one disgruntled wildlife outlaw would bite the other competitor in the behind every chance they got. Especially when it came to reporting any wildlife transgressions or suspicions negatively impacting the reporting gamekeeper. Bottom line, they did so not because they were such great conservationists but because they were greedy for what they considered were their share of the ducks and geese being illegally taken by a competitor.

Mentally keeping the madly feeding duck noises to the north and west so the wind would better keep me informed as to their exact location, I now changed course and walked back along the southern boundary of the duck club baited pond in question. Sure as God appreciated a mess of hot biscuits and homemade chicken gravy, there it was! On the southern side of the pond along the levee, was a windblown line of chaff from what appeared to be screenings from a rice dryer. In fact, the entire muddy-diked bank was heavily drift-lined with the evidence of the chaff. A line of chaff along the southern boundary of the shooting area, based on the normal north to south wind patterns, spoke to the fact that my bait was somewhere above my current location. Utilizing the old trick of using a flashlight and just letting a sliver of light slip through between one's fingers, I walked the suspect pond's south dike. By using that sneak-and-peek technique, I lessened the chances of being observed by the person or persons previously putting out the bait who might be nearby watching the area or spooking off prematurely the feeding ducks to my north. As I did, it became obvious that whoever was putting out the bait was a wise old cuss. The shallow suspect baited duck pond was full of naturally occurring dense marsh grasses. Sprinkling screenings (cracked seed, seed hulls, weed seeds, some whole rice grains, etc.) into the dense grassy portions of the pond, made locating and getting a sample of the bait that was used a bitch. Especially once the seeds were mixed in with the thick mats of standing and flooded natural vegetation. But as usual, the sharp-eyed ducks had discovered the bait and I had found the ducks. With that, the trap was now almost complete. Now in order to put together a case that would stand up in a court of law, the hard work began in earnest.

First, I needed a sample of the lure or attractant that was sucking in all the ducks to this hunting club in particular. That meant I would need to run my screened bait scoop in the area where the ducks were feeding in order to get a sufficient sample of the bait that would hold up in a court of law. Then I would have to identify the bait and roughly map out the extent of the baited area. Lastly, I would have to catch my shooter or shooters taking or attempting to take migratory waterfowl over, or going to or from the baited area without being seen in the process. Proving prior knowledge of the presence of bait was not an element of the crime or legal requirement placed on the enforcing officer in those days. Apprehending one taking migratory game birds over or going to or from a baited area were the elements of the crime (what must be proved) under the baiting regulations at that time during the 1960s.

"Taking" was defined as, "take, hunt, capture, kill or pursue or attempt to take, hunt, capture, kill or pursue." Knowing or having knowledge that the area was baited, which is difficult to prove, was not an element of proof required of the officer in a court of law. The old regulations were called "strict liability regulations" for a reason. Basically, if you violated the regulations and that could be proven, you were a goner in a court of law. Bottom line, the laws were written to conserve the wild resources of the land, not to allow the over harvest of a limited natural resource. And if one places out feed for hungry migratory game birds, they will come! When that happens, if history is any kind of teacher, birds will be killed. Lots of birds! Hence the reason the U.S. Fish and Wildlife Service by regulation, outlawed the use of bait when taking migratory game birds clear back in the 1930s! And since federal law superseded state laws, that definition of baiting soon became the law of the land at both the state and federal levels.

As an aside, the new baiting regulations as of recent times, have now been drastically weakened by crooked politicians, their politically powerful game-hog buddies and gutless federal wildlife agency bureaucrats. This I am told today in 2012 by special agents from the southern part of the states, where illegal baiting is almost what one would call a religious science. The politically powerful game-hog, duck-killing lads primarily from the States of California, Maryland and Illinois, were the ones most responsible for weakening the Fish and Wildlife Service's old, strict-liability baiting regulations. I guess those chaps just got tired of being pinched for shooting illegally over baited areas by state and federal conservation officers and having their names and less-than-honorable actions posted up in the local newspapers. So, they politically took on the sometimes-gutless Department of the Interior's U.S. Fish and Wildlife Service and the baiting regulations were weakened. As I now understand it, a weakening element of the crime of baiting under the new regulations has since been added. That is the element of "due care." Now the officer has to also prove the shooter knew the area was baited or suspected the area was baited. That new element is a real bitch to prove among dyed-in-the-wool outlaws—outlaws who, without hesitation and not surprisingly, will just pretend they did not know the area was baited. Even though they themselves or their trusted cronies had many times placed the bait into the area to be shot over. And in so doing, will now claim the same as the basis for their legal defense in a court of law. Just another step backwards in the conservation law enforcement arena brought on by brain dead, crooked politicians, their politically powerful game-hog buddies, and some timid, won't-buck-the-tide, gutless U.S. Fish and Wildlife Service agency bureaucrats. And now reportedly, because of sequestration and the flurry of constitutionally questionable Executive Orders initiated by the Obama White House in 2013, the Service's emphasis is shifting from protection of resident species of wildlife here in America, to those endangered foreign species such as rhino and tigers as a matter of national security... National Security... ? I would think that national security would fall under the purview of the Department of Homeland Security or the military. If that trend and direction of dopey thinking continues, the Service's law enforcement activities will soon become irrelevant when it comes to protecting domestic wildlife. What a sad ending of a proud tradition undertaken by honorable and dedicated officers from the Fish and Wildlife Service's old Division of Law Enforcement. A serious and proud migratory-bird law-enforcement tradition that dated back to 1918! What will be next under the Obama administration? Maybe allowing the wind power industry exemptions under the Bald Eagle Protection Act of 1940 to kill eagles at will by their wind generators so the President and his dopy supporting Democrats can continue their weakening attacks on the fossil fuel industry? If that travesty happens with the wind-power folks, then the oil and gas, power transmission, coal extraction, Native American and livestock entities will be standing in line at the government trough looking for their exemptions to kill eagles and other protected migratory birds as well... National Security? But, I once again digress.

After mentally marking the bait's location to my satisfaction as I watched the swirling mass of birds through my binoculars, namely those flying into, tipping, splashing, and vigorously feeding into and around the nearby duck blind's decoy set, I got the dickens out of the area. Having gotten what I initially came after and not being able to check out the area thoroughly enough for anyone watching the baited area, Dog and I headed for home before we were inadvertently discovered. To my way of thinking, it was best that the badge carrier made sure there were no other heartbeats rattling around in the area in question other than his, the ducks, that of his dog, and those of my two guardian angels. Bottom line, there is nothing worse for a law dog out to surprise someone doing that which they shouldn't be doing and in the process, getting surprised himself...

My Second Rule of Law Enforcement says, if you are going to sacrifice your body and miss important times normally spent with your family members for the sake of the critters, make sure you spend your time wisely in order to successfully apprehend and prosecute the culprits to the fullest extent of the law. To do otherwise is foolish and you will pay the physical price when you grow older because of a worn out, busted up and wasted body earned in the normally difficult wildlife law enforcement profession.

The next evening around ten o'clock after staking out the area from afar looking intently for any other sign of human activity in the baited location in question, Dog and I were back at the suspect baited duck blind on Jess Cave's Duck Club. Wading as quietly as I could, I slowly headed for the mass of still madly feeding ducks in a crouched over position. Finally realizing danger was near at hand, the ducks forgot their greed and fled the area in a loud roar of madly flapping wings, splashing water, flying duck poop, and quacking. Hoping no one else had heard their noisy departure that late at night, I hurriedly shuffled my feet out into the area where the ducks had recently been feeding. For you unwashed, another old game warden's trick of the trade is easily accomplished by feeling for the slightly hardened baited ground on the bottom of the muddy pond with one's shuffling feet. That is because when masses of ducks feed on the bottom of a baited pond—especially one that has been baited frequently in the past, the pounding impact of their many bills will slightly harden that immediate area's soft muddy bottom. Once that more or less firmer spot was finally located in the pond with my shuffling feet, I lowered my bait scoop and began dragging it around in that specific area in order to gather any physical evidence of a baited area.

As an aside, there is another trick of the trade all you budding game warden types out there will also need to be aware of. Many times, game hogs will place their illegal bait in and around their decoy sets in their immediate shooting area. Just think about the wisdom of that little maneuver. Most waterfowl shooters will set their decoys at the optimum killing range of their shotguns from their shooting blinds. So, why not place their bait at the optimum range of their lethal shotgun streams of steel shot as well? Plus, if you usually have a group of birds in the wild, where are they generally located? That's right. They usually will be in an area where there is food, another mess of feeding birds or decoys, or in a safe loafing spot occupied by other like-in-kind critters. Therefore, when you are in and around a decoy set checking your hunters, always keep your eyes on the ground if it is a field set, or looking at or into the water if it is a water set. If there are a lot of webbed tracks, feathers, and poop on the ground in a field set or muddy water and a lot of floating feathers in a watered shooting area from all the feeding activity, there very well could be bait there as well. If a boat is being used in the shooting area, casually look into the bottom of the boat when making your routine field inspections of the sportsmen. Many times grains of bait are spilled in the bottom of a boat transporting the sacks of feed out to the area to be baited. As a game warden in a heavy-use waterfowl hunting area holding deep-water duck blinds, always check the boats at the boat dock used to carry the hunters out to their blinds. Many times, there will be loose grains of bait in the bottom of those boats. That should tell you the area may be baited. However, don't let on as to what you have observed laying in the bottom of the duck boats. You still do not have a case. Remember, migratory birds can be fed by anyone. They just cannot hunt and kill those migratory game birds over a baited area. Just figure you have an illegally baited area and now your work to find such a site is cut out for you. Lastly, if your sports are shooting over a water set, casually eyeball the foot and lower leg areas of their hip waders when you are checking them back at the blind. If an area is baited, sometimes the mud and grains of bait will stick to the footed area of one's hip waders, especially if they are walking around in the water where the bait has been placed as they retrieve their birds. Remember what I have told you readers many times in my other books. If you are going to sacrifice your body and the well-being of your family because of your many work-related absences, make sure your time spent in the field away from your loved ones really counts. Also, be aware that the critters and the lay of the land many times will speak to you. Learn to be observant and listen. Anything you see that looks out of place from the normal scheme of things, go take a look. Many times the critters will give away a particular illegal situation. Learn the behavioral traits of the critters you are protecting and many times, they will talk to you if you are listening... If you do, you will be a better officer for it and the critters will benefit from your alertness and subsequent enforcement actions. Besides, being nosy and having lots of brass is just part of being a good wildlife officer on the wildlife field of battle. But, away now from teaching you readers the tricks of the trade. Let us quit goofing around and get back to the field of battle and the present story at hand...

The bait scoop I used had a metal lip on the mouth of its opening so it would scrape up just about everything laying loose on the bottom. Once the scoop was full of mud, grass, seeds and plant debris as indicated by its heavy drag, I lifted it up on my dragging rope and grabbed the steel bail attached to the front of the boxlike device. Turning on my small two-cell flashlight, I could see all kinds of foreign seeds in the scoop's muddy residue! In other words, seeds normally foreign to the bottom of a grassy pond in which I currently stood. Careful not to lose my seed contents, I sloshed the scoop back and forth in the water until all the mud had sifted through the screen surrounding the outside of the scoop. Then into a plastic evidence bag went the remaining grasses, seeds, and some chaff from the baited area. This action was repeated several times until I was satisfied with the quality and quantity of my evidence. Returning to the edge of the pond, I commenced marking in my notebook the scope of the baited area and how it laid in accordance with the blind's location. Satisfied with my night's work, Dog and I headed for our hidden patrol truck parked a long distance away. That is another thing. If you are a conservation officer and are going to work a suspect area on foot, make sure your patrol vehicle is parked a long ways away or at least well hidden. That way, if discovered, the bad guys don't have a clue as to your exact whereabouts. Like I said earlier, it doesn't do any good to be absent from your family and beat the hell out of your miserable carcass unless you are successful in running your miscreants to ground. Make every moment count because you only get one turn in the barrel on this planet before you find yourself crossing over the great divide in a pine box.

Then it happened! As we walked back toward my truck, I faintly smelled cigarette smoke halfway down the muddy dike surrounding the baited shooting area. Freezing for just an instant, then sensing someone was coming my way, as Shadow validated that concern by letting out a low deep rumbling growl, I quickly and quietly stepped down off the levee and ducked into a mess of weeds. Dog came with me and, holding her so she would be quiet, we crouched down in the weedy growth and waited. Moments later, two darkened figures quietly walked by me on the levee carrying what appeared to be full gunnysacks of something on their shoulders. One individual was smoking a cigarette, as evidenced by the soft red glow on its lit end. My two mystery guests walked right by my hiding place and went directly to the baited duck blind in question like it was old home week. Moments later, I could see and hear the men splashing and wading around in the duck pond. Not a word was spoken; just splashing noises were heard as the men walked around in the pond dumping out the contents of their sacks into the water. Then the splashing stopped as the men exited the pond and stood there on the bank looking over the baited area. Shortly thereafter, they came walking right by Dog and me once again. Not a word was spoken, but I could see that both men were now smoking and they were not carrying any full sacks on their shoulders, as they had been earlier.

Giving my two chaps thirty minutes to make sure they were gone and not coming back with more sacks of what I suspected had been bait, I crawled back up onto the levee and headed right back to the suspect duck blind. Quietly slipping out into the water, I once again shuffled my feet until they hit the semi-solid muddy bottom of the pond. Down went the scoop and, dodging flying ducks coming back into the pond from every direction on the compass, I dragged it just a short distance. Up it came and this time, it was loaded clear full of fresh screenings (weed seeds, cracked rice kernels and everything else under the sun ducks like to eat). Plus even in the pale moonlight, I could see the surface of the pond around the decoys was covered with a carpet of light colored floating chaff. Exiting the pond, I sat down and began noting in my notebook, under screened light from my small flashlight, the evening's events and times they occurred. In the space of about five minutes, I would say about one thousand ducks had flooded back into the baited area to feed on the free-and-easy grits. Soon they were making such happy feeding sounds that it about drowned out any other night noises. Rising and standing there quietly, I could appreciate why the federal government had earlier made the shooting of migratory game birds over a baited area illegal clear back in the 1930s. From what I had just experienced that evening and many others like it while working duck clubs in the Northern Sacramento Valley, it became very clear what an effective killing tool the use and placement of bait was. If baiting was once again legalized, there eventually would be nothing left of the migratory bird resource in its wild state for those yet to come to see, experience and enjoy. Particularly, once the shotguns went silent, as did their targets...

The next day was an allowed shoot day. It was a Wednesday and I expected to reap a harvest of shooters from Jess Cave's Duck Club's back shooting area, come hell or high water. However, it was not to be. There were still tornadoes of ducks slipping into my suspect baited pond that I could see from my distant hiding spot on the end of Harbison Road. After an hour of watching from my place of hiding, I realized my chaps had baited up the area so heavily that if they shot it, the whole world would quickly know what was going on because of all the flights of birds going to and from the area and the accompanying heavy shooting. So my clever shooters just did not shoot the baited area that day. My suspicions were confirmed an hour later when I observed three men with my binoculars in camouflage hunting apparel standing on the back side of Jess Cave's Duck Club in the tree line. They had their shotguns in hand and were looking thoughtfully towards the baited duck pond area. But it soon became apparent to my shooters that the horde of feeding ducks on their club would quickly warrant unwelcome outside notice, especially if it was shot over that day. Soon the three men disappeared from view. Sensing that would be their only action for the day, I started to leave.

Then the nearby Green Mallard Duck Club opened up, sounding like Cox's Army was on the march! That duck club was located west of my position at the end of Four Mile Road a mile or so distant. Digging out from my pack and swinging my 60-power spotting scope in that direction, I could see the air over one end of that duck club looked like a disturbed swarm of bees! The ducks were hauling into and out of the area like it was the end of the world. Anytime one had shooting like that, especially on that historically less-than- high-quality duck club, something was dead wrong and probably illegal to my way of thinking.

Scrooching deeper into my spotting scope, I could see the occasional duck fall and hear plenty of shooting. Damn, I thought, something is sure wrong with that picture. There was just too much shooting and numerous swarms of birds flying around in its air space for it to be normal in that usually poor waterfowl hunting area. That was unless the wind was howling and the rain was flying sideways. Then you could just about stand in downtown Colusa and shoot a limit of critters off Main Street, the air would be so full of low flying ducks and geese.

However, I am too far away to be able to sneak in and do any good at this time, I grimly thought. It was then that I remembered another of Grosz's Rules. That being, if bad guys have a hell of a good shoot and get away with it once, they generally will return for seconds at a later time at Mother Nature's trough because of their greed, egos and previous happy shooting experience on site. But, nothing precluded me from making another of my midnight inspections on that area and that was what I was about to do once the cover of darkness enveloped the land.

For the rest of my day, I ran through the rice fields of the Sacramento Valley sowing hate and discontent among those heavy on their trigger fingers who were ignoring the waterfowl bag-limit regulations. And in so doing, gathering up about a dozen lads doing what they shouldn't have been doing in the world of waterfowl. However, both Jess Cave's and now the Green Mallard Duck Clubs were not far from the forefront of my mind. And being built like an elephant, I had a memory like one as well.

The following Saturday was a shoot day in the valley and the weather report was for wind and rain. Those were two factors that always made for a great waterfowl-shooting day in the valley. Figuring my lads on Jess Cave's Duck Club would come into their shooting area from the south side near their clubhouse, that was where Dog and I had buried in. Finding a great hiding place along a line of trees growing out from a nearby drainage ditch, we arrived on site around three in the morning. Now some of my duck hunting readers reading these lines are probably wondering why one would arrive on the site in question so danged early. Simple. By being on site so early, it allowed those ducks scared off because of my earlier entry in the area to return. Plus, when that horde of ducks got up noisily off the water announcing my early arrival, the lads back at the clubhouse would be in their deepest of sleep at that time of the morning. As a result, they more than likely wouldn't hear the noisy lift off disturbance. And your early hour of arrival allowed the ducks plenty of time to return so when the shooters finally came out somewhat later, they would see lots of ducks like they normally would. In the bad guys' minds, that amount of ducks on their club meant they were the first ones there on the hunting site and the game wardens were not out and about or close at hand and in country. Just another of Grosz's Rules that I used successfully throughout the days of my career, much to the chagrin of many dyed-in-the-wool wildlife outlaws when they chose to shoot over baited areas, couldn't count the numbers of birds they killed, or foolishly did both.

About forty minutes before legal shooting time on that particular shoot day, here came three lads skulking down my levee trail toward the baited blind shooting area. By now, most of the bait was long gone, so if a dumb game warden happened along, chances are he would not sense or discover the presence of what little bait was left. But the ducks that had fed there earlier for several days would sure as hell remember the free grits. They would continue to return hoping for more of the free chow only to now get a face full of deadly lead shot instead of a bill full of grits. As an aside, lead shot was legal to use in those days when taking waterfowl. Today steel shot must be used to avoid depositing deadly, bird-killing toxic lead shot into the environment. Into the blind closest to the baited area my shooters hustled scaring away several dozen mallard and Northern pintail ducks still on the pond looking for more bait. Then quietly waiting for legal shooting time to arrive so as not to alert any game wardens listening off in the distance, two of my lads lit up and started smoking cigarettes. With that smoking action, I was hoping those two were the same culprits that I had almost stumbled into on my way out the evening the second time I had visited the suspected baited area. The time when I had physically collected my first bait samples and mapped the area in question. If that was the case, justice would be sweet in this particular matter. Particularly since they would have more than likely been the chaps carrying the two sacks of bait used to sweeten the pot that evening in my presence. If so, nothing like crossing the T. To you folks without any naval history in your backgrounds, "crossing the T" was where one line of naval ships was able to steam across the bows of another line of closing enemy ships, forming a T. In so doing, they were able to direct all one's guns on the top of the T to bear on the enemy's leading ships—a particularly devastating naval maneuver during wartime, one in which I hoped to figuratively approximate if those two smokers were also my ones who had placed out the bait in the first place.

Soon the sounds of whistling wings could be heard as small flocks of mallards and Northern pintail dove into the decoys where they had earlier found bait. What they found that morning was a little more lethal... Letting my three shooters bang away—note that I didn't call them hunters because of the lack of fair chase—I waited. That was until they had killed three ducks apiece. Then Dog and I sprang the trap before they killed everything in the air wearing feathers. Slipping out from my hiding place and sneaking down another long drainage ditch, I was able to sneak directly up behind and out of sight of my shooters. They were so engrossed in looking for airborne ducks to their front arriving over their decoys, that they never saw or heard me coming.

Remember another of Grosz's Rules? If they aren't expecting you, they won't see you until it is too late. Well, that rule, as expected, worked slicker than cow slobbers. Now standing there behind them, I scared off several smaller flocks of ducks trying to work their way into their decoys, with my obvious presence lurking there in the open like a rather large, but of course beautiful, badge carrying stork. As such, I waited for my turn in the barrel for the telling effects of discovery to occur with my three shooters.

Finally, one chap stood up in the duck blind saying, "What the hell is going on? That is the third flock of ducks that spooked off from our set of decoys."

Then he looked behind him and damned near fell through the front of their duck blind! "Who the hell are you?" he bellowed, as he recovered from his surprise seeing me so close at hand.

"State fish and game warden, Lads," I said, as I began moving towards my shooters.

"I don't care who the hell you are. You are wrecking our duck hunting," said the one with a cherry red face. A facial type and look seen all too frequently when I had checked duck hunters in many other duck clubs after some of the lads had been drinking a bit heavily for a spell.

"Well, I would like to check your birds, plugs, licenses, and duck stamps, if I may," I responded.

"Well, hurry up," said "Red Face." "You damned sure are wrecking our duck shoot and I don't appreciate it," he continued in a blustery tone of voice.

"Yes, Sir," I said, as I waded out to their blind. Setting down my bait scoop, I checked the lads' gear and licenses finding them to be in compliance with that portion of the laws of the land. Then without saying a word, I walked out into their decoys and began dragging my bait scoop looking for any left over and uneaten bait.

"Now what the damned hell are you doing?" Red Face bellowed.

To my way of thinking, I figured that fellow sure had a limited vocabulary. "I am looking for any signs of bait," I replied.

"What the hell?" said Red Face.

"Bait," I responded. "You know, any kind of feed that would attract ducks into the gunning range of your duck blind and shotguns."

"I need your badge number and name," bellowed out Red Face. Only this time, you could tell he was really getting pissed. "By damn, I paid good money to Jess Cave to hunt here, and you, sir, are going to hear about this damned intrusion from your superiors if I have anything to say about it."

About then I lifted up my bait scoop. In it was a slurry of mud, grasses and a spattering of bait screenings! That was all the evidence I needed to close the evidence loop in the case to my way of thinking. Sloshing out the mud in the bait scoop in the water, I wadded back to their duck blind. Then holding up the bait scoop, I showed my shooters the bait. I always liked to confront my errant shooters with the bait findings just retrieved from their immediate shooting area as they viewed my actions. That way, my time in court was many times vastly reduced or eliminated, if the illegal shooters saw the evidence first hand that I had against them while on site. Man, you could have heard a duck in the next county passing gas, it got so quiet. Even Red Face had nothing to say for once, which told me something about his knowledge of the bait being in his decoys.

"Gentlemen, I will need to see some driver's licenses," I said.

Then Red Face, who did in fact smell of stale and sour whiskey, said, "What the damned hell for?"

"Because all of you have been shooting migratory game birds over a baited area contrary to state and federal waterfowl hunting regulations," I said quietly, still holding my temper over the loudmouth's always challenging remarks.

"And if I don't?" bellowed out Red Face.

"Then you will go to jail right here and now in the town of Colusa," I answered, hoping at that point in time Red Face really wanted to dance in the marsh.

It was then that his two hunting companions spoke up for the first time trying to calm Red Face down. They were finally successful and I got down to the business at hand. "Are the two of you now smoking the cigarettes the ones who put out the bait last Tuesday evening?" I asked rather casually. Man, you talk about dropping a bomb in their midst. They both looked like they just had a mean-assed water moccasin drop into their canoe from an overhanging limb in a Louisiana marsh and they didn't have a paddle to dispatch such an unwanted reptilian surprise.

"How did you know that?" asked the short one.

"Because the two of you walked right by me that evening and I saw the both of you putting out several sacks of what appeared to be bait around your decoys," I replied.

"What if we say 'no?'" the short one responded curtly.

"Makes no difference, Lad," I said. "I collected enough bait from this blind when you finished putting it out that evening to choke a horse and I now have all three of you for shooting ducks over a baited area this morning. That is all I need for a case to proceed through the courts under state law or the federal Migratory Bird Treaty Act," I stated.

"Why didn't you arrest us when you saw us putting out the sacks of feed?" asked the tall one in a challenging tone of voice. With that, I had to chuckle. His verbal statement just added another nail to the legal lid on his shooting over bait coffin when it came as to evidence of the fact through his just uttered declaratory statement.

"Because it is not a violation to put out feed for the birds. Only if you shoot migratory game birds over it does it become illegal," I responded.

"Is this going to federal court?" surprisingly asked the taller of the two men.

"Not at this point, but I reserve that option based on any of your previous hunting violations and subsequent convictions," I said. With those words, all three men looked like they had just swallowed a rather large spoonful of castor oil.

"Yeah, we put the bait out. Jess is charging us an arm and a leg for hunting here and we haven't been doing too well. So, Jess suggested we should add some candy to the pot if we wanted to kill more ducks," the tall one advised.

"Your driver's licenses please, gentlemen," I asked once again. That time they were forthcoming. It was then that I discovered a little more about the three men shooting over the baited area. The one with the red face was none other than a municipal court judge from El Cerrito. The other two men, who had hauled out the bait, were neighbors, fellow golfers, and hunting guests of the judge.

After finishing up on the paperwork involving my three chaps, I headed for Jess Cave's Duck Club clubhouse and a meeting with Jess. In so doing, I knew an explosion of sorts was in the offing from the duck club's owner. That was if history was any kind of a teacher.

An explosion because Jess had little use for us game warden types and me in particular. There I spoke to Jess and advised him that his back shooting area was closed to all waterfowl shooting until I determined that the lure and attraction from the baited area had disappeared. Then I informed him that he was still looking at a ten- day waiting period after that before any waterfowl hunting could lawfully resume. It was then he began shouting and swearing at me telling me to get the hell out of his clubhouse and, that he would shoot ducks on his property any time he wanted. As I left, I advised Jess once again that if I caught anyone shooting waterfowl over that baited area until I had certified it clean of all lure and attractant, I would pinch those shooters in a heartbeat. That elicited even more angry talk and swear words from what I considered, based on my numerous previous official experiences with Jess, one who also probably should have left "John Barleycorn" alone. Come to think of it, Jess had a cherry red face that morning as well, and his breath smelled of stale whiskey every time he yelled at me.

I soon discovered all three of my shooting-over-bait chaps had previous wildlife violations and convictions from shooting dove during the closed season, taking dove over limits, and shooting dove over bait in the Stockton area. With that information under my belt, their three cases were filed into federal court in Sacramento. As a result of that federal filing action on my part under my U. S. Deputy Game Management Agent credentials, credentials that all California state officers possessed after they had successfully completed their one year period of probation, each man paid a $500 fine which was the maximum monetary penalty per offense allowed in those days under the Migratory Bird Treaty Act. No matter what Jess said about shooting that back waterfowl area whenever he wanted to after I had warned him about it being baited, no one shot it until I cleared it for legal shooting once again numerous days later. However, that wasn't the last run in or the most magical moment I had on that duck club for shooting waterfowl over a baited area. To read that subsequent waterfowl baiting story that was pure magic, one that originated on the Jess Cave Duck Club in California and ended on the windswept prairies of North Dakota, you readers will have to read that story in my book titled, No Safe Refuge, Chapter 7, "It's a Very Small World." If you want to truly see what happens when you piss off God doing bad things to His critters in the world of wildlife, read that one. That story will put you on the floor with laughter over a hard fought problematic success by a law dog and the matter of just how long the long arm of the law in wildlife law enforcement truly is. That story is truly one that reeks of "Lions, three, Christians, nothing..." It is not often one can catch three chaps shooting over bait and killing over limits of ducks in one state and, then do the same thing to the same three individuals in another state several years later... That case, still remains a classic apprehension in the annals of my wildlife law enforcement adventures. As I sit here writing the words of this story, I have to chuckle at how I was able to run that same set of rascals to ground years later.

As an aside, I later discovered who my unknown informant, up to that time, had been (he has since passed). It turned out to be a chap that Jess had verbally abused in front of the man's friends and a family member. Embarrassed over Jess's abuse and while present a duck season later when Jess had advised my three recently cited chaps about putting out the candy in order to have a better duck shoot, he saw his chance at revenge. A quick phone call later from that chap and I now had my chance. And when a game warden has a chance to pick up a dirty penny, he does so in a heartbeat.

GREEN MALLARD DUCK CLUB

Oh-dark-hundred the following evening after the Jess Cave's Duck Club baiting incident, found me slipping in on the Green Mallard Duck Club from my hiding place at the north end of Four Mile Road. My reason for being there at that goofy hour was twofold. One, because the heavy amount of shooting I had heard earlier while staking out Jess Cave's Duck Club was unnatural for that low quality of shooting success duck club. And two, my interest was piqued because of the highly unusual numbers of low flying birds I had observed earlier with my binoculars. Ducks and geese that had been swarming unusually low over a single blind on that particular duck club. To my experienced way of thinking, the unusual numbers and behavior of the ducks and geese were typical of waterfowl feeding in a baited area. As Dog and I got closer to that duck club's actual shooting area, we began hearing a familiar sound.

That sound was welcome to my tired old carcass but, on the other hand, was unwelcome to my practiced set of game warden ears as well. It was the sounds that massed feeding waterfowl made over an unusually heavily loaded unnatural chow table in a marsh that produced little in the way of food plants and now, one making very similar waterfowl feeding sounds like I had heard on Jess Cave's baited duck club nights earlier. Standing on the north end of the Green Mallard Duck Club and looking through my binoculars, I could vaguely see what appeared to be a blizzard of ducks, mostly mallards and Northern pintail, swooping into the area around one duck blind in particular located on the far east side of the club. Those observations were made easier because of the reflective ambient over-lighting effect open water produces. Those duck shapes discerned through my binoculars were calculated to be mallards and Northern pintail because of their larger sizes and characteristic familiar flight behavioral patterns. Sure as hell, I thought, someone has put a little sweetener in and around that suspect duck blind. I stood there for about thirty minutes watching to make doubly sure of my illegal baiting concerns and its exact location in relationship to the blind. Satisfied that I had a potential violation of the state and federal waterfowl hunting regulations, I returned to my truck. Grabbing my bait scoop from the bed of the truck, I headed back down the muddy farm road leading to my now suspected baited duck club and its eastern most blind in particular. Because it was a non-shoot day and now darker than all get out with the advent of arriving low based rain clouds, I walked out in the open like it was nobody's business. Walked out in the open, since the club members were absent the shooting area and the club did not have a full time gamekeeper living on site to physically catch me in the act of snooping around. Once on the club, I made a beeline along the northern edge of the marsh for the blind in question. Because of the open terrain and lack of cover, I soon spooked the ducks off their unnatural feed bag before I was anywhere near their specific location. But I had a pretty good idea where they had been concentrating and headed directly for that mental picture in my mind. For all my budding game warden reader types out there in this type of situation, all one has to look for are unusual numbers of flying or feeding waterfowl, muddy, stirred up water in the immediate area, and floating feathers on the suspected baited-water site. Once on the suspected site, look for numerous greedy ducks always trying to get back into the area in question, even though you are standing or working in plain view. That is plain and simply just another indicator of a baited watered area. And the later in the season it becomes, the more aggressive the waterfowl become in their feeding habits in order to maintain their vital fat reserves for life and the spring migration soon to come. Geese will also behave in a similar fashion as do ducks in like-watered circumstances.

Finally arriving at the blind in question, I unlimbered my bait scoop and got down to the business at hand. Walking directly out into the decoy set, I began dragging the bait scoop to gather up any evidence of wrongdoing. In two drags, I had all the evidence I needed of possible foul play, no pun intended. My bait scoop was almost half-full of fresh barley with just the first sample drag! The barley was fresh because it was hard as a rock and not yet soft and waterlogged from being in the water for a longer period of time. Brother, I thought, these lads have recently dumped a whale of a lot of bait into their shooting area. In fact, the barley was so heavily placed, that a lot of it came up with the mud sticking to my hip boots every time I took a step in the baited area.

I could sure understand why that club was heavily baited though. During my tenure in the valley as an officer, that club had never been a real consistent killer of ducks or one that attracted lots of waterfowl. Their blinds were not the best I had ever seen as far as placement or as a structural camouflage brush-up went. Additionally, their decoy sets appeared to have been placed by amateurs and serviced with crappy, always sinking, cheap, soft rubber decoys—rubber decoys that were half sunken many times because of the low streams of lead shot flying among them by poor shooters in the blind. Plus, their duck club was not one that I would say had the best surrounding natural waterfowl habitat. Lastly, they were more or less at the edge of the natural flyways the waterfowl utilized when they streamed off nearby Delevan National Wildlife Refuge to feed. Those combinations of conditions made for poor duck shoots at best, unless the wind was howling and the winter rains were flying sideways. Then, like I said earlier in my other writings, you could kill ducks anywhere in the Sacramento Valley during those kinds of weather events, especially as the stressed birds tried to find cover and a place to rest from the strong, energy sapping winds and usual driving winter rains. For my readers' edification, when flying, ducks and geese have to fly with their eyelids open. Raindrops painfully pelting the bare eyeball forces the birds to fly more slowly than they normally would, and has them flying only as much as is necessary to get to safety or a place to feed. Hence, the better waterfowl hunting during crappy weather events in the Sacramento Valley.

As my evidentiary work progressed, I documented the kind of bait and the extent of its placement locations in my notebook. Following that, I scouted out a good hiding place in which I would be out of the line of fire come the shoot day, yet was close at hand for an intercept and could still clearly see and not be seen during the anointed visitation day. Taking a final good look around, I got the heck out of there before I was by chance discovered by any other duck club neighbors in the immediate vicinity. Neighbors who would, at the drop of a hat, report any suspicious game warden activity to their like-in-kind duck club buddies. In the meantime, the mallards and Northern pintail flooded in around me for another free, fresh barley buffet that was almost knee deep to a tall nosing- around game warden.

Once back at my truck, I could hardly believe my luck. Two discovered baited duck clubs in under a week! Especially since finding one baited duck club or goose field a month was the usual find. Man, the Duck God is sure ringing my hell! I thought with a smile. With that bit of work in the bag, Dog and I were off to work the local duck draggers between Two and Four Mile Roads for the rest of the evening and into the wee hours of the following morning.

The following shoot day way before dawn, Dog and I hunkered down in a hide on the Green Mallard Duck Club in a typical cold, wind-driven rainstorm. As dawn approached, the wind continued kicking up as a normal winter weather system slid into the Sacramento Valley with a vengeance. Soon, the clubhouse lights came on and right at daylight, I had hunters moving throughout the immediate shooting area as they headed for the duck blinds of their choice. As nearly as I could tell, I had three groups consisting of two sports per group. Each group headed for a different blind. Then here came my two suspect over-bait shooters. They didn't tarry a bit but headed straight for the baited blind. In the meantime, their duck club shooting area was alive with overflying mallards, Northern pintail, Northern shovelers, and American wigeon. Yes, there are southern counterparts to the two northern species mentioned above and a European counterpart to the American species also mentioned. It didn't take long for all my sports on the duck club to begin shooting, and it was then I realized I might as well have been herding a mess of cats! Birds were dropping all over the area like flies and soon every blind occupied by shooters had shot over limits of ducks! Dang it, I was in a quandary. To quote a biblical term, "My Cup of Game-Hog Violators Runneth Over!" Well, maybe that was a direct quote from my homegrown wildlife law-enforcement bible instead of the real Good Book.

After recording in my notebook what each lad was wearing in every blind and their distinguishing facial features as best as I could in the driving rain through my binoculars, Dog and I crawled in the adobe mud away from our hiding place over looking our originally selected baited duck blind. Crawling together—yes, Dog would crawl on command—we headed for the far western side of the duck club's shooting area. I figured if I could do that without discovery, I could ambush and capture every dang one of my shooters once they figured they had enough and headed for their clubhouse. It took me the better part of half an hour to crawl to where I wanted to be without being seen, but I finally got it done. When I arrived, I looked like a well-used mud turtle and Shadow was now a brown Labrador instead of black. Gosh, was I ever a mess of adobe mud, weed seeds and cattail fluff from head to toe. But I was where I wanted to be and now, I had the proverbial twist on all of my waterfowl over the limit shooters. Especially once they arrived at my spot of ambush after they had left their respective shooting areas and were in route to their clubhouse.

Soon, my shooters were coming out from the duck club shooting area and, as nearly as I could tell looking through my binoculars, every one of them was very careful. Each man only carried out a legal limit of ducks. But that didn't matter. Even in the driving wind and rain, I had managed to get a fairly accurate count on each and every one of them regarding the numbers of birds and species they had killed. Thank God a No. 2 lead pencil will still write in a wet notebook under the worst kind of weather conditions.

Since all my six chaps appeared to be coming out more or less at the same time, I waited in the weeds at a choke point on their trail leading into the shooting area in ambush. Just as fast as they came within my gun range, I ground sluiced the lot. Then I made them sit down in a ditch out of sight so they wouldn't spook the others still coming my way. Group by group, my chaps arrived and forty minutes later, danged if I didn't have my mess of cats corralled!

I had not told anyone of them I had them for shooting over limits or, in the case of my particular two, for shooting over bait. I just told them as they arrived who I was, that they had a legal problem, and I would advise them of their illegality once all of their buddies had arrived so I only had to explain the problem one time. Once I had all of them sitting down on the canal bank in a driving rain looking like a mess of semi-drowned cats, I dropped the bomb about why my most beautiful presence was front and center.

"Gentlemen, I have identified myself to all of you as a state fish and game warden. I will cut through the chase because of the weather. I have observed and recorded all of you taking over limits of ducks since shooting time started this morning. So that there is no misunderstanding, I have been watching every one of you, recording the numbers of birds killed, the times you fired and the species killed as best as I could under the present weather conditions. And according to my notes, the least number of ducks killed over the limit by any one of you has been six! Now here is what I want all of you to do. I will need each man's driver's license and hunting license. Those I will keep with me until citations are issued later on for what each man did in violation of the law. Next, I want every one of you to go back to your blinds and bring me the rest of the ducks you killed this morning and left behind over your current limits for later retrieval. Now please don't leave any birds behind, toss any or try stomping them into the mud. If you do, I will add additional charges to the legal baggage you are currently carrying. In short, if the numbers you bring out don't match each individual's numbers in my notebook that is when the wheels are coming off your wagons. I will put my dog to work and I guarantee every one of you who tries to hide any ducks, rest assured, that the dog will find them. And in case the dog finds any ducks left behind, I will also cite the duck club for untagged birds, which is a federal charge that can be applied, and then additional fines will be levied against the duck club for those violations." With that, I paused and let what I had just said soak in, along with the pelting rain. Once again, no pun intended. My violation revelations and accusations went pretty well actually, because most of the members were fairly old men and didn't seem to want any kind of a verbal scuffle out there on the ditch bank, especially during a driving and cold winter rainstorm.

Having all of them leave their shotguns with me, back they went to retrieve their extra ducks they had originally killed and left behind. And in so doing, further nailed the lid on their coffin of illegality since they would be gathering up and bringing back the evidence against each and every shooter. In the meantime, I checked all their shotguns for plugs to make sure they were legal, which they were. Finally, all my chaps came dragging back to my ditch bank looking now like a bunch of thoroughly soaked muskrats. When everyone was accounted for, as were all the ducks according to my notes, the seven of us headed for the nearby clubhouse. Once there, the ducks were piled up outside in individual piles while the men went inside to change their clothing and dry out. In the meantime, I left Dog guarding the ducks as I went for the patrol truck, which had been hidden out of sight down the road near some parked farm machinery.

Slipping and sliding in the typical Colusa County adobe mud, I finally arrived back at the clubhouse with my vehicle. There I loaded all the ducks into the bed of my truck and had Shadow sit there with them. Then I went inside and filled out all the citations. At the end, I had chaps with over limits of ducks running from six to twenty- three in excess of the daily bag limit! I did not charge four of those outlying chaps for shooting over a baited area because the birds that they had shot from their distant blinds, appeared to be reacting to the windy and rainy conditions and not the presence of bait at the far eastern end of their duck club. However, for my two baiters, they received citations for taking migratory waterfowl over a baited area, and for taking and possessing over limits of ducks and Pacific white-fronted geese.

Finished with the paperwork, I drove back out to the duck club's hunting area where I had witnessed the earlier violations. Then just in case I had missed something, I spent the next ninety minutes on foot checking all the blinds for any birds intentionally left behind, as well as for any evidence of bait placement around those blinds not showing birdy behavioral indications of being baited. As expected, there was no bait to be found in the two other blinds that had been used that morning by my four other shooters. Then I went over to the baited blind and ran my bait scoop one more time to gather the last of the evidence I needed for the prosecution of that type of violation. By now, I, too, looked like a wet muskrat. Well, a rather large but beautiful one! Eat your heart out a young Robert Redford... However, that is where the comparisons between Robert and yours truly ended. He is a flaming liberal mouse-knuckle and I am and always will be a proud conservative American eagle.

Back at the clubhouse again, I filled the lads in on the fact that the eastern half of their shooting area was now closed to further migratory game bird hunting because of the lure and attraction of the baited area. In that discussion, I also explained that I had no legal authority to close off their private property, but I sure as hell could write anyone I discovered hunting in the area for shooting over a baited area. I also advised the club president I would let him know when the hunting ban on that part of their duck club would be lifted. Finished with the business at hand, Dog and I then went home, cleaned the ducks so they wouldn't spoil, and hung them in my garage to drain and cool out. They were later collected up and placed in my evidence freezers located on the Sacramento National Wildlife Refuge for safekeeping after Shadow and I had dried off, cleaned up and changed into dry clothing. For Shadow's part in the endeavor, she got to eat all the warm duck guts she could hold which, in every sense of the word, was a bucketful because that was the size of her boiler.

Some days later after that detail, my lads subsequently forfeited bail in the Williams Justice Court running from $350 to $750 each for their over limits. My two chaps shooting over bait paid an additional $500 for that little error in judgment. All their ducks were eventually donated under court order to several needy families in the area and the Colusa County Sheriff's Office to help feed the prisoners in order to keep the county's food costs down.

Not bad for a long and wet morning's work, I later mused. Shadow thought so, too, if the size of her full belly meant anything after eating all the duck guts she could hold. However, that was the last time she got to eat all the warm duck guts she wanted and in that volume. It almost took the strength of a fire hose at full power to clean out the back of my pickup a day later in which she had been riding...

"HOW COULD YOU SEE ME?"

One early morning while out and about in the Sacramento Valley during the waterfowl season, I received a radio message from the U.S. Fish and Wildlife Service's Agent in Charge, Jack Downs. Jack was the Service's Agent in Charge for the northern half of California. His office was located in Sacramento, and he was the supervisor over a number of what were then called U.S. Game Management Agents. Basically, officers who were federal game wardens and primarily enforced the Migratory Bird Treaty Act, Bald Eagle Protection Act, the Lacey Act, the National Wildlife Refuge System Act, Black Bass Act, and Migratory Bird Hunting Stamp Act. Plus, the wildlife laws for the State of California when the need arose, since all Jack's officers were also cross credentialed as deputy state fish and game wardens. Jack was one hell of a good catch dog officer and feared by a number of the Sacramento Valley's duck club members, who had a wild hair for violating the primarily federally enforced Migratory Bird Treaty Act. An Act that in part, regulated the migratory game bird (dove, ducks, geese, snipe, band tailed pigeons, etc.) hunting seasons, shooting hours, methods of take, and bag limits. On that particularly day, Jack was out and about in my state area of responsibility and wanted to meet with me. And for good reason, he did not discuss as to why for our meeting over the often times publically monitored state fish and game radio frequency.

Setting up a location in which to meet, I waited for his arrival. As I waited, I let my mind wander. I had always wanted to be a U.S. Game Management Agent ever since my college days at Humboldt State College as a wildlife student. However, up until then, that was not to be. There were only 178 U. S. Game Management Agents in the entire United States at that time, and it seemed the only way to get a position within those distinguished ranks, was to wait until someone was killed, died in the traces, or retired. And then when that happened, one had to compete with hundreds of other best-qualified applicants for the coveted position just vacated! If any of you readers out there are history buffs and understand odds, that is equivalent to a Chinaman's Chance...and that was after one had satisfied a four-year college degree requirement in a wildlife field of study and had successfully acquired a minimum of four years of experience as a state fish and game warden or other like in kind position in order to be considered entry level eligible. Truth be known, later in 1970, Jack approached and offered me a position as a United States Game Management Agent! However, that and the wonderfully storied career, which ultimately led to fulfilling that particular vision quest, will have to wait for another time and telling. But to my readers who are interested, those stories and adventures relating to that career can be found in my other wildlife law enforcement books dealing with my service as a federal officer, starting with my second book, For Love Of Wildness, and continuing on through with Defending Our Wildlife Heritage, No Safe Refuge, The Thin Green Line, Slaughter in the Sacramento Valley, Wildlife on the Edge, and finally, Wildlife's Quiet War. And if all goes according to plan, volumes one and two of my last wildlife law enforcement adventure books titled, Wildlife Dies Without Making A Sound, to be published in the fall of 2014 and spring of 2015.

What a morning and fateful meeting with Jack that turned out to be! Fateful in that the results of that get-together on a muddy farm road alongside a freshly harvested rice field, increased my abilities as a wildlife officer hunter of humans and sealed the fate of many of those killing son-of-a-bitches gunning on the dark side in the Sacramento Valley's world of waterfowl... Once he arrived, Jack typically got right to the point. "Tiny, [my nickname among the local wildlife officers due to my ample size] have I got a deal for you. Since you are bombarding the magistrate's court in Sacramento with more tickets than all the rest of my officers combined, not to mention the blizzard of state tickets that I hear that you are also filing, I brought you a present. I figured with this rather unique tool of the trade, you can more than double or even triple your catch of wildlife outlaws and then I won't have to work." We both laughed easily over Jack's teasing remarks as he opened up the trunk of his patrol car and produced a black, locked aluminum case holding the mystery item relative to the reason for his visit.

"What the hell you got there?" I asked.

"It is a Starlight Scope. It is like the one our troops are using in Vietnam and it magnifies all available light by a factor of fifty thousand. Imagine what use you can make of this tool on Colusa County's blizzard of late and early duck and goose shooting problems, not to mention your duck draggers and commercial market hunters" he said with a knowing grin. "And lastly, Tiny your outlaws cannot see it being used even if they are looking directly at the damn thing!" With those heartening words uttered to any hunter of humans with a soul, Jack opened up the case and therein lay a black, spotting scope like looking device.

"How does the damn thing work?" I asked, now all eyes and ears because if the darn thing did just half of what Jack said it would do in the increased light department at night as I hunted the lawless, man, I would have my wildlife outlaws by the throat! I figured with that device and all its reported magical powers and potential, plus my ability to get around on shanks mare, I would be able to lay waste to every damn, trigger pulling, late shooting son of a gun from the Sacramento Valley to the moon. And maybe even some of those duck killing son of a guns illegally shooting on the backside of the moon as well, eh? Ah, youth...

For the next few minutes, Jack gave me instructions on how the new scope worked and what to do and not do while using it. Not do, like not using it in daylight because it magnified all available light by a factor of fifty thousand! It sure didn't take this momma's boy long to realize the potential I was holding in my hands and the scourge it would soon become to my valley's run-of-the-mill late shooting outlaws, deadly serious local duck draggers and the few remaining insidious commercial market gunners still roaming the rice fields at night. Market gunners known for blowing up the feeding ducks at night by the hundreds and feloniously selling those ducks under the table to the Asian restaurants in the San Francisco Bay Area of California to be consumed as highly desired, rice fed, wild duck dinners. And to all you unwashed folks out there, there is nothing quite like a properly stuffed and baked, rice fed hen Northern pintail dinner with all the trimmings.

Before Jack and I parted company that fine day, he had me sign the paperwork involved with a loan from the federal government to the State of California for one Starlight Scope. Man, was that one hell of a fortuitous loan for me and an eventual scourge for many of those Colusa County night shooting waterfowl outlaws who were heavy on the trigger finger and slow of foot. Before all was said and done, I was soon to amass over $25,000 in fines in the state and federal courts from those who could or would not stop shooting within the prescribed shooting hours for migratory waterfowl in the Sacramento Valley. And, that was during the very first partial hunting season of use! That was at $25 for the initial violation and $2 per minute for the late or early shooting offense! With the use of that amazing device and a lot of long hours in the field, I caught chaps in the dark shooting up to six hours after legal shooting hours and many for shooting up to four hours before legal shooting hours! There were also over a dozen times that first year in which I caught late shooters shooting over limits of ducks in the darkest of nights using that device! With the use of that Starlight Scope during those darkest of nights, my duck identification skills learned as a wildlife student at Humboldt State's excellent wildlife program, all honed with my years of experience in waterfowl law enforcement, I was able to identify most species of ducks killed on the wing in the lime green field of that scope, especially when my shooters were shooting over water with its high light reflective properties. With those aids, I was able to relate to my much surprised, apprehended shooters the numbers of ducks shot, species taken and times each violator had shot. Man, to my way of thinking, I had died and truly gone to game warden Heaven with the use and aid of that instrument. Bottom line, figuratively speaking, use of that device meant ducks one, late shooters nothing and the Northern Sacramento Valley now became my Coliseum...

One of my first orders of business in the late '60s through the middle '70s after receiving the Starlight Scope, was to tackle the tremendous numbers of waterfowl early and late shooting problems in my patrol district in the Sacramento Valley. Problems associated with and initiated by many of my local fraternity of wildlife-duck-dragging outlaws, the few remaining commercial market hunters and the thousands of the run-of-the-mill-sportsmen early and late shooters that flooded into the valley every shoot day during the 107-day waterfowl season. Waterfowl, my primary enforcement concern during the late fall and winter months, could be taken one half hour before sunrise until sunset. Times other than that and the critters needed an opportunity to be left alone in order to feed, rest, and loaf. That's why there are the shooting hour restrictions for America's migratory game bird hunting sportsmen.

To you unwashed who do not hunt waterfowl, many times wintering birds would feed in the dark of night or the early morning hours in order to avoid any kind of human harassment. However, in many parts of the Northern Sacramento Valley in those early days right up into the middle 1970s when I was stationed there, there was no such rest for the hungry flocks of ducks and geese—no rest because of the vastness of the area, its tremendous numbers of acres of rice fields and a fair number of the rural folks acceptance of such illegal actions like duck dragging, late shooting and commercial market hunting. With those historic overriding factors, it seemed the local outlaws shot the hell out of the feeding waterfowl whenever they wanted or desired, day or night, as long as the critters were in the valley. And to my way of thinking, the local shooters figured the efforts of the outnumbered law enforcement officers in stopping such slaughters, be damned!

Even before and after the turn of the century, commercial market hunters had slaughtered the ducks and geese in the Sacramento Valley by the millions! I personally have seen turn of the century photographs, where over seven hundred Canada geese had been hung on a fence after a mornings shoot ... and in another, among the many such pictures viewed, where three hunters killed one hundred six geese in just forty-five minutes near the Sacramento Valley Town of Maxwell! Additionally, many of the local outlaw duck draggers would historically shoot into the feeding flocks of waterfowl in the dark of the night in order to fill their own freezers or those of their friends with the excellent tasting, rice-fed birds. And, did so in the darkness in order to lessen their chances of being captured by those of us representing the long arm of the law. In short, it is a hell of a lot tougher to capture an emboldened shooter under the cover of darkness, especially when that shooter knew the lay of the land and its tried and true escape avenues. As a result of the many years of wholesale waterfowl slaughter in the Sacramento Valley, I found that such night-killing habits died hard, regardless of how many conservation laws were passed to prevent such illegal actions. And continued into the 1970s, regardless of the numbers of state and federal officers that were afield or the sentences meted out to any shooters so apprehended. In light of the above history, the only thing that seemed to really curdle the milk of the outlaw shooters, was being apprehended selling waterfowl by federal officers working undercover. Many times, those so apprehended and prosecuted in federal court for feloniously selling waterfowl under the Migratory Bird Treaty Act, drew stiff sentences landing them within the federal penal system. That avenue of conclusion, slowed down somewhat those commercializing waterfowl but only slightly because chances of being apprehended were still slight or non-existent. Slight or non-existent because shooters of that caliber kept their mouths shut, and played any successes they had close to their vests. And traditionally, part of those clandestine successes were only shared with family or transacted with those trusted long time and known middlemen.

So, I quickly learned to work 18-20-hour days, 7 days a week in my district during the 107 days long waterfowl hunting season! Not only that but I worked the same crazy hours as long as I had shoot-able numbers of wintering waterfowl in the valley regardless of the seasons. That was until the birds switched from eating rice and other grains to green grass. When the birds switched from a grain to a grass diet they were not as good eating. It was then that my outlaw gunners finally left the birds more or less alone. Basically, I worked such crazy hours because of the total lawlessness during the waterfowl season in my area of responsibility in the late '60s through the middle '70s. After that, I changed from my State of California game warden position to that of a federal agent for the U.S. Fish and Wildlife Service, was promoted in 1974 to a Senior Resident Agent position and sent to Bismarck, North Dakota, as my new duty station. To be frank, that agency change only meant I worked still longer hours and more days of the week now that I was in charge of North and South Dakota, if that was possible. Plus, I had a very understanding bride who let me run because she understood I was on a vision quest to catch every trigger happy son of a buck in the valley come hell or high water! Lastly, I was a damn stubborn, thick-headed German and I doubt she could have slowed me down once I realized the degree of lawlessness swirling around me in the world of wildlife and the extreme need for the hard-working presence of wildlife officers in the field. Today I know that enforcement ethic and endeavor turned out to be impossible to accomplish. And my body bears the scars to prove it, as does that of my long-suffering bride. There were just too many outlaws to catch and contain. Just like in some misguided gun control legislation, it is not what is in the hand but what is in the heart when it comes to violating the laws of the land and those against humanity.

Now I don't know how many of you readers out there realize just how hard it is to hunt the most dangerous game, namely Man, in the dark of the night. In short, the individual who is hell bent on shooting waterfowl under the protective cloak of darkness and does so because he has most all of the advantages. He knows—I never caught many ladies late or early shooting—when and where he is going and what he is after. All the law dog knows is that the violations will be out there occurring somewhere and sometime, near waterfowl concentrations. And with that, the hunt for the most dangerous game or hunting the lawless is on. I say the most dangerous game because, according to the most recent FBI statistics, game wardens suffer a mortality rate that is nine times higher than any other type of law enforcement officer in the United States! In my own case for example, I was shot once in 1967 by duck draggers, and shot at intentionally or unintentionally another six times during the rest of my thirty-two-year career. Let me tell all you good folks out there reading these lines, being shot once or just shot at is more than enough for any chap to wrap his arms around! Especially if you were the size target I routinely presented. Being large in size when working the backcountry alone for the most part, among numerous armed individuals, many times has its advantages. However, there are also size considerations to be concerned about when lead bees are flying by one's carcass at 2,900 feet per second. To appreciate that concern, read in my book *Defending Our Wildlife Heritage*, the chapter titled, "Asia-1978." That will more than bring home the moment of flying lead bees and one's mortality...

Because of my knowledge of the lay of the land in the Northern Sacramento Valley, a good understanding of the waterfowl species behavioral patterns during fall and winter weather events, an understanding of the late and early shooting sub-cultural shooting fraternity, and where such activities were more than likely to occur, I was catching more than my fair share of those needing my attention. However, it was still somewhat of a crapshoot requiring a lot of intensity, focus, dedication to the moment, many long hours in every type of weather imaginable, luck, a pair of hard working guardian angels watching over my carcass, and damn good footwork on my part in order to put a dent in that type and degree of night-shooting lawlessness.

That was until Jack Downs called me that fateful and fortuitous day on my car radio. "Tiny," he said, "meet me on the Four Mile Road next to the Newhall Farms property adjacent to the rice fields they just harvested." The rest of that story became history. No two ways about it, a touch of Vietnam had just come from those rice paddies in Southeast Asia to those rice paddies in the Northern Sacramento Valley. But, let us get back to the story at hand.

That first evening of Starlight Scope use, with a strong northwest wind blowing, found me south of the intersection of Corbin and Lenahan Roads in Colusa County. I was in the middle of Section 14 and quietly waiting—waiting because, on numerous previously windy or rainy nights, I had an historical repeat lone shooter killing feeding waterfowl in that area, usually after ten o'clock at night. That shooter was a dedicated duck killer to my way of thinking and smarter than a kit fox. He would shoot only one shot at a time into low flying ducks from what sounded like a 20-gauge shotgun shooting low base shells. They made less noise. In so doing, that made it extremely difficult for an officer to echolocate on the shooter, especially during bad weather events. Then finished with his one shot, my chap would drastically and wisely change shooting positions to lessen his chances of apprehension in case the officers were nearby. He wouldn't shoot again for perhaps another fifteen to twenty minutes and then when he did, he just shot once and always from a totally different location. That scenario would be played out until around four in the morning. Then like magic, he would up and flat just disappear like a puff of dust in the wind. Probably one of the hardest individuals I had ever tracked in my career to date in the valley. I had stalked that lad at least a dozen times during my tenure as a state fish and game warden and was never successful in catching him. Hell, I don't think I ever even got close! But now my hopes were a little higher with my newest law enforcement tool. Especially if he showed that evening as I stood out in the center of the darkened harvested rice fields quietly waiting like a large German brown trout waiting for a foolish meadow mouse to come swimming by. This time, I carried a Starlight Scope in the game bag of my hunting jacket. That way I could carry it safely and, if I had to chase my chap, I could be hands-free as the scope rode safely in the game bag of my hunting jacket. As it turned out and as was the case on many stakeouts, nothing happened that evening in my targeted area. Oh, I had shooting all around me way after legal hours but I had my sights set on bigger, far tougher game that evening, namely my historical night shooting chap in Section 14, so, I held my water...

The following evening I had a repeat of the crappy winter weather. And guess who was standing like a bump on a log in the middle of that aforementioned rice field patiently waiting? You got that right, it wasn't Santa Claus. Yours truly and about eleven million ducks zooming around me like cannon shot at the battle of Gettysburg. And as usual, the critters were all looking for a place to drop down and load up with a meal of waste rice grains from the freshly harvested rice fields.

Boom! There he is! I thought as I spun around trying to quickly echolocate on my perennial extreme late shooter! Reaching into my game bag, I quickly retrieved my Starlight Scope. Unscrewing the lens cap and ocular cover, I flipped on the oscillator switch. Within moments, I could hear a faint hum as the machine internally came to life. Sweeping the field below me, I was amazed! For the first time in my life I could see in abject darkness! I was looking into a clear field of lime green, and there below me a distance away stood a solitary figure picking up a duck from the rice field. Hell, I could even tell that the species of the duck he had just shot was a drake Northern pintail by the white color of its breast feathers! God, you talk about excited! I had to be slobbering like a redneck's dog hanging his head out the window of a pickup as it rattled down the highway. I looked at my shooter totally fascinated now that I could watch for what his next move was to be. Putting the dead bird on a duck strap, my shooter commenced walking quickly to the west looking skyward at all the whistling shadows of low flying, eager to land and feed ducks. Following my lad and utterly fascinated with my newfangled law enforcement tool, I saw him walk about a hundred yards and then hide in the tall water grass on the backside of a rice check. Taking that as my cue and lining up his last seen position with a faint light from a faraway farmhouse, I began hurriedly walking in that direction. Now that was a real chore in a freshly rutted and harvested rice field because I didn't want to deep-step into something sight unseen and break an ankle. And I sure as hell couldn't use a flashlight without giving away my position. To all you unwashed folks out there, the normal human eye can discern the light of a candle from about ten miles away in the dark of the night! For my comparison readers out there, that is like having over one hundred forty football fields stacked end to end, a burning candle at one end and you can still see its glow from the other! Now one can see why it is so imperative to take care of your eyes. Especially if that chap is a badge carrier working alone, often at night. Again, to all you unwashed readers out there, being a game warden and able to see well at night is like having the sun at your back in the days of old as a gunfighter. Use of any light for assistance under my current set of circumstances would have been nice. But in so doing, with the distance factor and one's normal ability to see any far away faint light, meant I would go home empty handed that trip because of discovery by my clever outlaw. And for me, since I was sacrificing my body and time away from my family, I wanted to go home with a bucket full of trigger fingers if I had my druthers... So I learned to walk by shuffling my feet to aid my balance because of the deeply rutted muddy ground caused by the tracks of the rice harvesters, which if not careful, would cause me to take one hell of a spill in the ruts they had left behind.

Counting my steps, I stopped after walking about eighty yards. Then on went the scope. I had been walking all that time without the use and aid of the scope because it was hard getting extra batteries for the device due to their extreme need for military use in Vietnam. Jack had warned me about using what batteries I had in a conservative manner and I heeded his advice.

Sweeping the field below me with the scope, I saw my shooter approaching a large puddle of standing rainwater in the rice field. It had a passel of ducks on it and soon they rose into the air in alarm as they finally detected my shooter's stealthy approach in the darkness. When they did, I clearly saw my shooter raise the shotgun to his shoulder and fire. A small spark of light came from the end of his shotgun muzzle in the scope and two ducks dropped! Hot damn, I thought. This scope is slicker than cow slobbers, as thoughts of thousands of soon-to-be-caught late-shooting bad guys danced in my head. Then the scope went blacker than the inside of a long dead cow! No longer could I hear the faint hum of a working oscillator. The damn thing was deader than a glass doorknob on an abandoned North Dakota farmhouse out on a forlorn prairie hillside near the Town of Devil's Lake in the dead of winter. In my earlier excitement over the device's potential, I had forgotten to include a spare oscillator and an extra battery in my hunting jacket for my scope. Now, I was in crap up to my eyes and didn't have a shovel. Needless to say, my efforts in catching my shooter that evening proved the same as they had so many times in the past—fruitless. To make matters worse, my chap shot four and a half hours early that morning since anytime after midnight was counted as an early shooting violation! And I wasn't anywhere near him when he shot, no matter how hard I worked trying to outsmart and catch that rascal.

The next evening, I was in my chap's favorite shooting field once again, namely Section 14. And I was there with a new oscillator in the scope, and an extra oscillator and battery in my coat pocket as well. However, for the next week my lad never showed. Now I was beginning to wonder if he could have seen my scope when it had been directed at him earlier in the week. That and everything else under the sun in the way of concerns about being previously detected kept racing through my mind. And to make matters worse, my entire valley seemed to be blowing up around me with night shooting chaps, as I spent most of my dark time doggedly hunting my lone shooter. Be it duck drags or just plain late and early shooting, the valley sporadically rang with shots being fired once darkness descended and the ducks arrived to feed. Yeah, you are truly doing one hell of a good job, Terry, I thought with a grimace as I stubbornly carried on after my historically dedicated late and early shooting chap.

Then came the winter winds and now the rains once again. And your trusty servant was out and about in his favorite Section 14 hunting my night shooting nemesis once again. Now I was really feeling I was hunting the most dangerous game. It seemed every time I turned one corner, my shooter turned another and was out of sight and gone before I could even blink in frustration. However, that evening my guardian angels were telling me this was the night our friend would show. And show he did with his characteristic one shot right at midnight. Boom! Man, I was on my shooter's location like John Wayne was always on the bad guys in all his Westerns! Out came the scope and on went my oscillator switch. And, I couldn't see crap! I didn't realize heavy rain, like I was now experiencing, would screw up the scope. All I could see were millions of green raindrops reflecting back into my scope! If I hadn't been the kind, sweet, reserved, reverent, beautiful chap I was, I would have tossed that damned scope clear into Glenn County lying to my north! Suffice to say after four hours of fruitless searching and listening in that heavy rain, I gave it up as a lost cause. I remember arriving home and looking at myself in my bathroom mirror. You talk about looking like a drowned rat. It had rained so hard, even under all my rain gear, I was soaked. It was as if the gods were poking fun of me and my feeble attempts at catching my perennial night-shooting chap. However, one does not throw down a glove in front of a good game warden as a challenge like my shooter was regularly doing. A good officer will pick it up, and then the only way to get him off your trail is to shoot him. And, I had been shot once before by a worse wildlife outlaw than the one I was currently chasing and I was still on the field of battle...

Giving up on my lone shooting chap for the moment because of the awful valley winter rains, I went after some of my other night shooting clientele the old-fashioned way. That meant shanks mare and a lot of damn hard work. Suffice it to say, those violating shooting son-of-a-guns caught hell as substitutes for the chap I really wanted. If I remember the week I quit chasing my particular night shooting chap in order to get after those other rascals, I caught thirty-eight different late and early shooters screwing up by doing unto Mother Nature before

she could do unto them. However, she still had her Sword
For Mother Nature out and about, and this time, he had
the bit in his teeth. For you unwashed, it can be a real
chore sometimes when it comes to catching certain really
dedicated wildlife outlaws. But a good game warden is
sometimes like a feral cat. He will just keep on coming
and if he is a good hunter of humans, will be using all his
primal senses to catch his prey, no matter how elusive the
pursued chooses or happens to be.

Finally, I got a strong north wind with little rain one
evening. Perfect weather for my chap to be out and about
killing ducks to my way of thinking. With that break in
the weather, out I headed to Section 14 like a man on a
mission. Mission hell, it was a vision quest... Remember
Grosz's Rule? If a chap breaks the law and gets away with
it, many times he will return to the same area where he
had unfettered success in raiding Mother Nature's pantry.
However, being a creature of habit sometimes can be a
bad thing. And that evening had all those ear marks of
final destiny for my chap walking on the dark side of man,
no pun intended. I was out and about and the weather and
duck numbers were ideal for the moment at hand. The
hunt was on once again! And this time, the hunter of men
once again had the look of a happy, slobbering dog with
his head hanging out the window of his red neck owner's
speeding pickup, if you readers get my drift.

Sure as God made rice field mud that always gobbed
up on your hip boots when you were in a hurry, my
shooter was back on the field of battle and in fine style.
Boom! went his characteristic one shot. That time, I was
on him like ugly on a long dead cow in the July heat in
Colusa County. Sweeping the area with the scope, I
spotted my man in the lime green field of the Starlight
Scope. He was wringing the neck of a drake mallard and

419

looking right at me from about fifty yards away. For a moment, I thought he could see me using the scope and I froze! But that concern soon turned into thin air, as my gunner headed south at a ground-eating shuffle like he was still on the hunt. Looking off his direction of travel, I could see and hear a tornado of ducks flooding into the next rice check below his location. That was his destination, I thought. Not even bothering to put my scope back into my game bag that time, off I went in my own ground-eating shuffle in the darkness heading in that direction as well. It was always amazing to me just how strong the smell of blood, is in the air when a kill is in the offing... Plus I had a couple of guardian angels flopping around inside of my miserable carcass like they were trying to shake off all their feathers they were so fired up. Suffice to say, that was their way of letting me know my Christian had screwed the pooch one time too many, and the lion was once again in the proverbial Sacramento Valley coliseum...

Counting my steps, I figured I had traveled about seventy-five yards. Stopping, I flipped on my scope oscillator switch once again and took another gander. There, not forty yards in front of me, lay my chap on the backside of a rice check. The ducks in the next field were feeding toward him and he was content to just lie there until they got within easy gun range. Not this time, I thought. I was learning. That time, I kept my scope on and, using it as a guide, began sneaking up on the backside of my shooter. I got to within about twenty-five yards from my chap knowing the noise of the oncoming feeding ducks and his focused attention in their advancing progress would hide my foot crunching sounds on the previously harvested rice stalk stubble. Then it happened! The ducks spooked and rose up in a cloud of alarm. Ducks were going every which way including coming right at me. *Boom!* went my chap's shotgun, and it was so close that the muzzle flash blanked out my scope for an instant! Remember, the scope magnified any available light by a factor of fifty thousand. As I quickly discovered, a close-at-hand shotgun muzzle blast could cause the Starlight Scope fits. When the scope came back on moments later, I could see my chap using a small penlight to run down several ducks he had wounded when he had shot into the center of the fleeing flock. As he did, I moved onto his previous rice check and continued watching him picking up the ducks he had just shot. Moments later, he came almost right back to where I was now lying nearby on the rice check. Laying down my scope on the rice check, I reached in and grabbed out my flashlight from the game bag on the back of my hunting coat. By listening to his oncoming crunching footsteps in the rice stubble and judging that he was within grabbing distance, I turned on my five-cell flashlight.

"Yeow!" he screamed as he ran smack dab right into me! Dag nab it, I had waited too long and had misjudged his closeness. When I turned on my flashlight, he was so close that he hit the end of it with such force that I almost dropped the light! Quickly recovering, I lunged forward like a defensive tackle on a damn good football team. Down we both went into the muddy rice field full of dead crawdads, duck poop, rotting rice straw, dead carp remains, and mud from the force of the impacts from my tackle! But I had my man with a hold that would have taken a D-8 bulldozer to break! "Game warden!" I yelled, as I tightened my grip on the lad who had by now recovered from his surprise and was trying desperately to break away from my iron grip. Needless to say, one can't run very far or fast when a 320-pound game warden is hanging onto your goozle with a sure-fire death grip!

Soon everything was under control and I was able to identify one Jeff Cummings from the town of Willows. I later discovered he had always hunted this section of rice ground because it was one, which his uncle had leased and was farming. Then in the rotting rice field full of normal smells, all of a sudden I could now detect the strong smell of hot urine wafting by in the humid air. Checking out the front of the pants of my catch with my flashlight, I discovered my chap had wet himself when I reared up from the rice check in surprise and had put the King Kong grab on him. I think he figured a grizzly bear had him. Poor chap, if he only knew his California history. He should have realized that the last California grizzly bear had been killed in the late 1930s. If he only realized that he had been caught by a silken gilded powder-puff, and a beautifully wimpy one at that...

Sitting down together on the rice check once I had things under total control, I filled out a citation under the light of my five-cell. Then I advised he needed to sign the citation, which meant he promised to appear on or before the date on the ticket in order to settle the matter with the State of California. I also explained his option of forfeiting bail or appearing to personally to answer the charges I had lodged against his miserable late shooting, duck killing carcass. He was then informed that he was being charged with late shooting of waterfowl, To Wit, five hours and twenty-three minutes late. He was also charged with using a Winchester Model 12 pump-action unplugged shotgun to take migratory waterfowl. Why it was unplugged and fully loaded with five shells was beyond me because he characteristically only fired one shot at a time.

Then since things had quieted down, he asked, "How could you see me? It is pitch dark out here and, as well as I know the lay of this piece of land, it is even hard for me to get around. Plus, I never come out here to shoot my ducks unless it is pitch black. How could you see me?"

Then I dug out my scope from my game bag since retrieved from off the rice check and turned it on. Beckoning my chap for a look through the newest weapon in my arsenal, the man just gasped. Then he said, "You can see over two hundred yards away in the dark with this thing!"

"Yes, I can," I calmly agreed, like the scope was an end all to all our late and early-shooter law enforcement problems. It really wasn't, but it was a damn good start to my way of thinking. I could tell from the tone and tenor of what he said, plus the look on his face in the light of my now turned on flashlight, that he could not believe what he had just observed first-hand moments earlier through the scope in the abject darkness.

Striking while the iron was hot, I said, "Now, imagine how this is to be used on all your type, especially on the local drag shooters." For the most part, drag shooters were locals who sneaked up onto the feeding ducks in the rice fields at night and shot numerous times into those closely packed feeding masses, sometimes killing hundreds of birds at a time!

Jeff just looked at me for the longest time, then said, "Use of that device is illegal and chicken shit!"

"Yeah, well, you can think what you want. But it is about time the ducks had a friend, and if you want to try something as foolish as late or early shooting like this anytime soon, keep this in mind. I will be using this device in the future and, if I catch you doing this again, you will be heading for the lockup in Sacramento after a subsequent hearing and a finding of guilty in the Federal Court System by the U. S. Magistrate."

"Am I free to go now?" he asked caustically.

"You can be on your way, Jeff, anytime you wish. Just remember, take care of this violation or a warrant will be issued for your arrest.

And I will be just the chap happily serving it if it comes to that," I continued.

In a flash, my chap was gone into the dark of night that had here-to-fore protected his miserable carcass. Gone but not forgotten as I sat there in the dark watching him move out of the rice field through the scope. Then I watched him leaving in a vehicle he had hidden along Corbin Road. I had hunted that chap unsuccessfully for what seemed like an eternity. And now that I had caught him, it all seemed so anticlimactic. And in a manner of speaking, after I had picked up all his night shot ducks and was heading home for some much needed sleep, it was. I hadn't been able to run that lad to ground no matter how hard I had tried over my many fruitless earlier times in the valley. The country was just too dang big and he generally had all the advantages within his uncle's huge rice fields come the blanket of darkness. But now, a device saving men's lives in Vietnam was now saving the lives of my ducks in the Sacramento Valley. Either way, that was a good deal to my way of thinking.

My lad forfeited $550 in the Williams Justice Court fourteen days later. That was $25 for the base violation of late shooting migratory waterfowl, $2 for every minute in violation after legal shooting hours had lawfully ended up to a maximum of $500 and another $50 for the unplugged shotgun. His seized shotgun was forfeited to the State of California and later sold at a general auction for all fish and game seized property items. I have often wondered if whoever had purchased that shotgun at the live auction, ever thought of the history and the stories it could tell ... or just how many critters it had killed in its fifty-two-year history. Just to give my readers an idea as to what kind of a financial hit that was in those days, I made only $640 per month as a game warden during that same period of time.

But the best was yet to come. The day after I had caught Jeff, I stopped in Williams, a town known for their fair share of duck dragging and late shooting violators, and purchased a tank of gasoline for my vehicle. As the man pumped my gas, checked the oil and washed the windows—that was how it was done in those days—he looked into the front seat of my patrol vehicle through the windshield and spied my Starlight Scope laying there open in its case on the front seat.

"Is that the scope from Vietnam that allows you to turn night into day?" he asked rather off handedly and in a tone of voice that read nothing but Joe Casual.

"Sure is," I said. Kind of like blowing the smoke off the end of your pistol barrel after you had made a spectacular hundred-yard shot, I thought... Gee, I wondered, if my showing Jeff the use of the scope the evening I had caught him late shooting waterfowl, had anything to do with the rapid spread of the word throughout my outlaw community?

"Can you really see someone in a dark field about two hundred yards away?" my gas pumper asked, like he was trying to be Joe Casual once again. He was also a known to me as a local duck- killing outlaw.

"Sure can," I replied, like Joe Very Casual.

The gas pumper just shook his head, pulled out the nozzle from the gas tank and replaced the gas cap. "That will be four dollars," he said. Imagine that, four dollars for a full tank of gas...

I caught the gas pumper from Williams shooting waterfowl two hours late with the aid of the Starlight Scope three days later in a rice field just off Lone Star Road. Like Jeff, I let him look through it into the dark of the rice fields after the apprehension. The man couldn't believe his eyes. I never checked that old man shooting ducks ever again late at night. Like I said earlier, that type of scope saved the lives of many of our wonderful soldiers in Vietnam and was now saving my ducks back home in the rice paddies of the Northern Sacramento Valley. To my way of thinking, that was pretty ironic and very cool.

A DUCK CLUB AT THE END
OF ROAD SS

Checking duck hunters one evening in the Lambertville area in northern Colusa County, I could hear a lot of late shooting going on just to the north of me. Pausing to echolocate on the area in question, I surmised it had to be harvested rice field shooters banging away just to the northeast of the Sacramento National Wildlife Refuge. The sky that evening was full of scudding dark rain clouds and the wind from the northwest was picking up to about thirty miles per hour in the gusts. Damn, I thought. It is going to be another one of those historic Sacramento Valley winter nights in which one can wing shoot until they run out of shells or ducks, whatever comes first. It was good shooting weather because the clouds were low based and the local town lights from Williams, Maxwell and Willows would be reflecting off those clouds back towards the ground. When that phenomenon occurred, it allowed late shooters to keep on banging away at the ducks for hours long after legal shooting hours had since lapsed because of that artificially cast illumination. Sure as goats give good drinking milk, my late shooters to the north of me were having one hell of a field day at the waterfowl critters' expense. And from the frequency of the shooting, they were in no hurry to discontinue such illegal actions. Well, I had enough of that kind of stupid foolishness. I figured I was just the guy carrying the right kind of medicine needed for that kind of late shooting misery...

Gathering up my miserable carcass, I started out towards my hidden patrol vehicle from the duck club and its potential late shooters I had been watching. Keep in mind, my readers, a good wildlife officer always moves to the sounds of the guns for therein will always lay the root of any problems. Particularly when it comes to the critters and, many times, questionable human activity. Trotting down the small muddy levee surrounding my previously staked out duck club, I hadn't gone twenty yards when the lads I had been watching just moments earlier for any late shooting activity, opened up on a low flying flock of lesser snow geese! Dad hum it! I thought as I spun back around just in time to see my now three late shooters collectively unloading their shotguns into another flaring bunch of low flying geese accompanying that first flock they had just previously shot into. Trotting back to my originally stake out area and without any fanfare, I thundered out across the marsh after my close-at-hand late shooters. Once there and without any cutesy fooling around, like I was often want to do with my violators, I quickly rounded up and put the grab on my three late shooters. Heck, they were only shooting forty-three minutes after legal shooting hours—$111 per person in fines in the Williams Justice Court in those days! By the time I had finished administratively with my three lads for shooting late, it was now an hour and twenty-four minutes after legal shooting hours. And my suspect late-shooting lads to the north of my location were still banging away with the same ferocity, as were our G.I.'s were when they got overrun by several divisions of the Chinese Army on Pork Chop Hill during the Korean War in the 1950s.

Damn, it is so unique that such descriptors often come to my mind when writing my stories to emphasize a point. It brings back even more memories of an old college friend back at Humboldt, one retired army Major Sherwood "Scotty" Stutz. He had been there on Pork Chop Hill when it had been overrun by mass waves of Chinese soldiers. During one of our conversations in college since I was a warfare history buff, I asked Scotty what it had been like. Scotty advised what he most remembered, was when the Chinese attacked his positions, the first wave of Chinese soldiers had weapons and each succeeding wave had none! Then when someone was killed in the first wave, a soldier in the second wave would pick up the dead man's weapon and continue the attack... He also remembered he had four halftracks with quad .50-caliber machine guns positioned around his headquarters area. His last memories of those four vehicles were that they were backing up and they could collectively pour out more than eight thousand rounds of bullets a minute! In fact, the Major had been the officer who had ordered the friendly overflying air cover to drop their napalm on his dug-in positions just as they got overrun by the Chinese! Scotty still had the 9mm bullet scars stitched across his chest to prove that he had been there, had survived, and that war was just another phase of hell... But, back to the story and my war with the late shooters...

Leaving my Lambertville Duck Club late shooting lads, I took off running for my patrol truck like a bat out of hell. Jumping into the front seat, I burned my way out from that area and headed west for the old Maxwell-to-Willows Highway. Once on that highway, I sped north past the Sacramento National Wildlife Refuge in the darkness like there was no tomorrow. Power sliding the turn onto Road 60 above the refuge, I sped eastward toward Four Corners. The reason I was driving like a bat out of hell was because a late shooter could quit at any time. And in order to make a case that would stand up in a court of law, I had to see the shooter-taking waterfowl after legal shooting hours had ended. Hence me scooting along like a California brown bat...Dipping south on the turn by Road SS, I was now on Road 61. Sliding to a stop on a pull out, I bailed out from the truck and, in a cold driving rain and now steadily increasing wind, cupped my ears southward toward the area where I figured the earlier late shooting had originated. To you unwashed, cupping ones hands over his ears to concentrate any sounds in that direction in which one is looking was an old commercial market hunter's trick of the trade, a trick used to discern the nearby locations of quietly feeding waterfowl in the rice fields in the dark of night. And once the close-at-hand ducks had been located, the killing nature of the outlaw's intentions was put into motion. That trick of the trade was also used very successfully by us old game warden types as well. For once we located the feeding masses of ducks, we could sneak them as well and quietly position in next to the critters on a handy rice check. And then if the bad guys sneaked that bunch of ducks and blew them up,

429

guess what? Yep, I brought out more than one surprised duck-killing, night-shooting son-of-a-gun from the field to be incarcerated using such techniques. Standing out there in the elements like a damn ol' wet muskrat, I intently listened like a red fox would for mouse movement in a dense grassy field or under a thin layer of snow.

By now, the wind was really gaining strength and the winter's rain was beginning to slop down raindrops the size of duck eggs, no pun intended. Straining my ears for any telltale sounds over the hammering raindrop explosions off my rain gear, I now searched the lands to the south with my binoculars where I suspected my late shooters were located. *Boom-boom-boom-boom-boom!* went five quick shots from two different shotguns. Damned if they aren't just due south of me off Road SS, I thought, as I happily bailed back into my truck. To my way of thinking, the hunt was now on, big time! Turning my truck around, I headed down a muddy and badly potholed Road SS just a banging and a clanging. I figured at that point in time, vehicle noise be damned. The furious winds and driving rains would drown out any noises my vehicle was creating. Running without headlights and flipping on my cutoff switches so I would show no tail or brake lights when they were used, I steamed south as rapidly as I safely could in the rain swept darkness. I hadn't gone a mile when all of a sudden I was brought up short by a steel cable hanging from two large steel posts, which was strung across and blocking the road. The faintly seen cable had a white sign hanging down in the middle of it saying "No Trespassing—This Means You!" In fact, if it hadn't been for that white sign hanging down in the middle of the cable, I would have run full tilt into it in the darkness! Just another game warden hazard when one chooses to run in the darkness without the use of lights. Sliding to a stop just in time, I bailed out into a now-driving rain. Standing in front of my truck using it as a rain and windshield, I cupped my ears listening to my south once again. By that time, the air was now jug full of ducks looking for places to land and fill up on rice grains as foretold by the numbers of overhead whistling wings and their nervous, faintly heard aerial talking back and forth. Their numbers were additionally foretold by the numerous darkened flocks hurtling by not twenty feet off the ground in long, undulating streams as they used their fellow compatriots flying to their fronts as handy windbreaks. But other than that, nothing else characteristic of the late shooting fraternity greeted my ears for the longest time. I am too damned late to do any good this evening, I finally thought in frustration. Once again, keep in mind my readers, a wildlife officer has to see someone kill or shoot at a migratory game bird after legal shooting hours in order to have a late shooting violation occur under the federal Migratory Bird Treaty Act or like state fish and game regulations. Just knowing where the shooting came from and finding any chaps with shotguns and freshly killed ducks in hand in the suspect area, did not legally constitute a late shooting violation in any court of law.

I stood there for about another hour still looking, hoping and getting my tail end soaked by the driving winter rains. Looking for a telltale set of vehicle lights coming out from the field, light from a flashlight of returning shooters or nearby clubhouse lights going on pinpointing my suspect late shooting location, were my getting dimmer by the moment hopes. In fact, up to that moment in time, I was rewarded with nothing more than cold rainwater running down the back of my neck. Finally realizing my late shooters were through for the evening, I took my flashlight and headed for the locked cable gate in front of me. Using a small sliver of light through my fingers, I turned over the Master Lock to look for its identification number. It had been filed off to prevent anyone from using an unauthorized key to gain entry! That little move alone set off my alarm bells. Being overly suspicious anyway, I figured the landowners may have done that to keep the local game warden from entering their little out of the way shooting area. However, I always kept a ring of about one hundred of the most common keys for the locks ordinarily used in the valley by the landowners for just such occasions. But without a lock identification number, I would have been there all night trying each and every key I carried. Plus, this wasn't an area in which I was familiar. I was now in Warden Jim Hiller's law enforcement district in Glenn County. Jim was a long time, old school, California game warden friend from my Sacramento Valley patrol squad, who had just about completely burned out. He had been a fine officer in the '40s and '50s chasing the valley's deadly commercial market hunters and duck draggers during their heyday. During those times, game wardens were sometimes shot at like feral house cats or other vermin when they got too close to the local wildlife outlaws and their illegal activities. In turn, the men in green settled such altercations with their fists or a pistol barrel laid at a high rate of speed alongside one's head when the outlaws tried such deadly tactics. But time, long hours afield, eating lousy food, facing off against deadly odds, harsh weather, and hard work had taken its physical toll on his aging body. As a result, Jim's flame was just about gone as his worn-out body slowed and then began breaking down. Today, some forty- plus years later, my body understands what Jim was going through during that time of his life, more than likely, the main reason as to why Jim was not hot on my current late shooters' trail in a cold, driving rain and howling windstorm. It is hard to get-up-and-go when your body has got-up-and-went...

My game warden district was just immediately south of Jim's in Colusa County and I had plenty to do in my own area of responsibility. I hardly ever ventured into Jim's Glenn County patrol district because of my own never-ending heavy workload. However, now that I was hot on the trail of what I considered a mess of really serious and dedicated late shooting wildlife outlaws, all district line niceties were off the table and the hunt was on! I knew Jim would not be out and about in such crappy, cold winter weather. Jim was a worn out older man of slight build. It would have been better for him if he were sitting at home in the warmth of a fire with a toddy in hand and his tired feet resting up on a close-at-hand footstool to my way of thinking. And, he was...

So here I was, stymied by a damned locked gate on unfamiliar terrain and slowed by earlier late shooting activity that had occurred in my own district further to the south. Then I saw it! A faint light had just gone on in what I was later to discover was a duck club about a half mile below where I now stood. Those have to be my late shooters, I thought. They had late shot the harvested rice fields below their clubhouse earlier and are just now getting back to that facility. That's why the clubhouse light is just coming on this late in the evening, way after legal shooting hours have long since passed. Man, to my way of thinking, the fox was now in the henhouse...

Walking back and pulling my truck off to one side of the muddy road, I took off at a trot with my dog on shank's mare toward the suspect duck club. Arriving shortly thereafter, I quietly slipped unseen by the now well-lit duck club that was sitting on the west side of the muddy farm road on which I now traveled. Parked at the duck club were two vehicles whose makes, models and license plates I memorized. Looking through the clubhouse windows from the shadows of the road with my binoculars, I could see four men taking off their wet hunting gear, laughing a lot and beginning preparations for their supper. Slipping away in the darkness, I followed the road past their clubhouse heading south. I still had work to do if I was to be successful in capturing my late-shooting chaps at a later date. That was done because there was little I could legally do about their late shooting at that point in time since I had not seen them shooting. And if Sacramento Valley waterfowl late shooting history was a teacher, my shooters, since they had not been bothered by the long arm of the law, sure as house cats make good rifle targets, would be back!

Sometime later, I came to about a sixty-acre harvested and shallowly flooded rice field. Using my binoculars, I could tell the area was chockfull of feeding ducks and contained six duck blinds strategically located within the flooded rice field to elicit the best waterfowl shooting opportunities for their gunners. This has to be the place from where the late shooting I had heard earlier came from, I thought with a wet faced grin. What a neat and out of the way concealed spot to break the waterfowl sport hunting laws, zipped across my mind. However, their little late-shooting sweet spot had now been discovered. And, like a hungry rattlesnake slowly going down a rodent hole in the sagebrush, nothing good in the future was to come to its occupants if they didn't have a great and handy backdoor escape plan.

Leaving the area after committing to my memory banks a mental picture of the area, I hotfooted it back past their clubhouse and up the road to my truck. In short, getting the heck out of there before being inadvertently discovered. The way I figured it, I would wait until another like weather-wise non-shoot day came along—shoot days were Wednesdays, Saturdays, Sundays, and holidays in the valley—and return at that time for a closer, undisturbed look at the area during daylight hours. That would lessen the chances of being observed by the duck club members, and I could take my time scouting out the area so I could lay a trap and catch my late shooters red-handed the next time they decided to raid Mother Nature's waterfowl pantry during a similar rainy weather event. Plus, remember one of my main conservation officer's rules-if one illegally shoots an area and was not apprehended or disturbed, they would more than likely return again under the same circumstances for another dip into Mother Nature's cookie jar. And if my miscreants did so, they had better have a back door to their burrow when the game warden entered through the front...

Thursday late afternoon following, I was back on the scene of my suspected late shooters. True to form, the area was quieter than a car-hit chicken or sail rabbit on a Nevada highway. Moving around the area on foot, I surveyed the lay of the land. I also had a chance to visit each duck blind looking for any signs of bait. Bait I did not find, but I did find a mountain of newly fired shotgun shells with the fresh scent of burned powder still lingering inside the casing, letting me know the previous duck shooting had been pretty damned good and recent. With my field scouting accomplished and battle plan in mind, I returned to the deserted duck club proper. There I discovered the location of their duck-hanging facility used to cool out and drain freshly gutted birds. With that vital information under my belt, I left the area before being inadvertently discovered by the local farmer. But not before using my ring of keys and discovering the one that fit their lock back at the locked cable blocking the road to the duck club with the filed off identification numbers. Like I said earlier, a rattlesnake moving down an occupied rodent hole is not a good thing for its resident critter unless it has a back door, plenty of warning and is fleet of foot. And I sure as hell didn't see any backdoor in this immediate situation nor planned on giving my late shooters any advance warning my miserable carcass was in country. As for that fleet of foot thing, if my late shooters chose to run from their burrows, even weighing in at 320 pounds, I could still run an eleven-second-flat hundred yard dash...

Come the following Saturday and Sunday shoot days, I kept an eye open and an ear to the ground on my suspect duck club, all the while working waterfowl hunters in the northern zone of my district so I would be close to my target of opportunity. As it turned out eye balling them off and on from afar, the shooters on the suspect duck club were as clean as a hound's tooth when it came to any readily discernable hunting or late shooting violations. Sensing that there were too many of the other club members present who probably did not favor breaking the laws, I wrote off my late shooting patrol in that area on the weekends as a wash. However, the following Wednesday, when usually fewer club members historically shot the valley's duck clubs, I was hanging around in the area kind of like a feral cat. The weather report for the entire week was for crappy weather. Winter rain and winds were now in the forecast, weather events that were just right for the ducks, illegal duck shooters, and those hunters of humans chasing those doing what they shouldn't be doing to those in the world of wildlife who had little or no voice. And being a bit of a natural history historian myself, guess who was hanging around within earshot of the front of the burrow leading to my suspect rice field?

Right at dark, I slipped through the locked gate with my undercover county patrol truck but stopped short of the duck club proper. With that, I hid my vehicle among several parked rice harvesters not in use so it would not be readily observed or suspected. Then Dog and I, using the cloak of deepening winter darkness, slipped past the darkened duck club as we continued our trek toward their sixty-acre flooded rice field and suspected late shooting area. However, as we slipped past the clubhouse, I noticed the same two vehicles that had been there the Wednesday before when all the illegal night shooting had taken place, were now parked in the parking lot... The rattlesnake was now in the entrance to the burrow...

Hot dog, I thought. If you lads shoot late tonight, guess who will be there to welcome you to his Coney Island? Yep, you got that right. Dog, the super-sized tule creeper, and his trusty Starlight Scope were on the scene. That evening portended one of those "Game wardens-One, Late shooters-Nothing" looks about it emanating from my two now stirring guardian angels. Keeping that happy thought under my hat, I lumbered along towards my soon hoped for late shooter field of dreams. That I did by lumbering along out of sight in the bottom of a weedy adjacent ditch leading to the shooting area in question.

Right on schedule, I had four lads begin late shooting the flocks of ducks swarming over their freshly harvested rice field and shallowly flooded duck club hunting area. For my non-duck hunting readers, the ducks by that time of the year, had the legal shooting hours thing down pat, which were one half hour before sunrise to sunset. In those days when we had a lot of birds, twenty minutes after legal waterfowl shooting hours had ended, the ducks and geese just like clockwork, took to wing. As it turned out, I had two men in one blind and singletons in two of the other blinds. The way they were spread out over the club allowed for keeping the ducks moving within their sixty-acre harvested rice field, which, to my way of darkly thinking, allowed for the maximum killing effect. No matter from which side the ducks came to feed that evening, they had to run a gauntlet of shotguns in that cleverly laid out killing field. These aren't your usual run of the mill rubes, I thought as their heavy illegal late shooting commenced right on cue as if on a prearranged command. Those shooters have all the outward trappings of real killers when it came to night shooting those in the world of waterfowl. And truth be known, I would shortly have all the trappings needed to run such killers to ground in fine style...

Then the weather gods joined right in like they were pissed at all the ducks successfully navigating through the worst conditions they had to offer. The winds began blowing about a steady twenty knots out of the northwest and the rain was coming down in sheets and flying sideways. That always forced the winged critters, which had to fly with open eyeballs suffering the stinging rain pellets, to fly low and slowly so they could see. That was just what my gunners had apparently planned for, and they were exacting a heavy toll on my poor flying unfortunates, as Dog and I quietly swung into an intercept position. That kind of killing is OK though. The ducks have a friend this evening and this friend carries a hammer, I smugly thought, as the cold rainwater poured down the back of my neck with what appeared to be another Niagara Falls when it came to sheer volume. But by then, I was on the hunt and cold rain water running down my neck and back clear to my belt line, be damned. It wasn't the first time I had been soaked clear to my goozle and it wouldn't be the last as long as I remained a member in good standing of The Thin Green Line.

During periods of rain let up, I switched on the scope and I was able to individually identify my late shooters, who were now banging away two hours and forty-six minutes after legal shooting hours! As it so happened, they were killing the hell out of the ducks! Therein came the rub. All four of my chaps were out in the huge open, shallowly flooded rice field. They were smart. They were using the artificial light reflecting off their rice field's sheet water and the low based clouds reflecting the city's lights from the nearby Town of Willows, as a shooting prop in aiding them in the taking of the hungry ducks flooding into their gunning area. That, plus the howling winds and the fact that when my chaps walked around in the water picking up their dead ducks, they were all creating ripples in the water like feeding ducks made. All those ripples did was tell airborne ducks fighting the rain drops on their bare eyeballs, that there was food and feeding aplenty below and the welcome mat was out! The air around the shooters was full of swarming ducks until the scene looked like an overturned hive of bees! Brother, I think back on those days with wonder. Man, did we ever have ducks, especially mallards, American wigeon, Northern pintail and Northern shovelers in the Sacramento Valley in those historic days of yore.

To my readers, I apologize for not capturing in print what those spectacular days were really like when we had millions of migrating waterfowl in the Sacramento Valley. Their numbers were nothing short of astonishing and their behavior, when pressed by weather extremes, was nothing short of unbelievable. I only wish all of you could have experienced what I saw when Mother Nature really flashed all her goods for the world to see and enjoy as she collided with the weather. But alas, as these words were written in 2012, I think those days and duck numbers of old, are now in large part severely reduced. But when they were there in such memorable historic numbers, I reveled in their beauty, grace and life histories...

However, there was no way I could sneak in on any one of my late shooters to stop the slaughter without alerting and scattering the rest of their buddies to the four winds. Especially when my beautiful and loving presence became obvious right in the backyard of my illegal shooters. Basically my old way of running the shooters to ground, because of this group's careful duck blind field placement, was a no-go. So I then switched to Plan B. Figuring my late shooters were like coyotes, especially when it came to carrying out the huge loads of ducks they were killing, they would take the easy way out. In short, I figured they, like coyotes in the wild, would walk out using the road. That made for easier walking and, if anyone was heading their way, they could still see a country mile in the reflection off the water and from the low based clouds phenomenon reflecting the lights from the nearby Town of Willows. And once they spotted any form of perceived danger, like an approaching officer of the law, they would quickly become like a fart in a whirlwind and quietly fade off into the velvety nothingness of the darkness...

Instituting Plan B, I crawled down into another ditch running alongside what I figured would be near their escape road leading back to the sanctuary of their nearby duck club. From my new place of hiding, I could clearly see my shooters. But for the most part, because of the intense intervals of rain and low shots taken sometimes behind their blinds, could not get an exact count on the total numbers of ducks killed by each shooter. No matter how one cut it, this would be a bad dying night for the ducks and eventually an even worse one for my errant shooters... Especially once I got my hooks into their miserable carcasses for being a tad heavy on their trigger fingers, low skilled in their duck counting abilities, helpless when it came to being able to read a watch and understanding the waterfowl hunting regulations that pertained to shooting hours...

Then the unexpected happened! One of my shooters left his spot on the extreme western side of the duck club and began walking easterly toward one of his buddy's duck blinds. Looking through the night scope, I could see that man was carrying a duck strap loaded full of ducks. Pausing momentarily at his buddy's duck blind, my chap then continued on to the area holding the remaining two late shooters at the far east end of their killing field. It was then that I noticed my chap leaving the second shooter's blind was now carrying two duck straps full of ducks! Damn! I thought. That first lad is carrying off all the ducks! Arriving at the last two shooter's blind, my lad gathered up their duck straps and then, with signs of difficulty, labored toward my position by the road carrying four heavily loaded duck straps. Well, one thing is for sure. If he tries to run from me carrying all those duck straps heavy with birds, he is going to be run to ground by yours truly in short order, I thought.

Watching my lad leaving the last pair of shooters as he walked along a small muddy rice check toward the main farm road, I saw he was really struggling under his huge load of dead ducks. It quickly became apparent that my shooter was running straps full of ducks taken from

441

the shooters of each duck blind to a prearranged dropoff spot. Man, I was sure hoping he would run when he got close enough to my position for me to announce my presence. I had hardly full-force tackled anyone since my days playing college football and when I tackled someone, I could leave a mark! Now even more so since this lad had killed so many of my little feathered buddies! And in that anticipated collision, would certainly be a lesson in life for its outlaw recipient...

Then I got another surprise. My lad made it to the end of the rice check where it met the main farm road leading back to their duck club. Walking up onto the road, he began taking all the ducks off the duck straps and piling them onto the middle of the road. What the heck f I thought. Then taking the now empty duck straps, back he reversed his course, dropping off the empties at each shooter's blind. Then it dawned on me! The whole while he was hauling out the ducks on everyone's duck straps, all my other lads had quit shooting. I guessed they had ceased their shooting activity to check and see if anyone was the wiser as to their little late duck shoot. But, once that lad had returned with their duck straps, then had returned to his own blind and the coast was clear, the killing commenced again. Now they were shooting three hours and thirty-four minutes after legal shooting hours!

For the next hour, my four lads had at it like there was no tomorrow. Then they all quit on the top of the following hour as if preordained. Finally, here they all came heading toward the pile of ducks previously laid in the middle of the farm road at the edge of their shooting area. Arriving at that spot, all the shooters laid their ducks down in the same pile. Then two of the men picked up a rope and began dragging a heretofore unseen, stone boat like sled carrying all the ducks as they headed down the wet grass covered road toward their clubhouse. That is pretty slick, I thought. Instead of carrying all those duck straps full of ducks, they have just unloaded them into a stone boat like contraption that looked like a flat-bottomed sled. With that, the heavily loaded contraption could be dragged back to the clubhouse on the wet grass quite easily. Then if anyone like a game warden jumped them, they could individually split unencumbered to the four winds into the darkness, leaving their ducks behind. Later they could creep their ways back to the clubhouse with no ducks in hand and no over limit or late shooting liability attached. Pretty damn clever, I thought with a wet grin. But not clever enough...

Time for Plan C, I thought. Letting the men walk past Dog and me, I let them get a good thirty-five-yard head start. Then Dog and I quietly slipped in behind them walking in a crouch along the weedy edge of the ditch paralleling the main road. The men never looked back on their trail to see if anyone was following them. Remember one of Grosz's Rules—If they aren't looking for you, they won't see you. And these guys were as blind as a mole rat in the July mid-day sun when it came to observing the lad creeping along behind them with a wet grin on his very beautiful puss.

Walking back to their darkened clubhouse proper, my four late shooters entered their duck hanging facility. Turning on the hanging facility's lights and off-loading some of their wet hunting gear and duck straps full of ducks, the men headed back down to the stone boat sitting on the main road leading past their duck club. With that, the lads began making trips back and forth as they unloading the rest of their loose birds from the stone boat. Once all the ducks were unloaded onto the floor of their hanging facility, two of the men went inside the clubhouse while the other two moved the stone boat further down the road leading back to their shooting area. Soon the first two came back out from the duck club with a quart bottle of Wild Turkey® bourbon whiskey and four drinking glasses. By then, the movers of the stone boat had also returned. Rejoined back at the hanging facility, there was lots of excited talk as the glasses were filled about three fingers deep with the excellent tasting elixir and handed out amongst the happy outlaws. Happy over what they considered was a successful little illegal escapade, a toast was offered. With that ritual out of the way and a swill of damn good whiskey moved over their lips, two of my lads began picking the vent areas of each duck clean of feathers while the other two slit the ducks open around their vents prior to gutting. Watching the men with my binoculars through the hanging facility's open door, I guessed these lads had performed this little duck picking and cleaning ritual many times before...After a while, all four men stood around a fifty- gallon barrel lined with a huge garbage bag dumping in the feathers and duck guts. Man, how my dog, Shadow, would have liked to have gotten into that barrel of warm duck guts, especially on that cold and rainy night having been without any eats since way before dawn that morning, as had I. Hell, she would have loved that barrel of duck guts at any time of the day or night knowing her typical Labrador ability to eat anything not solidly bolted down.

Then came time for your trusty local game warden to make his beautiful and dainty Teutonic appearance. All my guys now had a snoot full or two of good whiskey and were trapped inside the hanging facility like a gunnysack full of unwanted kittens heading for a creek to be drowned. "Evening, Gents," I said, as I quietly and unexpectedly plugged the open doorway of the hanging facility with my more than dainty frame. Well, suffice to say, there was an instant explosion of surprise. The first casualty of my sudden and now-not- loved appearance, was the still half-full quart bottle of 101-proof Wild Turkey bourbon. The surprise of my unexpected appearance was so profound that in the instant melee that followed, the bottle of whiskey was mistakenly swept off the cleaning table and onto the hanging facilities concrete floor. Damn, that was one hell of a waste of good bourbon whiskey, I thought, as the bottle smashed into a million pieces of glass and thousands of drops of splattering, high- octane brown liquid to the four winds.

"Evening, Gentlemen," I began again. "My name is Terry Grosz and I am a state fish and game warden." With those words of greeting and salutation out of the way, I held up my silver star for all to see. I was dressed up in typical duck hunting grubbies at the time and not in uniform, hence the holding up of my badge recently retrieved from my shirt pocket. Somehow, I don't think that was what my cornered, duck-over-limit-shooting rats wanted to see at that moment in their lives. Especially since there appeared to be at least a hundred illegal ducks lying there on the floor in front of God and everybody and the most they could collectively possess if taken legally was thirty-two! At first, no one said a word. All they could do was look at the pitcher's mound-sized game warden standing in the hanging and cleaning facility doorway blocking all escape avenues. Of course, he was a beautiful looking pitcher's mound though and that had to count for something. Beautiful, hell he was an exceptional-looking hunk of a man, the truth be known.

Finally the fat one with a handlebar mustache said, "Good evening, Officer. You scared the hell out of us. Where the hell did you come from?" With those words, he casually dropped the mallard duck he was cleaning into the barrel full of feathers and duck guts, as if I wouldn't see his little sleight of hand. Fat chance! Besides, what difference would one little duck make when he still had the better part of probably a hundred freshly killed ones lying scattered around at his feet?

"Well, to tell you the truth, I have been here all along. I arrived on your duck club grounds long before you started shooting after legal hours and have been here ever since. During that time, I watched each of you folks late shoot and take over limits of ducks. And I did all that with a state of the art night scope fresh from the battlefields of Vietnam. In essence, I was able to turn night into day as I watched you gentlemen break several state and federal waterfowl hunting regulations like there was no tomorrow. And I suspect you were the same fellows doing the exact same thing last Wednesday on this club as well. That is why I am here this evening. And from what I saw going on out there in the field and what I am seeing here tonight, it was about time I came along to put a crimp in your collective styles," I said casually, like the spider to the fly. As you readers can ascertain, I was more than happy to win this one for the Gipper. Especially one over a bunch of lads who really needed some legal attention when it came to what I considered the sport of kings if done properly, namely lawfully hunting waterfowl.

Brother, it was at that point in time that I noticed a collective discernable look of abject worry flashing across my chaps' faces! Sensing something out of the ordinary as a result of those collective looks of abject worry, I said, "Why the long faces, Men? This little over limit and late shooting screw up on your parts can be settled with a citation and a fine. A hefty fine, mind you, but it is not the end of the world." Seldom did anyone go to jail in those days over a wildlife violation, especially one involving ducks. In those days, many judges considered wildlife violations a victimless crime and didn't really get too excited over offenses involving critters, particularly when it came to comparing them to the murders, incest, rapes, arson and other like human on human violations of the law then confronting the bench on a daily basis.

"That is what you think," said Mustache. "One of the owners of this club is a retired fish and game warden marine captain. When he finds out about this, we will be out of the club. And do you know how hard and expensive it is to find and join another good quality duck club here in the Sacramento Valley?"

"Well, Gentlemen, that hurdle is up to the lot of you to face. That is something the group of you should have thought about before getting carried away with this late shooting and duck-slaughtering escapade. Right now, I have this business at hand to square away. First, I need a count on all the ducks all of you killed by number and species. That includes the one you just quietly dumped in the barrel. Then I need to see some shotguns, duck stamps, hunting licenses, and driver's licenses if you would please."

When checked, their shotguns were plugged, their hunting licenses and federal duck stamps were all up to snuff. However, they still had the four hours and thirty-four minutes of late shooting and big over limit violations hanging over their heads. The total duck count was 104 ducks and the limit that year was eight ducks per shooter per day. Eight if taken legally and during legal shooting hours, that is. And since all the ducks had been taken after legal shooting hours, none could be lawfully possessed. Each man was then cited for shooting 4 hours and 34 minutes after legal shooting hours. Additionally, each man was also cited with possessing a joint over limit of 104 ducks. Jointly because I couldn't tell who had shot what, and when, so every man was in joint possession of the total of 104 ducks! They were additionally charged for taking over limits of ducks based on the numbers recorded in my notebook as to who took what.

None of those men cited ever showed up in the Williams Justice Court, but forfeited bail in the amount of $1,000 per man which was the maximum fine allowed in those days under state fish and game regulations for such violations! I swung the above cases into the Williams Justice Court instead of the justice court in the Town of Willows because the violation occurred on the Colusa-Glenn County line. In those days, that was an allowed legal practice when there was a jurisdictional question. That, plus, the judge in the Willows Justice Court was a wimp and prone to posting low fines no matter the type and degree of the violation. I just figured because of the grossness of the men's violations, they needed to stand before a real judge and that they did. The men were right. I never saw any of those four after that run in on that duck club ever again. From all appearances, their concerns about remaining with the duck club after being caught for gross wildlife violations were correct once the owner and former marine fish and game warden captain discovered their little boo-boo.

At our next fish and game squad meeting, Warden Jim Hiller, as I explained earlier in whose district the above violation had occurred, took me off to one side and thanked me for quietly giving him a hand with his problem at the end of Road SS. He retired shortly thereafter after many fine years of service in California and for its people during the '40s, '50s and '60s when the commercial market hunters were in full bloom and were of the ilk, if it came to shooting a close-at-hand pursuing game warden, some figured just go ahead and pull the trigger to rid yourself of such irritating trouble. Bottom line, it was easier to do that then spend time in the Big House over the market hunting and sale of migratory game birds. Can any of you folks out there imagine what that stint would be like, especially when gathered around a bunch of hardened murderers and the like, and have to tell them you were in the Big House over the mass killing and sale of ducks... Years later, Jim crossed over the great divide and joined those other members now long since passed who, at one time, formed what is known today as The Thin Green Line. Thank you, Jim, for all your years of excellent service in keeping the critters alive and for protecting the natural heritage for all the American people to enjoy in the years following.

The rattlesnake had finally made its way down the burrow and to the end of the hole that left no escape route for its unfortunate inhabitants. And then the snake rested...

THE WHITE MALLARD DUCK CLUB

Along with my numerous early and late shooting waterfowl problems in the Sacramento Valley, I had many other serious wildlife related problems as well. When the birds were flying low and slowly due to the onset of serious winter weather events, it seemed that the taking of over limits among many of my waterfowl outlaws and sports was the key to the kingdom! If those problems alone weren't enough to sink your bobber, I had over two hundred organized duck clubs that I frequented regularly within my assigned law enforcement district during the long waterfowl season: frequented because of the lawlessness they exhibited on most shoot days; bottom line, frequented because many of them had problems counting who had killed what and how many. There were more commercial duck clubs then that in the valley in my district, but that list of approximately two hundred were the ones that needed watching the most because of their past and present questionable legal histories. And one club in which I never ventured onto without writing some paper every time, was the White Mallard Duck Club located on the northeastern side of my patrol district. It seemed I could always take my pick of waterfowl violations once I was on that particular club during the waterfowl season. Be it over limits, untagged birds, no federal duck stamp in possession, shooting over a baited area or unplugged shotguns, there was always something of interest in the form of waterfowl violations that caught my attention. In short, all one had to do was take his pick of the poison once on site... It wasn't so much that many of the members didn't learn or know the hunting regulations but one of just plain arrogance on their part to my way of thinking. It just seemed in those days, that the members were wealthy, elitist, and obeying the conservation laws of the land was beneath their dignity. In short, most members just didn't give a damn. Not all the members, mind you, but enough were around who had such a strong disregard for the conservation laws, that I always made my enforcement trips on that club pay for themselves. But I had plenty of paper and got paid the same whether it was catching those folks or someone else breaking the fish and game laws of the land, so I did what I did best.

One particular fall shoot day, I had my trusty sidekick Reserve Deputy Fish and Game Warden Guy Bird with me. Guy was a good friend and worked in the Colusa County Assessor's Office as an appraiser. Guy was also a tremendous sportsman and crack rifle shot, hence his interest in and later becoming a Reserve Deputy Fish and Game Warden. The position of a Reserve Fish and Game Warden, one who held all the powers of a full time game warden, has not existed for many years since the late '60s because of the liability issues of such an unpaid, semi-trained position in the sue-happy State of California. However, when the program was authorized and operating, its volunteer officer corps freely served the people of California with distinction and honor. The two of us were not only great friends, but we managed to catch more than our fair share of wildlife outlaws when we worked in the county as a law enforcement team. Truth be known, based on our numbers of serious citations issued, we were pure poison to those who were a little heavy on their trigger fingers. You know, those who had trouble counting the numbers of birds taken in the world of waterfowl in the Sacramento Valley during those heady times.

One particular winter morning in the Butte Sink area on the eastern side of my patrol district, Guy and I prepared to launch our Grumman Sport Canoe, which had been borrowed from U.S. Game Management Agent Bob Norris (may God rest his soul). The Butte Sink was a historically storied watered area of ancestrally driven wintering flocks of hundreds of thousands of ducks and geese. In fact, so many birds would pile into that flooded and swampy area, that once the shooting began, I would frequently see one hundred thousand disturbed ducks and geese in the air all at one time!

Another time, Agent Pilot Al Weinrich (may he rest in peace) flew over an area in the sink named The Bean

Field by the locals and took a picture with his aerial camera of those flocks of resting birds below. He was later advised by the Service's research center, that there were over one million ducks and geese framed within his aerial photo! And in those storied days of the late '60s, the Butte Sink was home to over thirty wealthy, and I do mean moneyed, deep-water duck clubs. One of those duck clubs was named the Millionaire's Club. Does that more or less set the tone for such caliber of duck clubs on that storied hunting area?

Unloading the canoe from my vehicle at the water's edge, we attached our motor, shipped our necessaries, and set out for another day's adventures on the sink. It was around three in the morning and the Butte Sink was chock full of wintering ducks and geese at that time of the year. Probably wintering between five hundred thousand to one million birds, if I had to make an educated guess as to their numbers on site on any given day during the height of the winter waterfowl migration! With such storied stocks of aerial visitors, can any of my duck hunting readers out there imagine what the shooting opportunities were like on any given day of the waterfowl-hunting season? Yeah, you got that right...

To avoid detection by the various duck club gamekeepers who were always on the lookout for the fish and game law dogs, we launched our canoe in nearby Butte Creek. We did so because that area was located some distance away from the main area of the duck clubs targeted for that day. Paddling upstream, we stopped at a small, heavily overgrown feeder canal known to me that snaked easterly onto the backside of the Butte Sink duck clubs shooting area. Shipping our outboard motor so it wouldn't drag in the stands of dense aquatic weeds and cattails of the shallow ditch, we paddled and pushed our ways through the vegetation into the deeper watered sink hunting area proper. Soon we were in one of the finest waterfowl hunting areas in the United States and what a treat greeted our eyes and ears. Waterfowl habitat galore, and as I said earlier, from five hundred thousand to one million wintering ducks and geese on any given day resting therein. Man, you talk about a weedy-flooded timber paradise that to a conservation officer was pure magic, here was one in all its magnificence. Well, that was magnificence except for the thirty or so commercial duck clubs in the area, whose extremely wealthy members and their guests, were more or less legal part of the time on any given shoot day.

There was an aforementioned area just southwest of our position called The Bean Field. It was a large farmed area in the summer months that was later flooded in its entirety with the unharvested crop left on the ground for the birds to feast upon undisturbed when they migrated into the area in the fall and winter months. From the sounds of the Bean Field that morning as Guy and I paddled along now in deeper water, it held most all of the ducks and lesser snow geese in the world! The Butte Sink duck clubs never shot The Bean Field during the course of the regular season. The landowners of the various high class duck clubs, by not shooting the area, made it into a great natural refuge and a draw for every duck and goose in the immediate vicinity looking for a safe haven in which to land, feed, and loaf. Then as the birds traded to and from The Bean Field from other outlying wintering, feeding and migrating concentration areas, they in turn, provided almost unlimited duck and goose shooting for all the wealthy clubs in the sink. A great idea if killing scads of ducks and geese was first and foremost on one's mind. And in numerous duck club member's cases, that was always the considered course of action. More than just a few members from those exclusive duck clubs told me during field inspections, if they paid $50,000 (or some other figure) to join a particular hunting club, they wanted to kill $50,000 worth of ducks and geese or their waterfowl-hunting season would be a bust...

Therein laid the rub and that is where Guy and yours truly came in. With so many birds moving to and fro, as stated earlier, many gunners had trouble counting! You know, counting up to their legal limit of eight ducks and six geese per day and then stopping. From the historical numbers of chaps I caught with over limits of ducks and geese in my years as an enforcement officer while working in the Butte Sink, I would say many of my illegal gunners had failed Mrs. Wilson's third grade math class, big time! There were times in my later years as a federal officer in which I would catch so many shooters on those various clubs with over limits, that coming back to my launch point, my Grumman Sport Boat would only have several inches of freeboard! Only several inches of freeboard because I had seized and was carrying so many hundreds of pounds of illegally taken ducks and geese from those wealthy shooters who had difficulty in counting. And that was in a very stable seventeen- foot sport canoe with a three-foot-wide beam, capable of carrying many hundreds of pounds of weight in calm waters!

A week earlier, I had the occasion to drive by the White Mallard Duck Club on a routine patrol swing. As was usual for me, I had my windows down and my ears working overtime. Now that I think about that statement, I must have looked like a 320-pound bat or a kit fox... It was during that early morning drive by and, from the frequency of shooting on that club, realized maybe it was time I paid the lads another official shooting-grounds visit. After all, it had been ten days since I had last visited that duck club and on that swing, had only pinched eight lads with over limits of ducks. So with all that suspect shooting intensity in mind, that club's record in the poor counting department, and the ten day period since my last visit, I felt it was time they chanced upon my smiling face and lithe Teutonic figure once again.

Hence, the Great Grotz—that was me—and Guy ventured forth that fine morning so long ago into the storied Butte Sink. Paddling slowly to keep the ducks from going crazy and noisily leaving in alarm like a typhoon as we moved through the area in the darkness, we headed north to the White Mallard's shooting area. Based on the wind's direction and bird movement that morning, we selected a likely looking duck blind that we figured would be occupied and turn out to be a hot blind. With that selection accomplished, we looked for a likely looking hiding spot nearby. Finding one in the flooded timber in which we could hide, easily identify the ducks killed with our binoculars and yet not be seen by our shooters or anyone else like a gamekeeper casually passing by, we buried in. Removing a bundled camouflage netting from the bottom of the boat, Guy and I strung it out over the top of our canoe and us. That way we could still see up through the netting, look normal to our surroundings, and break up our outline so no one, including the over flying ducks, paid any attention to the somewhat odd-looking lump stashed in the brush alongside a nearby flooded tree line.

Then we got down to the really serious business at hand. That being a good game warden's breakfast. I had brought thick Molinari Salami and sharp cheddar cheese sandwiches heavily laced with mayo, jalapeno peppers, chips, and a half-gallon Stanley Thermos full of peppery-hot tomato soup spiced up with Tabasco Hot Sauce. How was that for a healthy spread of eats? As an aside, I remember what happened one time when I spilled some of my specially spiced tomato soup on the hood of my patrol truck when I was a game management agent a few years later. The spill ate the paint off the hood! But, oh my, it was great, especially on a cool, damp winter morning in a marsh full of loafing ducks, whistling wings overhead, a light breeze in the air and dozens of booming shotguns soon to be fired by future errant duck club clients who had trouble counting!

Sitting out there in the dark, the two of us had a feast as dozens of ducks buzzed into and out of the decoy set in the pond by our chosen duck blind. What a great morning that was! And, the best was surely yet to come if that area's illegal duck killing history was to have its say and rear its ugly head. You good folks out there reading these lines know what they say about history repeating itself. Hopefully, all of you also know what happens when one doesn't pay attention to the lessons history teaches us as well...

Shortly after legal shooting time arrived—wealthy clubs didn't have to send their members out any earlier because specific blind use was already pre-determined—the Sink came alive with the sounds of numerous running outboard motors carrying the club's shooters to their assigned blinds. Moments later, here came two men in a boat heading our way. They went straight to the blind we had selected as our target for the day. Docking their boat under the camouflaged brushed-up stilt blind where it could not be readily discerned by the ducks and geese flying into and over the area, they hustled up onto the blind's hidden shooting deck. It took a few minutes for our lads to get ready and then they got quiet as a field mouse pissing on a ball of cotton, as they looked skyward for their excellent eating, rice- and corn-fed winged quarry to come winging into their decoy set.

By now, the flocks of ducks and geese, which had been resting on the Butte Sink waters earlier, were alerted to the presence of human kind throughout the entire basin. The air was now filled with disturbed scads of birds trying to find a quiet place to once again light down and loaf. In fact, I remember my partner whispering to me that the air looked like someone had stepped on an underground nest of yellow jackets because there were so many flying objects in the air.

Soon four male and two female Northern pintail quietly dropped into the duck blind and set of decoys we had chosen to watch. They came so suddenly and quietly, that our two shooters were caught with their pants down. Suddenly, realizing they had ducks in their decoys, they blew up the swimming birds on the water! Only one duck escaped! I just shook my head in disgust. Here these rubes had the finest duck wing shooting in the world and yet they had chosen to shoot the birds resting on the water! Real sports, these guys, I disgustedly thought. With all the shooting going on around us, there were now disturbed birds in the air by the tens of thousands. Man, I only wish you folks reading these lines could have seen what it was like in those heady days of yesteryear! Soon three drake mallards dropped into our suspects' decoys and our gunners cleanly killed every one of them on the wing. By then, the shooting in the Sink from over two hundred guns from all the other thirty-plus duck clubs' members was something to behold and to my way of thinking, in full killing fury.

Then a flock of green-winged teal roared over our chaps' decoys. To you unwashed waterfowl sports, green-winged teal are the smallest ducks in North America. They weigh about ten ounces and have two motors and afterburners like an F-15 fighter jet! That little flock of birds roared into the decoys and, upon seeing our shooters quickly standing up to shoot at them, instantly went vertical. That's right, Folks, vertical! They went from flat-out flight over the decoys to vertical in a microsecond. And in so doing, they went from fifty miles per hour to over thousand miles per hour when they went vertical... Well, maybe not quite that fast but pretty damn close. Our two shooters simply emptied their shotguns into the thin air twenty feet below our little speedsters who got clean away. I just had to grin. That species of duck makes great eating because they are primarily seedeaters. However, you will work for them once they get into shotgun range, if you get my drift. But when they do and if you are a lucky or excellent shot, what an epicurean reward awaits, especially if you stuff and bake them for dinner. Guy and I now had our notebooks out on the seats of our canoe keeping track of what was going on with our shooters and double-checking the events among ourselves in case the issue at hand went to court. We kept track of the species of ducks killed, time of kill, and number of shots taken by each shooter. We also recorded when our lads picked up their kills and what they did with them once retrieved.

Then all hell broke loose! We had instant flocks of ducks coming into our shooters' decoys from four sides! They were shooting and reloading so fast, you would have thought they were trying to single-handedly stop George Pickett's charge of Rebs at the battle of Gettysburg in 1863, just as the Yankees had done! Twice Guy and I were hit with flying shot, and one of the recently killed ducks dropped within two feet of our hiding place. That doesn't bode well, I thought, especially if they come over here to pick up that duck and discover us sitting here before we are ready to spring our trap. Sure as hell is a hot place to be for Democrat defense attorneys from San Francisco, they would spy our little hideout and the jig would be up. Fortunately for us, our lads were deep into the killing mode and not into the process of picking up their dead ducks just yet. And that worked in our favor because they had just killed their last legal duck, a drake Northern pintail, and that put our lads at even limits of eight ducks each! Now, it was time for our shooters to leave since they appeared to not be interested in killing any geese or, if they stayed and continued with their duck shoot, it would be our time to shine...

But the ducks were still flying heavily into our decoy set, our friends were killing them like there was no tomorrow, and soon Mrs. Wilson would have to scold them for not counting correctly, if you get my drift. Then a large flock of American wigeon, a medium-sized duck, came barreling into the decoy set. Without hesitation, they landed in the decoys while our guys were reloading from their previous bout of shooting. Visible beyond the brushed up walls of the shooters' duck blind, those dumb wigeon sat there on the water in a tight bunch just asking for it. And true to the local outlaws' creed, the ducks got what they asked for! *Boom! Boom! Boom! Boom! Boom! Boom!* went six quick shots, slicker than cow slobbers, into the bunched up flock of swimming wigeon! Flyers and cripples from that flock immediately went every which way from Sunday. I leaned over and told Guy, "That is enough! They have just killed their last duck for today."

Throwing back our camouflage netting, the two of us gathered in the cover and threw it into the bottom of our canoe. If that didn't take the cake, with us in plain view off to one side of their blind, our two shooters acted like they were in a killing trance. They just continued shooting like nobody's business at a flock of drake and hen mallards zooming by overhead!

"Hey!" I yelled. "Don't the two of you think you have killed enough birds for today?" as it literally rained dead mallards around us!

Man, you talk about two stunned lads! Seeing our presence for the first time, they quickly dropped down and hid in their blind, like that would help them prevent discovery. Fat chance of that happening, I thought, as we quickly paddled their way. Fat chance, because our position was such that we could cut off their escape if they tried to load up and motorboat away. Seeing our errant shooters were continuing to hide in their duck blind like proverbial ostriches hiding their heads in the sand, Guy and yours truly began picking up their dead ducks. Guy and I picked up twenty-six dead ducks, or ten over their legal limit of eight ducks apiece. Then we paddled over to their blind. Since Guy was in the bow, I had him identify himself, step up into their blind, and check their licenses, federal duck stamps (no state duck stamps required in those days in California), and shotguns for plugs. As it turned out, they both were using unplugged shotguns, neither had a signed federal duck stamp, and now they were ten ducks over the limit! I would say Guy and yours truly had ground sluiced those two lads just like they had sluiced the group of wigeon earlier swimming in their decoys...

For you readers' information, the federal duck stamp has to be signed in ink across its face if one is in the act of hunting migratory waterfowl. That signing process validates the stamp. If that signature wasn't required, there would be those who would buy a stamp and let others use it when they weren't required to have it in their possession. That was the case that day. The White Mallard Duck Club used to have a cigar box full of unsigned duck stamps in their clubhouse. Anyone coming up to hunt who did not have a valid duck stamp in their possession, would just borrow one from the cigar box. Then when finished hunting and if not checked, that club member would just toss the borrowed unsigned duck stamp back into the box for someone else to illegally use. However, if out in the field hunting and seeing they were about to be checked, the sport would many times quickly sign the duck stamp procured earlier from the duck club's cigar box in order to save his cheating hide. The reason officers would write a citation for an unsigned duck stamp was because those monies raised from the sale of duck stamps went directly into land acquisition of wetlands for waterfowl. To be frank, by law, ninety-eight percent of the cost of the stamp went directly into land acquisition so the critters would have a place to call home. I would say that was one of the best deals going offered by the government. If one cheated and used a floater, or unsigned duck stamp, as we law dogs used to call them, then the land acquisition program was being shortchanged. There was no quarter given in that department by us law dogs for those trying to skate by the duck stamp laws. To do so, would only shortchange those sportsmen yet to come and the waterfowl using those vital wetlands purchased by the habitat acquisition proceeds from the purchaser of those stamps. Now you readers out there know why I always checked my waterfowl hunters for signed federal duck stamps and wrote the sport if they didn't have one properly validated by the shooter's signature across the face of the stamp in their immediate possession!

I began writing out the citations as our two sports grumbled about us trespassing on their duck club. That grumbling went in one ear and out the other just like mercury through my fingers. Wildlife officers have the right of trespass if they suspect migratory bird species are being taken in any area and then trespass is not a legal concern under the Fourth Amendment of the Constitution's search and seizure provisions. That is except on some super-secret military and submarine bases. Then an escort is required and usually provided for the wildlife officer in most circumstances. Trespass is generally not a concern because wildlife officers enforce conservation laws. And, if one has to get a warrant each and every time to conduct a field inspection of those suspected of breaking the fish and wildlife laws, there won't be much conservation taking place, will there? Under the Open Fields Doctrine, established from previous legal rulings in the federal court system, officers were allowed access to lands being hunted over when it came to federally protected migratory species. Additionally, as a state fish and game officer, I was also cross-credentialed as a Deputy U.S. Game Management Agent and migratory birds are a federally protected species. So, I didn't worry much about trespass concerns on a duck club's general hunting area because of my inherent legal authorities.

Finishing up the required paper work with our lads and seeing that the morning's shoot was already tapering off because many of the other shooters had already left after taking their limits of waterfowl, I backed off our canoe and headed directly for the shooting area's outlet canal leading to the White Mallard's boat docks. By beating a hasty retreat to the club's choke point for returning boat traffic, I figured maybe Guy and I could snatch off another shooter or two before the word got out about our hated presence on the club's shooting area.

We had no more than arrived at my selected cut-off point when I heard a boat motor coming our way. Hiding in a bunch of tall rushes, we waited until the boat was almost upon us before I paddled the canoe out into the boat channel and blocked it as we moved into plain view. Coming our way was a boat with two shooters. Seeing us and recognizing my magnificent figure from previous personal encounters, the man in the bow signaled with a lowered hand to the boat operator. The boat operator, whose one hand was on the transom of the boat as he steered the motor with the other, made a furtive move with his transom-holding hand. Immediately bobbing up in the wake of the now slower moving boat were four drake mallards he had just released to avoid their discovery in his possession by fish and game officers. Then our lad slowed and finally stopped his duck boat as Guy reached out and grabbed the side of the duck club member's vessel to steady it so a field inspection could be undertaken.

"Good morning, Gentlemen. Game wardens. I would like to check your birds, shotguns and licenses, if I may," I said. Then I pointed to the boat's operator and asked him to retrieve those four mallards he had just released off the transom with his right hand when he first saw us hove into view blocking the canal.

"Those aren't my ducks," he said stridently.

"Don't embarrass yourself. I clearly saw your partner in the bow signal you with his lowered hand of our presence, and then I saw you dump those four mallards off from behind the transom. They immediately surfaced in your boat's wake. I have very good eyesight, as does my partner, Sir. So please pick up your ducks and end with those foolish denials," I stated.

As our friend picked up his four ducks, we looked their boat over. It had sixteen drake mallards and Northern pintail laid out along the top of the boat's center seat. In the bottom of their boat were two large decoy bags full of decoys. To my way of thinking, if anyone tried to be helpful in a surprise game check, like laying his game out in plain view, a law dog should be on his toes for other wildlife related problems. Many times, I have discovered that the helpful ones are trying to get your inspection over quickly so they can be on their way. You know, like laying out their daily bag limit in plain view so all can see. That way the culprits figured, generally, you would be fast in your inspection and the sports could quickly be on their way before the good hidden illegal stuff was discovered.

As Guy checked their shotguns for plugs and licenses, I asked the bow man to hand me all their ducks.

"Why?" came a sharp instant reply.

"You chaps have a legal limit of ducks laid out across the seat. Additionally, the two of you are in possession of the four mallards the stern man dropped over the transom. That puts the two of you four ducks over the possession limit. Since the courts have ruled that the officer doesn't know in which order those ducks were taken for the over limit, they have ruled that all the birds in such a situation are to be seized in order to prove in a court of law that you did in fact have an over limit in your possession. So please pass me the birds," I responded. With that, all the birds were passed forward to me, followed by several "hands caught in Mother Nature's cookie jar" long faces now being exhibited by our shooters.

Guy checked out their shotguns and licenses and found them legal. Then Guy gave me the look and turning, said to our chaps, "I would like to look in your decoy bags, please."

With that, the lad in the bow of the boat asked, "What the Sam hell for?"

Guy looked over at me with a knowing smile saying, "Because sometimes we find extra ducks hidden in decoy bags. And since you folks usually leave your decoys out all the time on your club, two bags in your boat full of decoys are looking mighty suspicious." "You have a search warrant?" asked the lad in the bow. "I am an attorney, you know, and I don't think you have a right to search our bags of decoys without our consent or a search warrant."

"I do when I see a partial wood duck wing sticking out from the bottom of that first decoy bag and you already have over limits in your possession," I said with a grin.

"Oh, take the damn bag. We don't know who they belong to anyway. We just found them floating on our club and were bringing them back to the boat dock for storage," the attorney advised with a smart "your move" look crossing his face.

Anything to throw us off the issue, I thought. Since I knew what their defense would be if this issue went to trial, namely, "we just found the decoy bags floating by themselves and didn't know it was full of illegal ducks," I had a Plan B for just such an eventuality, especially in light of an attorney's "too smart for his britches" moves.

Sure as a gob of worms will catch a brook trout, that is if you are extra careful in your approach to the designated fishing spot so they don't see or hear you coming, the bags were loaded with freshly killed ducks when they were emptied out into the bottom of our canoe!

Twenty-seven assorted puddle ducks to be exact. "Well, well," I said. "What do we have here?"

"Those aren't our ducks," said the attorney stridently.

"Relax," I said with a timeworn grin of having been there and done this little dance of innocence in the marsh many times before. "We know you two more than likely took these ducks this morning, especially since I have pinched the two of you before for over limits of ducks in your possession on this very club. Plus, the ducks are still warm indicating they were freshly killed this morning. Then you hid them in the decoy bags hoping to sneak them back to the clubhouse. Nonetheless, since you are denying they are yours, I will take your word for it. We already have you and your partner for over limits, so you have your own set of legal problems to worry about. However, since that is your story, I will just issue the club a citation for untagged birds and the over limit found in the decoy bags on the club grounds since all the decoys have 'Property of the White Mallard Duck Club' marked across their bottoms. How does that sound? And since they were found in your boat, I am sure the club will send the two of you the bill for the untagged birds and over limits5 citations anyway. So in this case, all is fair in love and war."

Now the mouthy attorney truly looked sick. He knew I could charge the club for those two aforementioned violations and he also knew it would be easy to prove said violations under the Migratory Bird Treaty Act, especially since a person listed on the citation could also be a club when it came to violations under that Act's far-reaching legal language.

I then issued the lads citations for possession of an over limit of ducks—"possession," not "taking," since I had not observed the lads taking an over limit. Seizing all the ducks, I left them with an evidence receipt. Then Guy and I hotfooted it back to the clubhouse. There I issued two citations in the name of the White Mallard Duck Club to the club president for tagging and over limit violations for the birds discovered in the decoy sacks. Man, you talk about a hot club president. He got even hotter under the collar when our two chaps just pinched for over limits entered the clubhouse shortly thereafter while we were still present. I would say the fur, or should I say the feathers, really flew! Not so much over the violations by his club members but over the fact that the hated local game warden had caught and cited the club and some of its members once again for violation of the waterfowl regulations.

With that issue out of the way, Guy and I chuckled our way across the White Mallard's shooting area to that of another duck club and went back to work. Striking out on that club since that club's shooters had already limited out and left, we later found some high ground in the marsh and gutted our seized ducks so they wouldn't spoil. We then laid them out to cool in the shade of some nearby bushes.

Stretching out on our little island, Guy and I had another of our famously hot lunches, jalapeno peppers and all. Then it was cigar time, followed by a snooze while we waited to see if we would have any afternoon shooters on any of the Butte Sink duck clubs. Man, did we ever get a wonderful surprise before that day was done!

About 3:30 p.m., we heard the sounds of a nearby running outboard motor. It appeared to be back on the White Mallard Duck Club. Loading back into our canoe with our cooled-out evidence ducks, Guy and I began paddling quietly toward that outboard motor sound.

Locating the blind of our soon to be afternoon duck hunters with our binoculars, we moved into a stand of flooded cottonwoods and tied off our canoe where we could see but not be seen. From our vantage point in the timber, we watched two chaps getting up into an out of the way duck blind on the back side of the White Mallard Duck Club for a quiet afternoon duck shoot.

Most of the ducks and geese had already settled back down on the Butte Sink's now tranquil waters. But there were still numerous small flocks of incoming ducks looking for that special place to sit down, and, as a result, our two shooters had a good afternoon wing shoot. Realizing that most club members had already shot their ducks for the day, Guy and I were more than curious about our two shooters. Especially since their fellow club members had long ago headed for the club's bar and then the TV's to watch the afternoon's football games.

As it turned out, our two shooters stayed until the very end of legal shooting hours in order to get their full limit of ducks. Then as they began picking up and making ready to leave, Guy and I sprang into action. Dropping the outboard motor shaft, I quietly primed the motor, gave the starter rope a quick pull and the engine quietly stirred to life. Heading out into the channel, we headed straight for our shooters' blind from our place of hiding some forty yards distant. Arriving, I motored our canoe into their decoy area and then glided for the shooters' duck blind sitting off to one side. Surprisingly, our two shooters had yet to show themselves once they had obviously noticed and heard our approaching canoe and running outboard in their immediate area.

Nosing our canoe up to the blind's side opening, Guy stood up in the bow, then turned and gave me a big grin.

Turning back, he said, "Good afternoon. You know who we are and we certainly know who the two of you are."

Leaning over and looking past Guy, I was surprised to see our attorney and his "dropping ducks over the boat's transom" friend in the blind! Particularly since both of them had been cited for possessing over limits of ducks earlier that same morning by the Great Grotz and his trusty sidekick, Guy Bird. And now, here they were once again, only this time dressed in different hunting clothing with face coverings like turkey hunters routinely use. No wonder we didn't recognize them earlier during this second go around from our distant stake out position. Man, you talk about two hangdog faces now being exhibited by our shooters. They were two for sure prizes for the books. Neither man had much to say as Guy instructed them to hand over their second over limit of ducks for the day. They also did not have much to say when they were issued their second citations of the day for the same violations they had been tagged for earlier that morning! I could also imagine what it was like when the two of them were fined collectively $850 for their violations that fair day so long ago, in addition to, losing their hunting rights for the rest of that duck season! Back to Mrs. Wilson's third grade math class they went, I would venture, for a little help in their basic addition classes. Course, it was the White Mallard Duck Club members and then again...

THE WILLIAMS DRAG SHOOTERS

That fall after I had received the wonderful Starlight Scope from the U.S. Fish and Wildlife Service, I added two new tools to my wildlife law enforcement battle-kit.

After numerous successful and wonderful dark cycles involving the use of the Starlight Scope apprehending late and early shooters, the second acquired law enforcement tool was a pair of borrowed federal government hand held, line of sight radios. They were to prove invaluable when two or more of us lads were working sight-unseen in the pitch dark on extreme night or early shooting wildlife outlaws from different points of the compass or angles of attack. And the third new tool in my toolbox was my new faithful partner and dear friend, Sacramento Valley rice farmer, Tim Dennis. After all his crops had been harvested, he had spare time on his hands to give me a much needed law enforcement assist with another set of eyes, his knowledge of the land and more importantly his history of my local folks and finally, his physical presence. Tim was small in stature but large in heart. Additionally, he was as strap steel tough as a horseshoe nail, built like a fireplug and not afraid to take on any odds. As a civilian, he had ridden with me on a number of previous law enforcement patrols because of his dedicated interest in making sure there were wildlife resources left for his kids and those of others to enjoy. And even today, some forty-five years later as these words are written, I still have fond memories and a ten-gallon hat full of laughs and grimaces over some of the times we had working together. Particularly, some of the goofy stunts we pulled in order to run miscreants to ground. You know, it is amazing just how much devilment two very good friends can get into without even trying, especially when on the hunt trying to hold the conservation line in the sand in the world of wildlife law enforcement.

I have often thought back on some of the more dangerous stunts we pulled in our efforts to round up every trigger-pulling son-of-a- bitch in the valley doing to Mother Nature what they shouldn't have been doing: like wading in over our heads in icy winter waters after outlaws, when we belatedly discovered the waters to be deeper than the tops of our chest high waders; rolling over a fully-loaded canoe in the dead of winter in ten feet of Sacramento River floodwaters while not wearing life preservers; taking on groups of armed men violating the law when the odds many times were often better than three to one against us; operating a tippy air boat in dangerously high winds and deep, Sacramento Valley floodwaters; swimming ice-speckled waterways in an attempt to cut off escaping outlaws in twenty-degree weather with a half-mile walk back to the warmth and comfort of my patrol vehicle; going against whiskey-soaked game violators who were on the prod after they had been apprehended and were now ready to fight to avoid the embarrassment of being prosecuted; standing thigh deep in flooded, winter rain-swept unharvested corn fields for hours on end observing shooters and gathering evidence against those folks for doing what they shouldn't have been doing in the world of waterfowl; laying out on the cold damp ground in harvested rice fields in the winter protecting the feeding ducks at all hours of the darkness and then, when getting up to walk, discovered our freezing legs did not work for sour owl droppings; chasing fleeing deer poachers down dusty mountain roads at crazy speeds just three feet off the bumpers of their vehicles, full-well knowing one slip of the wheel and we were over the edge of the cliff and into oblivion; disarming armed and violent miscreants who were caught breaking the law and threatening to shoot if we moved a whisker and tried to arrest them; apprehending and prosecuting high-placed politicians seriously breaking the law, only to later find

471

they tried to use the power of their office and have me fired or moved to another duty station; and many more just as crazy game warden situations experienced while trying to catch those who thought they were above the law...

Once that joining of friends happened, the two of us became almost inseparable and patrolled the Northern Sacramento Valley working the wildlife outlaws with an increased vengeance. The Great Grotz—that would be me—and the Dirt Farmer—that would be Tim as I came to affectionately call him—fair-raised hell with our duck-dragging shooters, commercial market hunters, and every other type of wildlife outlaw in the Sacramento Valley of Northern California during the late 1960s and into the middle '70s. Let me tell all you readers out there, it was "Christians-Nothing and Lions- Everything" in that Sacramento Valley Coliseum, especially when it came to mowing down the slow-movers... With the combination of me with the authority and Tim possessing the historical knowledge, innate history of the valley, the lay of the land and her peoples, we were really deadly. And the sad thing about all our crazy exertions apprehending those who needed our attention, based on my thirty-two years of law enforcement experience, was that we more than likely only caught one-tenth of one percent of all the violators that were out there eating their ways through the carcass of the world of wildlife! A sad figure but based on my numerous years of law enforcement experiences, both nationally and internationally, those figures probably will hold true for all the wildlife officers success levels in the land... Hell, those figures will probably hold true for any type of law enforcement officer in the land, truth be known. As a follow up, how many of you readers broke the speed limit on the way to work this morning? Multiply those violations throughout the rest of your lives and you can see what I meant when I stated we caught less than one-tenth of one percent of all the violations that occurred in the world of wildlife law enforcement... Chaps who weren't just unmindful of the law but those dedicated in heart and soul to the destruction of wildlife for reasons known only to them.

In 1970, I relinquished my California State Commission as a fish and game warden for that of a federal commission as a United States Game Management Agent with the U.S. Fish and Wildlife Service. With that, I was then transferred to the San Francisco Bay Area. In 1972, I was transferred back to the Sacramento Valley to hold the line against those violating the waterfowl laws of the land once again. With that transfer, Tim and yours truly thundered through the rice fields chasing the outlaws once again. However, that catch-dog team was not to last. In 1974, I was promoted to Senior Resident Agent, as they were called in those days, over North and South Dakota and subsequently transferred once again. As expected, once I was moved and left California for the wind swept prairies and their wildlife related enforcement problems under the federal wildlife statutes, Tim and I were never to work together again. The last I heard years later was that he gave up the rice farming after his dad Charlie Dennis had passed on, along with his recently acquired Deputy Federal U.S. Game Management Agent commission, had remarried, and was working for a logging show somewhere in Oregon. We made a good team in those storied days of our youth and many wildlife outlaws paid the price for our excellent working relationship. I still miss him and his easy laughter and can do attitude to this very day, some almost forty-five-plus years later. I was blessed with being able to have had many great moments in time over my long career. Working with The Dirt Farmer, a great human being, was one of those moments...

For you non-Sacramento Valley chaps, dragging ducks was an illegal, time worn, killing blood sport and avocation by many of the locals carried out in the freshly harvested rice fields mostly during the hours of darkness. Dragging was nothing more than a number of chaps, usually numbering from two to four, sneaking out into the Sacramento Valley's rice fields after dark in the fall and winter months to locations where the night feeding ducks and geese abounded by the thousands. There, those chaps would concentrate on quietly sneaking up onto the feeding ducks. Ducks were shot by this method more commonly than geese because ducks were considered better eating. Plus, there existed a much greater illegal commercial market for ducks to be used in the form of duck dinners more so than for geese. Once the lads had sneaked into the fields, they would wait behind convenient rice checks until the birds had fed up close to their positions, sometimes no more distant then ten yards away. It was then the draggers would empty their unplugged shotguns, which were capable of holding more than three shells, into the unsuspecting masses of feeding birds. Usually when the ducks were in so close and ready to be ground sluiced or shot into on the ground, a pre-planned whistle would sound from one of the hidden shooters. That unfamiliar sound would cause all the feeding ducks to instantly raise up their heads in alarm. Then, the first shots would be slammed across the upraised heads of the birds killing huge numbers in that first deadly volley. As the ducks rose into the air in alarm flying away from the shooting occurring to their front, the shooters' shotguns' lead streams would then be loosed into the backs of the fleeing birds. By that method, the breast meat, which would be later eaten by the restaurant diners and duck draggers families, was not damaged. That type of shooting, rapidly done, would also be at the closest possible range to ensure the greatest kill possible. And once again, a slaughter in the Sacramento Valley would occur.

Often the gunners immediately after the shoot, note they aren't called hunters because of the lack of fair chase, would lie back down and wait to see if they had been discovered or were being pursued by the game wardens or federal agents staked out nearby guarding other feeding flocks in the various adjacent fields. If pursuit was not forthcoming after a short wait, the gunners would rise up and gather in what the Grim Reaper had sowed for them. From what I personally experienced after a shoot in picking up dead and dying birds or from talking to many of the experienced gunners over the years who would brag to me about their night shooting exploits, they could routinely kill anywhere from three hundred to five hundred ducks at a time on what they considered was a good shoot! Some old time market shooters from the nearby Sacramento Valley Town of Gridley, when interviewed years later for my book titled Slaughter in the Sacramento Valley, told me about having kills as high as a thousand birds after a very successful night shoot on massed feeding ducks. This they were able to do by using their Long Tom Remington Model 11 shotguns, which were capable of holding eleven to fifteen extra shells in their homemade extended magazines!

Often inexperienced shooters would have to settle for many less dead birds than that, especially if they shot when the ducks were at ranges not considered ideal for the greatest kill to occur. Frequently after such a shoot, the retrieved ducks would be hidden in the rice field killing area for later pickup by the shooters or a middleman buyer. Other times, as many as could be carried were gutted in the field to lessen their weight and then packed out and ditched in a culvert or similar hiding place along the nearest road for later rapid recovery. Routinely, those stashed ducks would then be picked up the next day and carried home after the gunners felt the kill site had cooled off and Johnny-law was nowhere to be seen or feared.

In later years, with the development and accepted use of mechanical pickers that were gentle enough not to tear the skin in the picking process, those birds taken from such night shooting endeavors would be transported to a safe mechanical picking facility for processing. Some local farmers who also outlaw-gunned, had picking facilities hidden in barns or sheds on their own property. There were several such set-ups south of Highway 20 in Colusa County of which I was aware and another one located in the Arbuckle area. The most unusual mechanical picking facility I knew about was one stashed in the back of a mortuary in a nearby Sacramento Valley town!

If the previous night's field shooting area was not being watched the next day by state or federal officers, the shooters would sometimes return during the daylight hours once they were assured all was clear to quietly pick up the remaining missed birds killed or wounded from the evening before. However, in the killing fields, dozens of birds would be wounded and crawl off to die or be eaten later by predators after the shoot. I can remember discovering a number of such previous evening's drag sites and, with two dogs working the nearby levees and rice checks in the area just shot, I many times recovered over two hundred previously shot and wounded birds in a morning! Another time, I picked up so many wounded and dying birds that when my dogs got back into the patrol truck, all the facial hair had been rubbed off my retrievers due to all the abrasive grasses they had run through retrieving the hundreds of cripples left over from the previous evening's shoot! Although I tried to use two dogs whenever possible, one time when I only had Shadow as my pickup dog, she worked so hard chasing all the hundreds of cripples from the previous evening's illegal shoot, that when she got back into my truck several hours later, her nose was no longer jet black but pink because she had rubbed off all her black nose skin running through the abrasive vegetation chasing cripples!

In most cases, those ducks killed and retrieved by my night shooters would be used to fill one's freezer or those freezers of the shooters' friends. And sometimes, although infrequently by the late '60s, those ducks would be moved into the commercial restaurant trade in the Bay Area of Oakland or San Francisco by middle men buyers. There they would be sold to select diners as rice fed, wild duck dinners. And let me tell you, there is nothing nicer to eat than a stuffed and baked, rolling fat hen Northern pintail that has been rice fed - legally shot, of course!

I also quickly discovered that unless the officer was right on top of the drag shooters immediately after the shoot, and I do mean right on their miserable carcasses, they would squirt off into the darkness like frightened jack rabbits greased with extra-virgin olive oil. You know folks, market gunners of that ilk were like child molesters to my way of thinking. They didn't advertise their ugly trade and they sure as hell were nowhere to be seen after the damage had been done... Then after the shoot, late arriving officers were left with only spent shotgun shells, feathers everywhere, splotches of fresh blood scattered about on the ground, and scads of duck poop as mute testimony to what violent evilness had just transpired. For my readers' edification, when violently surprised, often times ducks would poop like crazy when they lifted off, especially when greeted by a hail of lead shot. That, and of course, a mess of dead, dying, and crippled ducks were scattered about the area as mute testimony to the predatory nature of man once the smell of burnt gunpowder had wafted off into the damp night air.

And if the officer was close at hand when such a shoot had occurred, he had better be part greyhound when it came to running the shooters down... I can remember one race in which I chased a lone Town of Princeton drag gunner for the better part of a mile across numerous muddy rice fields and drainage ditches in the dead of night before I successfully ran him to ground. When captured by a flying tackle as the two of us sailed over a canal bank and into a shallow ditch partially filled with cold water, crawdads and rotting carp, I got a surprise. Instead of fighting or surrendering, the lad turned over in my arms in the slop, proudly raised his Remington Model 11 semi-automatic shotgun with a Long Tom (one that had been modified by a homemade magazine extender designed to hold and shoot eleven shells) into my face saying, "Terry, ain't she a beaut!" And to be quite frank, it was a beautiful piece of deadly homemade Sacramento Valley duck-dragging folk art. Unfortunately, it was also illegal as hell to use such a device when taking migratory game birds!

Today I still have that homemade magazine extender as a memento of that crazy rice field race in the darkness of night. One that ended up in the slop of a ditch after I was finally able to tackle my hard sprinting duck-dragging runner. When I pass, that piece of market gunning folk art shall be passed on to my special agent son, Richard. Passed on as a artifact of times long past when the men on both sides of the law were ingenious, fleet of foot and dedicated to their quickly passing moments in the annals of time...

Then I discovered my duck-dragging runner was a friend and all of 76 years old! He was strap steel tough and lithe as a willow branch and that old fellow sure could run. Especially with a 320-pound badge carrier with size 14EEEE feet hot in pursuit. Even in those days at that weight, I could still run a hundred yard dash in eleven seconds! After that event, my duck dragger, whom I shall call "Frank," and I remained good friends until his untimely death. I chose not to identify my friend because he still has living kin in the area and it serves no purpose in embarrassing those innocent folks who still have a great love and respect for their grandfather. He was a grand old man who was part of the fabric, folklore and legend woven into the illegal duck killing history of California's Sacramento Valley. But, he was also one hell of a duck killer, having told me one time he had killed and sold over a hundred thousand ducks in his lifetime! In fact, he had kept a journal of his kills and I still remember to this day looking at some of the earlier entries in that journal— Frank would only let me look at some of the early entries. The one entry I remember the most, was that of twenty-two canvasback ducks killed by Frank when he was only 11 years old. He sold them to his trusted Arbuckle middleman buyer for seventy-five cents each... In his later years during the '20s and '30s, many of his illegally killed birds were shipped by train to the Bay Area for sale into the restaurant trade. Little did I realize at the time at the end of that long chase, I was holding a living piece of early California folklore and history in my slop-covered hands. A piece of history, like all other scraps of history, that have long since disappeared without fanfare and are now almost forgotten in the musty eons of time... However, after Frank and I had picked up all the ducks killed and wounded from his shoot and had stashed them near a farm road, it was almost daylight. Both of us being hungry, I took him home and fixed breakfast. He sure loved my style of fried mashed potatoes and homemade biscuits. In fact, if I remember correctly, he came back for thirds! After breakfast, I issued him a citation for late shooting migratory game birds, use and aid of a shotgun holding more than three shells and for taking an over limit of ducks. It was then that he gave me his homemade magazine extender as a gift. After we both had cleaned up my bride's kitchen, I took him back to his stashed pickup and we went our different ways in our different worlds... Me to retrieve all the ducks he had killed and we had stashed and him to whatever he did best. Once again, I found my feet firmly planted in two different centuries of time with a man whose moment had come and gone, like the smell of burnt gunpowder in the damp rice-field night air after a deadly drag...

Today, every time I walk on my stiffened legs, struggle with my wrecked, arthritic lower back and both replaced, still not working worth a damn, metal replacement knees, I am reminded of those many law enforcement miles traveled. Miles I spent walking, running and chasing illegal gunners in those Sacramento Valley rice fields under the cloak of darkness as a young officer. And if I was young enough and physically able today, knowing what I now know, I would do it all over again in a heartbeat. Do it all over because, you see, wildlife dies without making a sound. And if the conservation officer isn't out there squalling like a smashed cat trying to subdue those illegal killers of wildlife, he or she is part of the problem as far as I am concerned! But once again, I slid off into the dustbin of times long past and digressed. Sorry for that my poor, weathered readers. Back to the original story at hand.

One winter morning about o-dark hundred, Tim "The Dirt Farmer" Dennis and I were working in the La Grande Road rice fields area of Colusa County. It had been raining for several weeks by then and many of my ducks were now feeding west of Interstate 5 in Colusa and Glenn Counties. That was a natural and historically occurring phenomenon because the hungry birds had previously fed out everything else closer to the national wildlife refuges, which were located on the eastern side of the interstate. And just as naturally, the long arm of the law in the conservation fraternity, was following those birds moving westerly as well because that is where the bad guys and illegal duck killing action would be. That was, if the northern Sacramento Valley commercial market hunting and duck dragging history was still my teacher.

To avoid chance discovery, Tim and I had hidden my patrol truck alongside a currently unused rice harvester at the edge of a freshly harvested rice field like any dirt farmer would do. As a further precaution, I had thrown my camouflage parachute over the vehicle just in case someone came snooping around looking for any sign of the local tule creeper in hiding. Everyone, and I do mean everyone, in that part of the country knew the looks of my unmarked, county undercover vehicle by then, so caution was a watchword. Then Tim and I had hotfooted it up into the cab of the unlocked harvester and were watching the surrounding, darkened harvested rice fields from our new vantage point. We had no more than gotten in place when a vehicle came slowly up Danley Road from the south toward our position. It had caught our eyes because earlier we had seen it stop several times, douse its headlights and sit for a while on the now largely untraveled county road at that time in the morning. I suspected what the chaps in that vehicle were doing were listening for any close-at-hand feeding ducks in the adjacent harvested rice fields. So doing, because starting and stopping was unlike the normal activity of high school kids when making out. Following that, the vehicle proceeded up the road, stopping at the intersection of Freshwater and Danley Roads. It was then that we saw the vehicle's interior lights come on. With our binoculars, we observed two lads carrying shotguns get out from the car and quickly head west at a trot into the darkened adjacent previously harvested rice fields. The drop-off vehicle then continued north on

Danley Road like nothing out of the ordinary had just occurred. Minutes later, that same vehicle turned east heading into the Town of Maxwell and disappeared from our view.

For the longest time, Tim and I heard or saw nothing else out of the ordinary. Realizing a drag was in the wind, we finally decided we had best get closer to the possible impending action, loaded up in my vehicle, and quietly exited our hiding place. Heading slowly and quietly south on Danley Road without using my lights, I turned off on the levee road running alongside the Glenn-Colusa Canal. Slipping and sliding in the mud from the recent rains, four-wheel- drive be damned, we moved far enough down the levee road so no one casually passing on the main road would see the reflection of my vehicle in the inadvertent sweep of their headlights. Parking the truck, the two of us then quickly headed out and back across Danley Road on foot. From there, we hotfooted it into the fields to our west toward the last sighting of our chaps who had been dropped off on Freshwater Road. The hunt was now on...

Arriving about dead across from the last sighting of our two suspect duck dragging chaps, I switched on the Starlight Scope now that we were close enough to see what was happening. There in the lime green glow of my scope to our west were my two shooters walking slowly in a crouched position toward a distant rice check! In the partial moonlight through the scope, I could see hundreds of ducks as they flew around like a living tornado, undulating up and down in mass, looking for places to light down and feed in the nearby rice fields. Even further to the west, I spotted another larger tornado of ducks swarming across that harvested rice field looking like the locusts during the plague in Egypt during biblical times. Figuring that would be the final destination of our two chaps based on their direction and speed of travel, we headed in that direction as well. Switching off the scope to save my precious, hard-to-come- by-batteries—the Vietnam War was in full swing, making battery replacements by a non-military affiliated agency problematic—the two of us continued walking across the harvested rice fields in a half crouch to avoid the chance of being inadvertently discovered by our shooters in the feeble moonlight. Then finding a close-at- hand location adjacent to where I figured our chaps had dug in, I set up shop on a water grass covered rice check. Switching on the night scope once again, I could see our lads had not moved from their previous location. They were still in the middle of the larger rice field and appeared to be near the head of a feeding carpet of ducks swirling their way towards their ambush rice check of choice. Figuring our lads would wait out the ducks until they had fed right up to where they were hidden behind the rice check, we went to work to counter what evil we knew was coming next.

Clicking on our hand held radios to the same channel, I sent Tim toward our soon to be shooting chaps while I guided him in the dark to almost their exact location with the scope and radio signals. Tim was using an earpiece on his radio so, no matter what changes in direction I gave him, our suspected field shooters soon to be, heard nothing of our conversations. Guiding Tim, based on what I was seeing through the scope, we began closing the trap on our soon to be duck draggers. Just like German tanks in North Africa in 1942, we closed in on our targets of opportunity in a pincher like movement.

To all you folks who have never worked or experienced such a natural phenomenon, feeding ducks works like clockwork. They feed all bunched up and travel like a huge flat snake moving along the ground hungrily eating every rice kernel they can find as they feel along in the darkness in the soft mud with their bills. The larger and greedier ducks, like Northern pintail and mallards, constantly raised up from the main flock and flew to the head of the living feeding carpet. By so doing, they were rewarded with more of the rice and, unknowingly, the most lethal part of the shot stream if they were ground sluiced by the deadly gunners located to their immediate front. Additionally, if there was any wind, the moving carpet of ducks would feed in that direction into the wind. That way if there was any danger suddenly detected, all the feeding birds had to do was open up their wings, which allowed them to quickly lift up and they were immediately airborne. However, many times that also worked against them. The drag shooters were aware of that feeding into the wind behavior and would constantly shift their ambush position so they were right at the point of that feeding stream of unsuspecting waterfowl. That way the shooters would be in among the thickest and nearest portion of the feeding flock and in so doing, guaranteed the highest kill numbers if their shoot went according to plan.

By now, my lads had adjusted their positions and were sneaking quietly along the backside of their rice check so they would be right in front of the feeding carpet of ducks once it arrived at the chosen ambush location. As our gunners moved, I changed Tim's course of approaching intercept as well. Boy, you talk about a plan of attack working slicker than cow slobbers. That method of our approach from two sides was really working beautifully. Then low-based storm clouds moved across the partial moon and it got darker than the inside of a dead cow. But the good old night scope, with its huge light magnification powers, still allowed me to see and guide Tim ever closer to my two soon-to-be drag shooters. Some of you readers may be wondering what the hell we were doing in not stopping the slaughter before it started. Bottom legal line, it was not a violation of any state or federal law to sneak up on feeding ducks at night. Only if you shot into them in the darkness were any state or federal laws violated. Therefore, we waited for the hammers to fall and the streams of killing shot to venture forth doing its deadly work before we made our moves into the action at hand.

For the briefest of moments, all hell broke loose! I could clearly see the flashing off the ends of the barrels of their shotguns and the black cloud of ducks rapidly lifting upward along with hearing the roar of thousands of frantically beating wings fleeing the scene. And those thundering wing sounds not only came from our staked out flock of ducks but from every other nearby flock in the adjacent, close-at-hand rice fields as well! Then, except for the numerous clouds of still fleeing ducks heading east towards the safety of the nearest national wildlife refuge, it was all over. My two lads had now laid back down on the rice check and did not move. It was obvious they were waiting and looking to see if any near at hand law dogs had heard them shoot and were now coming their way. And if so, they were prepared to flee into the darkness in the opposite direction. After about ten minutes of lying still as death, my shooters finally rose from their positions behind the rice check but kept carefully looking all around, as was clearly evidenced in the lime green field of the night scope. Finally satisfied that the coast was clear, I could see our lads in the Starlight Scope laying down their shotguns on the rice check and began running all around in the field in front of their recent firing position. Once there, I could clearly see them picking up ducks by the bucketsful and placing them on several duck straps, which are nothing more than leather straps with built in loops to hold the heads and necks of several ducks per loop.

I now began guiding Tim with our radio on the final intercept collision course with my duck dragging lads, as I moved in from the opposite side. As it turned out, the two shooters loaded up four duck straps with birds and then they piled up the remainder of their dead ducks along the edge of a nearby rice check for easy later retrieval. Walking back to their shotguns left on the rice check, they loaded their duck straps onto their shoulders and, staggering under their loads, headed out like two men on a mission. Soon they were walking alongside a long rice check that angled to the east. It was pretty obvious to me they knew the lay of the land very well. That rice check they were following would eventually lead them out and back onto Freshwater Road. I assumed from there, they would hide alongside the road until a prearranged time when their ride returned. Then they would hop into the getaway car and be off with their ill-gotten gains and no one would be any the wiser. With that, I suspected my shooters would return casually in the daylight as legitimate field duck hunters, retrieve the rest of the ducks piled at the edge of the field blown up from the dark of the night before and then scoot off into nothingness like cock roaches...

However, they still had the Great Grotz and the Dirt Farmer factors to contend with. I had Tim slowly walking toward my two lads who were exiting in his direction on the same rice check! Neither parties could see the other in the darkness, but I could. Over the radio, I told Tim to stop and get ready to spring the trap once his shooters got within grabbing range, which he prepared to do. Suspecting nothing, my two illegal shooters kept struggling towards my partner as they staggered under the combined weight of their four duck straps full of swinging dead ducks. When they were just feet apart so if they tried to turn and run Tim would be close enough to catch them, I gave the Dirt Farmer the signal. "Now, Tim! Turn on your flashlight! They are right in front of you!"

Watching the action through the scope, I saw Tim turn on his light when the two drag-shooting lads were just a few feet away from where he now stood. My scope then momentarily blanked out when Tim lit the area up with his flashlight. Switching the scope off, I continued moving along the base of the rice check towards the close-at-hand action. Then I could hear the yelling of surprise clear over to where I was coming from the opposite direction, fast shuffling in the deeply rutted field so I wouldn't fall or sprain an ankle. Our two drag shooters were so surprised to find they had been had from out of the dark that one of the chaps just flat fell down on his backside! Continuing to watch the action in the light of Tim's flashlight since my scope was now turned off, I saw Tim quickly disarm the two shooters just as I slid in behind the group and lit them up with my flashlight as well.

Tim now stood in front of me with two of the most forlorn looking chaps you ever saw. Two high school age lads, whom I quickly recognized from my drag-shooter intelligence files back at my office, which were from the nearby small Town of Williams. Two shooters who thought they were cutting a fat hog in the ass when they had sneaked into the field and had blown up the ducks. Then only to find it was the long arm of the law or, figuratively speaking, another type of pig if you will, that had clamped them in irons. Boy, you talk about two lads being shocked upon apprehension from out of nowhere! They were decked flatter than a flounder on a cooking griddle, to say the least. And it only got worse from there. As it turned out, both were juveniles from good local area families. Because federal law required one to be at least 18 before they could be cited into the federal court system, which was usually reserved for the worst offenders, that level of prosecution would not be an issue in the present case. But as juveniles over the age of sixteen, they could be taken before Judge Gibson in the Williams Justice Court under state law, if I so desired. However, I mentally put that prosecutorial action on hold, because to proceed would automatically generate a rap sheet for each of the lads. I did so because a better idea was now whirling around in my head. Recording all the information from our two very contrite lads and seizing their shotguns, I advised I would be in touch with them and their folks at a later date. Man, those words about parental notification sure didn't sit well with my two shooters at all, if the long looks on their faces in the light of our flashlights indicated anything to the casual observer! Faces made even longer, when the borrowed shotguns from their fathers were also seized! Letting them go, knowing they would not now give the pickup signal for their drop off driver, Tim and I made ready to head back into the field where their shoot had taken place. Our chaps then left the field and just began walking down the main road back to Williams as Tim and I hid their seized shotguns and duck straps full of dead ducks in a nearby culvert. Then we headed out into the rice fields once again. Locating the field just shot with our flashlights, we quickly discovered their remaining pile of ducks. For the next hour, Tim and I walked the field and rice checks with our flashlights collecting the dead, wounded, and dying ducks still scattered about and not picked up earlier by the two boys. Finishing, between the four duck straps seized from our shooters and our pile of recently retrieved ducks, we had a total of 213 dead ducks! Of those ducks, we had mostly Northern pintail and mallards. Remember me telling you readers earlier about the larger ducks being so greedy that they would generally fly to the head of the feeding duck column for the best opportunity to feed? Well, as expected, they got more than rice kernels as a reward for their greedy feeding behavior. With that chore finished, Tim and I spent the next several hours gutting the birds to reduce their weight and hauling all the ducks back to our vehicle. By sun up, we were heading to my evidence lockers located on the Sacramento National Wildlife Refuge, where the ducks were sorted as to species and placed in our freezers for later court ordered disposal. I purposely stored the ducks in those federal freezers because I anticipated Chief Federal Judge McBride would later distribute them to the poor in the Sacramento area. To those readers who never had the honor of meeting Judge McBride, he was not only a wise and honorable Chief Federal Judge but a great human being as well. That is one of the reasons he took it upon himself, using the federal conservation system, to acquire and distribute some very fine eating to the very poor in the Sacramento area. May God rest the soul of one of the finest judges I ever stood before...

For my readers' edification, the judge was a knowledgeable conservationist and a duck hunter who knew his waterfowl. When the judge went out on one of his famous duck distribution sorties to the poor of Sacramento, Judge McBride wanted only the mallards and Northern pintail, which were the largest and best eating, as presents for those unfortunate and needy souls. As such, at that time I had six different freezers located on the national wildlife refuge all full of sorted out ducks and geese. Six completely-filled, twenty-cubic- foot freezers! A good thing for the poor but a sad commentary on Man's greed for the waterfowl natural resources when one looked at the numbers of illegal ducks and geese those freezers would eventually hold. Freezers that I more than filled several times over every waterfowl season while gainfully employed as a state fish and game warden under my deputy U.S. Game Management Agent credentials and later as a federal agent in the Northern Sacramento Valley for the U.S. Fish and Wildlife Service. But the really sad thing is this. Just think about how many bad guys I missed and the numbers of ducks and geese those chaps killed illegally...More than once while working the Northern Sacramento Valley of California as a wildlife officer, I clearly came to the realization just how General

Custer felt in June of 1876 on the prairies of Montana...during his last moments.

Plus, there was another thing that bothered the hell out of me when it came to the numbers of ducks I seized or picked up in the rice fields after a drag or had seized from early or late shooters. Statistically speaking, half of all the ducks I picked up or seized, were females. Multiply those numbers eight to twelve-fold, which would have been the brood sizes of those females had they lived. Then multiply those numbers by the approximately eight thousand ducks I either seized or picked up in the rice fields taken illegally during my years in the area as a wildlife officer! 'Nuff said...

I waited for several weeks before I visited the two boys' Williams families. I figured I would just let the two offending lads stew over what they had done for a while. That might just be better than any subsequent trip to the Williams Justice Court regarding the matter. When I finally did drop the hammer and met with their families, both sets of parents were very upset over their heretofore-unknown sons' recent duck dragging activities. With that notification, both families took what I considered the appropriate action. The families subsequently got together and meted out the same punishment for the two boys. Part of that punishment was the revocation of all hunting rights for a solid year! Rights that meant a lot to the two lads, especially in light of the annual out of state deer hunting trips to Wyoming they usually went on with their fathers. Not to mention missing out on all the fantastic pheasant, duck, goose and dove hunting found throughout the valley for that year on all their friend's ranches! I also required that the boys tell me the name of their drop off driver, which they finally and somewhat sheepishly did. Additionally, I required them to testify if that Williams individual and drop off driver decided to fight the pending charges I was soon to lodge against him since he was over 18. In fact, that individual was way over 18 and a prominent Williams community member, who was using the boys to do his dirty work at night in the rice fields... I told them that if they did all that, I would not file on them in state court and start them off in life with a criminal record. Plus, I would return their shotguns, which had been seized the evening of their drag. They, aided by the urging of their parents, agreed to my requests. I later met with that drop off chap and advised him of the case I had against him. He was later cited for 18 U.S.C. 2, Aiding and Abetting, and I swung that matter into federal court in Sacramento. Aiding and Abetting was a charge that could be lodged against an individual for planning out an illegal action and then performing an act that furthered that illegal action. Like planning a duck drag and then facilitating that illegal action by recruiting and driving the shooters to the area where the illegal activity was to occur. Faced with the facts of the case, including having his two shooters agreeing to testify against him, he subsequently and quietly paid his $500 fine, the maximum allowed in those days under the federal Migratory Bird Treaty Act. After that, we never crossed legal paths ever again. Maybe that was because, after hearing the circumstances of the matter, Chief Federal Judge McBride removed the matter from the Magistrates lower court and put the issue onto his District Court docket. Once there and after receiving a guilty plea, Judge McBride also fastened onto the $500 fine a six-months-in-jail, six-months - suspended sentence, providing the guilty party never showed his face in his court ever again... Yeah, I probably would say that had something to do with the fact the Williams drop-off driver and I never again crossed swords on any wildlife related legal issues...

Today, those two underage lads of yesteryear have completed college and now have families of their own. I never again ran across those lads in the years following my stint in the valley doing anything illegal. The three of us never talked much about that surprise morning when our paths occasionally crossed in town or during community events. I think my lads had learned their lessons well. I later heard they were warning off their high school friends from dragging ducks because the chances were too great of getting caught saying, "Killing ducks in such a manner was pure and simply slaughter. Besides, Grosz has that night scope from the Vietnam War with him at all times and that device turns the night into day." You know folks, it is always nicer in the wildlife law-enforcement business to have some individuals see the light and turn from poachers into preachers... Thank you Special Agent Dave Hall for the poachers to preachers quote, may you rest in peace...

THE OLIVEHURST-MARYSVILLE
DRAG SHOOTERS

I had no more than gotten home from an all-night vigil on the Beauchamp Ranch sleeping—"freezing to death in the damp fields" was more like it—with about thirty thousand hungry rice-field- feeding ducks making sure no one blew them up when my phone rang. My bride just stared at me with her characteristic beautiful blue-eyed look, which said, "Hopefully you will have some time for breakfast with the family before hitting the fields once again."

Picking up the phone, I said, "Good morning, this is Terry."

"Mr. Grosz, I have some information for you. Tonight between five and six in the evening, Bert Rounds and Sam McKenna from Marysville, along with Bob Dunn and Darrel Mack from Olivehurst, are going to blow up the ducks. They have located numerous bunches of them feeding north of Cortena just off Bowen Road in Colusa County. Bert Rounds will be the drop off driver and the other three will do the shooting. After the shoot, they plan on meeting at the western end of Bowen Road around midnight with the ducks that they have killed. From there, they plan on taking them back to Marysville where they have a local Chinese buyer named Tom Chang. I tell you all this because I hate them damn Chinese who are buying up all them good eatin' ducks." Then my caller hung up without saying another word...

Slowly putting down my phone, I had to smile. I recognized the very distinctive sounding voice of my Japanese friend from Colusa, Tom Yamamoto, who was one of the best public, spirited informants I ever had. When that concerned public citizen and my dear friend spoke, I listened. He was always exactly right on the money with his information. Right on as to time, place, and the names of the chaps doing to Mother Nature what they shouldn't have been doing. In the seven years working with this giant of a man whom I regarded as the brother I never had, he had never been wrong once! He was one hell of a good man, honest as the day was long, of a great work ethic, an outstanding striped bass fisherman, a tremendous gardener without equal, and loved to eat ducks and upland game birds.

I could have pinched Tom in 1967 over a very minor deer-tag violation and had chosen not to do so because it was plain to me, not really knowing the man at that time since I had just moved into the area, that he had simply made a goofy mistake. As a result of that inaction on my part, even though the head shed in Sacramento told me to ticket Tom—which I had ignored—I had made an instant friend and informant like I never again had in my thirty-two years of state or federal wildlife law enforcement service! To this day, I still can't figure out how he came upon that quality of information provided from such a diverse bunch of normally very closed mouthed, wildlife outlaws that ran in the Sacramento Valley in those days. But he did and that kind of information came to me as regularly as a Swiss watch ran. Years later, Tom died on an operating table as doctors tried to repair a badly worn out lower back. Tom's loss was not only a real loss to humanity and especially to me personally but one to Mother Nature as well. May God rest his soul. As an aside, ironically, Tom had the same back problems that I now possess after many years of hard labors as a kid, like digging graves at age 9, working in a mill at age 15, logging in the woods at age 16, boat crashes chasing illegal salmon gill netters, backcountry horse wrecks while on grizzly bear patrols, a shoot-out in Thailand with Burmese insurgents, chasing wildlife outlaws over unseen cliffs at night, fist fights with Yurok Indians snagging salmon on the Klamath River in northern California, a helicopter crash in my early days as a firefighter, and just general wear and tear from my thirty-two years of law enforcement. My doctors advised me not to undergo such a lower-back repair operation because I would more than likely die from a stroke or heart attack due to the length of time under the knife, my age and because of the severity of the medical intrusion... But I digress once again. Damn, I have more literary wander in me than a kangaroo rat out looking for weed seeds on the floor of the desert during a drought. And, all the while having to eyeball a hungry red-shouldered hawk sitting high up on a Saguaro cactus some forty yards away...

Turning, I decided to have breakfast with my family, get a few hours of sleep, and then chase those duck dragging son of a guns once again until their tongues hung out. After breakfast with my bride, I slept until noon that day. Because of the tremendous pressure on the valley's wildlife resources, I got to where I could physiologically run on about four hours sleep per night in those days of my youth. Waking, I showered, dressed and then went to the Colusa County Sheriff's Office. There I exchanged my marked patrol vehicle for the county's unmarked fish and game undercover truck. That vehicle being a GMC four-wheel drive, which had been paid for with county fish and game fine monies for fish and game use. Moments later, I advised my dear friend and Colusa County Deputy Sheriff from Maxwell who was in the sheriff's office at the time, where I would be and the names of whom I would be chasing in his assigned neck of the woods. That way, if I ended up dead over a violent encounter from a run in with my duck dragging chaps, he would have a place to start his investigation in solving the crime. I had been shot three times in the back in 1967 by night shooting duck draggers and that was enough. Hence, my caution and possible duck-dragger information passed along to my deputy sheriff friend.

That Maxwell Deputy, a man named Fred Pilgrim, was a very unique but plain country boy type of individual and law dog from the old school. He was as quietly tough as they came and always a damned good backup when things got a little testy with the local outlaw crowd. In short, nothing scared him much. And uniquely, he came from a Sacramento Valley market hunting pioneer family from which one of his close kinfolk was sent to jail for selling ducks, a felony, or so as the local story so goes. Normally in a situation like that in Colusa County, home to many commercial market gunners, duck draggers and their kin of old, any surviving relatives would, as a matter of course, have nothing to do with the local game wardens. That was just the code of the county's local bands of wildlife outlaws and one not to be taken lightly or broken by other people living in the valley. However, that was not the case with Fred. He was a real man, an outstanding professional officer, and one not to mess with if you were on the wrong side of the law. In short, if Fred ever got on your trail for a serious wrong, the only way to get him off was to shoot him ... and if one was to do that, then that shooter would have a 320-pound game warden hot on his trail—a game warden who was an excellent cold tracker and, once in the above circumstances, would take no prisoners... Quiet Fred was but the genetics of a frontier lawman ran deeply in his veins if you readers get my drift. To my way of thinking, the good folks of Colusa County were damn lucky to have such a fine professional law enforcement officer and human being looking out for them and their kinfolk...

To illustrate that point, I remember one time being asked to back up Deputies Carter Bowman from the western Colusa County town of Stonyford and Fred Pilgrim during a very dangerous, if not life-threatening situation. I did that without asking what for, not that it would have mattered much anyway. The Colusa County deputies were always there for me in my time of need and I always made damn sure I was there for them when they called. Later that particular day the three of us went in on twelve heavily armed Black Panthers practicing military maneuvers in the county's backcountry. Those were in the days when many members of such a gang hated any kind of law other than the law of the jungle. All the men were heavily armed with Belgium made, semi-automatic weapons and were dressed from head to toe in military camos. If I remember correctly, Fred and Carter never even blinked an eye even though the heavily armed militants in a heartbeat could have shot all three of us all to hell. All that mattered to Fred was doing his job and backing up his friends and fellow officers. In fact, truth be known, I was the only concerned one in the bunch. Not over being killed, because I had long ago decided if that was God's will, so be it. But, because I had shot a rattlesnake earlier in the day on my way up to Letts Lake, a high mountain trout fishing lake in my district, to check fishermen and had forgotten to reload my handgun. So like a bonehead, I went into battle with only four live rounds in my .44 magnum. What a dummy! That meant I could only kill four of those Black Panther pukes before they shot the hell out of me! Fortunately, that escapade ended all peaceable-like, and the Black Panthers left our neck of the woods "PDQ" upon discovery by the local law dogs. But I digress as that is another adventure story for another time and place.

Meanwhile, back to the anticipated duck-dragging story at hand. Damn, Terry, you and that previously mentioned wandering kangaroo rat not staying on course, sure have a lot in common... Early that afternoon, I drove into the location Tom had described way before my ducks descended into the area to feed or the reported draggers had arrived. Turning onto Bowen Road, I put one of my favorite hiding-in-plain-sight tricks into play. Since I was sure none of my out of town outlaws knew my GMC county undercover truck, I parked it on the side of Bowen Road in plain view. Then I lifted up the hood on it like one would do when their vehicle is disabled. Lastly, as another trick of the trade ploy, I put a note under the windshield wiper saying the truck would not run and I had walked into town to procure the services of a wrecker. With that and a quick look all around for any other watching eyes that could give away my intentions, I hotfooted it out into the middle of Section 20 where I knew I would have ducks coming to feed once it got dark. In fact, I had staked out that very same field some two evenings earlier because of heavy duck numbers feeding in the recently harvested rice fields of both Sections 20 and 21.

Finding a heavily water grass overgrown rice check out in the middle of the nearest rice field in which to hide my rather ample carcass, I burrowed into the cover and out of sight like a big oP groundhog. But to all my regular readers, as you well know, a beautiful groundhog. If my work that night hadn't been so serious, it would have been another one of those classic wonderful evening's world of wildlife experiences. Come dusk, ducks by the tens of thousands began winging into my stakeout area from the nearby Delevan and Sacramento National Wildlife Refuges. During that time of the year, those two Sacramento Valley refuges were holding at least a million wintering ducks and geese between the two of them! And when the valley's two major refuges held such numbers of migratory birds like they were currently holding, the adjacent harvested rice fields soon were also filled up with happy and hungry birds come dusk. At first, the birds came into the suspect area in small numbers like Apache Indian scouts of old. Then like swarms of bees, the hungry ducks came in long typical "V" strings and once over the rice ground in which to feed, they dropped into their characteristically great, telltale cyclonic clouds! Man, what a spectacle! Only the Creator could have thrown that type of nature's event together and provided it for the enjoyment of a damn tired, but happy as a pig in a corncrib, tule creeper game warden type like yours truly. Talk about a sterling tribute to all those hardworking game wardens of yesteryear. A tribute to wildlife officers now long past, whose names and exploits sadly no one even remembers today... At the age of a worn out 73 as these words are written, soon, I will also be of that number of wildlife officers not remembered. But by gum, it sure was one hell of a wild and wonderful ride carrying a badge and a gun in defense of all of the critters large and small, even if one counted all the related chills and spills with a horse wreck or two thrown in for the added spice!

In the day's last light, I noticed a sedan slowly driving west along Bowen Road. Grabbing my binoculars, I zeroed in on that suspicious vehicle as I laid behind my water grass covered rice check. Slowly my suspect vehicle rolled to a stop and four men got out. Standing in the middle of an all but now deserted backcountry road for that time of the early evening, all of the men attended to a call of nature. However, I damn sure knew what they were doing. They were using the call of nature as a ruse to scout out the area for any suspicious looking vehicle that belonged to a game warden moving around in the vicinity. Seeing nothing but a world of flying, swirling ducks to their south in the now darkening of the evening rice fields, three of the men, sensing the coast was clear, hastily retrieved their gear and shotguns from their vehicle. Then sprinting out into the nearest empty rice field, three of the four men dove into the cover of a close-at-hand rice check and hid. With that, the remaining man casually got back into their car and drove out of the area like it was an everyday event not worthy of a second look. However, someone was looking with the intensity of that of a long-tailed weasel in the dead of winter, with an empty gut looking at a close at hand, scared all to hell field mouse...

For the longest time, no one in the field, friend or foe, moved. Then when it got sufficiently darker, my three lads began sneaking my way. Now I had a problem. I had chosen a good hiding place all right. But dang it, I was now smack dab right in the middle of about fifty thousand madly feeding ducks! If I moved to avoid being discovered by my cautiously approaching poachers, I would have spooked off all my birds and the three suspects as well. Cussing my stupid luck in picking an area right in the middle of the ducks' field kitchen, I quietly held my ground hoping I would not be discovered by either the ducks or my still slowly crawling outlaws.

Picture this in your minds. The air was so full of ducks barely zooming off the rice field surface, that to stand up, would risk being hit by a flying feathered cannon shot in the darkness. Lying there, I had ducks swarming and feeding all around me. Several times, thousands of ducks fed right up to my rice check and then over the top like a living feathered blanket moving hungrily from one harvested rice field to another. Lying stone cold still when that happened, I had ducks pass within inches of my face as they fed along. When many of those happily feeding ducks got to my inert carcass, they just walked right over my body to the other side like I was just another lump in the darkness of the trail! In fact, I had one duck poop right in my ear as he walked over my head! Like I said earlier, if it hadn't been for the seriousness of the moment, what a fulfillment of a lifelong dream that nature at her very best event turned out to be! No, not the poop in the ear, you knuckleheads. The experience of being in the middle of thousands of hungry, feeding ducks, many just inches away, and not paying me one bit of attention as long as I didn't move. It was like being back at the turn of the century in the Sacramento Valley when it was pristine and basically unspoiled by Man's greed, ego and stupidity. Lying there among so many living things, I could only think that such a wonderful experience for me was once again a memorable tribute to all those hard working game wardens and federal agents who came before me some fifty years or so earlier.

When that last tide of ducks had washed over me and I was more or less in the clear, I picked up my Starlight Scope that I had earlier laid out on the rice check next to me to see if I could locate my shooters to be. Nothing greeted my eyes in the lime green field of view of the scope except the scene of thousands of ducks feeding and flying every which way like an overturned hive of bees in the area of the next rice field. Then there they were! Not two rice checks away, my three lads were slowly crawling like maggots across the rice field directly toward my location on the rice check! Fortunately, the biggest feeding snake like carpet of ducks was now south of me. Because of that, my three lads could crawl my way without spooking too many ducks. And, by the way and manner they were slowly Army crawling in the muddy rice field, I knew they had "been there and done that" little maneuver numerous times before.

Slowly they continued crawling toward my rice check until they were maybe thirty-five yards away from my location! Finally, they holed up on another rice check and began watching the ebb and flow of feeding ducks to ascertain their exact direction of movement. Realizing the ducks were now moving off to their west, they began mirroring that movement so they could maneuver into the correct shooting position in front of the feeding stream of waterfowl. As they did, my shooters-to-be smartly kept to the backside of their rice check for the cover it offered. Soon they were out of sight once again. Realizing I had to stay close or I would receive a "no-capture" cigar for my efforts once the shooting began, I started carefully crawling on my rice check paralleling the same compass direction toward where my lads had just disappeared. Then my feeding ducks changed direction so they would be feeding into the light wind now streaming down from the northwest. That carpet of feeding ducks now came my way once again! Damn! I thought. Now I have to freeze or I will spook the ducks and my shooters-to-be as well.

Snuggling down alongside my rice check, I got as comfortable as I could as I waited for the inevitable carpet of madly feeding ducks to arrive. They never arrived! All of a sudden there was an explosion of shots that, even at that range, sounded like someone tearing a huge bed sheet in half! That was instantly followed by a loud roar of thousands of nearby and adjacent ducks madly fleeing for their lives. Speaking of lives, I was so close to the shooting action, that I got tagged with about a dozen shot in my tough-hided canvas hunting jacket and one stinging lead shot buried itself into the side of my neck! Unbeknownst to me, the rice check my lads had been sneaking along had turned south. In short, my three gunners were shooting into the feeding carpet of ducks placing me directly in the line of fire as I laid on my rice check just thirty-five yards away! That is why I got patterned with so many flying pellets. Fortunately for me, the ducks in front of the shot strings and between the shooters and me, took most of the lethal pellets. Otherwise, I may have fared even worse for the pellet strikes like possibly losing an eye! Rubbing my stinging and now bleeding neck from one of the pellets, I grabbed the Starlight Scope with my other hand. Turning it on and sweeping the field, I could see dozens of flopping and dead ducks littered about. Additionally, the ground was covered with numerous wounded ducks, which, unable to fly, were fleeing the area like a carpet of maggots leaving a cleaned out carcass. Sweeping the length of the rice check from which my shooters had just shot with the Starlight Scope, I saw nothing. It was obvious they had gone to ground after their shoot and were now lying down to see if anyone was coming their way. So, yours truly and the shooters just held their positions like barnacles on the side of a sperm whale. My trusty dog, Shadow, and always-constant companion as many of my readers have come to learn, was not with me that evening. She was home expecting a litter of puppies at any moment. So, she wasn't with me that particular evening and I sure missed not having her great eyes and ears in which to aid me in my hoped for capture-quest.

All of a sudden with shotguns in hand, my three lads burst out from behind their rice check in the lime green field of the night scope and began gathering up dead and dying birds like they were hundred dollar bills. Being that they were still carrying their shotguns that called for a change in my capture plans. No longer could I thunder out across the rice field like a German Panzer tank after my lads. To do that, especially out from the dark of the night in total surprise, might bring on another fusillade of shots. Only this time, clearly directed at me from close range. Now I would have to finesse my attack and capture plans. In the night scope, I could see that once they had picked up a load of ducks, my lads were bringing them back to their rice check and hastily dumping them into a hastily formed pile. Following that, they returned to the field for more of the same. Feeling that was their battle plan, I came up with one of my own. I would cross the upper part of the rice field over to their rice check. Once behind the cover that check offered, I would crawl along its backside, stopping immediately adjacent to their duck dumping spot. When anyone of the lads got within arms' reach encumbered with another load of ducks, I would ambush him at that time. Laying down my precious night scope on the top of my rice check so I could find it later and thereby freeing my gun and flashlight hands, I began crawling closer towards my three busy-as- a-mess-of-bees drag shooters'.

Finally arriving on the backside of their rice check by their duck offloading spot, I crawled to the top so I could hear and anticipate my next move. It was at that very moment I got my chance! When two of my chaps arrived at the duck pile at the same time, I pulled the trigger on my capture plan! Jumping up and lumbering over the top of the rice check like a cheetah after a gazelle—well, maybe a fairly large but always a beautiful cheetah—I turned on my flashlight and bellowed, "Game Warden! Hold it right there!"

Man, you talk about an explosion of humanity! In the confusion of the moment, one nearest lad continued running right at me and I neck-tied him in the crook of my left arm as he went by. When he did, I clamped down on his miserable carcass like a great white shark would do a seal pup. To my way of thinking, the only way he was going was with me! The other fellow turned in a heartbeat like he had been in such a position during his now ill-fated life and tried to run back into the safety of the darkness.

In so doing, he stumbled and fell over the earlier dumped, squishy pile of dead ducks on the ground by his feet. When he did, he stumbled, then nose-dived face first into the soft rice field mud like an errant Zero kamikaze fighter after an American carrier off the coast of Okinawa during the Second World War. In that fall, the man's shotgun barrel was inadvertently driven deeply into the soft rice field mud and then exploded with a loud crump! Instantly, both my two duck draggers and yours truly, were sprayed with flying rice field slop and mud from the shotgun's barrel ruptured in the explosion. An explosion caused when the barrel of his shotgun was driven deeply into the mud and then discharged. Suffice to say, when that happened, the plugged shotgun barrel assumed the shape of an opened up tulip flower... Dragging my gagging, neck-tied chap still firmly affixed in the crook of my left arm, I slammed into the other chap, who by then was stumbling back to his feet. That collision was when the rubber met the road...especially when 320-pounds of my most beautiful German fighting magnificence and majesty landed squarely on top of his struggling carcass. And of course, with the grace of a ballet dancer! Well, to be frank, maybe it was more like a clumsy crash on top of my second targeted lad when my feet like his, got tangled up in the huge pile of freshly killed ducks as well. And in so doing, toppled me head over hind end, gracefully of course... Suffice to say, the lad tightly held in the crook of my left arm was getting one hell of a ride... Quickly getting back to my feet and jerking neck-tied up with me, I shined my flashlight on the smashed as flat- as-a-sail-rabbit duck-killing chap lying there stunned as a car-hit chicken on the muddy ground at my feet. He was still trying to get his wind back from being semi-flattened out by my most beautiful two tons of weight—well, maybe beautiful to a hungry cannibal. Realizing sail rabbit was going to take a while recovering after being squished flatter than a flounder, I quickly splashed my light across the field for the other chap in their bunch of duck-killing son-of-a- bitches. All I saw was the rapidly disappearing fleeing hind end of my third shooter sprinting across the rice field for all he was worth. For all intents and purposes, I considered him lost to the ages as far as being captured by yours truly that evening. There goes that bear thing I keep alluding too. Remember, as I have told all you readers many times before in my other books, "Sometimes you eat the bear and sometimes he eats you." Well, there went another bite from that proverbial damn old bear from my now well-worn-out and chewed-up hind end when it came to catching my now-fleeing- for-the-safety-of-the-next-county, duck-dragging chap!

But, I still had two of my drag shooters and that was better than a poke in the eye with a sharp stick. Sitting neck-tied down somewhat roughly, I took their shotguns, unloaded them and then moved them off to one side so they wouldn't be the source of any further problems. Showing the lads my badge in the light of my flashlight, I asked for their driver's licenses. When they were produced, I had one Sam McKenna from Marysville and a Bob Dunn from Olivehurst. Once again, I had to marvel at the information my friend Tom always supplied. Like I said earlier, he was never wrong on any information he supplied. And I never asked him how he got such good information either...

"Well, lads, as I see it, you have a small problem. You are facing charges for late shooting waterfowl, over limits of the same, and I would bet unplugged shotguns once I check them out." And sure as pocket gophers can ruin a good lawn, when checked, their shotguns were unplugged, thereby adding the third soon-to-be-lodged charge for their little duck dragging boo-boo. For my readers' edification, there were no specific charges that could be lodged against one for drag shooting ducks under the federal or state's waterfowl hunting regulations. I just had to charge the outlaws caught with separate offenses, such as late shooting, over limits and the like. But either way, they all paid the same. Then with a "Do not run off and try to escape" warning since I now had their driver's licenses in my possession, using my flashlight, the three of us commenced picking up all the dead and wounded ducks that we could find. Once the three of us began picking up all the wounded, dead and dying ducks, I realized I would never be able to catch my drop-off driver of the group who was just as guilty as those pulling the triggers, especially, when he saw the flashlight being used so openly in the field, which was something no self-respecting duck dragger would ever do, because use of a light in such a manner signified the law was at hand and captures had been made. Since there was no way I was going to just let all the wounded and dying critters crawl off into the weeds and go to waste, I used my flashlight to aid in their pickup. And in so doing, was just out of luck when it came to capturing the equally guilty drop-off driver.

When finished with the cleanup detail, we had one hundred fifty-five dead ducks from my lads' little evening's wasteful shoot. Those numbers didn't reflect all the crippled ducks, which had been lightly wounded and had crawled off into the grasses to eventually die and/or be eaten by skunks, foxes or coyotes either! That number also did not include those wounded birds that had been able to get airborne and then moments later died in the air from their internal injuries. In that case, those falling dead birds would then be scattered to hell and back! For my readers' edification that did not think about that aspect of mortality from such a wasteful shooting, I offer the following example of what I speak. In 1970 as a federal officer, I witnessed such a ground-sluicing shoot on massed feeding ducks in a flooded cornfield during daylight hours in the Stockton Delta area of California. My three Italian shooters, after apprehension, the rest of the arresting state and federal officers and yours truly, picked up one hundred ninety-eight dead and wounded mallards and Northern pintail in the immediate killing field. However, right after that shoot and before I made my move to apprehend my three shooters, I observed with my naked eyes and then with my binoculars at a distance, another one hundred twenty-three birds falling from the just shot over flock of ducks as they died in the air from their wounds and fell to the ground! How many more birds died in the air and dropped to the ground after they had flown from my view only God knew... For those of you who might be interested in reading that story, see my book titled, *Defending Our Wildlife Heritage*, Chapter 1, titled, "The Parachute Squad." It is a story you will enjoy reading and is truly one in which I pulled the wool clear over the three apprehended Italian shooter's eyes. Those three Italian millionaires when asked why they killed so many ducks the way they did, shocked the hell out of me. Their response was they were hungry for a duck dinner... Millionaires and they couldn't pay for a domestic duck dinner...

Back at the ranch, I asked for the names of the other shooter and of their drop off driver. As expected, I got only silence for my efforts in return from my two apprehended duck draggers. That was OK with me though. The two I had apprehended would have to stand

509

for the violations on site. And, I was sure by the time my Williams Justice Court Judge got through with them, there would be more than enough in the fines levied department to go around for those other chaps who had participated in the illegal shoot and were now long gone but not forgotten. Especially when it came to sharing all the group's legal expenses. Particularly if they chose to lawyer up, and then splitting among themselves the subsequent associated legal costs and fees.

Walking back with their shotguns in hand to my Starlight Scope, I turned it on and took one final look around for my third shooter. Not surprisingly, he was nowhere to be seen in the lime green field of the night vision device. Returning to my two glum shooters standing nearby, we began the ordeal of hauling out one hundred fifty-five dead ducks. One hour later after hauling the ducks out in relays, we were back at my county undercover truck.

Since they had been cooperative up to that point, other than not giving me the names of the drop off driver and the third shooter, I issued them state citations on the spot for their violations. Then the three of us began gutting the ducks alongside the road and tossing the innards into a nearby ditch for the creepy critters to enjoy. Following that, I gave the lads a ride to the town of Williams and dropped them off at a gas station. I figured from there they would be calling some of their friends to come and get them. Since there was no way I could now legally connect the dots from that evening's shoot to those who were to pick them up and the escaped shooter, I headed home for some well-deserved sleep. However, not before letting Deputy Sheriff Fred Pilgrim know I was safely out of the field. Before hitting the hay, I took the time to hang all my evidence ducks in my garage to continue cooling out and draining so they could be useful as a food item when later donated to numerous needy families.

The next morning, my now very pregnant dog raised holy hell about being left home once again due to her advanced, soon-to-be- knee-deep-in-puppies condition; all you black lab owners out there know of what I speak, thirteen puppies in a litter not being unusual for such breed of dog. In her own way, she made her point very clearly that she was going along with me on the next patrol. With what I had planned for that day, I acquiesced to Dog and gently lifted her heavy body into the front seat of my truck. Later with her slowed but happy assistance, I managed to find another thirty-nine dead and dying ducks on the site shot over the evening before that had been missed during the first search. Those birds were gutted and, along with the previous evening's seizures, were eventually placed in my evidence freezers located at the Sacramento National Wildlife Refuge for later donations to needy families throughout the valley.

Two weeks later, my two chaps showed up in the Williams Justice Court accompanied by two other men. By then, I had run a records check, or a 10/28 and a 10/29, on the names of the four men previously identified by my informant, Tom. I had also viewed their mug shots and had reviewed copies of their rather lengthy criminal rap sheets that ran the gamut from petty theft and assault to breaking and entering. Approaching the two men accompanying my accused shooters I said, "Good morning, Bert, and good morning, Darrel," looking directly at the two newest members of the group as they filed past me to enter the justice court. Since the two of them had never laid eyes on me before, they looked back in pure shock upon my specific identification of the two. Looking Bert in the eyes, I said, "Next time you drop off shooters in my patrol district, you need to stay closer, Bert. That way when I catch them breaking the law, you can at least give them a ride home." Then turning to Darrel, I said, "And the next time you pull a shoot on my ducks, you had better hope it is not me catching you. Because if I do, I will throw your miserable carcass so far back into a holding cell, you will grow moldy before the authorities realize you are still there!" Suffice to say, both men were more than amazed that I had singled them out, even though we had never previously met and I sure as hell had not apprehended them the evening of the shoot. I am sure they couldn't figure out how the hell I knew who they were. But I knew... Later, Sam McKenna and Bob Dunn pled guilty to the charges I had levied against them, were found guilty and fined $1,000 each. They also had their shotguns forfeited to the State of California, including the one with the ruptured barrel.

I never saw those four chaps in Colusa County again. I know I didn't cure their dark-of-the-night duck-killing fever, and I am sure they just continued doing the same thing, only elsewhere in the Sacramento Valley. I have often wondered if my wildlife violators, especially the really serious ones, ever realized that God makes and cares for all the critters large and small. And someday, those chaps who are a little heavy on their trigger fingers, are going to have to stand before Him and explain why they had to kill so many of His feathered creations. They may just find as their punishment for such illegal activities, that they are being turned into ducks in their second lives and sent back to the rice fields in Colusa County so they know what it would be like to run the gamut of late shooters and duck draggers... The really neat thing about this adventure was that Tom, like always, was right on the money with his information. He was such a unique individual and wonderful friend. Looking back on my friend some forty-five years after his death, I guess one could say the impact of a powerful life like Toms' goes on in the poetry of the living. I was just happy I could contribute a verse to Tom's poem of life...

By the way, Shadow had a litter of twelve puppies several days later after the above event... Like I said earlier, typical lab, knee-deep in puppies. But, oh what a joy...

LATE SHOOTING BY THE LONG
ARM OF THE LAW

As the winter rain clouds once again scudded across the evening skies in the Northern Sacramento Valley and the usual accompanying winds picked up, I slipped and slid my way in the rice field mud hurriedly walking sight unseen toward two late shooters. The air was chock full of ducks winging off from nearby Delevan National Wildlife Refuge and, from their erratic aerial behavior, all were hungry as hell and eager to land somewhere and put on the feed bag. That was further exemplified by their low, wind-hampered erratic flight patterns and numerous dense flocks winging ever lower over the harvested rice fields looking for a safe place to land and feed. That aerial flying-low-to-the-ground display created a draw to even the most honest of duck hunters to stay and fire just a few more shots after legal shooting hours had ended before leaving for the evening. Particularly if their hunting success during the day had been less than satisfactory to their way of thinking. It was now forty minutes after legal shooting hours and most lawful duck hunters had long since left the rice fields. However, I still had my two shooters deep on the Newhall Farms area whanging away at every low flying duck coming their way. As the rains and winds refreshed themselves, in the fading light and in a crouched position, I continued trotting south toward my two late shooters.

Closing to within forty yards of my targeted shooters still sight unseen because they were looking the other way, I flopped down on the backside of a wet rice check. There I could watch my shooters through my binoculars and gather the evidence of late shooting needed to satisfy the elements of the crime and meet the requirements of a court of law if the case ever went to trial. Great, I thought. Neither of those two chaps even has an inkling that the long arm of the law is in country, and now I am between them and their vehicle parked along Four Mile Road and any chance of escape. The winds continued unabated and so did the numerous flights of low flying ducks winging their ways just barely over the harvested rice fields toward the next wind blocking rice check. Arriving at the next rice check, the straining ducks just barely lifted up over the rice check and then dropped back down toward the harvested rice field on the other side. There that close to the ground, the winds were less resistant because of the numerous blocking and higher rice checks lying ahead of their paths of flight. By that time, I was sure my two late shooters were in what I called a killing ecstasy over their ever increasing, low flying duck fortunes. The shooting was hot and heavy around my two targets and the killing was good if numerous dropping birds' broken bodies spinning out of the air was any kind of indication. So, I suspected, thoughts of being apprehended by the local duck cop and its subsequent ramifications were the furthest things from my shooters' collective minds at that massive, close at hand, duck flying miracle moment of time.

After finally being able to accurately count a number of ducks dropping and shots taken from each fellow after legal hours, I had the evidence I needed for a court of law. Plus, I now had enough of their late shooting foolishness and the killing that followed. Grabbing up my gear, I took off running right at my nearest late shooter using a handy, water grass covered rice check to my front for cover. Just like in Grosz's Rule, if they aren't looking for you, they won't see you, and he and his partner didn't. They were too busy looking skyward for the next low flying duck boiling over the rice check to their front to see the approaching freight train hammering down on them from behind. Well, a gorgeous and beautiful freight train, if I might say so myself. Trotting right up to the back of the rice check opposite where my two chaps were whanging away at the ducks, I slid to a stop. Satisfied with my positioning, I just stood there in all of my Teutonic magnificence in front of a thousand approaching low-flying ducks, the driving sideways falling rain, howling winter winds, and God Almighty Himself. Finally, one chap ran out into the rice field to his front to retrieve a close-at-hand drake mallard that he had just shot. Running back to his hiding place alongside the rice check, he looked right at me standing there in all my rain soaked beauty. I swear, his eyes were glazed over in the killing frenzy at hand during that moment in time. Without any sign of recognition of the wet as a muskrat game warden quietly standing there, he slid into the base of his rice check and began shooting once again at the next low flying flock of ducks streaming his way. Seconds later came the realization that he had just seen an unknown human being standing close at hand by his rice check, looking intently right at him in the dimming light of the evening. With that realization now sinking into the depths of his soul, he slowly rose up, turned, and looked directly at me now standing not fifteen feet away. In the blink of an eye, my lad dropped behind the rice check as if the hiding trick would save his miserable, late shooting carcass from the chap now eyeballing him like a hungry mink does a nearby, still flopping, recently caught, carp out of the water on a nearby grassy creek bank.

Walking up onto his rice check, I looked down at my late shooter as he tried hiding in the long water grass. Have any of you ever seen a grown man trying to hide in seven blades of grass? That is hard for even a pissant to do.

"Evening. How is the late duck shooting going?" I asked like Joe Casual. Believe it or not, my lad did not move a muscle or respond. I think he still considered himself hidden behind his seven blades of grass. Stepping off his rice check, I knelt down alongside my seven-blades-of-grass-hidden chap saying, "Make sure you are really hidden because the game warden is close at hand and is looking for you because of all the late shooting you and your partner are doing."

With those words, my chap realizing he was now a had dad, rolled over and sat up. "You win. But, you can't blame me for trying," he said sheepishly through a weak grin on his rain and field mud splattered face.

"No, I can't. But just remember, as a game warden I do this every day for a living. If you are trying to hide, you need to do it better. Like crawling into a hole and pulling the earth back over the top of you. State game warden," I stated once again, as I flashed my badge and credentials so he could see who he was officially talking to on that wind howling, horizontal rain flying evening.

"Yeah, I know who you are. The word is out that you are a big one and they weren't lying. How the hell did you sneak up on us without either me or my partner ever seeing you?" he asked.

"Piece of cake. You and your partner over there, who is also trying to hide now that he realizes that I am here, were too busy killing ducks to the front of you to look around. When that happens, you are easy marks to sneak," I replied. "Now, may I have your driver's and hunting licenses, please?" I asked. The lad began digging in his rain gear and soon a wallet appeared. That was soon followed with requested driver's and hunting licenses.

"You wait here while I go and retrieve your buddy before he tries to burrow into the mud like a crawdad and hide as well. In the meantime, your shooting is over for the evening."

Taking his licenses and putting them into my shirt pocket and unloading his shotgun, I headed for the spot where I had last seen his buddy shooting ducks. When I got there, his buddy was nowhere to be seen! Tracking his mud turtle crawl marks left in the soft mud along the base of the rice check, I took off after my errant late shooter at a trot. Soon, a hundred yards farther west, I saw his buddy furiously crawling along the base of the rice check for all he was worth. He looked like a big groundhog wearing rain gear and hip boots. I had to admit that lad sure could crawl fast though. When push came to shove, he was as good as any game warden when it came to his crawling abilities.

Trotting up alongside my fast moving crawler with the rambling rump, I said with a grin, "Howdy, Partner. If you will quit crawling, we can get to the bottom of this late shooting thing."

"OK, you caught me," said the rambling rump as he rolled over in the rice field mud, sat up and faced me.

Man, you talk about funny. In order to move faster and escape from me, he had discarded his ducks from his hunting coat as he rumbled along. All I really had to do was follow the trail of the freshly killed ducks he had chucked along the way and the rather obvious skid marks he had left in the rice field mud while trying to escape. On the way back, the two of us picked up his twenty-one freshly killed ducks! With that, things were not looking good for the rambling rump since the daily bag limit was only eight. Returning to the chap who tried to hide in seven blades of grass, I discovered he had killed a total of sixteen ducks. That too was an over limit sure as God made small live frogs and field mice great largemouth bass bait.

Sitting down on the nearest rice check, I began writing up my two late-shooting and over-the-limit chaps while shielding my cite book under the cover of my rain jacket. It was now seventy minutes after legal shooting hours. And as I sat there taking care of the paperwork at hand, I got madder and madder by the moment. I had at least four guns still shooting waterfowl to my immediate north! Damn it, it was now over an hour past legal shooting time or sunset! Who was ever doing the late shooting sure as hell had to know that legal shooting hours were long over to my way of thinking... Hurrying along with the paperwork at hand, I soon finished. With that, I hurriedly appraised my two lads of their legal obligations in the Williams Justice Court relative to their over limits and late shooting violations. Filling my game bag in my hunting coat clear full of seized ducks, I grabbed the remaining two handfuls and took off heading for my patrol vehicle at a brisk, mudslinging trot. But not before handing each lad their citations for late shooting and possessing over limits of ducks, along with once again detailed instructions for their court appearances or forfeiture of bail procedures.

While trotting back to my truck, I had pretty well echo-located my other four late shooters as being from one of the numerous small duck clubs located in the Lambertville area. Those small duck clubs located in that area historically didn't have very good shooting unless it poured down rain or the winds howled. And the weather conditions that evening, sure as hell made for perfect late shooting lawlessness opportunities for those club members so inclined to step over the legal line drawn in the sand, eh, rice field mud...

Back at my vehicle, I threw all the ducks just seized onto my passenger side floorboards, jumped in, and headed further north. Driving up to and stopping at the southern edge of the Lambertville area in question, I bailed out, climbed up into the bed of my county undercover truck and then up onto the top of the cab. From that vantage point with my binoculars, I was able to quickly locate my late shooters. I counted four, close together locations from where the late shooting was hotly occurring. As it turned out, my suspects were smack dab in the middle of the Lambertville duck club complex of over thirty individually owned, small shooting areas.

Jumping back down from the top of the cab, I drove for that duck club complex's interior. Once there, I hid my truck in an empty stand of bamboo, which had been planted as a duck club members' drive-in car blind. I left my Starlight Scope in the truck because I felt this late shooting group would be an easy capture because of their closeness to me. Besides, heavy rainfall made it hard to see subjects with any definition because of the scope's propensity to reflect light back off the raindrops. Then Dog and I took off on foot at a ground-eating trot. The air was alive with ducks flying every which way by then, as they looked for a place to alight down and feed. And in so doing, they were giving my late shooting gunners to my front plenty of easy low flying targets at which to shoot. Like my two earlier late shooting subjects previously apprehended, these gunners were acting like they had shot few ducks until the recent bad weather had arrived as well. When the intense wind and rains had started in the late afternoon, their shooting success had steadily increased by leaps and bounds. Not wanting to miss any killing opportunity, my four lads were blazing away killing all they could kill on their normally low duck producing duck club as if to make up for lost time on other previous poor shooting days.

Identifying my late shooting gunners' exact locations, I began my stalk but soon quickly realized I had a problem. My gunners appeared to be watchfully interconnected on their small in size duck club. All four were shooting on one club, but they were located at four different points on the shooting area's external boundaries as if almost by design. Kind of like what a set of real outlaws would do who had been in this extreme late shooting circumstance numerous times before. Or, like crooked law enforcement officers would do to protect their escape options if approached by a fish and game warden... No matter which way I tried sneaking my late shooting chaps, I always had to contend with one, who if I was spotted, could give a warning to the others. And if I physically grabbed off any one of the four, the others would quickly notice his absence of shooting and would more than likely vanish into the howling winter winds like a puff of burnt gunpowder. And if that fleeing option was exercised, I would be left holding the bag with only one culprit contained therein. Being greedy, I knew losing any one of this group of extreme and dedicated late shooters would not do. Plain and simple, they needed to be captured and put to bed. Plus, my two guardian angels were now stirring within my wet as a muskrat carcass because a good case to be made, in their estimation, was close at hand. Yet, case or no case, those two damn guardian angels hardly stirred in this kind of weather for any reason unless a good catch was close at hand. That was because they said the wind mussed up their feathers... But at least they were on the prod and so was I. Circling out of sight from the still heavily shooting group, I discovered two golf carts that had been converted into duck club hunting transport buggies hidden off to one side of their immediate shooting area. They were covered with military surplus parachutes and, in the darkness, I almost walked right by them. Realizing they were more than likely vehicles belonging to my four late-shooting chaps, I went into my Plan B capture mode.

Using the sliver of light through the fingers trick with my flashlight, I discovered the muddy levee all four of my chaps had walked out on. I soon discovered what a gift that levee turned out to be because it led directly into my four suspects' immediate shooting area. Humans being creatures of habit, I figured if they had used that muddy levee to enter the shooting area it stood to figure they would also use it to exit. Positioning myself where I could count the numbers of ducks killed by each shooter, I dug into a dense patch of handy rushes like an alligator snapping turtle. Since all four of my chaps were shooting over a pond, they could shoot even longer than normally in the darkness because of the reflected light open water provides. Finally positioned where I could clearly see and gather evidence for a court of law, I recorded and waited like a large bullfrog waiting for the soon to turn deadly approach of an innocent duckling intent on catching a water skipper. Yes, my unwashed readers, bullfrogs do commonly catch and eat reckless ducklings.

By now, my lads were mostly shooting ducks they could see that landed on the water in their decoys. When they did, they would only shoot one shot at a time to reduce their late shooting fingerprint. And in so doing, reduce their chances of being apprehended by any game warden in the area trying to echolocate in on their exact shooting location. Pretty damn savvy violators, ran through my mind. That type of behavior of just cautiously shooting those birds on the water when the air was full of low flying birds, told me I had a set of real dedicated been-here-before killers... Anyone exhibiting such low to the ground late shooting behavior, with shotgun sounds-baffled by low growing plants, would be damn hard to catch unless the officer was right in the shooters' back pockets. I was too damn big to fit into my shooters' back pockets but you could bet your bottom dollar, I was so close to their miserable carcasses that it was the next best thing... Before long, I had each of my chaps for taking an over limit of ducks and for late shooting. By now legal shooting hours had been over for two hours and still my lads shot those ducks landing in the water in and around their decoys like there was no tomorrow. At two and a half hours after legal shooting hours had ended, my lads uncharacteristically fired their last shots into several large flocks of low flying ducks massed overhead. Then it got as quiet as a church mouse during Sunday services in a house of God full of cats and it stayed that way for another forty minutes. Those guys were not moving at all. It was almost as if they were waiting for the long arm of the law to appear and if he did, they would quickly disappear into the surrounding marsh like puffs of dust in the wind. These guys are good, I thought. But there was a major problem. There was a pitcher's mound sized, badge carrying type of fellow in between their shooting locations and what I suspected were their two escape vehicles. And that lurking in the reeds chap was one patient son of a bitch, especially if he could eventually gather up all his late shooting sheaves in one arm gathering felt swoop.

Three hours after legal shooting hours had ended in rain-swept total darkness and over the howling winds, I could faintly hear the squishing sounds numerous hip boots make when walking in nearby levee mud! I still couldn't see anyone because of the darkness, but from their walking-in-the-mud sounds, they were coming my way. Then about twenty yards out from their vehicles and my location, the walking noises on the muddy levee ceased. Then except for the sounds of falling rain and the gusts of wind, it became as still as the proverbial Angel of Death when she is eventually approaching each and every one of us for reasons known only unto her.

For about the next twenty minutes, the only noises I heard were the wind, rain, and flocks of ducks and geese calling softly as they flew low overhead. Then there it was! Once again, I could hear the faint sounds of walking in the mud, but this time the squishing-step sounds were reduced in number and moving quietly. Moments later, one chap quietly walked by where I was hidden in the rushes on the side of the levee road. He was not carrying any ducks or a shotgun. Dog never made a sound. She just watched the walker from our place of cover and so did I. Walking past me, that individual went directly to the hidden vehicles. A few minutes later, I briefly saw a light flash from the vehicles as if signaling the other three chaps still in the marsh that the way was all clear. Then I could hear a lot of hurried squishing sounds hip boots make in the mud as their owners hustled toward their parked vehicles. A quiet rumble from Dog let me know my three chaps were now very near and then they walked right by me carrying what appeared to be loads of ducks and shotguns like they were innocently returning from a church social. Well, this was one church social when those who had eaten the left out in the sun too long spoiled homemade potato salad would soon pay the price...

Letting them walk right by me, I waited until I could tell they were at their vehicles, which were just a few short yards away. Taking that as my cue, I rose from my place of hiding, turned on my flashlight, and strode right into my surprised group of four late shooters. Man, you talk about four chaps jumping like a bunch of bugs on hot rocks when my five-cell light went on! I don't think those chaps could have passed a whiff of gas between the four of them because they were so startled. That priceless moment of utter surprise was one for the books.

"State fish and game Warden, gentlemen. Please lay your shotguns down. As long as you are holding them, it makes my dog very nervous and mean as a snake." With those words, I quickly flashed my flashlight's beam on Shadow standing alongside my right leg and then back to my four surprised chaps. I did that so they could see that I was making no idle threat about my monster-sized dog being in country. Plus, that kind of a show of force always tended to even the odds no matter what kind of law enforcement situation presented itself.

Boy, you talk about words bearing fruit, the guns just flew to the muddy ground! It is almost like these chaps have been in the presence of a large mean assed dog in the past, I thought cautiously. Once I saw the shotguns were out of the immediate reach of my lads, I had them take three steps away from them. With that, Dog and I walked over to their shotguns. "Sit," I commanded Shadow and she quickly obeyed sitting alongside the four shotguns laying in the mud. That way, if anyone changed their mind about possessing their shotgun, there would be more than a tussle in the offing in order to accomplish that deed, if you readers get my drift.

I asked the lads for their hunting and driver's licenses after flashing them my badge in the light so they could truly see who I was. There was some grumbling over my request but soon they were forthcoming in a surprising sort of way. Each man handed me his open wallet. On one side of the open wallet was a driver's license and on the other side a bright and shiny prominently displayed deputy sheriff's badge!

Ignoring the display of badges, I again asked for their driver's licenses. Then an Asian gentleman said somewhat brusquely, "We just showed you our driver's licenses."

"Yes, you did," I said. "But we as a matter of agency policy aren't allowed to handle anyone's wallet. So, would all of you remove your driver's licenses from your wallets and hand them to me?"

"Didn't you see our badges?" asked the Asian gentleman, now with an arrogant sharpness creeping into the tone of his voice.

"Sure did," I said, as I began looking at their driver's licenses now being brusquely handed over by two of the other lads. As it turned out, all four of my chaps were from the City of Sacramento and were deputy sheriffs in and for Sacramento County!

"Now that you know who the hell we are and what we represent, where the hell is your professional courtesy?" the Asian lad asked sharply.

"I left that at home when the four of you decided to late- shoot waterfowl, a violation of state and federal laws," I replied professionally. However, there was now a slight edge creeping into my professional tone and tenor of voice. In short, a response that was easy to understand when asked such a dumb-assed question by an obvious dumb ass!

"Then what the hell is the matter with you? These three are captains, and I am a lieutenant. Doesn't that mean anything to you?" snapped out the Asian.

"Sure does. It means every one of you should have known better than to put me in such an awkward position as a fellow state peace officer," I said, with an even more getting-truly-pissed-off tone and tenor now ringing sternly at the edges of my voice.

"Don't ever let me catch you in the Sacramento area," said my Asian officer in a truly threatening tone of voice.

"If you do and if I am breaking your laws, I would hope you would extend to me the same professional courtesy I am extending to the four of you," I quietly replied.

"Count on it, Asshole," curtly replied my Asian.

With that, I began the paperwork after checking their shotguns for plugs, their hunting licences, and duck stamps. Then I counted out each man's ducks. Two of the lads were four ducks over, one was six over, and my Asian chap was seven over. Additionally, my last recorded shots at the large flock of low circling mallards were two and a half hours late per man, a flock they all had the opportunity to collectively shoot at and happily did so based on my observations.

Then my Asian lad who couldn't leave well enough alone began again. "What are the fines for our chicken-shit, no-account, piss-ant fish and game violations?"

"It is $25 for the late shooting offense and $2 per minute for every minute you are over. Each of you can figure that out based on what I have entered on your citations for minutes late shot. As for the over limits, it is $100 for shooting an over limit and $25 for each duck over. Again, each of you can figure that out based on the numbers of ducks I charged each and every one of you for taking over the legal limit. That is unless any of you have been convicted previously for fish and game violations. Then the fines for these late shooting and over the limit violations could be higher. But, that would be up to the judge once any previous history of fish and game violations is made known to his honor. Additionally, all of you will lose your ducks because of the late shooting and over limit violations since they were taken and possessed illegally. Are there any other questions?" I asked with a grin in my heart. Those lads knew better then to pursue the matter any further regarding their recent actions. It was clear to all us wet-as-muskrats standing on the levee that evening that their actions had been carefully planned and carried out with evil and deliberate intent. And in so doing, my ducks, and now my shooters, had paid the ultimate price. Now it was time for those lads to pay the piper and that they did some twenty days later.

All four of my law dogs from the Sacramento area forfeited bail and did not appear in the Williams Justice Court. As for their over limits of seized, late shot ducks, they were later distributed to four poor, hardworking Mexican farm-worker families in the area.

It was unfortunate that one branch of the long arm of the law had to address another in such a situation. But that is one reason why the arm of the law on one end of such a situation is so long and far reaching. What is good for the goose is also good for the gander, no pun intended. After that little episode, I later drove very carefully in the City and County of Sacramento making sure I obeyed all the traffic laws...

A LUCKY CATCH

The sounds of heavily pounding winter rains on the roof of our new home in Colusa woke me up about three o'clock one fine morning. That rain event was soon seconded with the realization that my brick home was also being heavily buffeted by the storm's strong winds striking the north face of my residence. When such weather events occurred in tandem in the Sacramento Valley during any ongoing waterfowl season, they foretold a major duck and goose-killing day by the sportsmen was in the offing because the ducks and geese would be flying low and slowly as they moved about in the heavy rains and stiff winds. And when the low-bird-flying events occurred, the sportsmen throughout the valley took advantage of the slow flying and close in range-winged targets.

Not being able to go back to sleep since I was physiologically and game-warden-biologically accustomed to running on about four hours of sleep during every twenty-four-hour period of time, I quietly got up, dressed, and headed for the kitchen. There I began planning out a lumberjack breakfast knowing with the kind of weather I was facing and the numbers of hopeful sportsmen who would be out and about in the valley during such a shoot day, I would be looking at a very long day afield. Boy, if I only knew what a string of oddball cases, called in my lexicon a game warden's stew, I was to make during the next flurry of hours before my head finally rested on a pillow once again...

I also knew those kinds of shotgun-sound-dampening weather events would bring out my extreme late shooters, duck draggers and the few remaining commercial market hunters in the valley as well—bringing them out from under the slime of their rock piles with high hopes of successful killing escapades soon to follow, especially once the dark of the night and scads of hungry ducks once again descended into the rice fields to feed.

Moving my anticipated workload for the day to the back of my mind, I concentrated on assembling and making my lumberjack load of breakfast grits. For all you willow thin wimps out there who are eternally watching your waistlines, you might turn away from reading the following hell-bent-on-election breakfast narrative... Into the toaster went two thick slices of my wife's homemade bread, the best homemade bread in the world, I might add. Let me tell all you unfortunate readers out there, there is nothing quite like the smell of freshly made homemade bread cooking in a toaster on a cold, rain swept winter morning. That is unless you would have access to some of my wife's outstanding homemade pie with its melt-in-your-mouth crusts! Then into one cast iron skillet went a mound of mashed potatoes from super the night before, followed by heavily spiced and previously sautéed in butter, chopped onions, minced fresh garlic, diced fresh tomatoes, jalapeno slices, and celery bits. Into a second skillet went five farm fresh eggs, and into a third went about a pound of bulk pork sausage. Those were the days in which I could really put away the grits. But those were also the days in which many times I would not see the bottom of a cast iron frying pan or a plate of food for another eighteen to twenty hours either! That and walk five or more miles in the rice fields and marshes every day during California's busy 107-day waterfowl hunting season checking duck and goose hunters... Ah, youth.

Rooting around in the refrigerator, I discovered half a homemade apple pie. Now to all you unwashed folks out there reading these lines, therein was a piece of Heaven. Knowing my love for pies, early on in our married life my wife set about teaching herself how to make good pies with crusts that literally melted in your mouth! That she did practicing from a Betty Crocker cookbook given to her by my mother the Christmas before our marriage in 1963. After lots of trials and errors trying to make good pies, Donna had succeeded. Truth be known, she had succeeded beyond my wildest dreams! Without a doubt, today my bride makes better pies than my North Dakota farm gal mother ever did and that is going some! Sorry mom...

Soon the kitchen was awash with many great smells, especially the sausage, which had come from my dear friend and a man, I consider to this very day to be my brother, So Han "Sonny" Park. Sonny was a butcher among many other community-helpful traits and friend to all at Chung Sun's Market in Colusa. Now, Sonny was a man who knew his meats like Mozart knew his music. To a manner of speaking, Sonny was such a great butcher that he put a square to every circle when it came to his friendship and the fruits of his profession! And that was partly understandable because he was an engineer by academic training in college. And the other part of his outstanding character was because he was such a damn good human being and thoughtful individual when it came to the needs of all the other folks around him in the Sacramento Valley. Man can't ask for a better brother than that!

Getting out a plate, I turned and there stood my blue-eyed bride with a sleepy but beautiful smile. Setting down the plate, I gathered up her small frame into my arms and gave her a hug and a smooch. Talk about a real woman, there was one for sure. She was a school marm, a damned good one I might add, and needed her sleep. But there she was, up at three in the morning so she could have breakfast with her hardly ever at home but much-loved husband. To all my law enforcement type readers out there, I only hope you have been blessed with a mate such as the one I have had now for over fifty- two years of marriage. If you don't, then you will struggle as a law enforcement officer in our rather dynamic and dangerous profession. An officer of the law must have a fortress, like a great mate, to always come home to. If you do, that means you can function in your profession at one hundred ten percent and more than likely make it to retirement. If you don't, well...

Finishing breakfast and giving my bride one more hug that had to last her all day and I suspected into the coming night, I gathered up all the gear needed for the blustery wet day ahead. With that, I headed out into my garage to feed my dog and constant field companion, Shadow. I knew that day, with the wind, rain, and it being a shoot day in the valley, we would be afoot and on horseback on the hunt for at least the next wet and cold eighteen hours. That was if it was a short day... But what a blessing to be able to hunt the most dangerous game in such a wildlife resource rich Northern Sacramento Valley environment during such a fabled winter weather event. Particularly since wildlife and the local outlaws liked to move around a lot during such blustery times, making for a unique day in the life and times of any good game warden. Damn it, today I am so busted up at age 73 that I couldn't even hunt and catch a field mouse without getting my last part over the fence kicked by said critter. Enjoy all your blessings, my able-bodied readers. It is just a matter of time before you will also age out and then have to meet that same field mouse...

With that, off Dog and I went to the Four Mile Road area just northeast of the Line Dennis farm. The evening before while on patrol, I had noticed a tornado of about twenty thousand hungry ducks descending into and feeding in that area's freshly harvested rice fields just north of Line's main farm buildings. I figured I would babysit those critters for a spell that would more than likely be using those freshly harvested areas that fine blustery morning. I did so because any time you mix man and wildlife such as I had observed, you will many times have problems. If I had observed such a massive tornado of ducks working that area the evening before, so too could those walking on the dark side of man in the world of wildlife. And let me tell you, there were shooters of wildlife inhabiting the valley who were every bit as good at killing the critters as I was at hunting humans. And if those chaps turned to the dark side in the world of wildlife law enforcement at any given moment, I would more than have my hands full corralling such individuals...

Sliding my county undercover patrol truck in between two idle rice harvesters on Line Dennis' farm some fifteen minutes later, I rolled down my lee side window. That way, I wouldn't have a bucketful of cold, winter rain and noisy wind pouring in on me had I lowered the windward side window. Then I listened intently to the outside whispers of nature over the quietly drumming and, to me, musical sounds of rain on the metal roof of my truck. I knew that the ducks were out there all right in the adjacent rice fields as evidenced by their characteristic flowing water feeding sounds they made faintly over the music of the wind and rain. And, I could also hear them calling overhead by the thousands winging to and from the immediately adjacent Delevan National Wildlife Refuge. That they did as they traded back and forth into the freshly harvested rice fields that were within yards from where I was now staked out. And for such numbers of feeding birds to be that close to a main road in the outback, meant that mortal danger could be just a trigger pull away. Slouching down in my heavy coat for the warmth it offered, I sat there quietly lost in my thoughts as Dog snored in the front seat of the passenger side of the truck. For about forty minutes nothing unusual happened. Then I heard the unmistakable sounds of a vehicle's tires crunching on Four Mile Road's graveled surface just a few yards away from where I was parked and hidden from roadside view. Swiveling around in my seat and squinting through the openings of the harvester parked alongside, I could just make out the darkened shape of a vehicle slowly coming down the road from the north. It appeared to be a four-wheel drive pickup and it was running without lights!

The lights out thing was a commonly used trick of the trade by game wardens, agents from the U.S. Fish and Wildlife Service, and duck draggers alike in the Sacramento Valley in those days. The outlaw thinking was that running without lights, you wouldn't be so readily observed if the wildlife officers were close at hand. Additionally, one who was outlaw-bent could be more effective in locating and subsequently sneaking up on the feeding ducks on foot that were located in the rice fields alongside the roads; use of headlights would spook close-at-hand feeding ducks. Law dogs also used that same technique to sneak up unobserved and then later to aid them in apprehending those of the lawless nature who had evil duck-killing thoughts on their minds. I was the only game warden working in the area at that time of the morning and I knew from the lack of radio traffic with the sheriff's office that none of my federal counterparts was out and about either. So, what did that leave? Yep, you chaps got that right! Dang, some of you readers just might make good game wardens yet.

That suspect darkened pickup stopped on Four Mile Road just across from the rice harvesters that I was hidden behind and quietly sat there for a few moments in the dark. Then, of all the lucky things to happen, here came the vehicle being quietly driven over to the rice harvesters behind which I laid in wait. Since I was well hidden behind the harvesters and it was still darker than all get out, the lads in the mystery pickup didn't see my vehicle. Nor did they see me when I stepped out from my truck because I had earlier flipped on my cutoff switches and therefore displayed no dome lights when exiting my vehicle. Quietly walking over to the driver's side of the darkened suspect vehicle, I could faintly see my three occupants had all the windows partially rolled down. Like me earlier, they were attempting to locate some nearby feeding ducks. Then if they did, I assumed several of the men would exit the vehicle and it would leave that area with the driver to avoid suspicion or discovery. Those two passengers would then quietly sneak out into the close-at-hand field of feeding ducks, blow them up, and then wait hidden alongside the road for their drop off driver in their vehicle to return. When the pickup driver returned by signal or prearranged time, he could pick up the shooters after the shoot, quickly load up their ducks, and split the area into the darkness without anyone being the wiser, especially at that hour and remote rural location in the morning.

Well, all hope of dragging ducks by my lads in the pickup went out the window when I quietly slipped up to their vehicle on the driver's side, flipped on my flashlight, and identified myself. You know what they say about a bird nest on the ground. With that in mind, I just figured I would spoil their little illegal shoot and preclude them from killing a mess of my ducks in the process. Man, talk about scaring the crap out of three chaps with evil thoughts on their collective minds! My arrival was so sudden and unanticipated, the lads inside did something to their shorts that their wives would have to wash out later... As it turned out, the pickup contained three well known to me duck draggers from the nearby Delevan area. All had eyes as big as dinner plates when their nemesis daintily showed up and, figuratively speaking, mightily took a dump in their collective mess kits. Talk about being surprised and embarrassed all at the same time over being caught with their pants down! It was a classic wildlife outlaw ground sluicing surprise, to say the least, on a windswept, rainy morning now around four o'clock. And since I was so close and had greeted them by their first names, they didn't dare try to bolt and run, much less breathe! Getting the three of them out from their vehicle, I scooped up the three shotguns they had in the cab. All three of their shotguns were fully loaded and unplugged carrying five shells each! I couldn't do much about the unplugged shotguns because I had not observed any of them taking migratory game birds with them. But I sure as hell could do something about the loaded guns in a motor vehicle on a way open to the public. California law did not allow one to transport a loaded shotgun or rifle (one with a live round in the chamber) in a motor vehicle on a way open to the public in those days.

I don't know about California's laws today but I would bet their gun laws, because of their idiot stick, liberal politics and mentality, are really goofy and even more restrictive than they used to be. However, as for the loaded rifle or shotgun in a motor vehicle law, I supported that one because it made good safety sense. But, I digress...

I then proceeded to write up each of my Delevan chaps for the loaded gun violations. True, at the time they were at the edge of a private rice field. However, I had observed them coming directly off a public way, namely Four Mile Road, onto the private rice field. As such, the shotguns were loaded on the public road before they came onto private property so I nabbed them, because I had sneaked up on them before they could do anything really stupid like trying to quickly unload them in the crowded cab of their pickup. They were written up in fine style because I knew in the immediate case, I couldn't take my three Delevan lumps of clay from Hell and mold them into angels in any given lifetime. Finishing my paperwork, I let the lads go with a rather stiff warning about blowing up the ducks when the local law was so close at hand. And in so doing as a force multiplier, made it sound like state and federal officers were currently in the darkened rice fields as thick as western wood ticks on the back of a mule deer during springtime in the Rockies. Boy, you talk about three whipped and embarrassed pups because the locals considered it bad form to be caught by wildlife officers, especially me! I guess to the locals' way of thinking, it left some sort of a permanent stain on one's kilts if caught by a lowly fish cop like yours truly. But no two ways about it, it had been an easy and welcome catch by the local fish cop and a great way to start off my morning. A lucky catch, if you will, but one that was damn sure needed when it came to those three known duck-dragging poaching son-of-a-guns. Maybe I hadn't caught them red-handed with a load of illegally taken ducks but I sure as hell had put an "apprehended soon to be convicted" stain on their collective kilts, one that wouldn't wash out as easily as the stain in their shorts when I had announced my presence earlier from just three feet away.

Two weeks later, my three embarrassed chaps forfeited $50 each in the Williams Justice Court for their little "loaded gun in a motor vehicle on a way open to the public" error. Damn, I loved it when the good Lord gave me a one up when I was hunting the lawless. Lucky catches like that one involving three historically lawless chaps, sure helps to make up for the broken body I suffer today and salves the old carcass regarding the numbers of hard core chaps I missed in my early days as a state and federal wildlife officer.

Returning to my truck to get out of the wind and rain, I got a grin on my face that soon broke out into a wide smile. I did so because it was in this exact area a funny happened to a local duck-dragging outlaw a number of years earlier. It seemed that those state and federal officers had staked out these same fields on which I now sat. They had sneaked into the area in mass to sit on about fifty thousand feeding ducks. Ducks that routinely stormed off the adjacent Delevan National Wildlife Refuge at dusk and onto the Line Dennis rice farm located just across the Four Mile Road. As was the course of history of the area, if the officers saw such a mass of birds arriving in the rice fields, so did the outlaws. So here you had a mess of officers staked out in the fields quietly sitting on the ducks and as it turned out, a mess of duck draggers, unawares of the officers' presence, sneaking those same bunches of birds to pull a drag. Well, the drag was pulled off like clockwork and the duck dragging party was soon happily joined by the wildlife officers. Then, the foot races were on! As the local story goes, one outlaw ran for the area in which I was currently sitting hoping to escape. Sure as a cast-iron frying pan full of fried brook trout makes a meal fit for a king, our running-for-his-life outlaw headed for Four Mile Road in the hopes his pickup driver was close at hand. And if so, would rescue our outlaw's fleeing hind end and the two of them would drive off, frustrating the pursuing, hot-on-the-outlaw's-heels game wardens who would be on foot.

Sure as God loves fools, little children and game wardens, our fleeing outlaw upon reaching Four Mile Road just ahead of his federal pursuers, observed his pickup driver coming down the darkened road running without using his headlights. Remember what I said to all of you readers earlier. Running without headlights in the dark was a common trick by the duck draggers and fish and game wardens in the days of old. Hell, the good officers of today still run without using their headlights when trying to be sneaky! Anyway, back to the story. Our fleeing duck dragger raced for his pickup vehicle, stopped it, jerked open the driver's side door, pushed over its driver and said, "Let's get the hell out of here. There were game wardens all over that field watching that same bunch of ducks we just blew up and now, they are hot on all of our trails!"

That was when Fish and Game Warden Bud Reynolds (may God rest his soul), reached over the front seat from his position in the back seat and handcuffed our duck dragger to the state's patrol car's steering wheel! That move was followed by the words, "By God you are right, Partner. That whole field and this car are clear full of game wardens!" Whereupon, the first of several of those duck draggers that day that had blown up the ducks in the same field years earlier upon which I now sat, was captured. With a grin on my face over my recent three just-as-easy captures and a little bit of humorous history from days past under my belt, I started up my truck with a another laugh on my lips and a grin in my heart.

"ZORK" KILLERS

Since my day had started off in such a fine fettle, I figured I would continue my travels because the duck-shooting moment was so young. Knowing the cat was soon to be out of the bag, I picked up my kilts and moved on. I was sure once my three recently-captured outlaws got anywhere near a phone, they would be calling all their other poaching buddies with the news of my location and much hated presence. Since my outlaws were now more than likely in the full Paul Revere mode, I got on my iron horse and got the hell out of Dodge so I could keep my whereabouts a mystery. Heading over to the adjacent Delevan National Wildlife Refuge, I pulled into the state-run, waterfowl-shooting area's headquarters. Sensing blood in the water with all the eager hunters jammed into the small parking lot for the morning's duck hunt, I advised the lads running the public shooting area that I would be working off the parking lot No. 2 area that morning. That way they wouldn't drive by in a marked vehicle and screw me up as I watched my sports in a covert capacity. They were happy for the extra law enforcement help, so Dog and I split. Parking my unmarked county patrol truck in the parking lot like everyone else, Dog and I headed out into the shooting area on foot with shotgun in hand. The shotgun I carried, a double-barreled ten- gauge, to look the part of another eager duck hunter, was empty so that I could not be accused of hunting on government time and money by anyone I apprehended. And any chap being pissed off by his apprehension would be looking at me, the arresting officer, for any reportable flaw in my performance or character.

By now, the shooting area was swarming with all kinds of bright-eyed and bushy-tailed waterfowl hunters. It was still pretty dark, so I was able to walk freely in the excited crowd as they ventured out on foot into the different marshy shooting areas. Taking my time, I moved into an area where I knew all the migratory non-game birds that could not lawfully be taken, or "zorks" as I called them, would use as an early morning flight-crossing to get away from the sporting crowd once the shooting disturbance had busted them off their roosts. Once central to my anointed location, I lurked in some tall reeds like a mongoose. Well, a big but rather handsome mongoose. Soon legal shooting time was just about upon us when, sure as good homemade chicken gravy is so thick that a fork will stand upright in it, here came a stream of zorks freshly spooked off their roosts. In short, they were getting the hell out of the way and off the shooting area from all the marsh-invading noisy crowds of hopeful sportsmen.

Broork! went the alarm call of an American egret as it passed over three nearby sports. *Boom! Boom! Boom!* went all three sports shotguns blowing the poor zork clean to kingdom come! Sadly, it looked like someone had just shaken out a feather pillow when the magnificent bird took three loads of No. 4 shot at such a close range! Damn, Boys. It sure helps to know your birds and what the dickens you are shooting at, I thought, as the big mongoose quickly slipped from his hiding place to put the grab on the three zork-shooting rubes before they blew the hell out of the rest of the fleeing protected non-game birds streaming out of the area. As I slid over to my chaps, one of my rubes had just waded out into the marsh and retrieved their kill. As he returned, he said, "What the hell kind of goose is this, Angelo?"

Stepping over to my now bunched up lads, I said, "Maybe I can help you guys." With that, I took the shot-all-to-hell bird from my shooters and held it high for all to see. I did that just to see what kind of reactions and attitudes my lads would exhibit when they realized the error of their sporting ways.

"Damn, Gino. That is one skinny snow goose. Look at them long legs and that stabber for a bill," said a short, dumpy looking lad who looked like he had just emerged from a ragbag.

Then it got as quiet as drifting cottonwood fluff in late summer over a beaver pond in the high Sierras, as the men realized maybe what they had just shot probably wasn't such a fine-eating snow goose after all. "Maybe we better bury that one," said Angelo, "He may just be illegal to shoot. He don't look like he has much in the way of eats on his carcass anyhow," he continued.

"We can maybe make him into spaghetti sauce," hopefully said a man named Pauli.

By now, except for what had just happened to the zork, I was almost in hysterics. Here were the "Three Stooges" incarnate. In short, these three guys didn't belong in the wild hunting ducks. They didn't know a duck from a house mouse. Then Pauli said, "Maybe we ought to toss that bird into the tules. Just like Angelo said, it might not be legal. Do you know what kind of bird that is, Mister?" he asked, turning my way hoping I had a happy response to his question.

"Yes, I do. It is an American egret and is illegal to kill," I said.

"Then we best breast it out, ditch the carcass and hide the meat," said Pauli, as he reached for the bloodied bird's carcass in an attempt to remove it from my hands.

By now, the refuge shooting area was a mass of shooting, madly fleeing waterfowl, and anything else possessing wings along with a drop of survival common sense. As it continued getting lighter, I let my three rubes down gently and took the time to give them some lessons in overflying bird identification. Then all three of my chaps received citations for taking a protected migratory non-game bird, To Wit, one American egret. Since they all had shot at the bird, that little mistake cost each of them $150 in the Williams Justice Court. Pretty expensive eats, I might say. I know Italians are known as great cooks but to cook an American egret would be one hell of a challenge. They had better use a lot of garlic and butter if they ever choose to cook and eat such an evil-tasting critter. But, as a point of fact in the above matter, the coon-asses in Louisiana kill and eat the damn things every chance they get. So, I guess American egrets can't eat that badly with the right cook close at hand. 'Course, Cajuns are some of the finest cooks on the planet. Having worked in that neck of the woods in my later law enforcement years, I would say the Cajuns could make the sole of a rubber boot good to eat... Looking back on that apprehension of my three Italians and the unfortunate zork, I guess that could be counted as a lucky catch as well. Being right alongside my three illegal shooters sure made it an easy catch anyway.

After the above mess, Dog and I moved deeper into the center of the public shooting area and took up a position where we could watch all my close-at-hand sports in a 360-degree area. For the next hour, I saw lots of ducks and geese falling to the sporting guns. It was then I noticed another pair of zorks, or long-billed curlews this time, slowly winging my way flying low over the marsh. Keeping an eye on my totally protected, low-flying migratory non-game birds, I happily watched them as they headed for the southern reaches of the refuge boundary and away from the danger of the deadly public shooting area. They had almost made it off the shooting area and to safety when I saw a heretofore-unseen lad stand up from a dense mess of reeds and shoot twice. Both protected birds folded like a house of cards in a puff of feathers and dropped like stones into the water. Soon my shooter was en route to the two dead birds and so was the local game warden. By the time I got there, after plowing through knee-deep mud and water holding ten thousand years of goose crap and tule roots, about ten minutes time had elapsed. The mud was deep and I was plain physically worn out from being deep into the 107-day long California duck and goose season, so it took me longer to get to my zork shooter than I anticipated. When I finally did arrive, I was confronted by a stocky Eastern European swarthy-looking chap with the two recently shot birds hanging proudly by their necks from the belt holding up his pants.

"What you got there, Partner?" I asked, already knowing what he had.

"A couple long-billed stabbers," he happily reported.

Showing him my badge and credentials, I said, "Lad, I am sorry to tell you this but you have a couple of long-billed curlews."

"Yeah, like I said. A couple of long-billed stabbers," he replied once again before I could further identify his problem to him. "Back in Hungary, these are considered the best eating birds going."

"Well, that may be, but here in America these birds are totally protected," I said.

"But why? They are really good eating," he continued insistently.

Then I took a good look at the two birds. Both of them had their throats cut from stem to stern! "What happened to the necks of these birds?" I asked in dumbfounded amazement.

"I cut their throats. If you don't, they will stick you with their stabbers," he said with finality and a little bit of disgust in his voice because I obviously, being a wildlife officer, didn't realize just how deadly these birds could be with their stabbers...

"They can't hurt you," I said in surprise.

"Are you sure? Because back in Hungary, they tell you to cut their throats quickly or they will stab you," he continued.

"Well, as I said earlier, here in America they are protected. It is against state and federal laws to kill them," I flatly stated.

"Well, that is the problem with your laws here in America. Those birds are good eating, should be killed and I plan on cooking them up," my shooter now argued in a more than determined fashion. After another lesson in bird identification, I got down to the business at hand. My Hungarian fellow wasn't too happy at being cited for killing such deadly stabbing birds, but he finally accepted what I had to say and took his citation.

However, getting that citation adjudicated later took some doing. The man went to the Hungarian Consulate and raised hell over being cited for killing "two good eating birds." The Consulate in turn raised hell with the Williams Justice Court. Having enough of the shooter's political tomfoolery, I contacted Jack Downs. Jack Downs, the U.S. Fish and Wildlife Service's Agent in Charge in Sacramento, who advised the Consulate to have their man pay up or he was going to have the citation removed from the state court system and transferred to the federal court system for adjudication and, possibly from there, the shooter would find himself going to jail upon conviction for his violation of the Migratory Bird Treaty Act. The $150 fine money was soon forthcoming without any further whimpering on the part of the Consulate.

Once again, I would consider that case a lucky catch as well. Just imagine, how many times does an officer of the law get to be so lucky in watching a pair of zorks hastily leaving an area and almost escape the danger, only to get illegally smoked at the last second in front of his eyes by someone who needed a good smoking as well?

Those two zorks now rest in the Fish and Wildlife Service's water bird teaching collection in Glynco, Georgia, at the Special Agent Basic Training Academy. There, the new agents not only learn to identify such birds and those critters possessing such dangerous stabbers but, as of 2013, they also learn their life histories from Special Agents and outstanding waterfowl instructors Rich Grosz and Patrick Bosco. Two seasoned waterfowl instructors who are soon to have a book jointly published on the facets of waterfowl identification for public use—an area of game bird identification that is badly needed by the run-of-the-mill waterfowl sportsmen and the youngsters entering the sport. And the really neat thing about that waterfowl identification booklet is that it is so durably constructed, the sportsmen can carry it with them to aid them in waterfowl identification right in the field. How cool is that?

WOOD DUCKS

Having enough of what was fast becoming a typical game warden's stew on the western side of my patrol district, I left the refuge and headed for the eastern side of my district to see what kind of devilment I could stir up. No pun was intended when talking about creating a game warden's stew when it came to making a variety of cases in such a short period of time. And from the initial looks of things, I was on a roll and had a feeling that my day of goofy wildlife oriented cases was just beginning. Turning down Laux Road somewhat later, I soon found myself heading for Davison's Duck Club. Warren Davison, the owner, and I were good friends. Having had such a good morning in the case apprehension department, I figured I would stop by and visit with my friend and his wife. Well, as usual in the world of wildlife law enforcement, the Gods stepped in and I figured wrong!

Passing an ancient oak tree infested swampy area on the northern end of the Butte Creek Farms Duck Club, I heard two quick swampy sounding shots coming from the flooded area as the characteristic deep booming sounds of a shotgun resonated over the water. As a matter of course, good weather or bad, I always drove with my truck windows down so I could hear any unexpected shooting going on around me. Plus, it made it easier to pinpoint any near at hand and unexpected shooting. From the sounds of the flooded, timbered swamp shooting I had just heard, it sounded to me like there was only one shooter and that chap who was not too far away.

Knowing the water in the flooded oak timber was waist deep, I stopped and hurriedly changed from my usual winter footwear of hip boots into my chest high waders. Leaving Dog to guard my truck, I headed out across a small freshly harvested milo field. Moments later, I was at the edge of the flooded timber from where I had heard the earlier shooting. I stood quietly for a few minutes just listening and looking because I knew this area was home to many wood ducks, one of North America's most beautifully plumaged birds. But, they also carried a daily bag limit of only one in those days because of their low population numbers. That species of waterfowl was almost shot to the brink of extinction in the early 1900s because of their demand as mounted display taxidermy specimens brought on by their unique and beautiful plumage. Only recently after their population numbers had biologically recovered, had the wood duck once again been placed in the bag limit as a sporting game bird. And for someone who didn't know their duck identification very well, which included many, many duck hunters of yesteryear and today, the possibility of an over limit always existed when one was hunting in a wood duck concentration or roosting site into which I was now heading.

Within moments, I could hear the very distinctive sounds of wood ducks calling as they either swam or flew my way. Their beautiful plaintive calls preceded them and, from the stressed sounds of their vocalizations, something was worrying to those little guys. That was soon followed by another loud booming sound a shotgun makes firing over a densely wooded and flooded area. With that, the dozen or so little wood ducks swimming in my direction rose into the air in terror. *Boom! Booom!* went the shotgun twice more as I hurriedly tried to locate the exact position of my shooter in among the numerous flooded oak trees. Moving deeper into the area, I tried moving slowly to reduce my preceding ripples in the water which would give my presence away to my now nearby mystery shooter. I also kept oak trees between my shooter's approximate location and myself because he did not, as of yet, know I was there. And as such, the trees kept me from gathering a faceful of unintentional lead shot which always made for a delightfully moving and memorable experience...

Moving as quietly as I could, I was soon deep into the flooded oak swamp. Throughout the branches above my head flitted dozens of wood ducks, and swimming nearby were several more. If I hadn't been on the hunt, I would have enjoyed the wild wood duck moment of that day. I had discovered this little cherry patch of prime wood duck roost habitat some years back as a game warden but I had told no one of its existence. It was the only wood duck roosting site I was aware of in my district and I damn sure didn't want anyone else to know about it and quickly shoot out the area of that uniquely beautiful species of waterfowl. Now I had someone who had found my little wood duck roosting area and my guardian angels were telling me a strike was near at hand.

Then around a huge oak tree, about ten feet in diameter, came a smallish, longhaired man, which to me was the perfect picture of a poacher par excellence. He was a ragged-looking little man vastly in need of a few meals and, from initial outward appearances, a shower or two as well. His ragged flannel shirt hung on his sparse frame like the had-seen-better-days rag it was, and covering his head was a beat up old felt hat appearing to be of at least Civil War vintage. As for his shotgun, a pump action Winchester Model 97, it was nothing short of being an antique even in that current day and age. One, which I never would have shot for safety reasons because of its age and problematic dangerous hammer, set up. To you unwashed, the gun possessed a small hammer spur, which was prone to accidental discharge. Especially when in full cock and about to be let back down due to its small size and the possibility of slipping from one's thumb when possessing cold or wet hands! Holding my hidden position, I let my slowly moving, wood duck shooting lad continue his approach. He then shot two of the beautiful male wood ducks out of their roost high up in an oak tree not twenty yards from my position. It was then I discovered that he had about a handful more of the beautiful little birds dragging in the water from a duck strap hanging loosely on his sparse frame. Slowly, my poacher kept coming towards my oak tree in order to retrieve the two latest birds he had just shot out from their roost tree. And just like Grosz's Rule states, if one is not looking for you, they will not see you. My chap was looking skyward into the tree branches for more wood ducks to roost shoot when I stepped out from behind my tree. He was so engrossed in the killing that he never even saw me until he heard me softly splashing water as I slowly moved in his direction.

My startled poacher turned quickly upon hearing me slipping out from behind the tree next to where he stood. Then as if by blind instinct, he swung the barrel of his shotgun my way! However, by then that move was too late. I was on him and had the business end of his shotgun's rather large bore barrel in my hand pointing it away from my rather ample and somewhat beautiful carcass. I had been shot three times before with a shotgun by a poacher in 1967 and didn't cotton to being in the line of fire ever again. Hence my quick defensive action when it came to controlling the end of the barrel of his shotgun.

"What the hell! Who the hell are you?" he shouted.

"State fish and game warden," I said in a clearly understood tone of voice. That, plus I was in full uniform that day. "Let go of your shotgun," I commanded. It was a moment or two before that command registered and he finally complied. No two ways about it, my chap was a little on the goofy side and now thoroughly battle rattled by my surprise entry into his heretofore quiet wood-duck-killing world.

Now in command of the situation, I pointed to the badge on my uniform shirt to show the man once again so there would be no unauthorized and goofy actions on his part, if you get my drift. He just nodded after intensely looking it over carefully through a set of rather squinty eyes like maybe his ownership of a set of eyeglasses might have been helpful.

"You have permission to hunt on this private property?" I asked.

"I wasn't aware you couldn't hunt here," he fired right back as his composure quickly returned, as did the challenging look in his eyes.

"I take that answer as a 'no,'" I replied.

"I am not sure where to hell I really am," he finally blurted out. "I parked my boat over yonder in that there slough and just walked over here when I saw a flock of them wood ducks fly into these trees. I figured this was a roost site jest like they have back in Arkansas, so I came after them good acorn-eating little devils."

"Well, you are trespassing and hunting on the Butte Creek Farms Duck Club lands," I said.

"Well, like I said, I didn't really know where I was. I just parked my boat and took off walking after them ducks. Them little guys is damn good eatin'," he continued, as if that good eating thing would counter my earlier trespassing question.

"I need to see a hunting license and a driver's license," I said, as I shucked the shells from his Winchester shotgun into my hand. As expected, it was unplugged. Over my many years of checking sportsmen using Winchester Model 97s, I have found a large number of them to be unplugged. They are always a good bet to check for not being plugged, for all you budding conservation officer law dogs out there reading these lines. Then he handed me his hunting license. Again as expected, he did not possess a federal duck stamp as was required by law. No State of California duck stamp was required in those days. Checking his license more closely, I discovered he was another of the infamous unwashed from the town of Olivehurst, California. Taking a look at his ducks, I saw that he had taken seven of the little wood ducks, or six over the limit! Like I had thought earlier when I viewed my chap for the first time, he just looked like what I had pictured in my mind as to what an old time, dyed in the wool, backwoods poacher would resemble.

Letting him go for the trespassing violation, I wrote up my chap for no federal duck stamp in possession, using an unplugged shotgun to take migratory waterfowl, and an over limit of wood ducks, To Wit, six over the limit. All his birds were seized because they had been taken illegally with the use and aid of an unplugged shotgun, much to my little fellow's chagrin. My chap later forfeited bail in federal court to the tune of $350. Where he got that amount of fine money, which in those days was like a month's wages, I had no idea, but he paid up just like a penny slot machine.

Several weeks later, I was reading U.S. Game Management Agent Hugh Worchester's classic California waterfowl outlaws book from the days long past, Hunting the Lawless, A book that is now considered a rare book. In it, I ran across the name of my wood duck poacher who had been apprehended by Hugh for dragging ducks in the Sacramento Valley's rice fields in the early 1950s! As an aside, before I left the Sacramento Valley in 1974 to accept a new position in North Dakota as a Senior Resident Agent for the U.S. Fish and Wildlife Service, I had apprehended nine of the same subjects caught by Hugh years earlier during his storied federal career who had been mentioned in his book. It just goes to show that the illegal killing of wildlife for many people is simply genetics. Once in their blood, it is like a disease and the only way to placate it is through unmitigated killing until that urge is satiated.

Come to think of it, I never did have or make the time to visit with my friends, the Davisons, on their duck club that fine day. There was just too much work that needed to be done due to the inclement weather, the sky being full of waterfowl and hunters under every leaf. Sadly, that was the last time I could have seen my dear friend, Warren, alive. He died shortly thereafter. You know, folks, you will never know when that bend in the river will come into your life. You had better enjoy the fishing while you have the chance...

THE JUDGE AND CLOSED SEASON
PHEASANTS

Since it was now past lunchtime, I kept heading north and east toward the old California Duck Club. That was one duck club that always gave me fits because of its members and their lawlessness when it came to the sport of hunting. In short, it gave me a bad case of the vapors first as a State fish and game warden and, later as a U.S. Game Management Agent. So in order to cause the most gas possible to its not so God-fearing, non-law-abiding members, I always paid them visits when in country. I did so in the hope of seeing my beautiful face all the time, many of my shooters would square their sails and do things legally. Like I said earlier, that particular winter shoot day had already proven it was a good one for the duck hunters. With the north winds and rains, along with the Butte Sink nearby and its hundreds of thousands of resting waterfowl, the folks on the eastern side of my patrol district were having the waterfowl shoot of a lifetime, particularly in the Northern pintail killing department. In fact, by the time I entered the club that morning, many of its members had either already limited out and gone home or were at the clubhouse relaxing or watching the football games on TV. Realizing I would do no good with the field shooters since they were mostly finished for the day, I headed for their clubhouse proper. Sailing in on the road to the duck club, I passed their gamekeeper parked and talking with several of his members. Since he was also less than honorable and a pain in the backside, I kept going even though he tried to hail me down. Realizing the only reason he tried to hail me down was to stop me in plain view of the club and give his members a heads up the law was in town, I didn't fall for that old trick. If I had, some of his less than sterling members would see the roadside action, and in so doing, suspect I was en route to their club, and if they hurried, they could make right the many wrongs that always seemed to accompany that club when it came to the excess numbers of ducks and geese in their members' possession.

So being game warden polite, I waved like the goofball I was as I passed the madly gesturing for me to stop gamekeeper and kept going. Soon I could see his pickup just a-flying down the road behind me in my rearview mirror. That was all right, though, because I now had the lead and would be in and among his remaining club members before they could spit. Moments later, I was at the clubhouse. Hurriedly exiting my vehicle, I walked over to where many of the lads hung their gutted birds to cool out in their duck club's screened in hanging facility. Right off the bat, I could see that many of the freshly killed ducks had not been tagged as required by federal law when stored in a temporary abode.

To those of you who do not know about what I am saying, it is simple. When federal waterfowl hunting regulations first came out, one had to keep in their immediate possession and transport their own, freshly killed migratory waterfowl. However, that imposed a hardship on the sporting public. So the feds changed that specific regulation, allowing the birds to be tagged with the taker's printed name, signed name, place where taken, date taken, and species taken. Ancillary to those regulations were others, which allowed for temporary storage at other than the hunter's personal abode, like a duck club hanging facility. In short, if you stored your birds anywhere other than at your personal dwelling, they had to be tagged as described above. That is name, rank and serial number, if you get my drift. Those new regulations also allowed hunters to transport other people's birds just as long as the tagging criteria were met. However, as in any regulation, there was room for those with a dark soul to illegally rattle around within. In the case of the tagged-birds regulations, many times outlaw shooters would use them to their benefit. That is, shoot a limit, tag the birds, then go back out and take another limit that same day. Those walking on the dark side would then bring in their second limit that was illegal, and forge or doctor someone else's name on the tags like they had been there earlier in the day and had personally taken those birds. That way, everything would look legal on the surface and aboveboard. Then when the double-bagging outlaw went home, he would take both bunches of birds like they were all legally taken. Many sports felt that since they had paid $20,000 to join a particular duck club, they wanted $20,000 worth of ducks. Hence, the illegal use of the tagging system to enable the shooter to feel like they were getting back their investment and at the same time, cutting a fat hog in the ass. If ever stopped while in transit with the illegally tagged birds, many a crafty outlaw had already taken the time to call ahead to his crooked buddy, whose name he had illegally used in the tagging process, and alerted him as to the phony transport action. At that point, it was almost impossible to catch the outlaw. Almost... But I won't put to print how the officer could break that criminal code and sever the illegal transport chain for obvious reasons. Therefore, anytime I examined tagged birds, I was always looking for those sports trying to pull the wool over the local game warden's eyes. And as I have stated many times in my other books, it is not nice to illegally mess with Mother Nature or her minions for that matter.

Knowing the bird hunting had been excellent that day, I swung into action. Moving quickly among the numerous bunches of tagged ducks in the hanging facility, I began checking the tags on the birds as the game keeper drove up and hastily ran into the clubhouse to warn the members that I was on the duck club grounds. My plan was to catch the lazy outlaws who had brought in extra birds and, instead of promptly tagging or hiding them, had gone into the club for a drink and a little bragging time. Within moments of my arrival, I began finding extra birds that had been freshly killed and placed in out of the way places. Or other bunches of birds wearing funny tags that spoke to ducks or geese being taken the next day, a signature that looked phony as a nine dollar bill, a hastily scribbled illegible tag, one with lots of blood covering all the needed data to throw the game warden off his feed, or the like.

Shortly thereafter, I was snagging illegal limits of birds left and right because I had caught some of the more crooked members and the gamekeeper flatfooted before they could scam the system. Throwing three suspicious limits of drake Northern pintail into the front seat of my truck, I told Dog to watch 'em. Then hustling back into the hanging facility combat zone, I saw a heavy set man grabbing a bunch of birds from another hanging facility by his bunkhouse and take off running like the roadrunner does when a coyote is hot on his trail. Well, you readers know what it is like if prey runs from a predator. That is nothing more than an invite for pursuit. Off I went just a-flying after my suspect. Well, sort of slow flying but the black smoke was soon pouring from my smokestack like an old time locomotive pulling a steep grade while towing a heavy load. Rounding the corner of the bunkhouse hot on the trail of my runner, I saw my portly chap open up the lid to a wood box and throw his illegal stringer of ducks inside. However, he was not fast enough and I caught him in the act. Striding up to the wood box, I flung open the top in his presence. Remember all my San Francisco types, not an illegal search under the Fourth Amendment to our Constitution because I had seen my runner chuck the ducks inside. No warrant was required if the officer observed the illegality. Therein laid the stringer of ducks just thrown and another limit of ducks laying underneath! That second limit had been previously hidden there by another club member as a precaution against the chance arrival of the nosey game warden. Hot dog! My game warden stew was thickening up like a great New England clam chowder as my variety of oddball case-making continued.

Grabbing up the stringer just thrown by my portly chap, I noticed a lot of oddball brown and red coloring in his stringer. What the hell? I thought, as I whirled that stringer of ducks around for a closer look. Well, well, well, what would two hen and two rooster pheasants be doing on the man's stringer of ducks? Especially when pheasant season was not yet open, and the killing of hen pheasants was never allowed, I wondered with a huge knowing grin.

"Those aren't mine," said the portly, duck-tossing one.

"Well, I beg to differ with you. Since I saw you running with and then throwing this mess of birds into the wood bin, I would say you were in possession of said stringer of ducks and what appears to also be closed season pheasants!"

Motioning for the portly one to follow me, I grabbed up the two stringers of birds, which I had just discovered and pulled from the wood box. By now, the gamekeeper who had just arrived at the backside of the clubhouse to where I was creating hate and discontent, was fit to be tied. Especially when the portly duck club member told him as he accompanied me to my patrol truck, "If you can't keep this bastard away from here or at least give us some early warning of his presence, you can be replaced you know." Boy, those stinging words from my portly one sure set the hair on my gamekeeper's last part over the fence. So much so, that all he could do was sputter out excuses as to why I had slipped through his member-protective net

Back at my truck, I also tried to sort out the three stringers of ducks previously seized since my arrival. Since all had names on the tags that I couldn't cold track back to a present club member or a guest and no one admitted to that boo-boo, I got out the citation book. In short, I just fired up a citation issued to the club since no one was forthcoming on that illegal duck tagging mystery. By doing it that way, I had a valid citation and figured I would just contact the federal magistrate and see if I could get the bail upped to address this never-ending problem on that particular duck club. For my readers' sake, under the Migratory Bird Treaty Act (M.B.T.A.), a federal citation could be issued to a club because a club was described in associated M.B.T.A. regulation language as a "person" or the same as the one pulling the trigger. And since I was also a cross-credentialed Deputy U. S. Game Management Agent, I was legally allowed to file my cases in federal court and, as a result, "Katy, bar the door."

However, for my portly one, I had him stone cold by the stacking swivel. "I need to see your hunting license and driver's license," I said.

Digging around in his wallet, he finally proffered the needed paperwork. Looking down at the man's last name,

I thought, Terry, this name is sure familiar. But from where? Then it dawned on me. Several times I had worked the abalone tides along several north coast counties of California while on special covert assignments during the storied "ab tides." In each circumstance, I was assisting the local fish and game wardens that were already known to many of the local poachers, hence my working there in an undercover capacity. This was part of the state's officer exchange program to other fish and game squads needing extra assistance during a specific area's high recreational-use times. In that particular case, I was assisting during very low-tide cycles when abalone were the most exposed and accessible to the taking of over limits. The portly man standing before me was none other than one of the local north coast judges whose court my abalone citations were therein adjudicated! That is, since I was not a local officer, my citations were filed through the local game warden into that judge's court. Oh no, I thought! Any future ah cases I make up on The Sea Ranch in Sonoma County will now go into the toilet if this judge puts two and two together and discovers I am his duck and pheasant-citing officer. Well, I have been in hotter water than this in the past, so, so be it, I thought with a grimace as I continued the administrative work associated with the cases. After all, the laws of the land are supposed to apply to everyone. That is except to a number of those associated with the Obama administration...

Finished, I provided the judge the information that I would transfer the untagged bird matter to the federal authorities in Sacramento. I also advised he would be notified forthwith as to the bail and any future court dates in that jurisdiction. Then I whipped out my state citation book and wrote him a citation for possession of closed season pheasants. Man, you talk about a hopping mad judge!

The last time I saw that man, he was eating the gamekeeper's last part over the fence clear off for not keeping me at bay so he and his fellow club member wildlife outlaws would have time to hide their illegal bounty. And man, let me tell you, it was a hind-end chewing to end all hind-end chewings to say the least.

That judge ultimately forfeited $50 in federal court for the untagged ducks and another $375 in state court for being in possession of the closed season pheasants. Plus, he lost his birds, which were later donated to a hardworking poor Mexican farm hand that had seven children.

From then on in that judge's jurisdiction, whenever I assisted the state game wardens on abalone patrols as a state officer or later on as a federal officer, I just handed my citations over to Elvin Gunderson, a great and hardworking local warden. That way he would file them under his name and the abalone cheats would have their pound of flesh extracted for raping that poor California mollusk resource, a resource that many California "sports" raped with aplomb in that day and age.

As these words are being written in 2012, the abalone resource in California, due to its overharvest both legally and illegally and in part due to the increasing, highly protected and expanding sea otter population whose favored food item is abalone, is in serious trouble. However, a major reason for its demise is its commercial value in the market place as an outstanding food item.

My wife and I have a couple of dear married friends, Ernie and Lynn Eaton in northern California, who put on an abalone dinner that would knock out your eyes at twenty feet it is so good every time we come to visit. In order to do so though, he orders his abalone from a legal commercial abalone farm. When he does, he pays $100 per pound for that abalone steak! With such prices and California's population growth and diversity, it is easy to see which way the abalone resource in California, despite the best efforts of its hard working and out gunned game wardens, is ultimately heading. Like many other critters, I am glad I had the opportunity to see and protect the abalone resource when it was in its heyday. I am also saddened that my efforts were not great enough to prevent its slide towards its population downturn and possible destruction.

A CAR MAKES A GOOD BLIND

By now, my bottom was dragging. What had started out as a nice day was quickly turning into a game warden's stew of oddball events. Especially, as far as when it came to making a weird mixture of unique wildlife related cases. I had loaded gun violations, the illegal taking of protected migratory non-game birds, wood duck over limits, waterfowl tagging violations, and now the possession of closed season pheasants by one who supposedly upheld the law, namely a judge! Hell, my day was just getting underway and my game warden's stew of oddball case variety was starting out in fine style! All I needed now were a couple of chopped onions, some celery, fresh garlic, carrots, chopped beefsteak tomatoes, and I would have a real game warden's stew. As I was soon to discover, it was only going to get better and better as that crazy, wet, windy, wintery day and a goofy game warden lumbered on in the world of wildlife law enforcement field of battle.

Leaving the old California Duck Club and a mad gamekeeper with most of his hind end eaten clear off by some of his recently ticketed members, I headed north for Putnam Road. I had no more than hit Putnam Road when I noticed a huge tornado of lesser snow geese funneling down into one of local rice farmer's, Terrill Sartain, harvested rice fields. There must have been twenty thousand geese blanketing the ground in white already, and another ten thousand noisily circling around in the air looking for a place to land and join the party as they are wont to do. As for the noise with all the excited calling that many geese can generate, it was unbelievable and wonderful to my ears all at the same time! To all you unwashed readers out there, there is nothing quite like Mother Nature all decked out in her splendor and finery when she rears up and lets herself go. How I lived for such moments like that in the world of wildlife! Knowing it was just a matter of time before someone got into that mess of birds and did something really stupid, I parked where I could watch the scene and yet not be readily observed by anyone casually passing by.

Digging out two non-chocolate type Payday Candy Bars, I shared one with my dog Shadow. She was great. Eating that Payday Candy Bar, she slobbered all over my front seat as she intently looked out the passenger side of the truck's open window watching all the snow geese. But, the presence of all those geese in no way slowed her down from worrying her favorite, peanut covered candy bar. Fact be known, all I had to do was say, "Get the duck," and she would have been out the window into that field of geese, candy bar and all, looking for a critter to bring back to me.

Lord, I still miss that dog to this day. Especially being able to wrap my arms around her massive neck and giving her a big hug. Gosh, how writing these words hurts inside and brings tears to my eyes as I put the ink to print. To all my dog-loving readers out there, you know of what I speak when it comes to having such a fine animal as a friend and longtime constant companion. And then, when it is time, losing that animal to the ages, especially one that had saved my life early on in our relationship! But you readers will have to read that hair raising story in one of my earlier books titled, The Thin Green Line, in the chapter titled, "Dogs." That story will give all you readers out there a pretty good idea of the odds most game wardens on a nationwide basis face daily. Bad things can happen in the blink of an eye in the world of wildlife law enforcement and unless one has two guardian angels faithfully working as his partners, he will soon join them...

Down Putnam Road came a sedan driving slowly from the north. No big deal. Many people would stop or slow down to watch such a spectacle of so many noisy lesser snow geese doing what they liked doing best, namely eating and visiting. That slow moving sedan passed below me and was soon out of sight. Ten minutes later that same vehicle came back, only this time driving north. Still no big deal. They were probably returning from or visiting one of the many duck clubs in the area. Then it drove out of sight as it headed towards the Colusa to Gridley Highway further to the north. Forty minutes later, that same sedan drove south on Putnam Road once again! That time, I went into full alert. From where I sat with my binoculars, I could see one driver and two passengers. But what caught my eye as the car slowly drove south by my field of geese was that both passengers were sitting inside the car in the front and back seats facing the huge goose spectacle with their windows rolled down!

Crawling into my binoculars for a closer look, I really began eyeballing my suspect vehicle. Then sure as my thick, homemade chicken gravy is the world's best, shotgun barrels exploded out from the front and rear passenger window openings of the vehicle! Six shots quickly boomed out across the noisy goose field, raining down lethal lead shot on those nearby geese feeding closest to the road. For a microsecond, all the geese went instantly quiet. Then with a thunderous roar, the entire flock went airborne rising up out of harm's way. In the meantime, all three of my chaps from the sedan threw open their car's doors. All three men ran into the field quickly picking up dead and dying flopping snow geese by their necks. Chasing down the cripples, the men would grab the birds by their necks and, with a vicious twist, wring the birds' necks breaking them in the process. Then running back to their car, they would toss the dead geese into the back seat and then hurriedly return to the field for more just as fast as their legs would carry them.

That is when I stopped looking and sauntered out from my hiding place. Well, not really did I saunter forth. One does not do much sauntering forth with a ⅞-ton GMC pickup with the biggest cubic inch engine money could buy back in those days, herded along after a bunch of idiot stick bad guys by a fellow with a leaden foot, if you readers get my drift. Up Putnam Road I snaked in my truck. Steaming up to the front of the suspects' car, I flipped on my siren for its effect. The air, heretofore still filled with noisy, milling snow geese overhead, went totally silent for a second. Then the goose noises started up again as many retreated overhead for the safety of the nearby Butte Sink. However, there was no safety for my three chaps still picking up snow geese in Terrill's rice field. They were hurriedly picking up the spoils of their little illegal shoot until the siren let everyone, including God, know that I was there. Stepping out from the truck, I let Shadow loose so she could round up the many cripples moving away from the kill zone before they escaped off into the tall grasses surrounding the rice field. Then I began walking across the rice field picking up dead and crippled geese as I went. By now, my lads looked like they were in worse shape than the geese they were carrying. It was obvious their beautifully planned snow goose shoot had just turned into that brown liquid smelly stuff one usually finds on his shoes after walking in a public park full of dogs led around by their untrained owners.

My lads just stood there in the field with their hands full of dead geese and now long and getting longer faces. Walking over to them, I said, "State fish and game warden. Keep picking up the birds, Lads. I don't want the cripples running off and dying a slow death from their wounds or ending up in the mouth of a predator. Only this time, throw all the birds you are picking up into the bed of my patrol truck. And take those out of your car while you're at it and do the same with them as well. And when removing the birds from the back seat of your car, make sure you don't leave any. Because I will check out your car before I leave to make sure no illegally taken snow geese remain in your possession."

About then I saw a pickup roaring down from the north on Putnam Road toward my location. The truck skidded to a stop by our two rigs and out jumped a very mad farmer and landowner named Terrill Sartain. In fact, he was so mad over the trespassers who had just moments earlier shot into the field of geese that he didn't even recognize me in the heat and emotion of the moment.

"You son of a bitches! Get your asses over here before I start shooting," he yelled. And he could back up his threat if the Browning 12-gauge, semi-automatic shotgun in his hands and his mad-as-hell flushed face meant anything to the casual observer!

"Terrill, I have these lads. You can put that shotgun down," I cautioned, as I took another crippled goose from Shadow's mouth and wrung its neck.

With my words and the recognition that followed, Terrill snapped out of his anger, settled down somewhat, and then walked over to where I was standing. In so doing, I could tell he was still really pissed off if his red-flushed face was any kind of a read. "By God, Terry, I am damned glad you are here. Otherwise, I would have shot these bastards. I was saving these geese for a shoot tomorrow with my friends, Roy Rogers, Dale Evans, and Andy Devine. Now those bastards have frightened the hell out of the geese and ruined my planned hunt. And, damn it, there is no way I can contact my friends to tell them to stay home now that the geese are gone. They are in a private airplane coming here, even as we speak, and I don't know how to reach them and tell them to turn back around and go home because the goose shoot is ruined!"

"Don't sweat that, Terrill. I think that if we finish picking up the rest of the dead and dying geese and then quickly leave this field, the geese will return and be available for a shoot tomorrow if you want," I counseled, as I scanned the sky eyeballing the thousands of still hungry geese flying over the area.

There were still numerous hungry stragglers flying overhead so I hustled my lads and the last of the dead and wounded geese out of the area. Taking my lads over to

Terrill's office, I issued the shooters citations for taking migratory game birds from a motor vehicle, possession of loaded shotguns in a motor vehicle on a way open to the public, aiding and abetting for the driver who allowed the shoot to take place by using his car as an unlawful, power-driven blind to get up on the geese, and over limits on my shooters, To Wit, forty- three over the limit of six white geese per person per day, a total of sixty-one geese. A week later, my contrite shooters had collectively forfeited a total of $1,250 for their little lapse in judgment in the Colusa Justice Court.

As I had predicted, later that afternoon the snow geese returned to that same rice field to feed. That time, Terrill had a bunch of his Mexican farm laborers sitting in company pickups alongside the roads surrounding that huge field. The next day as I had predicted, Terrill and his movie star friends had one hell of a lesser snow and white-fronted goose shoot in that same field.

Oh, by the way, Terrill even had his Mexican laborers clean all the geese, which I later donated to their families as authorized by the Colusa County District Attorney's Office—donated under an official arrangement that allowed me to donate such large illegal kills before any court action occurred so the meat wouldn't be wasted or reduced in quality by freezing, just as long as I had witnesses to the event and pictures to back up my claims. As for Shadow, she got to eat an early lunch. She got to eat all the warm goose guts she could hold as the Mexicans cleaned the birds. The Mexicans thought that goose-cleaning detail was the cat's meow. They had a big dog wolfing down a mound, and I do mean a mound knowing Shadow, of the goose guts. Later that day, rain or no rain, Shadow rode in the back of my patrol truck. It always amazed me how a gallon of rich duck or goose guts could fire up a hardworking dog's digestive system, especially second hand, if you get my drift and no pun intended!

FREEZE DRIED

After my get together with Terrill and my shooters had ended, I crossed the Sacramento River on the old Princeton Ferry so I could finish out my day working the north central part of my patrol district. It was during that afternoon, that I ran into one of the many bizarre wildlife cases I was fortunate to make during my state and federal career.

Moving west down Norman Road, I chanced upon a Northern kestrel, which is a species of small hawk. It was sitting on a power line and fluttering like it was having a hard time balancing on the wire. All of a sudden, it dropped off the wire and fell into the weeds below the power line! What the heck? Did that bird just get electrocuted? I thought, as I braked to a stop alongside where it had just fallen into the weeds under the power line.

In those days, I was also a waterfowl identification instructor at various State Fish and Game squad meetings. As such, I was to provide waterfowl identification training to the game wardens prior to the start of waterfowl season in Region II. But I also wanted to expand that teaching program to include bird of prey species identification as well. That I wanted to do since bird of prey identification was also a weak point for many game wardens of the day—so weak, in fact, that every type of aerial predator many of them ran across resulted in them being called a "chicken hawk," even on their citations! Hence the need for me to institute a bird of prey identification training session as well. Stopping to pick up the kestrel that had just fallen off the power line and see if electrocution was a problem for my bird species, I rustled around in the roadside weeds. Also, if I could find him, his carcass would be mounted as a study skin by Ron Cole, my friend who was a curator at the University of California at Davis. From there, the specimen would go into my teaching collection for later use as a study skin by my bird-identification deficient officers.

Rooting around in the weeds, I finally located the little male kestrel and got the surprise of my life. Picking up the dead bird, I discovered a blowgun dart firmly driven deeply into the bird's chest! Standing there holding that little guy in my hands, I was shocked down to the toes in my hip boots. What the hell? I thought, as I slowly removed the dart deep from within the kestrel's chest. Holding the blowgun dart in my hands, I just stood there transfixed in amazement. Hell, we weren't in the jungles of Brazil where the use of blowguns was common! What the hell! Then my game warden mode of thinking went into high gear. That little bird of prey had been shot elsewhere and had managed to fly off and die in front of me with the dart firmly stuck into his breast muscle and its internal organs. My amazement soon turned to anger. This bird's wound was fresh. Whoever was shooting birds with a blowgun was either one hell of a killer or a nut case but a damned skilled one. And since this kill was fresh, that meant my shooter was probably still close by.

With that, I bailed back into my patrol truck and began running every back road I could find in the immediate area. I didn't know what I was looking for, but figured I would know it when I found it. An hour later of hard, dirt, farm-road running and searching found me heading west on Packer Road. About halfway down Packer Road, I spotted a sedan pulled off to the side of the road. Suspecting that may be my blowgun shooter, I stopping and grabbing my binoculars, got an eyeful!

Coming out from a walnut orchard was a tall, lean individual. He was dressed from head to toe in camouflage clothing, his face had been painted in camo colors and he was carrying a blowgun in one hand and a dead bird of some sort in the other! Wanting more definition on what was occurring, I grabbed my spotting scope off the front seat, quickly balanced it on the top of my steering wheel and focused it so I could see better. My chap with the blowgun unaware of my presence, opened up the trunk of his car, unscrewed the blow tube into two pieces, and laid the blowgun inside. Then he smoothed out the feathers on what I had now identified as a male Northern flicker. Reaching into his trunk, my chap pulled out a woman's nylon stocking and carefully inserted the flicker head down into the stocking after he had rolled the bird up in a blanket of cotton gauze. The bird was then placed into the trunk of the car and the lid was shut. Turning, it was then that my lad saw my truck parked down the road apiece. Looking hard at me for a moment, he then reached inside the front seat of his car and extracted a pair of binoculars. Then he took a really long, hard look at me quietly sitting alongside the road. By now, I was sure my blowgun-wielding chap had spotted me looking at him with my spotting scope. Hurriedly putting away his binoculars, he got into his car and headed west on Packer Road at a high rate of speed until he came to a southern turn in the road. Realizing he had nothing but a deeply rutted, muddy farm road ahead of him requiring four-wheel drive for safe passage, I saw his taillights suddenly glow red.

Pulling up behind his vehicle in a blocking fashion so he couldn't back away from the muddy road trouble he was in, escape, and outrun my truck with his car in the process, I calmly shut off my engine. Unlimbering my tired frame from the truck, I approached my chap. As I did, I could see him intently looking at me in his rearview mirror. The look on his face said it all...

"Afternoon," I said, "State fish and game warden." I don't think I saw a man's Adam's apple go up and down so much as I did that day on my now-captured chap. "I would like you to open up your trunk and hand me that Northern flicker you just loaded into it a while back. That species of migratory bird is totally protected by the Federal Migratory Bird Treaty Act and California state law. And unless you have a state and federal scientific collecting permit for taking such a species, your take and possession is illegal."

Opening up his car door, he said, "You stay right here and I will get it for you."

"No, I don't think so," I countered. "I want to see what else you have in the trunk. Plus, I plan on seizing your blowgun if you do not have a valid state and federal migratory bird scientific collecting permit."

With those words, my chap just went white in the face and sat back down in the front seat of his car like he suddenly had a load of liquid mercury just dumped into the rear of his pants.

"You all right?" I asked, figuring he was about to have a stroke or heart attack.

My chap just nodded and then got out from the front seat and faced me. "I will not let you look in the trunk of my car. Not without some kind of a warrant. I know my rights," he said.

"Well, let me explain to you how I see it. First of all, I observed you through my spotting scope with a protected migratory bird species in hand. Then I witnessed you putting that bird into the trunk of your car. Since you have not produced a scientific collecting permit allowing you to take and possess such a species, that gives me probable cause to look in the trunk of your car. If you insist in not letting me do so, here is what I am going to do. I will arrest you on the spot for the illegal possession of a protected migratory bird species and haul you off to the Colusa County Jail. Then I will get a wrecker and have them haul your car to the sheriff's office impound lot in Colusa. That will be followed with a trip to the county attorney and the judge to procure a search warrant. Then I will come back, open your trunk and see what you have in there as you cool your heels in the Colusa County Jail. And lastly, I will see to it that you will be taking a trip to federal court in Sacramento over the illegal possession of that federally protected bird species. So, that is your roadmap to ruin unless you cooperate and open up the trunk so I can see what is inside."

I just stood there looking at my chap with the nervous Adam's apple. For the longest time, he just stood there thinking over what I had just said. Dejectedly removing his car keys, he turned and walked back to the rear of his car. Hesitating for a moment as if realizing once he opened up the trunk he was really in trouble, he finally reached down and opened up the trunk. I then had him step out of the way for my safety and a better look-see. What a surprise I got! The first thing I spotted was two steel-tubed blowguns and a mess of darts! The darts matched the one I had pulled from the chest of my little kestrel earlier in the day. Then there were two homemade plywood boxes with partitions. Kind of like what one would see in a case of wine to keep the bottles separated so they would not break in transit. In each of the slots of those boxes were various cotton wrapped bird species stuffed inside a woman's nylon stocking. In all, I pulled out eighteen freshly-killed protected migratory birds that had been recently collected by my blowgun shooter. There were robins, Steller's jays, yellow-billed magpies, Northern flickers, avocets, long-billed curlews, and the like. Every species I pulled from those stockings were freshly killed, state and federally protected migratory birds!

Turning, I asked for his driver's license. Once in hand, I asked my chap why he was killing all those bird species. As it turned out, he was a taxidermist from the San Francisco Bay area. A freeze- dried taxidermist at that. To you unwashed, freeze-drying in those days was a new art form in the taxidermy trade. In short, the taxidermist procured a species of critter and positioned it into the pose he wanted the animal to look the most life like and natural. Then the animal was freeze-dried: guts, hide, feathers, goozle, and all. When finished, the critters come out looking so life like that while checking a freeze-drying shop in Martinez a year or so later as a federal officer, I got a huge surprise. Walking in to inspect that taxidermist's freezers, I steered clear of what I believed was a pet coyote sitting in a chair by the counter. It turned out to be a freeze- dried specimen and I couldn't tell it from a live one at first glance...and I was a trained wildlife officer!

So, it seemed my freeze-dried taxidermist was making the rounds in Colusa County collecting every bird specimen he could tag with a blowgun dart. And, to be sure, my chap was every bit as good with his blowgun as anyone living in the Amazon jungle. I sure as hell wouldn't have wanted him shooting at me.

After finishing all the citation paperwork and seizing his gear and the birds as evidence, I let him proceed on his way. Then, I contacted Ben Crabb, a United States Game Management Agent located in the San Francisco Bay Area where my recently cited chap had his shop located. When my shooter arrived home, guess what? Ben was waiting for him and tagged him again for having a mess of protected migratory birds in his possession. Birds in his freezers and freeze dryer that were later discovered when his taxidermy license for migratory birds and shop facilities were inspected as allowed under the man's migratory bird taxidermy permit. As a result of Ben's discoveries, my blowgun chap subsequently lost his federal taxidermy license and paid a large fine in federal court in San Francisco! Two weeks later, my chap forfeited $1,000, the maximum allowed under the Migratory Bird Treaty Act in those days, for fines in federal court in Sacramento for the illegal taking and possession of protected migratory birds. Ben had caught his lad in the San Francisco federal court jurisdiction and I had caught my lad in the Sacramento jurisdiction for charges of taking and possessing numerous protected migratory birds. As a result, our chap paid the piper in two separate legal jurisdiction for two separate but related federal offenses.

I have to admit, that was just one of the weirdest cases I ever made in my lengthy state and federal careers. And all because I had the opportune moment in time to observe a little kestrel falling from a power line. Who says if a tree falls unobserved in a forest it doesn't make a noise? Boy, that little kestrel sure made one hell of a lot of noise, if you get my drift. Once again, the powerful play of the poetry of life within the world of wildlife law enforcement went on around me and I was able to contribute a verse...

LATE SHOOTERS OFF ROAD H

Finishing up with my blowgun chap, it was just about time to go after those soon to be late shooting waterfowl at the end of the day. Crossing Interstate 5 and traveling west, I headed for one of my favorite waterfowl late shooting honey holes. The area to be worked had a history of high feeding duck use associated with what seemed to always be a mess of late shooting chaps who just couldn't help themselves when it came to breaking the law. And because of the continuing high winds and driving rains, tonight would be a late shooter's paradise because of all of the low flying ducks. Accompanying all that historical late shooting banging and clanging, would also be attracted one beautiful and wonderfully handsome game warden, namely me ... of course! Sitting off at a distance overlooking a mess of harvested rice fields, I waited until almost the end of legal shooting hours. Then with the now-driving winter rains, howling winds, big smells Dog from all her goose guts lunch at Terrill's earlier in the day, and yours truly, the vehicle slipped onto the north end of Road H. Grabbing my binoculars from the seat, I took a gander down toward the far end of the road where I spotted four vehicles parked alongside an irrigation ditch. No one was in sight so I surmised my lads were still out in the field hunting waterfowl. Slipping the truck into first gear, I slowly drove down the mud puddle riddled, deeply potholed road. Arriving quietly, I parked my rig in among the others sitting there for the cover it offered. Then I noticed four lads coming in from the fields like most legal duck hunters will do. Two of the four knew me from, shall we say, previous legal business encounters during the current waterfowl season. Knowing what I was up to, they all stood around to see if I was going to treat those still shooting after hours in the field as I had treated them. Not to worry, Lads, I thought. I have had a long, hard day and a plethora of wildlife cases to show for my efforts. To my way of thinking, a few late shooting violations wouldn't hurt being added into this wonderful game warden's stew of unique cases I am now in the process of figuratively making.

Upon my arrival, I gave my chaps still shooting in the field the usual ten-minute buffer at the end of legal shooting hours for differences in times on their watches. Following that, Dog and I headed out on foot into a now worsening driving rain. To my immediate south were two gunners still banging away at the low flying ducks trying to find a place to light down and eat. Off to my west were two more chaps who were a little more selective in their shooting but breaking the law when it came to late shooting ducks just the same.

Figuring I could ambush my late shooting lads to the south and still have time to head across and gather up my shooters to the west, I set my miserable carcass into motion. By now, it was forty minutes after legal hours, and the air was jug-full of hungry ducks zipping every which way but loose. My two gunners to the south never saw me coming, and soon I had ruined their evening's late shooting activities. True to form, they were so busy killing low flying ducks in the heat of the moment that they never saw me in the darkness lumbering across the muddy, freshly harvested rice fields like a T- Rex. Like Grosz's Rule says, if they aren't looking for you they won't see you. And looking skyward all the time as they late shot ducks, is certainly not conducive to seeing the local game warden coming one's way. Trying to keep our encounter to a low roar so the lads to the west wouldn't know I was in country, I quietly procured my chaps' driver's and hunting licenses. Then telling them to present their illegal birds so I could get an accurate count as to numbers and species, they were then asked to meet me back where they had parked their vehicle. I also advised that to run from the law once back at their vehicles would not be a smart move since I had their driver's licenses in my possession. And if they chose to run and through that action, deny any illegal activity on their part, a warrant would follow. Finishing with that piece of business, I took off after my last two late-shooting field shooters to the west. Two shooters who were making sure that every danged duck that flew by in range got shot at with a killing gusto.

As those shooters continued shooting, twice I saw ducks fall to their guns as I closed in within grabbing range. However, I soon discovered I had a deep ditch to cross and that took a few moments as I carefully navigated the deep water, an old barbwire fence that I didn't want to rip my rubber hip boots, and deep mud. Once on the other side of the ditch, I took stock of my shooters' last location. That turned out to be a chore. They must have sensed Johnnie Law was in the field because all of a sudden they realized the other late shooters had gone as silent as a bunch of mice pissin' on a ball of cotton. My shooters to the west, taking that as a suspicious cue, then went as silent as a German Type VII submarine when chased by a sub-hunting destroyer during the Second World War in the Atlantic. Figuring I had been had, I crossed back over the field in the growing darkness to cut them off from their vehicle. Pausing on a great intercept location, I found nothing but rain, wind, and hungry ducks flying across the rice fields like cannon shot. Never one to be without a Plan B, I took off at a trot once again. They had to eventually return to their vehicle, so, I trotted across the muddy rice fields in that direction. Arriving back at my truck, I scooped up my Starlight Scope and took a look. The heavy rain didn't help my field of vision but, as near as I could tell, my chaps were now long gone from their previous shooting location. Gone, vanished, kaput, or maybe gobbled up by the hungry ducks and geese. Sure as God made bears always hungry for more grits, especially just before hibernation, my shooters had simply vanished from their previous late shooting location.

But then I got a break. Who says God doesn't like fools, little children, and game wardens? The wind and rain abated somewhat. On went my Starlight Scope once again for another look-see. My chaps, sure as all get out, had vanished from their last shooting location. Figuring I had a couple of real classic and savvy outlaws on the run, I went to Plan C. Turning around three hundred sixty degrees and looking at every point on the compass with my scope where they might be, I finally spotted my previously-identified late shooting lads coming towards their vehicle from the far north end of the road! Boy, those late shooting suckers are slicker than cow slobber, I thought. Or, someone from the four hunters who had arrived back at their vehicles earlier must have somehow warned them of my presence...

Those suspicions were confirmed later when one of my legal sets of hunters made ready to leave. As one hunter passed me en route to his vehicle, he quietly said, "Those other fellows were flashing their lights from their vehicles when you were at the south end of the field chasing that first bunch of late shooters." Then he kept walking so as not to tip off the other two hunters that he had given them away as he passed by. As it turned out, the light flashers were the two I had written up earlier in the year for shooting waterfowl fifty-nine minutes late in this same rice field...

Taking off without a word, I, too, headed north on an intercept course. Keeping the scope turned on, I kept track of my two "too smart for their own damn good" late shooters. Finally, about one hundred yards from our rigs, I made contact with my chaps. Man, you talk about two surprised lads when they were finally caught in a rainy night almost as dark as the inside of a dead cow.

"Evening, Lads," I said as I stepped out from the edge of the road much to their abject surprise. "State fish and game warden. Do either of you know what time legal shooting hours ended this evening?" Neither one responded with the correct time which told me neither of them had the foggiest idea what time they had to stop shooting that evening. Then I asked to see their watches. Only one was wearing a watch and it had the correct time.

"Well, Fellows, the last time the two of you late shot this evening was fifty-eight minutes late. And, that was at that large flock of American wigeon that passed over your heads. One of you killed a bird from that flock, and then the two of you spent some time looking for it in the dark before you found it," I said.

"No, that wasn't us, Officer. You have us mixed up with some others. We were hunting north of our car," replied the taller of the two.

Turning on my scope, I asked the man who had just denied shooting late to look through it. When he did, all he said was, "Whoo-eee. He has us dead to rights, Sammy."

"By the way, you might tell your friends who flashed their car lights to let you know I was in the area, that they get an 'attaboy' for trying, but not from the local game warden. Let them also know they had better be as right as rain in the future, or they will have me to contend with again," I said in a tone of voice not to be misunderstood as to its full meaning.

Together the three of us walked back to the parked vehicles where they were issued citations for late shooting waterfowl along with the other two previously caught late shooters, who were still waiting for me by their vehicles as they had been instructed to do after being apprehended in the field. Then turning to the two light-flashing chaps looking on, I said, "Maybe next time you ought to honk your horns, too. That would be a better signal to your friends that I am in the field." It was now pretty dark, but you could tell those two lads were looking a little sheepish at being caught red handed trying to screw the local game warden. That probably would have happened had I not had my Starlight Scope and a couple honest duck hunters ratting them out. It always amazed me when other shooters tried to warn their crooked buddies that the law of the land was afoot and about to ruin their little illegal shoot. They were doing nothing but eventually destroying the sport they loved by allowing others to continue their illegal killing and wildlife stealing ways. And did so without any thoughts about what they were leaving those still yet to come in the way of natural resources. Continuing, I said, "You light- flashing chaps need to remember that you can't bite a porcupine in the ass." Their only retort to that statement was the sound of cold winter rain drumming off their rain gear.

Two weeks later, my first two late shooters forfeited bail to the tune of $105 each. My other two lads, who failed to get away even with the flashing car lights' warning, each forfeited $141 each.

Finished and running on empty after a long but very productive day, Dog and I headed for home. I was thankful I had eaten a large breakfast that morning because between then and now, all I had eaten was a Payday Candy Bar. But what a game warden's stew I had created on that unusual day. I had apprehended a total of seventeen chaps for everything from loaded gun violations to killing protected migratory birds with a blowgun. In that daylong process of making a game warden's stew, I had collected a total of $4,317 in fines for the State of California and Uncle Sam! To say the least, I was so damned tired and hungry, my large bottom was dragging and my big guts were eating the little guts. But, a happy camper over the day's results I was.

Pulling into the driveway of my home—I had called the sheriff's office earlier and had asked them to call my wife and let her know I would be home for supper—I let Dog down from the truck. She headed for her doghouse and before I had cleaned up outside in the garage sink, I could hear her loudly snoring. Opening up the backdoor to my kitchen, I was met by several glorious smells: freshly made buttermilk biscuits and a pie, not to mention something with beef in it. Hugging my bride, she said, "Sit down before the phone rings. I will have your dinner served shortly."

I did as I was told—hard to believe, eh?—and soon I was facing four steaming hot biscuits fresh from the oven and a plate of thick and rich homemade stew. That stew was loaded with onions, potatoes, tomatoes, garlic, green peppers, celery, chicken broth, carrots, and large chunks of the tenderest beef you ever ate. How was that for a perfect ending of a great day? I had put together a game warden's stew of numerous violators running from A to Z. Then coming home, I was met with a home-cooked stew par excellence made by the world's best wife. Man, I had it made. Falling to, I soon foundered like a bull in a green alfalfa field. But I did manage to leave some room for one of my bride's freshly made, world famous, homemade blueberry pie. Man, talk about dying and going to Heaven...

Just minutes before midnight that same day, I was once again tiredly parked behind the two rice harvesters on the Line Dennis Farm where I had earlier apprehended my three lads from the Delevan area with the loaded shotguns in their vehicle. The night air was blessedly full of the whispers of hungry ducks and geese quietly passing overhead. Shadow was snoring in the front seat of my truck and the vehicle was gently rocking in the wake of the wind from the winter storms pouring out of the northwest. And me? I was once again ready for my next game warden's stew or whatever the Chief Game Warden in the Sky had lined out for me...

Afterword

The face of history says, "Whisper my stories when I am gone. For to speak loudly will bring shame to the many who came before me walking on the dark side of man in the storied world of wildlife law enforcement."

—Terry Grosz

I know one thing. This journey as a state fish and game warden and later as a federal agent was started many years earlier with hope in my heart and a keen eye fastened on the horizon because the conclusions were uncertain. After many trials and tribulations on that Heaven sent world of wildlife law enforcement journey, it finally has ended in this book, the last of my adventures. I am now in the winter of my years, my eyes have dimmed and I have more metal in my body from my many surgeries than a World War Two battleship! As a result of all of those maladies, I am no longer fleet of foot. Hell, I can barely walk I am so busted up at the ripe old age of 74 in the year 2015 when this book came to print. To the best of my knowledge, the time most of the stories in this book were first drafted in 2012, out of my entire North Coast Fish and Game Squad and later my Sacramento Valley Squad there are only four of us left alive from groups of good men once numbering twenty-one officers collectively!

Soon, I, too, will be just a faint memory, like those other officers of The Thin Green Line who came before me or trotted alongside my miserable carcass on the fields of battle in and for the world of wildlife. However, as I wait to die like we all must do—since death is just another part of life—unlike many others of my ilk, hopefully some of my efforts will be represented by a few words written in a long forgotten musty book like this one. Just another book of wildlife law enforcement adventures placed on an out of the way shelf in the back corner of someone's home waiting to once again be discovered. To discover, read its pages, laugh and enjoy its historical and sometimes hysterical pratfalls and adventures from a time long past, written by a man who by the time of reading those lines in that book, is now dust...

However, physical conditions and ethereal travels aside, I was blessed on this epic world of wildlife 32-year law-enforcement adventure with the world's best wife, a body that more or less held together and a supporting cast made up of two sons, a daughter, and eventually two feather-worn guardian angels. I won many battles and more than likely lost just as many more in the world of wildlife arena. However, during those more than three decades of time on those hallowed fish and game law-enforcement fields of battle, I thankfully served my God, the critters, and the American people. Served, I would like to think, with distinction and honor. In turn, I was rewarded with many beautiful moments of nature, met some truly unique individuals both good and bad, experienced many things ethereal, and lived times that few other people today will ever have the opportunity to experience and enjoy. They will fail to experience, enjoy or even realize because many such moments in time are now a long past part of history or, in many instances, have disappeared into the dust bins of time...

Thank you, Lord, for the many blessings you have given to me and mine throughout the years. I rode with you, Lord, and I have no real complaints. It has been and will always be a pleasure to have been in Your service... And lastly, thank you, Lord, for teaching me the further backward into history I looked, the further forward into the future I was able to see...

I am sure glad that God loves little children, fools and game wardens. So let it be written, so let it be said!

Some of you have said—especially my Native American friends—that in my lifetime I always lived in the "borderland" between this world and the other. I have often thought during my many quiet times in the fields surrounded by the world of wildlife, that the "borderlands" were my genesis and will eventually lead into my point of exodus. That being said, I will someday see all of you across the Great Divide.

Fear not when that happens, because we can then return to the times of thick prairie sod, buffalo grass, clouds of passenger pigeons, the rumbling thunder of the bison herds, campfires with old friends who have passed before, all punctuated with the music of happy wilderness "song-dogs" ringing in our ears. And with that wilderness serenade, we will experience the cold, clear nights with sparkling necklaces of stars winking the stories of the adventures of our earthly travels overhead in some long forgotten intergalactic style of Morse Code...

One of the many thoughts I always carried with me during my thirty-two hard years of putting those in the business of extinction out of business, was that all of God's creatures had a place in the choir! And I tried to make sure that God's choir was every bit as good as is the Morman Tabernacle Choir...

And last but certainly not least, I would like to thank my wife being that this is my last wildlife book in which she figured so prominently in all of my world of wildlife law enforcement adventures.

Excerpt from Wildlife's Quiet War

Tule Fog
"Catch Me If You Can"

During many winters in the Northern Sacramento Valley there always occurred a unique duck and goose-killing weather-assisted phenomenon. That phenomenon was a very dense, ground-hugging fog. That fog sometimes lasted for weeks on end and is locally known as the "tule fog." I am not sure what causes the tule fog meteorologically to occur but with its occurrence the killing of ducks and geese by sportsmen and outlaws hits high gear. Hits high gear because the dense fog makes the flying ducks and geese virtually blind to the dangers awaiting below in the form of the gunning sportsmen. That is, except for the lordly Canada goose. When that species is moving around in the tule fog, they are as quiet as a bunch of mice pissing on a ball of cotton. All the other species of geese are frantically calling in the tule fog because they are so damned lost, and in the process, giving away their locations. And in so doing, many times ultimately "giving away" their lives as well. But not the Canada geese because for some reason they recognize the danger inherent in Mother Nature's dense gray blanket and what lethality many times lies below, especially if one is discovered within gunning range. They slip in and are gone before you even knew they were in country or can raise your shotgun for a killing shot. For some reason, that is just one of Mother Nature's flukes of nature. A fluke welcome to the lordly Canada goose but not so much to the lowly hunter trying to bag such a magnificent and many times difficult and wary bird to lure within gunning range.

In short, many times the fog is so thick that the ducks and geese have one hell of a time finding their ways around. That includes finding places to eat as well as safe places to land and rest. To those experienced in such natural occurrences, a large harvested rice field, skillful use of a good duck or goose call, and a pocketful of shot shells are all one needs in "greeting" such a "soon to be a critter in the pot" phenomenon. That killing opportunity went double for many of the Sacramento Valley's local outlaws possessing a gleam in their eyes, evil thoughts on their minds, and a wicked desire in their hearts to clean out Mother Nature's duck and goose pantry during such a climatological phenomenon.

When the Northern Sacramento Valley tule fogs were in their usual numerous and top dense forms, all one had to do for a good waterfowl shoot was to walk out into an open harvested rice field and listen. Soon one could hear the sounds of numerous lost ducks and geese flying by and many times calling in the dense fog. If one listened carefully, he could also hear the birds' wings hitting one another as they flew around in confused, dense flocks overhead. When the experienced shooter heard those sounds, he would give a couple of quick calls on his duck or goose call. Then listening carefully, he would be rewarded with the sounds of birds' wings hitting each other as they frantically turned around in mid-air towards the sounds of that guiding clarion call on the ground. Carefully listening, the shooter could hear the whistling wings of the flock of birds coming by once again. Only that time, the confused birds would be much lower and flying more slowly looking for the caller on the ground. The smart shooter would wait until the sounds of the near-at-hand birds had barely passed his position. Then would give a couple of quick calls once again. Instantly, the caller would be rewarded with the sounds of flying ducks or geese once again adjusting their flights and quickly turning around. In the process, all followed once again with the giveaway sounds of slapping, colliding wings from the confused flyers now almost overhead.

When that happened, the shooter needed to be ready because within moments he would be swarmed with low-flying ducks and geese looking for the caller on the ground. In short, he was swarmed by close-at-hand, confused birds trying to find a place to land where they last heard the shooter using his call. Then killing began big time because the birds would be fog-blinded, flying slowly, densely packed and in very close gunning range. And with that, based on the inclination of the shooter, the killing or overkilling began. Those sounds of fast and furious shooting during such foggy conditions would be the needed clues for the nearby law enforcement officer, if he was worth his salt and using his ears, to begin the "hunt" for his fellow man.

With the advent of the tule fog, the badge carrier would find his days filled with hard, long work hours trying to corral those taking advantage of the confused and easily killed birds.

Two reasons for the hard work and long hours were paramount. First, the fog concealed the gunner and, if he was so inclined to slaughter, he had the cover and opportunity to do so. Secondly, the confused birds made killing large over limits easier by their closeness, slower speeds, and their overall eagerness to land in order to get the hell out of the dense, vision- robbing fog.

However in my particular case, I had a third very personal reason for the extra hours worked. Every time the heavy tule fogs rolled in, without fail, I would usually get teasing phone calls from the same "voice." Those phone calls would go something like this when I answered the phone. "Is this Terry Grosz? If so, I will be out and about this fine duck-killing day in the fog. Catch me if you can,"...*click*. And with those challenging, maddening words, the phone would go deader than a car-hit great horned owl. That was usually when I had more damn ducks and geese in the valley than there were Democrat defense attorneys in hell. And my caller had been doing so with his challenging phone calls ever since I had arrived in the valley as a game warden in 1967 and continuing into later years after I became a United States Game Management Agent. Those maddening phone calls seemed to me to be coming ever since the Great Auk had marched into the silence of history (To my unwashed readers, the Great Auk was a penguin-like bird whose numbers were the first to be shot into extinction by American hunters. The last known pair were killed on their breeding grounds off the Atlantic Coast in 1844!).

Later, as the local U.S. Game Management Agent assigned to a Sacramento Valley county that didn't "cotton" to conservation officer types because of many of the locals' past illegal market hunting histories, both my wife and I began getting challenging calls incessantly when the tule fogs rolled into the valley from my unknown challenging outlaw (before caller I.D.). Or even worse, my wife would get calls from the same "voice" saying, "Mrs. Grosz, you need to come down to the

Sheriff's Office. Your husband has just been shot in the face with a shotgun and we need you to come in and identify the body... " *click.*

When such phone challenges, as I called them, rolled my way, I would gear up and head back out into the wildlife field of battle. To my readers, you must remember several things. Things that my local outlaws always seemed to forget. First, it is not nice to mess with Mother Nature or her minions. Second, I knew the Northern Sacramento Valley like the back of my hand. And for the most part, I knew where my ducks and geese would more or less be congregated. With that information and the weather factored in, I would head for my historical hot spots in the hope of catching my "challenging caller" in action. And you could bet your bottom Carson City Morgan silver dollar, if I did manage to cross my caller's path, he would get some "challenging" action as well...

Well, one fine tule fog day, just as sure as Mrs. God makes great gooseberry jam, elder berry jelly, and beer biscuits for Her Fella, I got my usual "catch me if you can" call. This call I was used to, not only due to the now commonly occurring, foggy winter weather events, but now because of the familiar sameness of the tone and tenor of my caller's voice as well. A voice that was so distinctive to my way of thinking after hearing it so many times, that all I needed was to hear it spoken to me face to face. When that happened, you could bet your bottom dollar my caller would be treated with the utmost kindness, patience, loving care, and professionalism...

The only problem I had, well, I had more than one even though I knew my district, was one of time and space. I had a federal law enforcement district that encompassed many thousands of square miles of the Northern Sacramento Valley's wonderful rice farming grounds. This area was commonly used extensively by just about every "waterfowler" for hunting the excellent-tasting, rice-fed species of waterfowl during the winter months. Especially so when the tule fogs arrived. I also had more than three hundred operating private and commercial duck clubs in addition to all my local, unattached field gunners. Just try to find one chap and his familiar voice in that stack of rice straw, goose droppings, tule roots, and spent shotgun shells, if you will. Then throw into that "soup" the covering effects of the dense fog and the great waterfowl hunting going on just about anywhere a duck or goose could drop their feathered behinds. With all those factors, one ultimately had a hat full of hornets even if he was a skilled conservation officer, if you get my drift. Bottom line, the officer held a hand of aces and eights (hopefully you readers know your Deadwood, South Dakota, Wild Bill Hickok history in the late 1800s and what such a hand held for him...), and the wildlife outlaw, a straight flush. But, God was the dealer in such a "card game" and after all, He did in fact create all the critters who had little or no voice, didn't He?

To give all you readers a taste of just how bad the fog could get for the birds, how about this. Several times during my years in the Northern Sacramento Valley, I observed ducks and geese trying to land in the lighted, wet city streets at night thinking it was water. They were that confused by the tule fog... Or they landed on the flat tops of buildings holding a little rainwater from the latest rainstorm thinking it was more than it really was. Or, when driving down the highway, one could only see three white stripes ahead in the road at a time!

When those great wet fogs rolled in, I would average apprehending anywhere from thirty to forty shooters a week with over limits of ducks and geese and for other collateral violations! Just imagine how many more illegal waterfowl shooters throughout the vast Northern

Sacramento Valley I missed! Then multiply that by the usual number of tule fogs that rolled into the valley in the winter months annually. Suffice to say, Custer had better odds when it came to knocking the Indians out from their saddles with his single shot, trap-door 45- 70s, during his little skirmish in 1876 in Montana. Truth be known, it seems history has revealed that less than forty Indian warriors were ever killed by Custer's men...! Kind of gives you readers an idea as to the odds I faced even knowing the area as well as I did.

As I was saying before I got carried away, that fine morning so long ago after receiving my usual "catch me if you can" phone call, I loaded up my faithful Labrador retriever, Shadow, into the back of my truck after only three hours of sleep between the two of us, kissed my bride goodbye, and disappeared into the swirling foggy mists. Knowing that just about anywhere I went that morning, I would have "some business" to attend to because I had so many wintering ducks and geese in the valley (over a million!), along with a bushel basket full of lads with itchy trigger fingers who couldn't count for sour owl droppings, off I went with a happy heart.

For starters, I headed west down Highway 20 towards a small local town named Williams. About the time I approached Lone Star Road, my guardian angels were doing "flip-flops." That was their way of telling me some "catching" was in the wind, eh, fog, if I minded my P's and Q's in that historic specific gunning area. With those "warnings in the wind," I turned south on Lone Star Road. Arriving at the junction of Meyers and Lone Star Roads, I stopped, got out of my truck, and listened. By then the tule fog was so thick, I couldn't see more than thirty yards in any direction. But I could still hear, and being blessed with a set of ears like that of a great horned owl or a kit fox, I put them to good use.

Off to my east I heard just one shot. Thinking nothing more about that one shot, I continued standing there in the road bathed in the swirling foggy mists listening because I always had a policy of "moving to the sound of the guns" when "hunting humans." The more guns I heard, the faster I moved! I figured that way I would always be in the middle of anything hitting the fan, if you get my drift. As it turned out, that morning's fog was so thick and wet, any sounds of shooting seemed very distant and almost soft-sounding in nature. True to form, I heard little of interest in that neck of the woods up to that point in time.

Just as I was getting back into my truck so I could "cast my net elsewhere for some little fishes," like the Good Book says, I heard my "one-shot" shooter again. This time from the sound of it, he had changed positions, moving slightly to the northwest.

Then my instincts and guardian angels clamoring around inside my being got the better of me. Why only one shot in such fog with so many birds aloft? I asked myself. Having hunted in such conditions, I never had less than a mess of ducks or geese responding to my calling at any given time. To my way of thinking, only shooting one shot at a time under such potentially great hunting conditions now began piquing my interest. Perhaps "One-Shot" was a serious killer and didn't want to bring any attention to himself, I thought. Self, I thought, maybe we need to fathom that shooter out and examine his intentions more closely. Especially if this "one-shot shooter" is using that technique to throw any "human-hunting law dogs" in his vicinity off his trail.

Picking up and moving east, I stopped just shy of Ohm Road, bailed out, walked a short distance from my vehicle, and listened once again. Listening carefully, I could tell the air was full of birds by all the calling and "wing slapping" I was hearing. Then just north of me towards the Colusa National Wildlife Refuge, I heard my one-shot chap have at it once again. Moments later, an alarmed mess of ducks swished loudly over my head in the fog numbering at least a hundred. I will bet you that is the flock my chap had just shot, I thought, now starting to get really interested in my "one shot at a time" shooter.

To my readers, I had always found over the years that a lone shooter was a proven good bet for a pinch. Be it hunting without a license, no duck stamp, an over limit, or some other sort of chicanery, "singletons" as I called them, when checked, usually were "money in the bank." And my one-shot shooting chap could very well fall into that category with the tule fog, tons of birds, and all, I now surmised.

Hiding my truck among a mess of idle parked farm equipment, I gathered up Dog and took a look at the compass I always carried. With that, I took a bearing on the echolocation of my shooter's last shot. Hopping a small ditch alongside the road, Dog and I headed northwest into the swirling mists. Coming to my first rice check in the field, I paused and listened for the longest time. True to form, the air was filled with nearby ducks and lesser snow geese trying to find a rice field in which to land and feed. They knew from their "onboard natural compasses" and instincts, there was a rice field below them. But damned if they could chance a forty-mile-an-hour flight downward without knowing where the ground was. To do otherwise meant a smashed bill full of rice mud and possible broken bones at the airspeed they routinely traveled.

Boom went my shooter and, from the sound of the fog- dampened shot, it came from the northwest once again! Only this time it sounded like it was about 150 yards distant from where I now stood. Once again within moments of the shot, the air was filled with the whistling wings and ghostly, fog shrouded sights of alarmed and fleeing ducks and geese. With that, Dog and I again moved northward towards our shooter heading for the next rice check in the field and the cover it offered in the process.

About the Author

Whether as a professional in the field of wildlife law enforcement or as a prolific writer, Terry Grosz has distinguished himself with a kind of passion, dedication, integrity and professionalism that often exemplify Humboldt State alumni. The beginning of his 32-year career in wildlife law enforcement came in 1966 with the California Department of Fish and Game in Eureka. After several years and a transfer to Colusa, he was hired by the U.S. Fish and Wildlife Service (FWS), moving into increasing responsibility for conservation and wildlife law enforcement in successively larger geographic regions, from jurisdiction over the central half of Northern California to finally Assistant Regional Director for Law Enforcement where he supervised FWS's wildlife law programs covering 750,000 square miles.

When Grosz became the FWS Senior Special Agent, he wrote regulations, policy and procedures, responded to congressional inquiries, provided advice, guidance and expertise. But it wasn't just a desk job. He also traveled throughout Asia assisting foreign governments in curtailing the smuggling of wildlife and establishing cooperative international law enforcements programs. In all the various positions held by Terry, he supervised agents who protected wildlife from being smuggled or imported illegally into the US, protected eagles from being poisoned or trapped, and more.

In 1998, Grosz retired from the FWS and began a second career as a prolific writer, and has since authored and published fourteen wildlife law enforcement memoirs and seven historical novels. Clearly, he's got a lot of material to work with. Many of his stories have hilarious moments and hair-raising adventures, some others are sad and tragic, they are all about the men and women who work as wildlife conservation officers trying to preserve our natural heritage for future generations.

Find more great titles by Terry Grosz and Wolfpack Publishing at http://wolfpackpublishing.com/terry-grosz/